Jesse Feiler

Sams **Teach Yourself**

Drupal

in **24** **Hours**

 800 East 96th Street, Indianapolis, Indiana, 46240 USA

Sams Teach Yourself Drupal in 24 Hours

ISBN-13: 978-0-672-33126-8

ISBN-10: 0-672-33126-8

Library of Congress Cataloging-in-Publication data is on file.

Printed in the United States of America

First Printing November 2009

Trademarks

All terms mentioned in this book that are known to be trademarks or service marks have been appropriately capitalized. Sams Publishing cannot attest to the accuracy of this information. Use of a term in this book should not be regarded as affecting the validity of any trademark or service mark.

Warning and Disclaimer

Every effort has been made to make this book as complete and as accurate as possible, but no warranty or fitness is implied. The information provided is on an "as is" basis. The author and the publisher shall have neither liability nor responsibility to any person or entity with respect to any loss or damages arising from the information contained in this book or from the use of the CD.

Bulk Sales

Sams Publishing offers excellent discounts on this book when ordered in quantity for bulk purchases or special sales. For more information, please contact

U.S. Corporate and Government Sales
1-800-382-3419
corpsales@pearsontechgroup.com

For sales outside of the U.S., please contact

International Sales
international@pearsoned.com

Associate Publisher
Greg Wiegand

Acquisitions Editor
Loretta Yates

Development Editor
Kevin Howard

Managing Editor
Patrick Kanouse

Project Editor
Mandie Frank

Copy Editor
Barbara Hacha

Indexer
Tim Wright

Proofreader
Sheri Cain

Technical Editor
Todd Meister

Publishing Coordinator
Cindy Teeters

Designer
Gary Adair

Compositor
Mark Shirar

Contents at a Glance

Table of Contents

About the Author

In 1998, **Jesse Feiler** wrote *Database-Driven Web Sites*, one of the first books about the marriage of databases and the web. This relationship between databases and the web has grown and encompassed blogs and Content Management Systems (CMS), culminating in Drupal.

Jesse is the author of numerous books on Mac OS X, FileMaker, the web, and various other technologies, such as Bento, mashups, and Facebook.

Jesse has worked as a developer and manager for companies such as the Federal Reserve Bank of New York (monetary policy and bank supervision), Prodigy (early web browser), Apple (information systems), New York State Department of Health (rabies and lead poisoning), The Johnson Company (office management), and Young & Rubicam (media planning and new product development). He also consults with small business and nonprofits in areas such as publishing, production, web technology, and contact management.

Active in the community, Jesse has served on various nonprofit boards, including HB Studio and Mid-Hudson Library System, as well as zoning and planning boards. He has conducted trustee training sessions for Clinton-Essex-Franklin Library System and other groups.

Feiler's website is www.northcountryconsulting.com. It is, of course, powered by Drupal. Downloadable files, updates, and discussion forums for this book are located there.

Acknowledgments

Many people have contributed to this book, not least the large community of Drupal developers and users.

At Sams Publishing, Loretta Yates, acquisitions editor, helped shape this book through the editorial process. It's been a pleasure to work with Kevin Howard and Mandie Frank, who, in various ways, helped make this book as clear and strong as possible.

At Waterside Productions, Carole McClendon has, again, provided the support and assistance that's so important to an author.

We Want to Hear from You!

As the reader of this book, you are our most important critic and commentator. We value your opinion and want to know what we're doing right, what we could do better, what areas you'd like to see us publish in, and any other words of wisdom you're willing to pass our way.

You can email or write me directly to let me know what you did or didn't like about this book—as well as what we can do to make our books stronger.

Please note that I cannot help you with technical problems related to the topic of this book, and that due to the high volume of mail I receive, I might not be able to reply to every message.

When you write, please be sure to include this book's title and author as well as your name and phone or email address. I will carefully review your comments and share them with the author and editors who worked on the book.

Mail: Greg Wiegand
         Associate Publisher
         Sams Publishing
         800 East 96th Street
         Indianapolis, IN 46240 USA

Reader Services

Visit our website and register this book at www.informit.com/title/9780672331268 for convenient access to any updates, downloads, or errata that might be available for this book.

Introduction

You have probably used Drupal without even knowing it. It is powering an ever-growing number of websites around the world. In some cases, it is chosen because it is open source software and the price is right: There are no annual license fees or up-front costs. In other cases, it is used because it lets people put up websites with many sophisticated features and put them up remarkably quickly. Still, other sites choose Drupal because of its sophisticated security mechanism that allows you to manage contributions and site management by many people.

Who Should Read This Book

This book is aimed at direct users of Drupal—the people who use it to develop websites, rather than the end users who visit Drupal sites (often without even knowing that Drupal is playing a role). If you are about to start a Drupal project, this book gets you up to speed quickly. If you are thinking about a Drupal project, you will find out what you need to know to carry that thought into action.

If you are already working with Drupal, this book can help organize your experiences. Drupal has changed dramatically over the past few years, and many of those changes have involved Drupal incorporating suggestions and ideas from various sources. What you had to write PHP code to accomplish in Drupal 4 often has been implemented directly in Drupal 5 and Drupal 6—and now in Drupal 7. The bar to entering the world of Drupal is much lower than it ever has been, but you may need a roadmap to the new and often simpler world.

Drupal Versions

As this book was written, the conversion from Drupal 6 to Drupal 7 was under way. Once a new version of Drupal is available, users begin to convert their sites to use the new Drupal. Although Drupal is committed to keeping content safe from version to version, some aspects of the user interface (that is, the interface you use to build the Drupal site) change. In addition, contributed modules and themes that can be used with Drupal may lag behind the official release of Drupal. For that reason, you will sometimes find alternate URLs and ways of doing things for the two versions. Because the transition was not complete at the time of writing, visit the author's website (northcountryconsulting.com) for updates to the new features.

How This Book Is Organized

This book is divided into four parts that will get you quickly up to speed with Drupal:

▶ Part I, "Getting Started with Drupal," shows you how to administer Drupal and work with its basic concepts of modules, notes, and images.

▶ Part II, "Socializing and Communicating," deals with the aspects of Drupal that implement modern social websites. These include comments, discussions, polls, user bookmarks, and even user-contributed content along with organizational (taxonomy) tools and search techniques that help people navigate a website that may be growing through dynamic contributions.

▶ Part III, "Creating a Site," puts it all together as you learn how to create pages, use themes, implement primary and secondary menu systems, use Drupal's workflow management tools, handle events, use calendars, and learn how to actually take your site live.

▶ Part IV, "Appendixes," consists of two appendixes with additional information on updating Drupal and the background of Drupal.

Special Features

This book includes the following special features:

▶ **Chapter roadmaps**—At the beginning of each chapter, you will find a list of the top-level topics addressed in that chapter. This list enables you to quickly see the type of information that the chapter contains.

▶ **Q&A**—At the end of each chapter is a Q&A section that explores some of the topics raised in that chapter.

▶ **Workshop**—In this section, you will find a brief quiz to help you remember the high points. Workshop sections also include a few activities that you can use to test your knowledge of the material in the chapter.

▶ **Try It Yourself**—Numbered lists of steps to complete tasks (such as installing a Drupal module) help organize the material. You can use them as a checklist for your Drupal development.

▶ **By the Way**—These notes provide additional commentary or explanation that doesn't fit neatly into the surrounding text. You will find detailed explanations of how something works, alternative ways of performing a task, and other tidbits to get you on your way.

- ▶ **Did You Know?**—This element gives you shortcuts, workarounds, and ways to avoid pitfalls.

- ▶ **Watch Out!**—Every once in a while, something can have serious repercussions if done incorrectly (or, rarely, if done at all). These elements give you a heads-up.

- ▶ **Cross-references**—Many topics are connected to other topics in various ways. Cross-references help you link related information, no matter where that information appears in the book. When another section is related to one you are reading, a cross-reference directs you to a specific page in the book on which you will find the related information.

Downloads and Support

Updates as well as a number of files are available from the author's website (northcountryconsulting.com) and from the publisher's site (www.informit.com/title/9780672331268). There also is an RSS feed from the author's site that provides information on updates to the modules used in this book.

A Note on the Figures

Because each package of modules can be updated separately within a given release of Drupal, the interfaces for the various modules can differ from the interfaces shown here. In addition, remember that you can access a Drupal website using any browser and operating system that you like. The fact that most of the figures in this book were generated using Mac OS X and Safari reflects the author's preference and nothing about Drupal.

HOUR 1

Using Drupal and the Twenty-First Century Web

What You'll Learn in This Hour:

▶ Introducing Drupal and Content Management Systems

▶ Learning to Talk CMS

▶ Getting Started with Drupal

Introduction

The beauty and power of the web are derived largely from the simplicity of its basic concepts. With minimal training, almost anyone can learn to put up a basic web page using HTML. And almost from the beginning, an enormous backlog of web pages to be done began growing. In the two decades since the web began, we've tried 0to tame that backlog with the usual technology tools: all of them are some variation on automation (templates, reusable components, style sheets, and the like). For a while, it seemed as if blogs with their incredible ease of use might be the answer, but at the same time, new web technologies and features were emerging that blogs couldn't handle.

Drupal, a Content Management System (CMS)—or content management framework, as many call it—is the preeminent tool that marries open source, sophisticated yet simple databases for content storage and manipulation, and high-level tools that generate the actual HTML and CSS code for pages. Many people believe that website development can now be sped up by an order of magnitude (yes, 10:1). In this hour, you will see the basics of how Drupal does it and how you can change your life (or at least your website) with Drupal.

Drupal: The Short Version

Drupal is a tool for building, managing, and presenting a website. It is open source software, so there is no explicit charge for using it.

> ### What Does "Free" Mean?
>
> Open source software is free in the sense that you do not have to pay money to use it, but it carries the wish that users will pay for it in other ways, such as by participating in discussion boards, offering to test new features, and possibly even contributing to the code base itself. In addition, you may have other costs for customization, support, and the hardware on which to run it.

Like much software that powers the web, Drupal doesn't run in the way that a word-processing program or spreadsheet runs. It sits on a web server ready for action, and it flies into action when that web server receives a request to display a page. Drupal responds to the request by interacting with the rules and information that have been stored in its database; the result of this response is almost always a web page that is returned to the user's browser. For the most part, input to Drupal consists of requests for pages (sent via Hypertext Transfer Protocol [HTTP]) that, after processing, are returned as pages of Hyper text Markup Language (HTML).

The database that powers Drupal (which can be MySQLor PostgreSQL and, in Drupal 7, SQLite) also lies in wait most of the time. It springs to action when Drupal sends a request for data or, in the case of developing a site, when Drupal sends a request to store information or rules about how the site is to be structured and displayed.

The primary exception to this is an optional job that runs periodically on the web server (a *cron* job) to do maintenance, such as indexing the site for searching. If you do not have access to cron on your site, Drupal provides *poormanscron*, which does the same sort of periodic processing, although it is actually triggered by events on Drupal.

Thus, to access a Drupal website or build one, you use a browser to communicate with the site, which must be installed on a web server. (The web server can be your own computer identified as *localhost* or with its own IP address.)

More technical information on how Drupal functions and how you build, manage, and use websites is provided throughout this book.

Getting the Terms Straight

In this web-based world, some of the terminology that has applied to the application-based world of word processors and spreadsheets (along with web-authoring tools such as Dreamweaver and Microsoft's Expression, which is its replacement for Front-Page) needs to be replaced. Here is a description of terms that are used in this book. Some people may use them in slightly different ways, and some people may use variations of them or even other terms to mean the same thing. As Humpty Dumpty says in *Alice in Wonderland*, "When I use a word, it means what I choose it to mean, neither more nor less." These are the choices for this book.

Developers

The word ***developer*** in the Drupal world means pretty much what it means through-out the software world: A developer is someone who develops code. In the world of Drupal, that code is most often PHP: Hypertext Preprocessor (a recursive acronym). On the database side of things, the code consists of SQL queries.

Users

As far as this book is concerned, *users* of Drupal are people who directly interact with Drupal as Drupal—that is, they are building, maintaining, or managing websites with Drupal.

End Users

End users are people who visit the websites created by Drupal users. Most of the time, they have no idea they are interacting with Drupal: They are interacting with a web-site ***through*** Drupal.

Web Pages

In the Drupal context, a ***web page*** is the same as it is in any other context: HTML that may be enhanced with JavaScript and Cascading Style Sheets (CSS). The difference is that Drupal creates that page on-the-fly when the user requests a page. The page that is generated combines the information that is required with the visual appearance determined by the Drupal user when the site is being created. (Like all web pages the visual appearance is modified by the end user's browser and operating system.)

Because Drupal pages are generated dynamically, the designs and rules for generat-ing them do not have to be repeated for each possible page in the website. In fact, the underlying data along with the designs and rules can create large numbers of pages on demand without any further coding. This is why dynamic websites using tools such as Drupal along with application servers such as WebObjects from Apple, .NET from Microsoft, WebSphere from IBM, and Oracle OC4J are so cost effective. However, this structure can confuse users who want the format for one particular page to be tweaked. That tweak will either apply to all pages of that type, or you will need to create a new type of page. To provide tweaks and customizations on each page defeats one of the main benefits of dynamic websites because you are back to the world of handcrafting each page. Drupal's block structure can provide a good deal of customization by displaying or not displaying blocks on specific pages; it is a good balance between handcrafted tweaks and generalized customizations.

Designers

As you will see, the visual appearance of a website and its pages in Drupal can be accomplished by developers in code and—most often—with CSS. In general, this book refers to developers and end users rather than designers.

What Content Management Means and How It Helps You

A Content Management System (CMS) stores and retrieves content that can be text, audio or video, images, and any other types that are relevant to the CMS and its users. This much is done with a database. But, CMSs add some additional features to basic storage and retrieval:

▶ A CMS normally provides the capability to **version** the content that it stores. Versioning means keeping track of multiple versions of the same item along with information about their sequence (and which is the current version); versioning may also allow for manual or automated comparisons to show the differences between versions.

▶ A CMS also typically provides for **workflow management**. This enables you to specify the steps that need to be taken as content moves through the system. For example, the workflow for a book chapter in a book such as this begins with the author writing a first draft; then, a review by a technical reviewer; then, an editor reviews the manuscript for grammar, usage, and style. The workflow continues with all comments being merged and returned to the author.

▶ Finally, a CMS generally provides the capability for a number of people to work together on the same content. Version control and workflow management are key tools that allow a collaborative process to culminate in the production and publication of final, consistent, and reviewed content.

Drupal and CMSs

Drupal is a CMS, and, for many people, it is the preferred CMS. From now on, this book focuses just on Drupal, even though some other CMSs may have some of the features described.

Focus on Content: What

The primary focus for Drupal (and any CMS) is the content. On traditional websites, the content and the presentation are generally treated together; sometimes, it is hard to separate them. When it comes to Drupal, it can be simple to separate content from presentation. Here is how you can do that:

▶ Content is **what** is on the website.

▶ Presentation is **where** it is (and what it looks like).

When you start to think about your website, if your first thought is, "This is what people will see on our home page," you are thinking about the presentation. If you think through the idea that content is the **what** and not the **where**, you may find yourself in the heart of CMS-land. This is one of the key features of Drupal: Because content is the key, its location (the **where**) need not be unique.

When you think about your website's home page and envision an article in the lower right, you probably are not thinking that the same article might appear on another page and might appear in the upper left. You also are probably not thinking that the article might have a short version, such as its first paragraph (commonly called a **teaser**), and a full version. When placed in the lower right of your home page, the teaser might appear with a link labeled More; when appearing in the upper left of another page, the article might appear in full. In Drupal, it's the same article, but it behaves differently in different places.

The **where** of Drupal content is not a location on a page; it is a location in the database that powers your Drupal site. This means that content for your website can appear in multiple places on the site, but it also means that content for your website can exist without appearing anywhere on the site. If you have developed websites by writing HTML, you probably have encountered this issue. You may have web pages that you do not upload to your server so that you can use them to store content you may need some day. You may keep content in word-processing documents or spreadsheets so that you will know where it is (you hope) when you need it. With Drupal, you create the content whenever you want to and store it in the Drupal database. You can specify tags to categorize it, add images to it, and indicate a teaser along with many other features. It sits in the Drupal database until you need it. And, as you will see, you can even search unpublished content so that you do not have to remember where you put it but can find it when needed.

Focus on Usability: How

Websites in the twenty-first century have become faster and more flexible (particularly with technologies that allow for partial page loads). In addition, the widespread use of social networking sites, such as Facebook, has raised expectations in many users that they can participate in the sites that they use to a greater extent than ever before. More and more, people expect to be able to bookmark content on the sites that they visit; they also expect to interact with sites by sharing them with friends and to keep up with them by subscribing to automated news feeds. Shopping carts for purchasing items are also expected, along with the ability to comment on content and provide formal ratings for content and products.

All these intense social interactions are available in Drupal—most of them in the basic Drupal installation.

Focus on Collaboration: Who

With its built-in workflow management and versioning tools, Drupal is ready for collaborative websites. Many Drupal sites are built by a single person, but many others are team efforts. Even when a single person develops a Drupal website, that person usually plays a variety of roles, such as writing and collecting content, planning the site, uploading files, monitoring the logs, and wishing that there were someone else to help out from time to time.

Because Drupal is ready for collaboration, and because there is no Drupal software to run (you just use your browser), Drupal collaboration happens easily on the website itself. By setting access controls, you can let people manage different features of the site without worrying about security problems. You can set up workflow management so that the various people know what is going on as they work together; you do not have to rely on separate email messages because Drupal will send the right messages to the right people at the right times after the workflow is set up.

With traditional websites, allowing people to create and edit pages means that you have to give them access to the web server—usually by giving them the File Transfer Protocol (FTP) login information for the site so that they can move files to and from the site as well as within it. With Drupal, you can allow specific users to create, modify, delete, and use different types of content: There is no single FTP login information to pass around.

Because Drupal is ready for collaboration, you can seriously consider constructing websites in a new way. Being able to allow people to modify the site without having to turn the keys of the website kingdom over to them expands the pool of people who can create and maintain your site. Not only does this spread the work around, but it also can create a different type of site, a site with multiple creative and editorial viewpoints.

After you set up the security settings of who has what type of access to what parts of the site, and you have implemented workflow management as needed, people can focus on maintaining the site. And that is all good.

Except that there can be a problem. Do not go looking for trouble, but in the back of your mind, tuck this little thought: After the access and workflow rules are set up, you may have automated tasks out of existence. Having the keys to the website kingdom can be a bit of a thrill, or at least a power trip for some people, and when the responsibilities are spread around and automated, a bit of push-back may occur. It may even be you who feels a bit threatened as other people gain access to the site's internals that heretofore were yours alone.

Organizing the Drupal Project

If you think of Drupal as a tool for developing and powering a website, you will miss much of its significance. Drupal can support a wide range of interactive features ranging from polls, comments, and user-created content (all supported in Drupal core), to e-commerce shopping carts and end user created bookmarks and collections. In the world of the twenty-first century web, these interactive and collaborative features are becoming increasingly important.

Web User Identities

Another major feature of the modern web is the use of real and verifiable identities. With the rise of social networking sites, such as Facebook and LinkedIn, more people are becoming used to an Internet in which online personas are real people. This has dramatically changed the web from a place of shadows and suspicion to something more like the real world—with about the same degree of shadow and suspicion found in the real world. Drupal supports automatic verification of email addresses for site registrations, and that is an important first step to providing a safe, secure, and honest web environment. When you register and provide an email address, Drupal can be configured to automatically send a message to that address with a temporary password. After you log in, you can change your password.

By the Way

Before you start working with Drupal, it is important to have a project ready to go. In many cases, that comes automatically: The idea for the website is the starting point, and Drupal is the tool to implement it. If you just want to bring yourself up to speed on one of the most exciting technologies on the web today, create your own project to work on. A personal website will do, but you can also offer to create a website for a friend, business, or nonprofit organization. Trying to learn any technology in the abstract is difficult.

With the website identified, organize the Drupal project. If it is your personal website, you are the designer, user, manager, and everyone else. If it is a site for an organization, you are playing only some of those roles. Take a few minutes at the start to identify the roles and who will play them.

Implementing the Management Structure

Welcome Management to the Party

With Drupal, you can create a full-featured website without writing any HTML, CSS, JavaScript or PHP; you can take advantage of Drupal's database interface to store the website's data without knowing any SQL. (In all fairness, many Drupal sites are maintained by people with these skills, but they aren't necessary.) Until now, the technical barriers to building and discussing websites have been significant for many people. Final decisions about printed brochures and advertising are typically made by management, but when a website substitutes for or augments the printed media, the website decisions are often made by technical people alone.

Because the technical barriers to Drupal website development are so low, many organizations find that management can reclaim its normal role (of managing the organization's communications). In addition, because Drupal allows so many interactive and social features, such as e-commerce, user-contributed content, and end-user blogs, the decisions about which of these features to implement and how to manage them must be management decisions.

For a new Drupal site built from scratch, the first step is to determine who is responsible for the site. This may be an individual, group, or committee. Technical knowledge is not required for this management role, but a clear understanding of the organization, its purpose, and the website's role in carrying out that purpose are required.

At the beginning, the main tasks of the management team are to determine what features are on the site and who has access to them. Because Drupal allows a variety of levels of security for various users, you do not have to live with a simple password/no-password level of security, and this means meetings and discussion. It cannot be emphasized enough that these are business meetings, not code reviews. Although you may wind up writing new code in Drupal, for the most part, you will be using the built-in Drupal security code to implement the business security rules you are developing.

Browse Drupal Features

Look ahead at the chapter titles in the rest of this book to see features that you can implement easily. You may not have thought about e-commerce, but that technology can allow you to sell file downloads and provide access to special website services and features. Likewise, the interactivity of polls and forums can transform your site into a dynamic environment. Before setting up a meeting to plan the management structure, consider reading the first three hours and completing the activities listed at the end of each hour. Those activities will provide you with an agenda for your first Drupal project meeting.

Did you Know?

GO TO ▶
For more on deployment issues, see **CHAPTER 2, EXPLORING DRUPAL,** p. 17 and **CHAPTER 3, SETTING UP AND INSTALLING DRUPAL,** p. 29.

Planning for Implementation

Drupal can run on an in-house server that is accessible from the outside or on an in-house server that is available only from within your organization. It can run on a shared server or a colocated server. Although you can move a Drupal site from one environment to another, it makes sense to explore the options right at the beginning, especially because some of the research may take time to track down options and prices.

Try It Yourself ▼

Beginning the Drupal Organization Chart—Roles and Responsibilities

As you have seen in this hour, Drupal is a CMS, and the focus is on content, so that is where your Drupal org chart begins. Start to identify the content for your Drupal website. If you are converting an existing website, it is not enough to say "everything on our current website." Take the time to identify what is on the website at least by category or content type.

Converting Websites to Drupal

One organization that is converting to Drupal was an early adopter of web technologies, and its site began in earnest in the late 1990s. Today, it has more than 1,000 pages, most of them handcrafted with raw HTML. A little arithmetic shows how easily such a website can evolve: If you add 100 pages a year for 10 years, you wind up with 1,000 pages. 100 pages a year may sound like a lot, but it's only two pages a week. For an organization with programs, conferences, events, and news items, this is par for the course. Looking forward, the organization can see that Drupal will help it manage an ever-increasing amount of information, but it is taking the Drupal opportunity to convert only some of the 1,000 pages.

By the Way

As you start to plan your Drupal site, consider these steps. As you will see, these initial decisions are management decisions involving no technical issues. Work with pencil or on a whiteboard, and leave lots of blank space; you will revise this plan as the project proceeds. As you work, strike a balance between doing the homework and planning that will make the site easier to implement and discuss, versus turning the project into creating an org chart and diagram rather than a website. At this stage, generalities are fine. They will start you thinking, and, with luck, you will start to free-associate and come up with other items for your plan.

1. Identify the types of content—the **what** of your site. Work with generalities, such as "meetings" or "items for sale," rather than a specific meeting or item for sale. A good general rule is that each type of content you identify should behave in different ways from the other types of content.

2. For each type of content, decide **how** it will be presented. (Multiple answers are fine where appropriate, but resist the urge to choose all presentations for all types of content.) The following are a few of the basic ways in which you can present content using Drupal's technologies:

    ▶ **Stories and articles**—Drupal 6 calls them **stories**, Drupal 7 calls them **articles**, and you can call them items, essays, thoughts, or whatever you want. Whatever you call them, they consist of a title, text, and, possibly, one or more images. Using CCK, you can add additional fields to the basic content type.

    ▶ **Images**—Images can be attached to stories, but they also are their own content type for Drupal. An image can have a title with text accompanying it, so in some ways, it is like a story, but the emphasis is on the image.

    ▶ **Forum topic**—Drupal supports forums that are divided into topics to which people can add their own comments. Making an area of interest into a forum topic is one way of presenting it.

    ▶ **Blogs**—Drupal allows users to create their own blogs. You can create a blog for a specific type of content and use it to add new information over time.

    ▶ **Polls**—Drupal's basic poll functionality lets you create a poll to which people can respond. As with all Internet polls, this is unscientific, but it comes with certain safeguards, such as not allowing multiple voting, provided that you require people to log in.

3. For each content type, decide **who** will present it. This choice may apply to all items within a specific content type or only to some of them. Your choices are basic:

    ▶ Anonymous authors from the web team. These are the unsigned stories and articles that you find on most websites.

▶ Signed articles from the web team. Drupal can manage the identification of authors for you. A signed article can be signed with an author's name or a phrase, such as "By the Web Team," or "From the Management."

▶ Anonymous contributions from end users of the website.

▶ Signed contributions from end users of the website. (Drupal can take care of managing registration, login, and verification of user email addresses.)

▶ In addition, Drupal content types allow you to provide the capability for people to post comments. You can allow anonymous comments from people who are not logged into the site.

You can also confine comments to people who are logged in with a verified email address.

4. For each content type, decide who will make these decisions in the future. When first planning the site, it makes sense for several people to talk through the issues, but in the long run, it makes sense to delegate the decision-making process after the guidelines have been discussed. Depending on the site and the people involved, you may want to create a kind of appeal process for thorny issues that may arise in the future. If you are the sole manager of the website, you can obviously skip this step.

Summary

This hour presented the basic concepts and terminologies behind Drupal. You have seen how the emphasis on content can be played out on a website and how you can organize your project around the management issues that will arise.

Q&A

Q. *Which of the following technologies do you need to know before using Drupal: PHP, SQL, HTML, XHTML, and CSS?*

A. None of them. If you want to customize themes or develop your own modules, you need to be familiar with them. For most Drupal users, a passive knowledge of them can help. (Passive knowledge means being able to recognize syntax and follow it, but not necessarily being able to write code from scratch.)

Q. *What is the difference between users and end users in Drupal?*

A. As used in this book, users are people who directly use Drupal to create and manage websites. End users are people who visit the site and may not even know it is powered by Drupal.

Workshop

Quiz

1. Where is Drupal data stored?

2. What are the three main characteristics of a Content Management System (CMS)?

Answers

1. In a database.

2. Version control, workflow management, and collaboration.

Activities

Work through the task to begin planning the Drupal org chart. The importance of including people who currently are not involved in managing websites (because they are daunted by the technology) cannot be overestimated.

HOUR 2

Exploring Drupal

What You'll Learn in This Hour:

▶ Finding Your Way Around Drupal

▶ Exploring Drupal Sites

▶ Looking at Drupal's Structure

This hour provides a brief overview of the various Drupals (the project, the websites, and the association) and what they mean to you. It also shows you some examples of Drupal in action and gives you an overall look at how Drupal works.

Wandering the Worlds of Drupal

Drupal is a Content Management System (CMS), a community of users, and an organization (The Drupal Association) that provides support for Drupal by providing marketing and conference support. The founder and president of Drupal is Dries Buytaert.

The Drupal website is www.drupal.org. It is your source for the latest information about Drupal, the downloadable code, contributed modules, and discussions. The home page is constantly updated with the latest news, as you can see in Figure 2.1.

You can create an account so that you can log in to the site. Certain functions of the site (such as posting comments) are restricted to registered users. All of this is handled by Drupal itself because, as you might expect, the site is powered by Drupal.

As you can see in Figure 2.2, a section of the site at groups.drupal.org contains information about events and job listings. You can join specific groups, which often relate to a geographic area or a particular industry.

FIGURE 2.1
Visit drupal.org
for the latest
information.

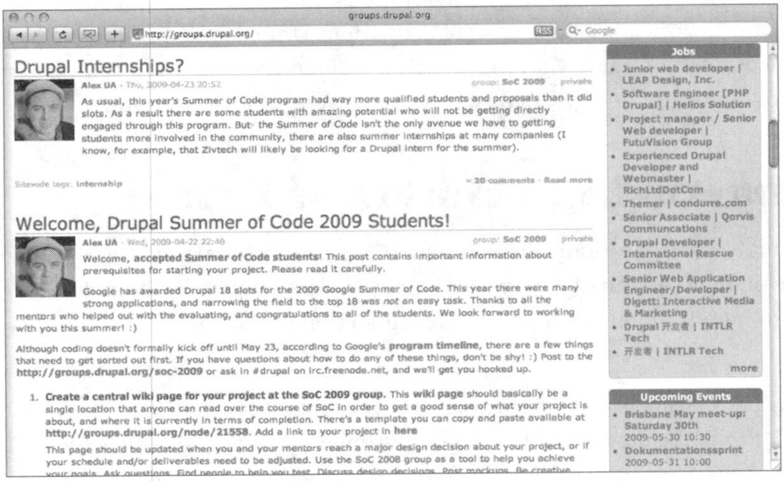

FIGURE 2.2
Use groups.dru-
pal.org to
explore jobs and
events.

Finding Drupal Information

Search the Drupal site for information as you build and maintain your site. If you
get an error message that you don't understand, search for its text. (Most of the
time, error messages show up in your site's log.) If you find items relating to the
problem, always check the date of the posting and the version of Drupal to which
it relates. In the last several versions, Drupal's capabilities have expanded dramatically, and a number of optional modules have now moved into Drupal core.
For that reason, problems (and solutions) that were relevant to Drupal 4 and 5
may not be relevant to later versions.

Identifying Drupal Sites

Drupal sites are all over the web, and they are proliferating rapidly. As open source software, Drupal itself is free, and that is obviously a big attraction. If you look at the websites powered by Drupal, you will see commercial sites as well as a large number of nonprofit and governmental sites from around the world.

There Is No Drupal "Look"

Out of the box, a Drupal site can have a specific Drupal look and feel, just as any out-of-the-box website has default settings that can identify its origin. Like many other websites, Drupal's internal URLs can identify the site as a Drupal site. However, tools such as Pathauto are among the downloadable modules that allow you to automatically customize Drupal's URLs to make them friendlier to people (and, coincidentally, remove the Drupal syntax).

Similarly, when you download Drupal, you get several default themes that specify the look of the site. Many people do not customize them at all, whereas others do minimal customization. Still other Drupal users download the many other available themes and even write their own. Thus, an identifiable Drupal look is possible, but not required.

About the Images in This Book

These are images of live sites at the time the book was written. Like any website, they are subject to change over time, so they may look different when you explore them.

The Drupal site shown in Figures 2.1 and 2.2 show a default theme that many people use. But, other Drupal sites have very different looks.

The American Recovery and Reinvestment Act of 2009 is a massive program to handle problems caused by the economic crisis that became apparent in 2008. A special government website at www.recovery.gov was created quickly to track the activities and investments carried out through the program. You can see its home page in Figure 2.3. Yes, it's a Drupal site.

Although there is no common look to Drupal sites, sometimes the internal URLs have an appearance that identifies them as Drupal URLs. For example the URL http://www.recovery.gov/?q=content/act suggests to many people that it is a Drupal URL because its query part (?q=content/act) has the hallmarks of Drupal. It is not necessarily a Drupal URL, because the actual syntax of a URL's query part depends on the requirements of the page that will process it.

FIGURE 2.3
Drupal powers
recovery.gov.

Later in this hour, you see how Drupal handles these URLs. In addition, you will see in Hour 6, "Managing URLs: Cleaning, Redirects, and Pathauto," how to modify these URLs to more standard formats using the Pathauto module.

Drupal is often used for commercial sites large and small. Figure 2.4 shows the site for City Market/Onion River Coop in Burlington, Vermont.

FIGURE 2.4
Find out this week's specials using Drupal at City Market in Burlington.

Sony Records has hosted a number of Drupal sites, many of which take advantage of Drupal's multilingual support. Figure 2.5 shows the Swedish version of artist Pink's site. As is often the case, only some of the text is translated. In some spheres, English, French, or another language carries an extra cachet.

FIGURE 2.5
Visit Pink's Swedish site (courtesy of Drupal).

Perhaps inspired by Pink, the New York State Senate unveiled its own Drupal site, shown in Figure 2.6.

FIGURE 2.6
The New York State Senate has joined the Drupal world.

Finally, Figure 2.7 shows the author's site, which used the Drupal Zen theme at one time. This downloadable theme is designed specifically for customization. Switching from one Drupal theme to another can be a simple process, although in some cases, customizations may need to be reimplemented.

FIGURE 2.7
The author's site at www.north-countryconsult-ing.com provides information and serves as a test site.

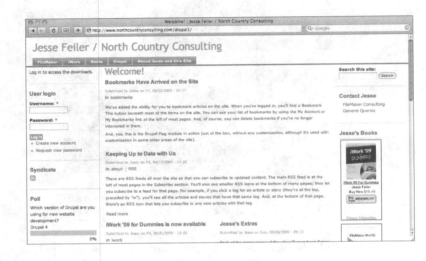

As you can see, there is no common Drupal "look." Many of the sites shown here have been built with customized themes (the look-and-feel), but the Drupal site shown in Figures 2.1 and 2.2, as well as the author's site shown in Figure 2.7, are built using common Drupal themes that you can download and modify. Depending on your site and budget, you can choose the path you want to take: a downloadable theme, a totally customized theme, or a slightly customized downloadable theme.

Finding Drupal Sites (And Seeing What They Can Do)

Go To ▶

HOUR 24,
"**CUSTOMIZING
THEMES AND
THEIR CSS**,"
FOR MORE ON
CUSTOMIZING
THEMES.

There is a Drupal Showcase discussion on drupal.org (drupal.org/forum/25). Sites are listed as discussions with comments and suggestions, as well as links to the sites, as shown in Figure 2.8.

Browse through the list to see what people are doing with Drupal. In describing their sites, people often provide insight into the process, such as why they made certain choices, how much time it took, and what (if anything) they would do differently next time.

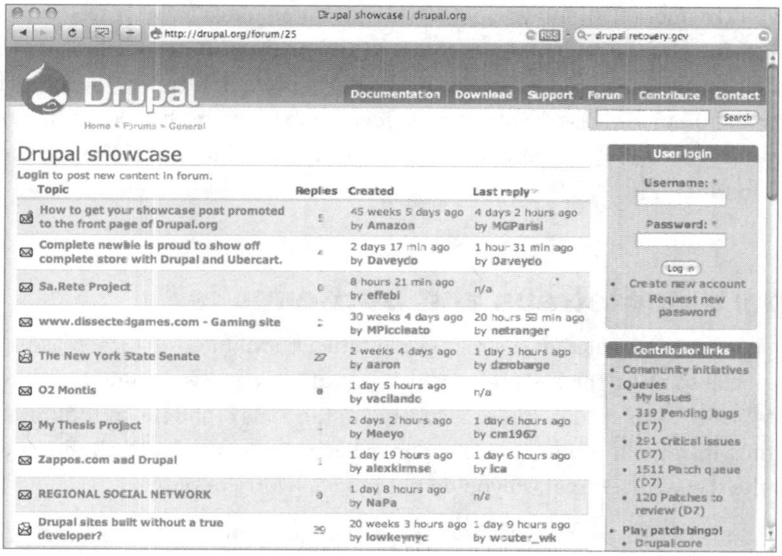

FIGURE 2.8
Browse the Drupal showcase to get your own ideas.

How Drupal Works

One of the great features of Drupal is that you do not need to write code to use it. However, it is useful to have a basic understanding of how Drupal manages its content, and that understanding can come from a superficial look at some of its code. Do not worry: There is little code in this section, and the most important message to take away is that Drupal's architecture is a sturdy one; it can be extended and modified by developers who have already been given specific places to customize Drupal. By using these customization structures, you can add significant new features to Drupal without jeopardizing the overall stability of its operations. You need have no fears about downloading additional modules from the Drupal website and installing them in your copy of Drupal.

Go To ▶
HOUR 3, **"SETTING UP AND INSTALLING DRUPAL,"** FOR MORE ON INSTALLING DRUPAL.

Rewriting URLs

This section describes the overall architecture and a bit of the specific implementation for Drupal running on Apache with mod_rewrite enabled (the most common configuration for Drupal sites). You can also run Drupal using Microsoft Internet Information Services (IIS). Use the URL Rewrite module for IIS 7.0 to replace the .htaccess file; information and downloads are available at www.iis.net/extensions/URLRewrite.

By the Way

When you download Drupal, you get a folder that you place on your web server. The most basic installation is to place its contents in the appropriate location—either the site's root or a subfolder. Note that it is the contents of the folder, not the folder itself, that you should place on your site. A subfolder can be used in the URL, as in www. northcountryconsulting.com/drupal1; alternatively, you can point a domain or sub-domain to that folder.

Drupal's Bootstraps and Bottlenecks

The .htaccess file is located at the root level of the Drupal file structure. It is a simple set of Apache settings, the key one of which is that all requests coming into the direc-tory in which Drupal is located are redirected to the index.php file in that directory. By the time they get to index.php, they have been reformatted, but all that is done behind the scenes by Drupal, so you do not have to worry about it.

The request is then routed into bootstrap.inc, a file in the includes folder of the working directory, as you can see in the following code. This means that every page request goes through the same logic that can check for various conditions.

```
define('DRUPAL_ROOT', getcwd());

require_once DRUPAL_ROOT . '/includes/bootstrap.inc';
drupal_bootstrap(DRUPAL_BOOTSTRAP_FULL);
$return = menu_execute_active_handler();
```

The $return variable contains the main section of the Drupal page to be returned to the user. After some error checking in index.php, the page is rendered with

```
print drupal_render_page($return);
```

Within that function, the page is rendered with this code:

```
function drupal_render_page($page) {
  // Allow menu callbacks to return strings, or bare content arrays.
  if (is_string($page) || empty($page['content'])) {
    $page = drupal_get_page($page);
  }
  // Modules alter the $page as needed. Blocks are populated into regions like
  // 'left', 'footer', etc.
  drupal_alter('page', $page);

  return drupal_render($page);
}
```

This means that every request for a Drupal page goes through the same bottleneck where additional processing (such as modifying URLs) can take place, and every request to render a page goes through a similar bottleneck where different types of additional processing (such as placing blocks in regions of the page next to the main content) can be performed.

This is a common structure for modern web applications. Facebook applications, for example, consist of a Facebook frame that is created by Facebook independently of the app. The app is called by Facebook to return the center portion of the frame, and Facebook merges them together.

Using Hooks

Drupal's **hooks** are somewhat similar to bottlenecks. At specific moments, such as when content is about to be viewed, stored, or deleted, or when a user has just logged in or logged out, Drupal checks the modules (including ones you have downloaded and installed yourself) in case one wants to be involved. Thus, a module can modify the data to be displayed or it can do something to reflect the users log in or log out. The implementation of these hooks is provided in the code for each module. (Not all hooks are implemented in all modules.) Each hook has its own syntax, and it is named with the module's name.

For example, the hook that is called when a node is about to be viewed is defined as shown in Table 2.1.

TABLE 2.1   Node View Hooks

Version	Syntax	Return Value
6	`hook_view($node, $teaser = FALSE, $page = FALSE)`	$node (possibly with changes)
7	`hook_node_view($node, $teaser)`	$node (possibly with changes)

By the Way

How New Drupal Versions Work

The example shown in Table 2.1 illustrates the process of implementing a new version of Drupal. Sometimes, module developers need to change their code to adjust to changes in Drupal's core. Here, for example, the second parameter in hook_view change from a true/false indicator for $teaser in Drupal 6 to a more flexible parameter, $build_mode that can have values of "full", "teaser", or others in Drupal 7. Such changes do not happen in each version, but from time to time, internal structural changes are necessary for the long-term development and implementation of Drupal. The process is that, at a certain point in the development of a new version of Drupal, the code is frozen. At that point, while testing continues, module developers can safely make the changes necessary for their modules to run in the new version. (Often, no changes are needed.) That is why it can take a period of time for modules to be available for a new version of Drupal even after its release.

For a module called `mymodule`, the actual implementation in the module file would be `mymodule_view` or `mymodule_node_view`.

Unless you are writing your own module, do not worry about this, but it is useful to understand how Drupal manages its operations. If, for some reason, you are tempted to bypass Drupal's event-dispatching mechanism, you will break the hook structure. (Fortunately, it is not easy to bypass the event-dispatching mechanism.)

Drupal's File Structure

The whole functioning of Drupal depends on this combination of `.htaccess` and `index.php`. For it to function properly, the files must be in the right place. If you start to move them to improve on the file structure, you will break this robust structure.

The file structure does allow for several types of optimization within this structure, and you should consider them before you start your installation. Figure 2.9 shows the basic structure of a Drupal folder. You can see the `index.php` file; `.htaccess` is hidden. Two folders should draw your attention: `modules` and `themes`. These contain the files for modules and themes that either ship with Drupal or that you can download.

FIGURE 2.9
Review the Drupal file structure.

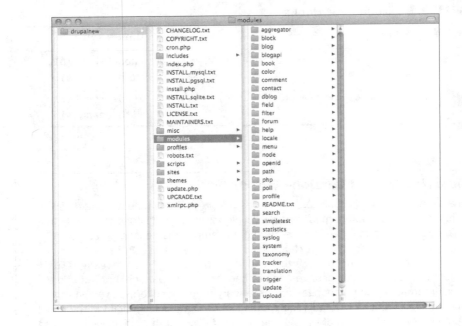

The temptation for many is to download modules and themes into the relevant folders. However, notice the `sites` folder in Figure 2.10; within it is an `all` folder, containing its own `modules` and `themes` folders. Those are the folders into which you should place your downloaded modules. That means that the main `modules` folder contains only the modules that were downloaded with Drupal itself. The ones you have added are in their own folder. This can make maintenance and updating much easier.

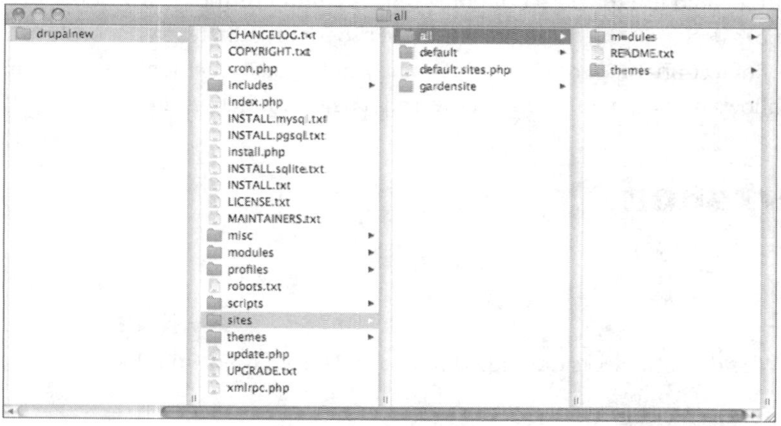

FIGURE 2.10
Use site-specific folders for modules and themes inside the sites folder.

Furthermore, you can add additional folders within the sites folder, each with its own modules and themes folders. That way, a single Drupal installation can serve several sites with several sets of themes and modules. All this works because of Drupal's runtime structure.

Summary

In this hour, you saw how Drupal is organized and how it is used in various websites. Drupal's structures—both the structure of the organization and the structure of its software—show you how you can feel comfortable downloading new modules for your website from www.drupal.org.

Q&A

Q. What is Drupal's copyright status?

A. Drupal is distributed under the GNU General Public License version 2 or later (www.gnu.org/copyleft/gpl.html). All contributed modules by third parties must be distributed under the same license. Drupal is free in the four ways covered by the GPL—free to use it, free to change it, free to share it, and free to share changes you make to it. Obviously, to make this possible, the source code is distributed.

Q. *Is Drupal object-oriented software?*

A. Drupal 7 is the first version of Drupal to require PHP 5, so it is the first version that could use the object-oriented implementations that PHP 5 supports. Drupal's design is object oriented in the sense that it adheres to the basic principles of object-oriented software, particularly in its use of the hook mechanism that allows any module to extend (override) default functionality.

Workshop

Quiz

1. Why do bottlenecks and hooks matter to Drupal users and developers?

2. Is there a Drupal "look?"

3. Does Drupal require Apache?

Answers

1. They provide a safe and stable environment for implementing new modules. Users need not worry about destabilizing their Drupal environments by installing new modules.

2. No.

3. No, you can use other web servers, including Microsoft IIS 7.0 with the URL Rewrite module installed.

Activities

Study the Drupal Showcase (drupal.org/forum/25). Browse to see what people are doing and what types of projects they pursue with Drupal. You may want to specifically read the descriptions that often mention how long it took to develop a Drupal site (be prepared to be pleasantly surprised). Then, use the search feature to search the listings for features you are interested in adding to your site.

To find other sites that use Drupal, browse the jobs listings at groups.drupal.org/jobs. Not only will you see the available jobs, but you'll see the companies that are using Drupal and what they are doing with it. Notice, too, the time frames for the projects that are listed.

Setting Up and Installing Drupal

What You'll Learn in This Hour:

▶ What You Need for Your Drupal Site

▶ Understanding Drupal's Version Structure

▶ How to Do the Installation

This hour shows you the process of setting up and installing Drupal. The Drupal site (drupal.org) and the author's website (www.northcountryconsulting.com) provide additional information about installing specific versions of Drupal and using specific types of servers and hosts.

Try a Test Installation

For your first Drupal installation, it is a good idea to plan to throw it out when you are finished. That way, you can experiment without worrying that you will live to regret your choices. Having thrown out your first Drupal installation, you will find that your second one is much easier and faster. That is because, if you do make a mistake (or two or three), you can take care not to repeat them when you set up the real site. If your first attempt is going to become your live site, you will have to go back and repair any mistakes. This applies to the most basic installation as well as to taxonomy categories and terminology for the objects you are creating in your Drupal site.

Did you Know?

Planning for the Next Installation

Yes, before you take the first steps to install your first Drupal website, start planning the next installation. As the Internet and the software world have changed over the last few years, almost everyone now understands that software (much less websites) are not eternal. They require periodic maintenance and attention.

Vendors of commercial products are increasingly adopting a current-and-one-prior policy with regard to support: The current version and one prior version are actively supported with bug fixes and other forms of support. In addition, special upgrade pricing is usually limited to registered users of one prior version, although this is periodically changed for marketing reasons. Drupal, too, is on the current-and-one-prior schedule, although, of course, upgrade pricing is not an issue with free software.

Some products are revised annually, particularly if they are tied to the calendar (such as tax software). Other products, including operating systems and major productivity tools, are typically revised about every two years. It used to be that changes to operating systems set in motion a cascade of necessary revisions to end-user tools, but the cost and unpopularity of such cascades has made them less common.

Nevertheless, cascades occur. In the open source world, where there is no direct cost for the software, they are less costly than for commercial software, but the need to install new versions of supporting software still exists. For example, with Drupal 7, PHP 5.2 or later is required, although with Drupal 5, PHP 4.3.5 or later is required.

Drupal's release schedule is published on the Drupal site. In addition, the release plans for the supporting software are well known. As you start to plan your Drupal site, take a moment to check out the schedules. Where you have choices, select the choices that will have the longest life.

Planning for Drupal

Drupal runs on a web server and stores its data in a database. The code for Drupal itself and contributed modules is primarily PHP. Other common web languages and protocols, such as CSS and JavaScript, are also used, but they rarely need to be considered: If you have a web server, it will almost always support them.

You also need an Internet connection if you intend to allow people to visit your site. You can install Drupal on your own computer and allow only people on your network to access it; you can even install it on your own computer and access it yourself from that computer. This is a common testing environment.

Get the full requirements for Drupal installations at `drupal.org/requirements`. As you install and test Drupal, watch for error messages. If you cannot immediately diagnose the problem, copy the error message and paste it into the search box on drupal.org. Most of the time, you will find several items or comments that report on or solve the problem.

> **Repeat as Necessary**
>
> You may have to go through this section more than once because the versions of Drupal, database, and PHP are all interrelated.

Setting Up Hosting

Your hosting environment typically includes both the Internet connection and the web server. It frequently includes your database as well. If you already have a website, the easiest choice may be to install Drupal on that host. Just check that the requirements in this section can be met (and try a test installation to see if you encounter any errors).

Your hosting choices are the same as for any website—your own server, a colocated server at a hosting service, or a shared server. If you are using a shared server, make certain that it supports the products and versions that you need. In addition, you need to find out the vendor's plans for upgrades to new versions. For example, some shared hosting services that provide PHP support took two years to make the transition to PHP 5 from PHP 4. At first, PHP 5 was an option, but then support for PHP 4 was dropped.

If you need a shared hosting vendor, the best choice for many people is to use one that already runs some Drupal sites. You can find a list of Drupal hosts at drupal.org/hosting. The absence of a host from this list is not necessarily an indication that it cannot host Drupal. (For example, Network Solutions provides a number of open source products, including Drupal, with automated installation scripts to its shared hosting accounts, but it is not on the list.)

Setting Up the Software

PHP and the web server are the primary software. PHP 5.2 or higher is required for Drupal 7 and recommended for Drupal 6. If you are using a shared hosting service, the versions they support are important as well as their upgrade policy. In many circumstances, Drupal will need to send email using PHP. Particularly on shared hosting servers, you might need to contact your vendor to enable this. Remember this is email sent from PHP and not the normal email application or web page you can usually access to send and receive email on your web server.

Download a Bundle

If you need the software, you can install all of it in a free open source download. XAMPP is the cross-platform version that contains Apache HTTP Server, MySQL Server, PHP, and Perl. The versions are regularly updated to the current releases. It is available at www.apachefriends.org/en/xampp.html. You can search Wikipedia for a list of AMP Packages to find specific versions for Linux, Windows, Solaris, memory sticks, and more.

As for a web server, Apache 1.3 or Apache 2.x on Mac OS X, Windows, or UNIX/Linux is the recommended choice. Drupal also runs on Microsoft Internet Information Services (IIS) 6 or IIS 7.

The most common modifications needed are enabling the mod_rewrite extension for Apache or the Microsoft URL Rewrite Modules for IIS 7.0 on IIS. If you do not do this, Drupal will still run but will not be able to create clean URLs. See Hour 6, "Managing URLs: Cleaning, Redirects, and Pathauto," for more on mod_rewrite.

Working with Microsoft

Microsoft's relationship to open source software has evolved over the past few years. It has reached out in a number of ways and has sponsored some Drupal events.

On a shared server, you may or may not have access to the PHP initialization values in php.ini. (If you do not have direct access to it, contact your hosting service; it may either give you access or make the change for you.) One common value on shared servers that might need to be overridden is the memory setting. It is often set to 16MB, but changing it to 32MB or 64MB will prevent some Drupal memory errors. Drupal is designed to be as fast and efficient as possible, but at some points in its processing, memory requirements can spike. The memory issue is a commonly misdiagnosed Drupal problem. It often occurs after you install a new module and then go to the modules administration page to enable it. That is a moment when memory can spike. Removing the module appears to solve the problem. It can then recur when the same module or another one is installed. Instead of blaming the error on the modules, increase the memory limit to handle these spikes.

Other common php.ini settings that may need attention are the following:

▶ `register-globals` **off**

▶ `session_save_handler` **user**

▶ `safe_mode` **off**

Setting Up the Database

Drupal core has a database abstraction layer that makes it possible for it to use many types of databases. At the moment, MySQL and PostgreSQL are supported. Table 3.1 shows the versions that are required.

TABLE 3.1 Drupal Database Requirements

Drupal Version	MySQL	PostgreSQL (pgsql)	SQLite
6	4.1 or later	7.4 or later	
7	5.0 or later	8.3 or later	See drupal.org/requirements

Shared hosting packages often limit the number of databases you can have, and they may also limit the creation of databases so that they are done only through a script on the shared server. In addition, some hosting services that provide scripts to perform an automated install of Drupal and creation of its database may not allow you to access the database features such as optimization and data export. This matters only if you need to extract all the data (as when you move to another host). If you are using a host-provided script to set up the database, make certain that you have access to all the functions that you might need for its maintenance. You may need to contact the hosting service to do this.

You need the following permissions for the account that Drupal uses to access the database: SELECT, INSERT, UPDATE, DELETE, CREATE, DROP, INDEX, and ALTER. Contributed modules may need CREATE TEMPORARY TABLES, LOCK TABLES, and other permissions (they should be identified in the module documentation). As noted, you need the ability to create a new database whether with the CREATE DATABASE command or by running a host-provided script that executes the CREATE DATABASE command only after checking that you have not used up your quota of databases and any other constraints the hosting vendor may have implemented.

Selecting a Drupal Version

This is the easiest part: Select from the current or the prior version after having checked the release schedule. Also, if you know the modules you want to use, check to see if they are available for the Drupal version you select.

The numbering convention for Drupal has two numbers: a major version and a release. Drupal 6.13 is thus the thirteenth release of Drupal 6. The number might be followed by -dev to indicate that it is in development. In the listings on drupal.org/project/drupal, you will find an indication of the recommended release for each version of Drupal.

Module numbering uses a similar approach. Because modules are specific to versions of Drupal, the module incorporates a Drupal version but not a release in most cases. Thus, the Panels contributed module can be numbered 6.x-3.0-rc1. The first part indicates that it is for Drupal 6; the x shows that no specific release is targeted (this is the common case). Following the hyphen, you find the module's numbering. This is version 3 of Panels, and this is the first release (zero); -rc1 indicates that it is a release candidate (other common indicators are alpha and beta). Depending on the developer and the complexity of the module, you might see several release candidates as the module's latest release is frozen and the last bugs are fixed.

Getting Ready

You are now ready to install Drupal. Double-check your hosting settings, create a simple HTML page (such as a Hello World greeting), and upload it to the server. Make certain you can access it from your browser.

Also, make certain that you can access your database host. Create a new database and create a single table in it using phpMyAdmin, MySQL Administrator, or MySQL Query Browser. (You can remove this database as soon as you have tested it.)

If you do not regularly use PHP, create a one-line PHP program to check the PHP settings on your server with the following code:

```
phpinfo();
```

Save it and place it in your server's web root (where you successfully placed the Hello World page) and run it from a browser by typing www.myservername.com/phpinfo.php. You should see your server's PHP settings.

If you cannot create a database and a table, or if you cannot create and run a PHP program, you will not be able to install and run Drupal. Particularly on shared hosting servers, much of the customer support is provided for the initial setup, so don't be shy about asking.

Creating a Drupal Directory

Now, designate a directory for your Drupal files. It can be the root level of your website, or it can be a subfolder that you create specifically for Drupal. If you want to keep your Drupal files in their own folder, you can place a PHP file at the root level of your account to move to that folder. Particularly with shared hosting, you may already have an index.php file; if you do not, create one with this code:

```php
<?php
    header("Location: http://www.mysite.com/mysubfolder");
    exit();
?>
```

If you do have an existing index.php file, you can move it to your subfolder or incorporate this code into it.

If you are using localhost to test your Drupal installation, you are done. If you are using a separate server, you may decide to keep a copy of your Drupal site on your own computer for safekeeping. If so, create that directory now.

By the
Way

Using Relative Path Names

Within your Drupal folder, the names of files and subfolders are the same whether you are running in `localhost` on your own computer or in a path to an IP address or a domain name (which in turn may be a subdomain or a folder within the domain). Rather than repeating this throughout the book, files and folders within your Drupal director are identified by relative path names that begin with a dot. Any relative path name that is not otherwise identified is relative to your Drupal folder wherever you may have placed it.

Try It Yourself

Creating the Database

On a shared server, you may run a script from the hosting provider to create a database; in many cases, phpMyAdmin is provided for your use. If you have the ability to create your own database (on a host or on your own computer), use MySQL Query Browser to create the database. It is available for free download at MySQL GUI Tools (dev.mysql.com/downloads/gui-tools/5.0.html). Versions for Windows, Mac, and Linux are available. This package also includes MySQL Query Browser.

1. Log in to your MySQL on your database host, as shown in Figure 3.1. You will need the IP address of the database host unless you are using localhost. You also need your MySQL user name and password. These should have been provided when you created the MySQL account. You also need to know what port number is used (3306 is the default). The Stored Connection pop-up menu lets you choose from connections you have already used; it also has an option to save current settings with a name that is added to the pop-up menu.

FIGURE 3.1
Log in to your
MySQL account.

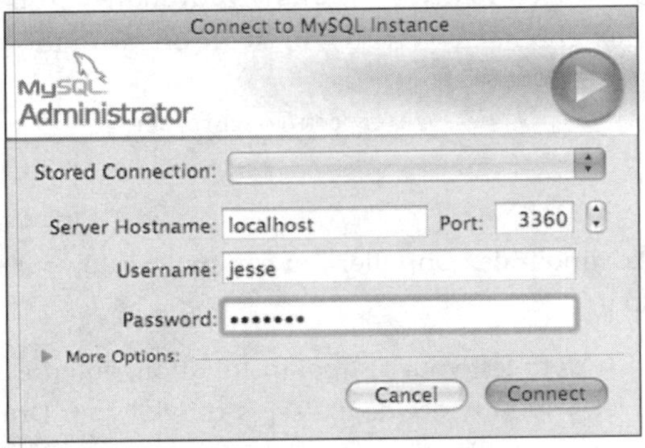

2. Create the database. The syntax for creating a database is CREATE DATABASE
   <database name>, as shown in Figure 3.2.

FIGURE 3.2
Create your data-
base.

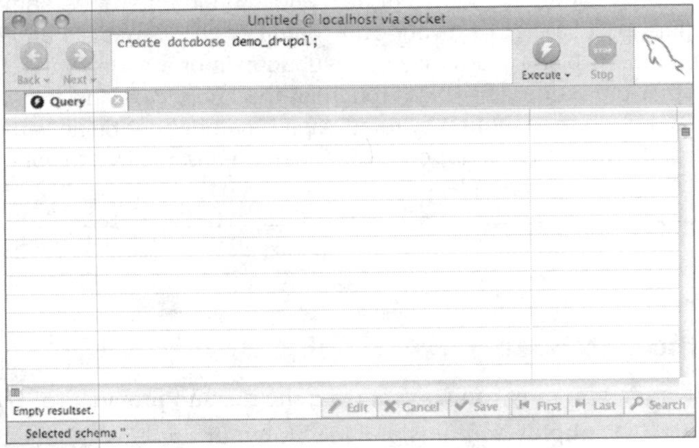

3. Create an account for Drupal to use for access to the database. If you have
   been running in an unsecured environment (such as using the root account
   and a blank password), you absolutely must create a new secure account. You
   can do that in MySQL Administrator. (If you have used a host script, you will
   probably have already provided the database name and account/password
   information.) Figure 3.3 shows how you can modify a user account in MySQL
   Administrator. You create a new account with the button at the lower left (the
   image of a person and a +).

   Each account can have different privileges for different locations. If necessary,
   open the account with the triangle to left of the account name and add a

location with the location add button. (The location add and delete buttons are the pair to the right of the account add and delete buttons below the user list.)

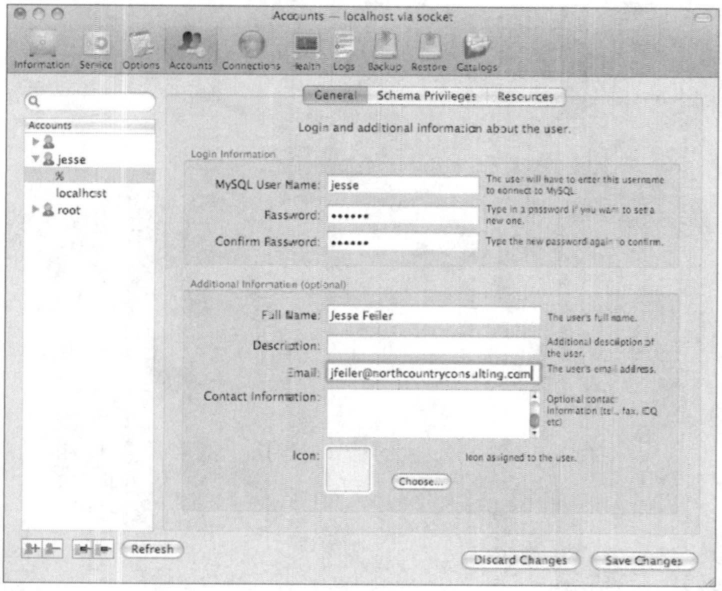

FIGURE 3.3
Create or modify
a database
account.

4. Set the location for the user privileges, as shown in Figure 3.4. For testing, localhost is a common choice; for production, you usually know the IP address of your database server, and that is the safest setting. (You can change it if you change hosts.) You will be setting privileges for the account that Drupal itself uses, and not for your individual end users.

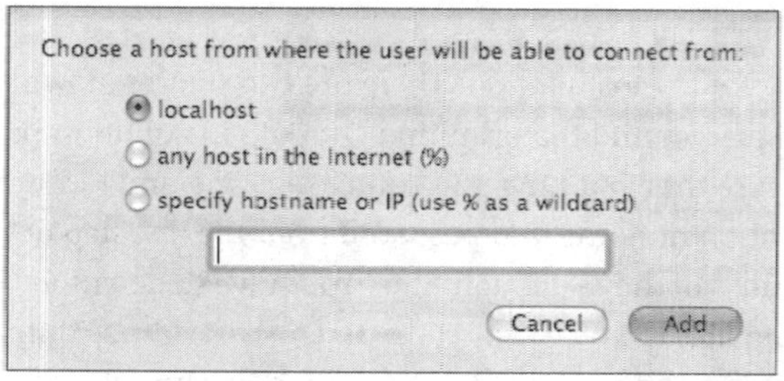

FIGURE 3.4
Choose a loca-
tion.

5. Use the Schema Privileges button at the top of the MySQL Administrator window to set the privileges. Choose the database that you created by clicking it; then, select the privileges from the list at the right and move them into the Assigned Privileges column, as shown in Figure 3.5. You should allow only the

privileges that Drupal needs (SELECT, INSERT, UPDATE, DELETE, CREATE, DROP, INDEX, and ALTER) and additional privileges that contributed modules may need. (CREATE TEMPORARY TABLES and LOCK TABLES are common.)

FIGURE 3.5
Set the privileges for the database.

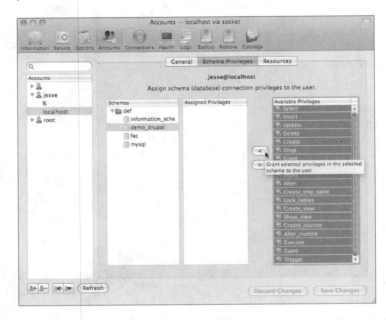

6. Write down the database name, location (server hostname in Figure 3.1), Drupal database account, and password. You will need them for the installation.

Try It Yourself

Installing Drupal

You are now ready for the installation. There are two phases: downloading and placing the files on the server and then running Drupal's installation program. Before you begin, make sure that you have the database name and location as well as the Drupal database account name and password from the last step of the previous task. Also, make sure that you have enough time. You have to download Drupal and then possibly upload the files to your own server. If you are adding contributed modules, you need to download and possibly upload them. The Drupal installation process is automated, but it takes some time. Depending on your Internet connection and the number of times you have done this, installing Drupal can take from a few minutes to an hour or more.

1. Download the current version of Drupal from drupal.org, as shown in Figure 3.6. Download links are on the main page. It comes as a compressed file; expand it into its component files and folders.

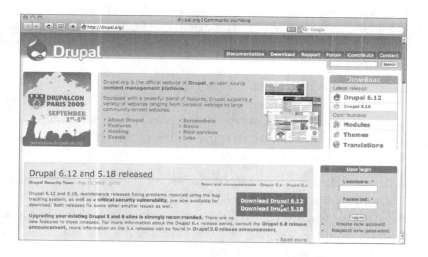

FIGURE 3.6
Download Drupal.

2. Create the settings.php file. You will find default settings in
`./sites/default/default.settings.php` inside the expanded download.
Copy this file and rename the copy to `./sites/default/settings.php`, as
shown in Figure 3.7. (The copying and renaming is a good idea in case something goes wrong: you can revert to default.settings.php without having to
redownload all of Drupal.) Make sure that `settings.php` is writable for the
installation process. When the process is complete, you can make the file
read-only.

FIGURE 3.7
Create set-
tings.php.

3. Move the downloaded files to the server. The folder you downloaded will normally be named with the Drupal version—something like `drupal-6.12`. You

can leave that name or rename the folder as you see fit. Depending on how you set up your URLs on the site, this name may be visible, so it is a good idea to remove the version from it. If you do not want to use a subfolder, move the contents of the downloaded folder (not the folder itself) to your web server root directory.

4. Launch the installer. Use your browser to open www.myservername.com/mysubfolder/install.php or, if you are running on your own computer, localhost/mysubfolder/install.php. If you installed the contents of the downloaded folder in your site's root, the URLs are www.myservername.com/install.php or localhost/install.php.

5. In Drupal 7, there is now an extra step at the beginning of the installation process. As shown in Figure 3.8, choose the installation profile you want to install. In addition to the standard installation, a minimal installation now exists with only the required modules enabled. The minimal installation is not for people just getting started. In fact, it can make life more difficult for beginners. The minimal installation is designed primarily for module developers who want to test their module with a minimal of interactions with other modules. This step is shown in Figure 3.8.

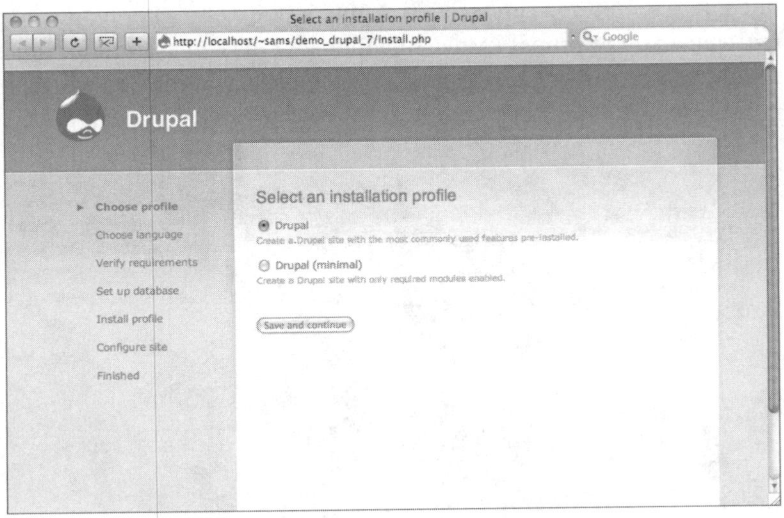

FIGURE 3.8
Choose your installation profile.

6. Choose your language. English is the default, but you can also find instructions for other languages, as shown in Figure 3.9.

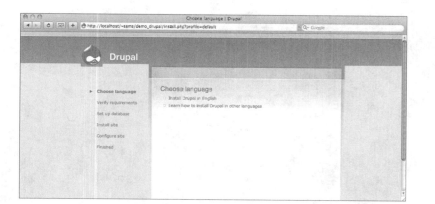

FIGURE 3.9
Choose your lan-
guage.

7. Set up the database. Provide the database information that you wrote at the
end of the previous task, as shown in Figure 3.10.

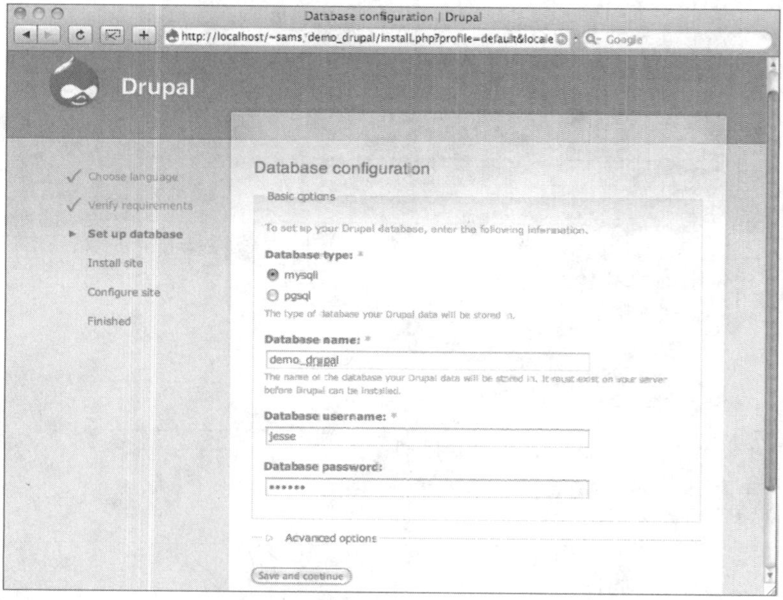

FIGURE 3.10
Provide the data-
base log in infor-
mation.

8. If needed, provide the advanced options, shown in Figure 3.11. Although it is
included as an advanced option, the hostname is required.

9. Configure the site, as shown in Figure 3.12. Set the email address for Drupal to
use in sending its emails.

FIGURE 3.11
Set hostname
and other
advanced
options.

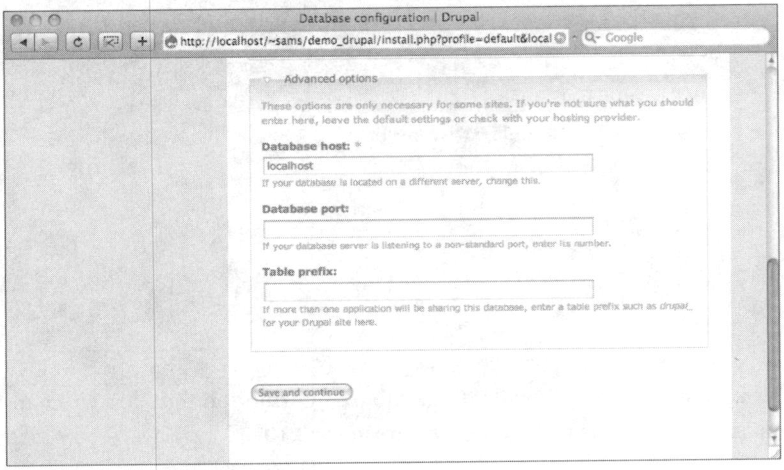

FIGURE 3.12
Set the site's
email address.

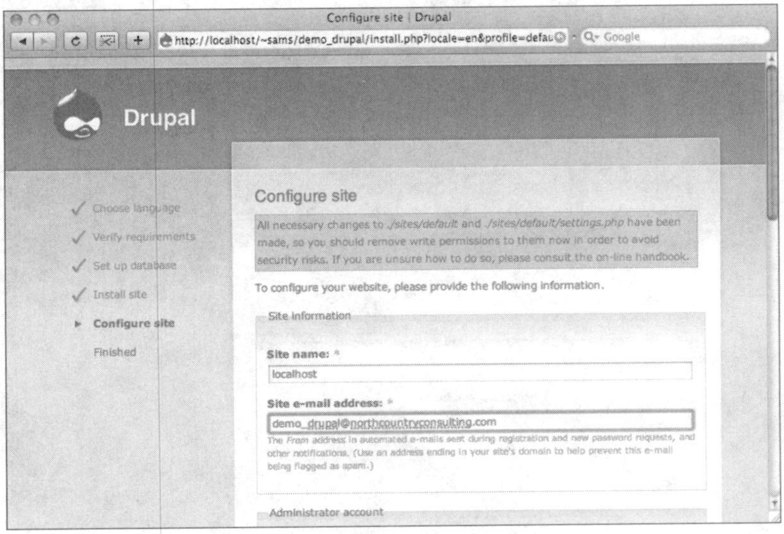

10. As advised in Figure 3.12, make `settings.php` read-only.

11. Create the administrator account. This is a superuser account with total access to the site. (It is sometimes called the primary account.) One of the most important tasks for you to carry out after you have created the site is to create another account with more limited administrative permissions. Figure 3.13 shows how you set up the administrator account.

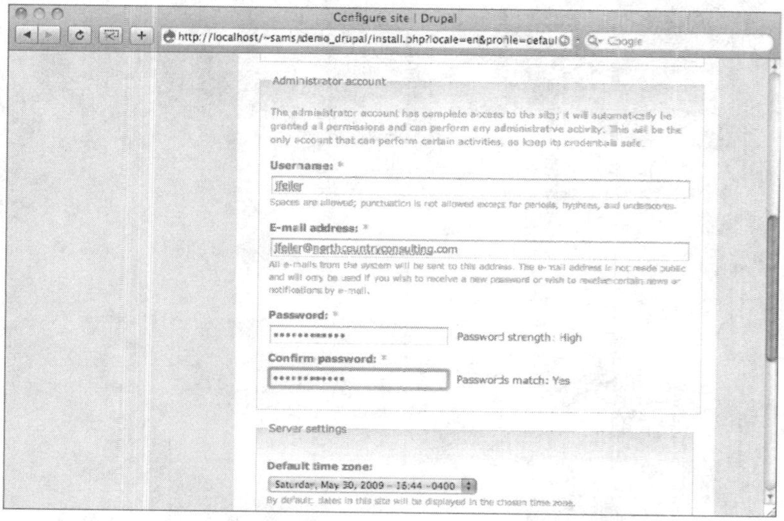

FIGURE 3.13
Create the administrator account.

12. Select your time zone and the options to use clean URLs and to automatically check for updates, as shown in Figure 3.14. If you want to use clean URLs, enable the mod_rewrite extension for Apache or the Microsoft URL Rewrite Modules for IIS 7.0 on IIS. (There is more on this in Hour 6.)

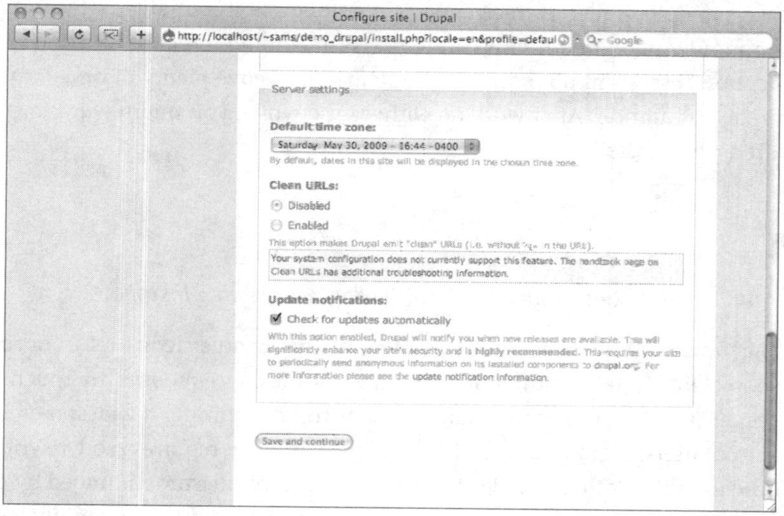

FIGURE 3.14
Set time zone and options for clean URLs and updates.

13. At the end of the process, you get any error messages that may have arisen. A link on that page lets you continue to your site, as shown in Figure 3.15. You are now running Drupal.

FIGURE 3.15
Move on to your site.

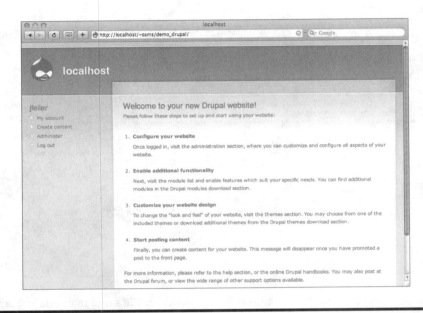

Summary

This hour showed you how to install Drupal. You need a web server to which you have access to upload files. It must support a database for Drupal's use (MySQL is most commonly used), and it must support PHP, including the mail function. Perhaps the most important point in this chapter is this: Leave plenty of time for your first Drupal installation. After working with it for a while, you might want to start over with a clean install.

Q&A

Q. *What are the consequences of not having mod_rewrite installed?*

A. The immediate consequence is that you cannot enable clean URLs. For some people, this is just a matter of cosmetics, but the consequences are much deeper. The `ImageCache` module, which is rapidly gaining a widespread base of Drupal users, requires clean URLs, and that, in turn, requires mod_rewrite functionality. Because the vast majority of Drupal sites are managed by people who turn on **mod_rewrite** (unless it is already turned on), it is rapidly becoming a de facto requirement. It is so much taken for granted that, for example, if it is not available, `ImageCache` simply does not work properly. It is worth the effort to turn on clean URLs.

Q. *Likewise, what happens if I don't have mail working from PHP?*

A. You can run Drupal without it sending mail. After all, many websites do not send mail themselves. However, your Drupal site will be so limited that such a site is usable mostly for testing. For example, if you use your own computer as localhost for a test installation, the fact that it cannot send mail is not going to be a serious concern for your testing.

Q. *If I follow the advice to throw out the first installation, what do I have to do?*

A. Drupal stores information in two places: its own PHP files that you download from drupal.org and in the database table that you create for it. You can use a tool, such as My SQL Administrator, to select all of the tables in your Drupal database, and then drop them. The database will be empty. Alternatively, drop the entire database and create a new one. Dropping all the tables seems to have no adverse consequences and is a little faster. You can simply remove all of your downloaded Drupal files and replace them with newly downloaded files. Do not think you can speed things up by reusing settings.php. For a clean install, you want a settings.php created as described in this hour.

Workshop

Quiz

1. What databases work with Drupal?

2. What is the purpose of the Drupal 7 minimal installation?

3. Do you have to set up tables for Drupal?

Answers

1. MySQL and PostgreSQL (pgsql) work with Drupal 6 and Drupal 7. SQLite works with Drupal 7.

2. It is designed for module and theme developers to use during testing.

3. No, you only have to create an empty database.

Activities

Take the time to do a test Drupal installation as soon as you can. This is particularly important if you are running on a shared server or on your own computer. Even if you do not plan on creating your site for weeks or months, getting to the final page of the installation sequence will let you feel confident that your environment, including its database and PHP version (not to mention the Drupal version), are working properly.

Similarly, if you will be running your site on a different server from your test server, install Drupal there as soon as possible. If you will be relying on an administrator of a shared web server to update a version of PHP or to modify your shared settings, it is important to get that process started as soon as possible.

Administering Drupal, Themes, and Modules

What You'll Learn in This Hour:

▶ Learn How to Administer Drupal

▶ Working with Modules

▶ Changing the Appearance of Your Site with Themes

Introduction

In this hour, you will finish the initial administration of your Drupal site. The installation from Hour 3, "Setting Up and Installing Drupal," is just the start of your Drupal adventure. By the time you complete it and look at Figure 3.15 at the end of Hour 3, you know that your software was downloaded properly from the Drupal site and uploaded properly to your own site. The database is functioning and has been populated with the necessary tables, and the first user (with total access) has been created. This hour builds on the installation with your various settings. For most Drupal sites, administration of the site is an ongoing process. You may enable or disable various modules that are part of the basic installation, and you may download, enable, or disable contributed modules from drupal.org/project/modules. Likewise, you can customize themes or download new ones.

This hour explores the basics of Drupal site administration that you will do many times as your site grows. As is true of all websites, site administration is not just something you do once.

Figure 3.15 at the end of Hour 3 suggests a three-step process of configuring your site and its administrative settings, adding additional functionality with new modules, and customizing the site's appearance with themes. This is a logical sequence, but not a necessary one.

Interacting with Two Interfaces

There are many ways to navigate Drupal's administrative interface. For example, you can use menus and submenus. There is an Administer menu with submenus, such as Content Management and Site Building. Rather than navigating submenus, you can click Administer or one of the submenus; the page that is displayed may have further links on it. You can also type a URL to go directly to the administration page that you want. Many people use all these ways of navigating.

Just to make things interesting, the excellent revisions to the user interface in Drupal 7 have occasionally moved administration pages around. In the cases where this has happened, this can affect the Administer menu, its submenus, and the various pages through which you navigate. And the URLs have sometimes changed.

With Drupal 7, an administration toolbar is available at the top of the page to the primary user and to other users for whom you have granted permission. (If you have followed the sequence of hours in this book, you are still running as the primary user, so you will see it in Drupal 7.) This adds a third component to navigation: menus and submenus, the URL of the page to which you are going, and now a toolbar button (and possibly two for certain tasks).

To provide a range of information, this book normally handles administration navigation as follows:

1. The menu and submenu links are given. These use the menu and submenu names and locations from Drupal 6. At the time of publication, Drupal 7 was not yet released and the code was barely frozen, so more users needed the Drupal 6 menus and submenu links. In the next edition. Drupal 7 will be the default and Drupal 6 will be the variant.

2. A URL is given in parentheses following the links. These URLs are relative to your Drupal root, which could be something such as www.yoursite.com, www.yoursite.com/drupal_test, or drupal_test.yoursite.com. Remember to add the /?q= so that admin/content/forum is www.yoursite.com/?q=admin/content/forum. In the cases in which Drupal 7 is different from Drupal 6, two URLs are provided. Thus, regardless of your menu and submenu structure, you should be able to get to the page you want. Here is an example of such a reference:

```
Administer->Content Management->Content (D6: admin/content/node D7:
admin/content).
```

Getting Started with Administration

If you click the Administer link at the left of the window in Drupal 6, you will see the submenus shown in Figure 4.1. You can also get there with /?q=admin in Drupal 6 or Drupal 7. In the preliminary version of Drupal 7, the page is the one shown in Figure 4.2.

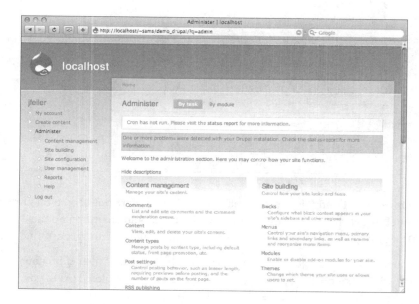

FIGURE 4.1
Administer Drupal 6 from the Task view.

As you can see in Figure 4.1, each submenu (such as Content Management) can have its own submenus (such as Comments, Content, Content Types, and Post Settings).

Note the absence of the menu from the left side of the Drupal 7 page. (This is part of a larger menu reorganization that is discussed in Hour 21, "Working with Menus.") Instead of the menu at the left of Figure 4.1, there are links at the top of Figure 4.2.

The main area of the page, shown in both Figures 4.1 and 4.2, organizes the administration by task. Within each task are the specific administration commands. Using the links at the top of the Drupal 6 page or the tabs at the upper right of the Drupal 7 page, you can switch between the task view and the module view, shown in Figure 4.3 and Figure 4.4.

Because the Navigation menu is present at the left in Drupal 6, you can always click Administer to get back to the pages shown in Figures 4.1 and 4.3. In Drupal 7, the Dashboard button at the top returns you to the pages shown in Figures 4.2 and 4.4. Although the look and feel is different, it is the same basic operation.

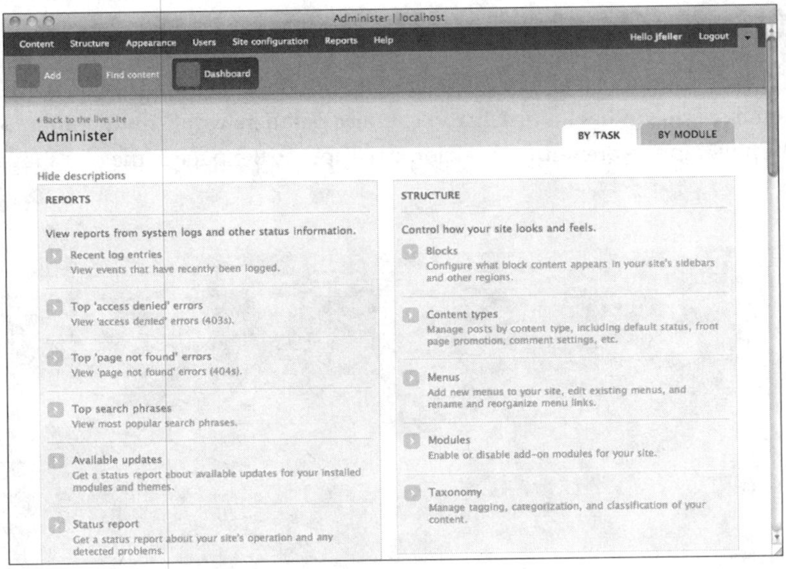

FIGURE 4.2
FIGURE 4.2
Adminster Drupal 7 from the Task view.

You will see that, in addition to a change in the design, there has been a bit of reorganization between Drupal 6 and Drupal 7. There is a guide to mapping the Drupal 6 to Drupal 7 commands at the author's website (www.northcountryconsulting.com).

This hour covers the submenus of administration, but not all of their submenus. Some of them will be explored later when specific functionality is explored. Also, you will

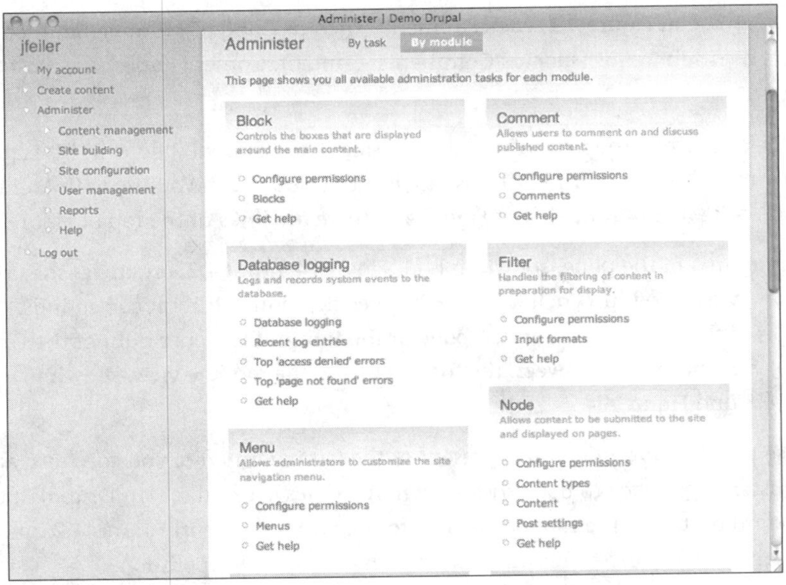

FIGURE 4.3
Adminster Drupal 6 from the Module view.

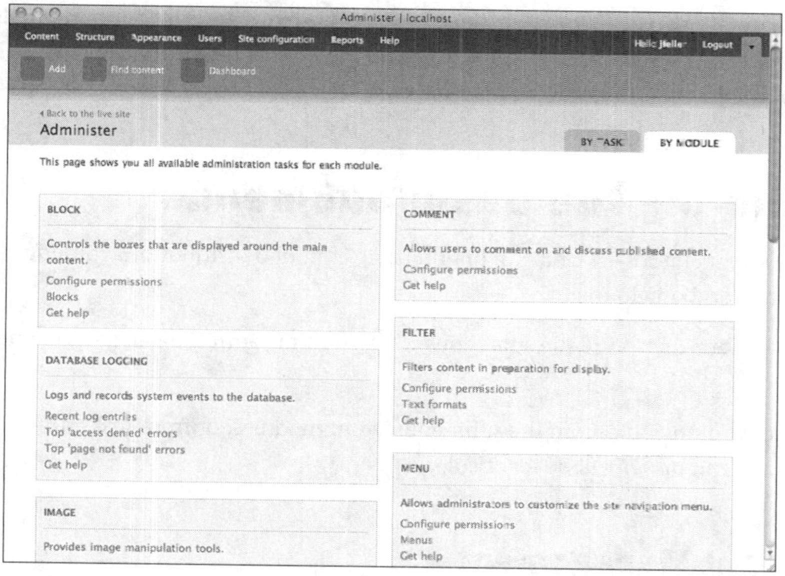

FIGURE 4.4
Administer Drupal 7 from the Module view.

see new items added to the Administer menu as you add and remove modules. For now, your primary objective should be to learn how to use the administration tools.

It is not uncommon to find a warning message at the top of the administration page. If you have set Drupal to check for new versions of software, this is where you will find such information. In addition, you will find messages, such as the one shown in Figure 4.1, that alert you to conditions to which you should attend. If you get such a message, click the Status Report link. That will open the page shown in Figure 4.5, which shows the full extent of the problem.

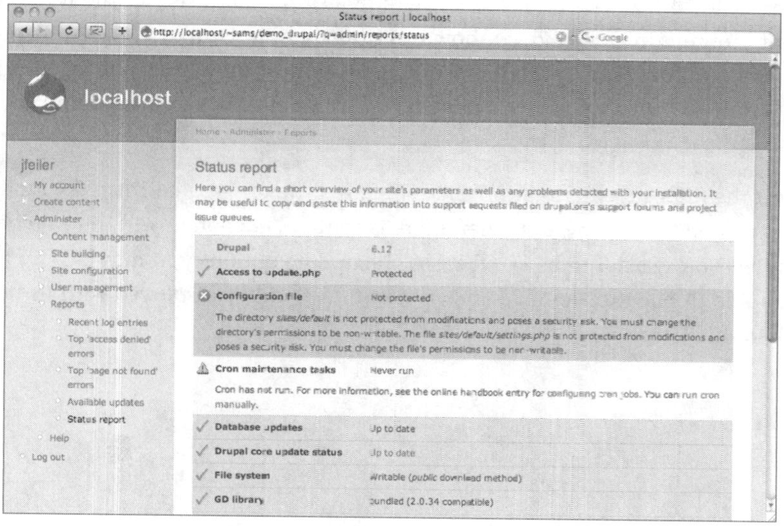

FIGURE 4.5
Resolve issues (particularly security issues) promptly.

In this case, the access permissions need to be adjusted. This is a common problem after the initial installation. The `settings.php` file must be writable during installation, but thereafter, it should be read-only.

Exploring the Basic Submenus

As you see in Figures 4.1 and 4.3, after a basic Drupal 6 installation, you have five submenus and a help menu.

If you do not want to use the submenus, click Administer in the Navigation menu at the left.

Whether you navigate from the submenus, from modules, or from tasks, the settings pages you end up on will be identical.

Content Management

The Content Management section of administration has all the settings you need to manage content. Notice that the actual creation of content is not an administrative task—the Create Content menu is just above Administer at the left of Figure 4.3, and in Drupal 7, the Add button performs the same task. Although it is not a hard-and-fast rule, for many sites, content creation is a more widely allowed function than the administration of content; Drupal separates content creation from content management in part to allow different settings for those two areas for users.

Remember that content in a CMS is stored in the database and does not have an intrinsic location. You can locate content by using Administer, Content Management, Content in Drupal 6, as shown in Figure 4.6. In Drupal 7, the same page is opened from the Find Content or Content buttons at the top, as shown in Figure 4.7. Note that in Drupal 7, tabs let you use this same interface for managing content and managing comments.

Select the filtering criterion and click Filter. In a newly created Drupal website, there is no content to display, but when there is content, each item will have a check box that lets you select it to be acted on by the update options you may choose (such as changing publication status). Each content item will be displayed with its title and a link to the item.

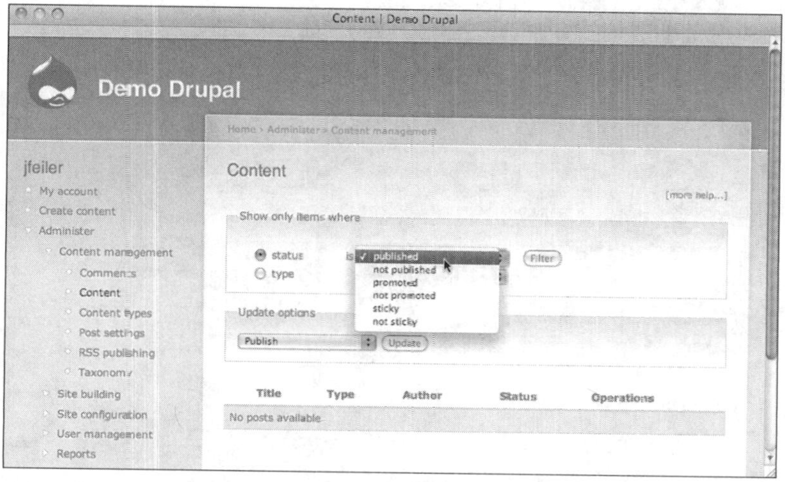

FIGURE 4.6
Manage content
in Drupal 6.

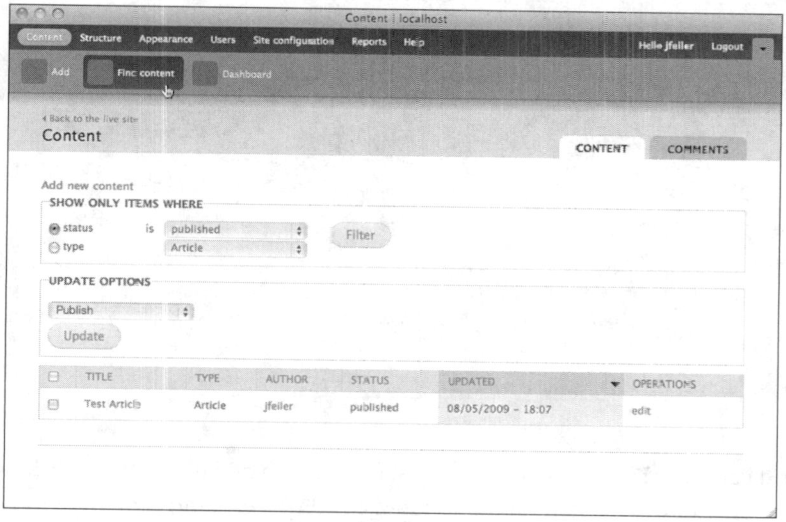

FIGURE 4.7
Manage content
in Drupal 7.

The other submenus for Content Management manage settings in general rather than for a specific item of content. The Content Types submenu is explored in some detail here. Not only does it give you a sense of the Drupal user interface, but it also shows you how you can use settings to streamline user content creation. The Drupal 6 Content Types submenu is shown in Figure 4.8. In Drupal 7, this page is accessed from the Structure button at the top and then from the Content Types link, as shown in Figure 4.9.

GO TO ▶
You find more about stories, pages, and other basic Drupal content types in **Hour 5, "Using Drupal Nodes,"** p. 75.

This is a common Drupal interface to a list of items. To add a new item, click Add Content Type at the top right of the window. To edit an existing content type, click Edit or the name of the content type. To delete a content type (with a chance to cancel the deletion), click Delete.

When you click Edit, you have a series of settings that control how that content type is managed. (The Add button provides the same interface, but all the data is blank; the Edit button lets you edit the settings that are already in place.)

Out of the box, Drupal has two content types installed: stories (Drupal 6) or articles (Drupal 7) and pages. You already know what they are because you have seen and used web pages many times; stories and articles are the elements that appear on pages. Depending on your background and the tools you are using, you may refer to them as stories, items, articles, or by some other name. Rest assured that the difference between stories (Drupal 6) and articles (Drupal 7) is mainly one of nomenclature.

As you can see in Figure 4.10, there are three parts to the story content type identification:

▶ A Name is required. In Drupal, names are usually visible to users or end users. They frequently are capitalized and must be unique within a given namespace (such as all content types). (Names of stories themselves need not be unique.)

▶ An internal Type or Machine Name is required and is used by Drupal internally. Within a given Drupal namespace (such as the content types), these types are required to be unique. Although types are used internally by Drupal, they may be visible to end users in URLs.

▶ An optional Description gives you the ability to enhance the user interface for people who will be entering data from the pages shown in Figures 4.8 and 4.9

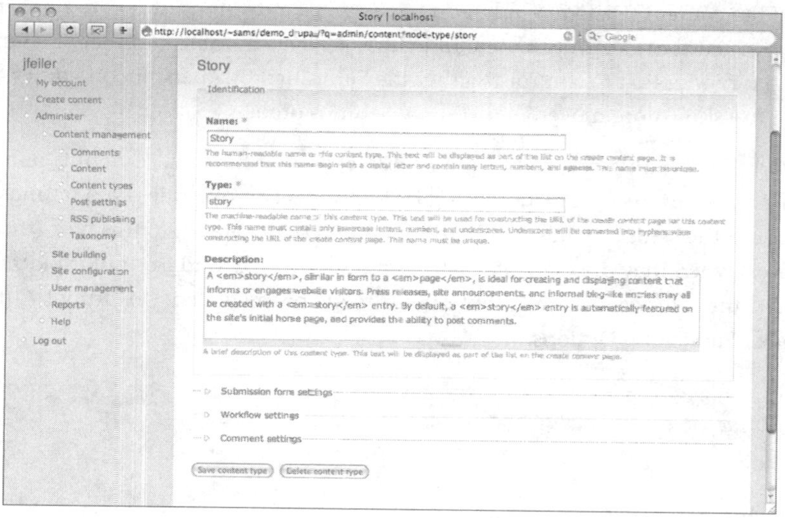

FIGURE 4.10
Identify your content type.

This combination of name, type/machine name, and description is common to all content types and many other entities within Drupal.

In the submission form settings, shown in Figure 4.11, you set up the interface that users see when they are creating content of this type. You can change the labels for both the title and body of the content that will be created. A title is required, but you can have a blank label for the body of the content. (Note that, in Drupal 7, having a blank label for the body means that there will be no body field.)

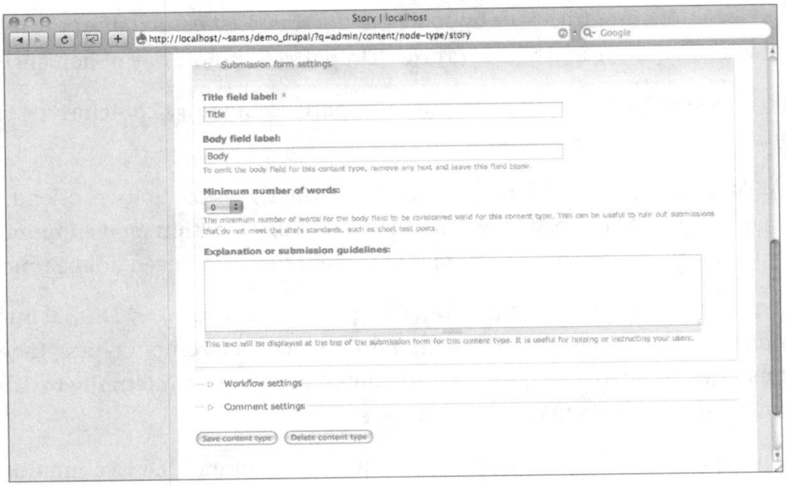

FIGURE 4.11
Add submission
form settings.

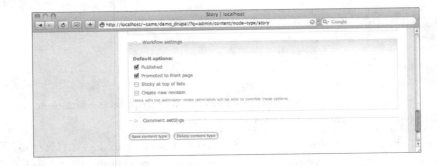

As you can see in Figure 4.11, you can set a minimum number of characters for the body of the content (Drupal 6 only), and you can add free-format text to further clarify the content that is being created. In Drupal 7, the minimum number of characters and a new option to control whether the Submitted By <person> on <date> post settings are shown are moved to a Display Settings area.

The Workflow Settings, shown in Figure 4.12, let you set how the content is published. As you can see from Figure 4.12, certain users can override these settings; for other users, the settings you select here will apply to all content of this type (that is, all stories) when they are created. Changing settings here (and in similar places) will not affect the settings for stories that have already been created. (In Drupal 7, these are called Publishing Options.)

FIGURE 4.12
Manage work-
flow publication
settings.

The last group of settings for stories consists of Comment Settings, as shown in Figure 4.13. As with workflow settings, some users can override these, but for other users, these are the settings that will apply to all newly created stories.

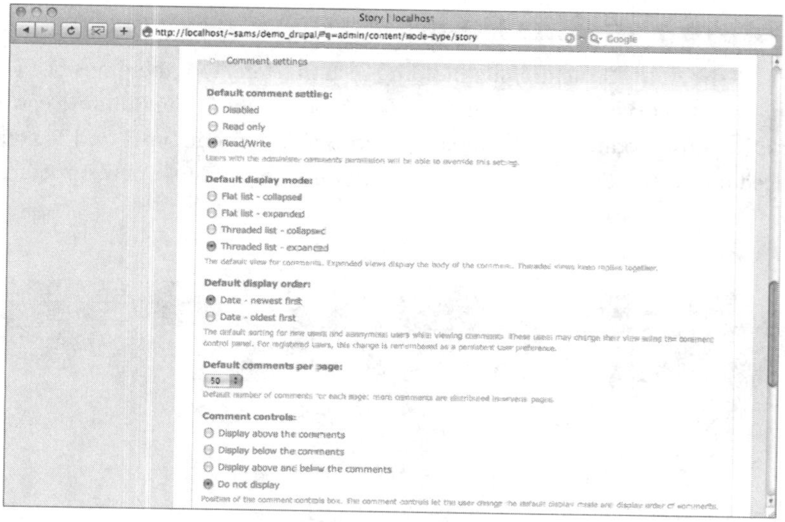

FIGURE 4.13
Create comment settings.

GO TO ▶
There is much more about comments in **Hour 10, "Using Polls, Comments, Discussions, and Feed Aggregators"** p. 159.

The final section of comment settings is shown in Figure 4.14.

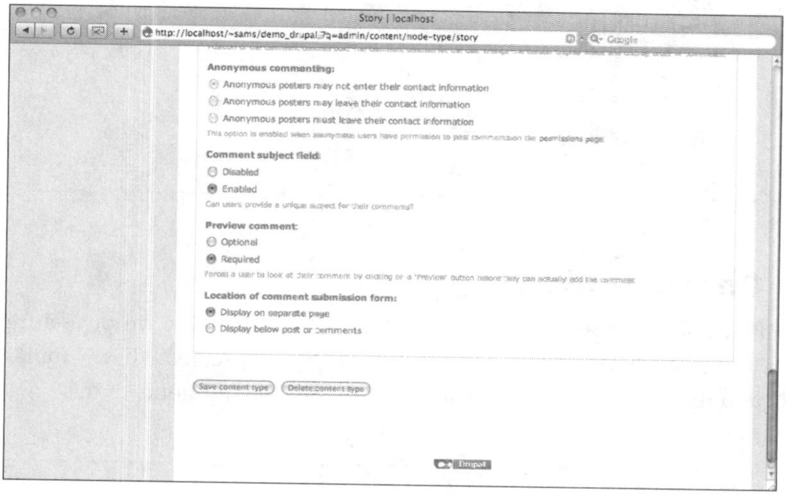

FIGURE 4.14
Finish comment settings.

The most important part to notice is the Save Content Type button at the bottom of the window. Next to it is a Delete Content Type button. Remember that Drupal is a web application; if you navigate away from a page, your changes are gone if you have not explicitly saved them.

Structure and Site Building

Figure 4.15 shows the Structure/Site Building section. Here, too, there has been rearrangement between Drupal 6 and Drupal 7. In Drupal 6, Site Building consisted of Blocks, Menus, Modules, and Themes. In Drupal 7, Content Types and Taxonomy are placed in the new Structure area, and Themes are moved to a new Appearance section.

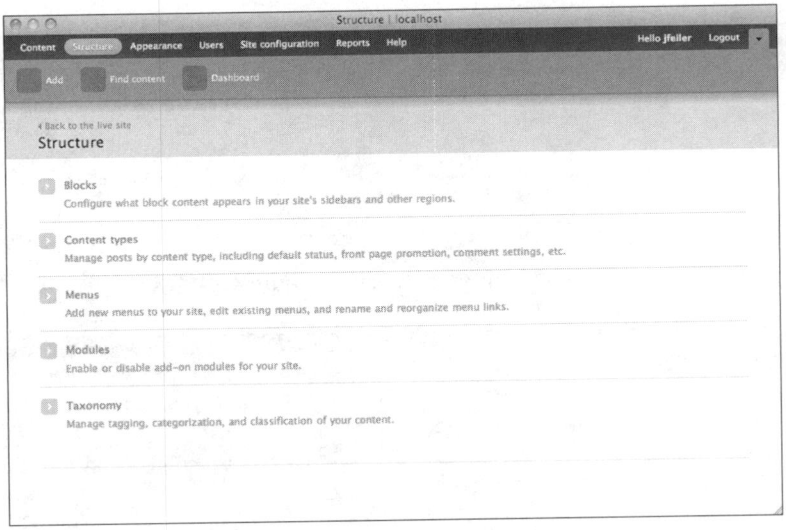

FIGURE 4.15
Building your site and its structure.

GO TO ▶
Modules and themes are so important that they have their own sections later in this chapter. You can find additional information about themes in **HOUR 18,** **"CHOOSING A THEME,"** p. 313, and a detailed discussion of menus is provided in **HOUR 21, "WORK-ING WITH MENUS,"** p. 355.

Site Configuration

Site configuration submenus are shown in Figure 4.16. Here, the various settings for formats and functionality within the infrastructure are specified. These submenus are described in the context of their functionality in the relevant hours of this book.

▼   **Try It Yourself**

Taking Your Site On- and Offline

One of the most important tools in this hour is Site Maintenance. It lets you take the site online and offline. Anything that might leave your site in an unstable or unfinished state should be done with the site offline. Fortunately, a great many management and maintenance activities can be done with the site online. For example,

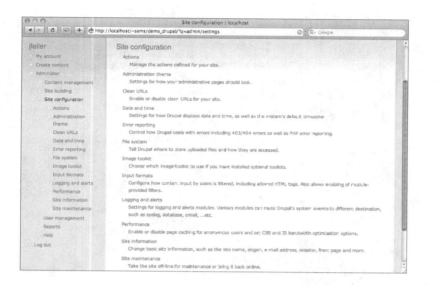

FIGURE 4.16
Configure the site.

content creation is almost always doable with the site online. As you will see in Hour 5, you can set the published status of new content. By creating new content and marking it unpublished, it will be viewable only by administrators and other types of users you specify. Your end users can have access to the site without you worrying about it.

If you are experimenting with a new Drupal site, now is a good time to take it offline if it is visible to the public. If you are experimenting on localhost or in an area of your server that is not accessible to the public, you do not have to worry.

1. Log on to your Drupal site and choose Administer, Site Configuration, Site Maintenance from the Navigation menu or from Site Configuration, as shown previously in Figure 4.16. This opens the page shown in Figure 4.17.

2. Although the site is offline, that does not mean you cannot access it. You can log in with your default user account by going to ./?q=user, as shown in Figure 4.18.

3. Remember to bring the site back online and update the message if necessary. If your account and password are remembered by your browser, you may be able to log in to the site while it is offline without taking any special steps, and you may forget that the site is offline.

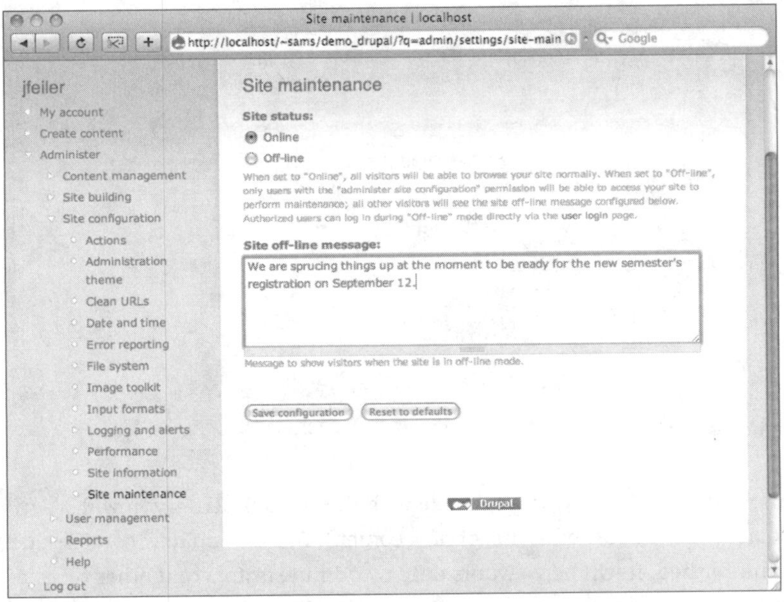

FIGURE 4.17
Take your site
on- and offline.

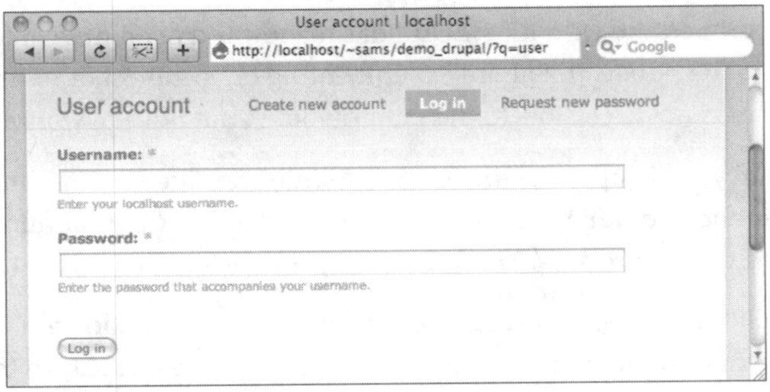

FIGURE 4.18
Log in when your
site is offline.

User Management

Manage user accounts in the User Management area of Drupal 6, as shown
in Figure 4.19. In Drupal 7, Permissions, Roles, and User Settings are in Site
Configuration; Users is under the new Users button.

If you have followed the sequence of this book, you now have only a primary
account on your site—the first account created as part of the installation process is
an account with unlimited powers. One of your first orders of business is to create
additional accounts. (If you want to jump ahead to Hour 8, "Managing Users, Roles,

and Permissions," feel free.) For now, what you need to know is that in addition to the primary user, Drupal automatically supports two types of users: Anonymous users are visitors to your site who have not logged in; authenticated users are users who have registered with an email address and have responded to Drupal's automatic verification process. These are identified as roles, and you can add more roles. Each role can have an unlimited number of users.

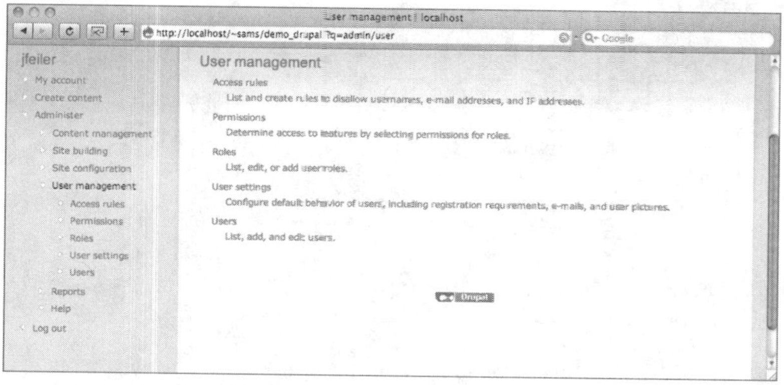

FIGURE 4.19
Manage user accounts.

In the User Management section, you can manage individual users and the roles and permissions of Drupal's security mechanism. Roles and permissions are common modern security mechanisms. You define a role (perhaps one of the built-in roles, such as authenticated or anonymous users), and then you set specific permissions for that role. To give additional permissions to a user, you assign that user to a specific role that has those permissions. You do not assign permissions to an individual user.

Reports

The reports submenu is shown in Figure 4.20.

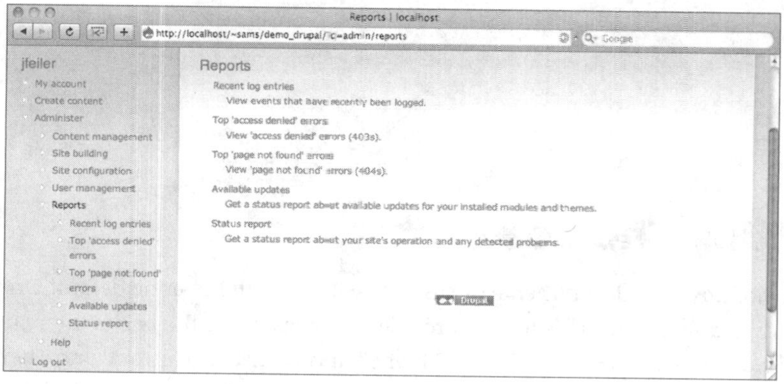

FIGURE 4.20
Use the reports submenu as needed.

Drupal automatically collects the information that you need to manage your website. Most people look most frequently at recent log entries and at the status report shown in Figure 4.21.

FIGURE 4.21
Review the status report periodically.

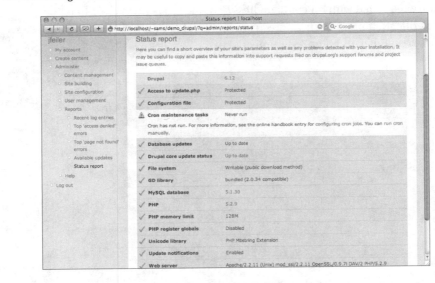

Help

Finally, the Help links shown in Figure 4.22 let you get to Drupal help and assistance on the Drupal site and on your own computer. The Help page in Drupal 7 (shown here) is more extensive than Drupal 6.

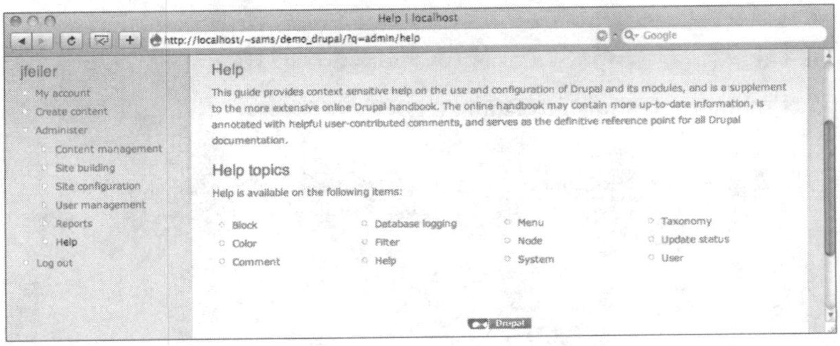

FIGURE 4.22
Help is available.

Setting Themes

You do not have to select a theme or customize it: You will have the default Drupal theme available to you. This section provides an overview of the basics; more details are provided in Hour 18, "Choosing a Theme" and Hour 24, "Customizing Themes and Their CSS."

Figure 4.23 shows the themes that ship with Drupal 6.

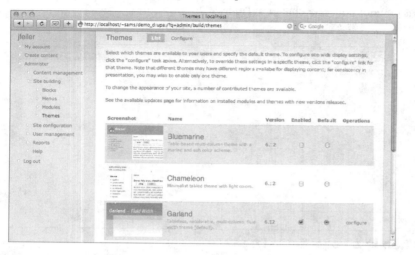

FIGURE 4.23
Drupal ships with default themes.

You can enable any of the themes by clicking the check box for that theme. Only one of the enabled themes can be the default theme. It is used as the site's theme unless you have allowed users to select their own theme from all enabled themes in which case they can change from the default theme.

You can configure themes by clicking the Configure button at the top. You can choose to configure global settings for all themes or the settings for the current default theme. (You can use the configure link at the right of the theme if you want.) Figure 4.24 shows an individual theme (Garland) being configured. You can change the color scheme from the pop-up menu; if you unlock specific colors for links, highlights, and so forth, you can change them individually.

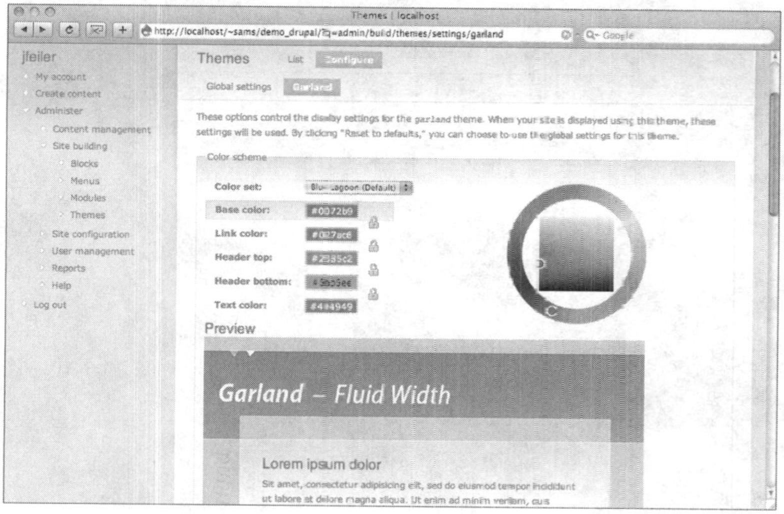

FIGURE 4.24
Configure settings for all themes.

As you continue down the page, check boxes let you control the visibility of certain items on your pages, as shown in Figure 4.25.

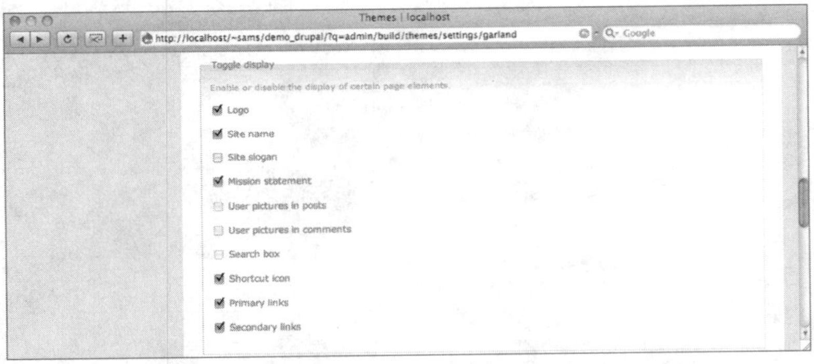

FIGURE 4.25
Configure standard content for your theme's pages.

Finally, in Figure 4.26, you can set paths to your custom graphics. Remember to click the Save Configuration button when you are done. Some people who are new to Drupal navigate away from the page and lose their work. This is particularly an issue when you are filling in a multipage form. Usually, each page needs to be saved separately.

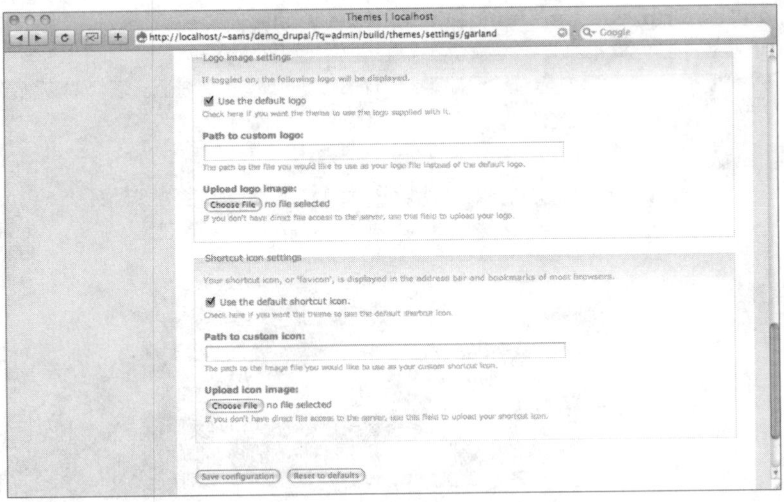

FIGURE 4.26
Provide custom graphic file paths and save your settings.

When Is a Logo Not a Logo?

Each theme handles these items in different ways. One variation often involves the site logo. Some themes allow you to set an image for the logo that is larger than a typical small logo image. In these cases, you can use a large graphic (possibly the width of the page) as a "logo."

The Configure button at the top of the page lets you configure the selected theme, but the Global Settings button lets you configure defaults, as shown in Figure 4.27. This is particularly helpful if you are switching themes, as you decide which one to pick for your site.

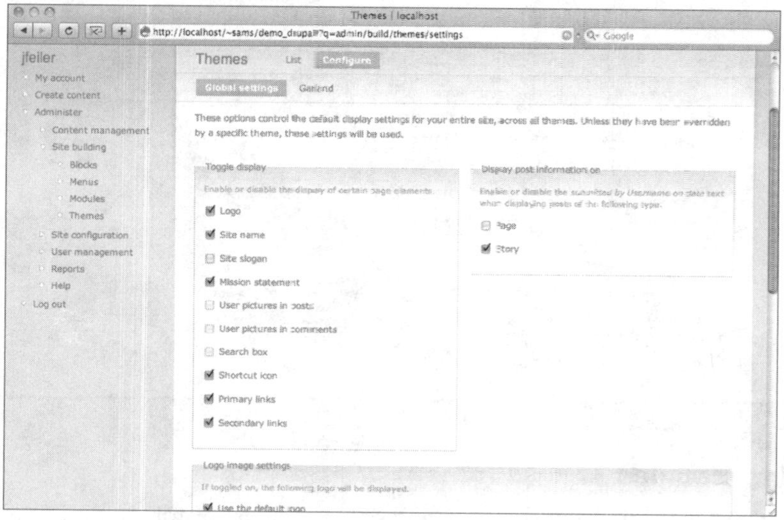

FIGURE 4.27
Set global set-
tings for all your
themes.

Introducing Modules

The final focus of your administration tasks is managing your modules. In fact, this may be the most important (and most common) task you perform.

Configuring Modules

As you have seen, Drupal consists of numerous PHP files that implement its function-ality. These consist of its core functionality and optional functionality that you can enable using the module administration page, shown in Figure 4.28.

You will see dependencies among modules; that will often explain why you cannot enable a module. Also, if a module is required by another enabled module, you can-not disable the module that is in use by the other enabled module.

Note the important links at in the text at the top of this page. The most important is a link to update.php, which must be used after you have updated a module. It will make any necessary database modifications for the new modules. It is important to back up the site before running.

FIGURE 4.28
Configure your
modules.

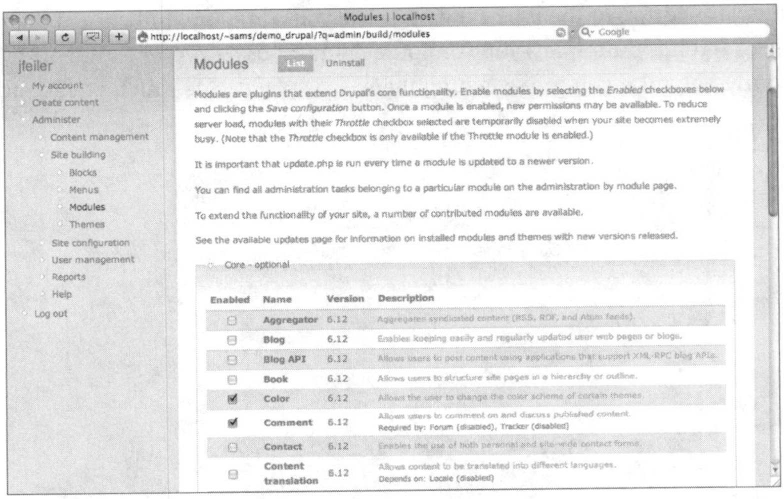

▼ **Try It Yourself**

Finding Modules

The modules shown in Figure 4.28 are part of the standard distribution of Drupal 6.
You can download additional modules from drupal.org/project/modules to add new
functionality to your website.

1. Go to `drupal.org/project/modules`. You can search the modules for a word
   or phrase, as shown in Figure 4.29. Make certain you use the Search Modules
   box rather than your browser's own search (which will search the Internet) or
   the Drupal search box (which will search the entire Drupal site).

   Note that, as the URL of this page suggests, you are actually looking at Drupal
   projects. Projects can contain themes or modules. In the case of module projects,
   there may be more than one module in the project.

2. You can explore an individual module more fully at its own page. These pages
   all have the same basic layout, as shown in Figure 4.30.

3. Download and version information is shown at the bottom of the module's
   page, as you can see in Figure 4.31. Make sure that you select a module version
   that matches your Drupal version (Drupal 6 or Drupal 7). Modules almost
   always need some revisions from one version of Drupal to another. Also, at the
   bottom of the page is a link to a page with all releases, as well as an RSS feed to
   the releases. After you install a module, Drupal will remind you about updates.
   But, if you are interested in a module that has not been updated to the current
   version of Drupal, or if you are interested in a module that has certain features

▼

in development (or on its "wish list"), subscribing to the RSS feed can let you know when it is ready.

FIGURE 4.29
Search to find
modules.

FIGURE 4.30
Read about the
module before
installing it.

Modules in This Book

All the modules discussed in this book are listed on the author's website at www. northcountryconsulting.com. In the Drupal section, you will also find an aggregated feed of the updates for those modules.

By the Way

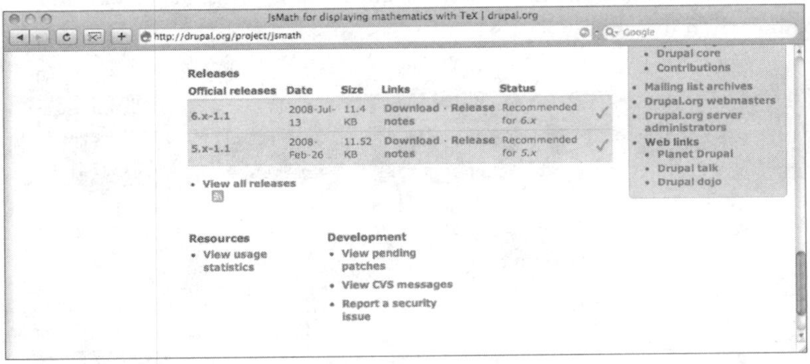

FIGURE 4.31
Learn about the
module's version
history.

4. For the modules discussed in this book, a summary of the module's download
location, administration links, and permissions (discussed in Hour 8, p. 127) is
provided when the module is introduced. In addition, modules whose authors
have committed to having them ready for the release of Drupal 7 are indicated
with the D7CX code. Table 4.1 shows such a table.

TABLE 4.1   WYSIWYG Module Reference

Download from	project/wysiwyg
Enable in section	User Interface

D7CX

Permissions

Use WYSIWYG profiles and assign them to roles as
described in this section.

Administration

Administer, Site Configuration, WYSIWYG
(admin/settings/wysiwyg)

5. Check the usage statistics, shown in Figure 4.32. These are provided automatically starting in Drupal 6. The numbers do not necessarily let you know how
good the module is. A module that addresses a specific issue may have few
users. However, in such a case, it is likely that the module developer will
respond to an email query from someone interested in the topic. The usage statistics are merely a guide.

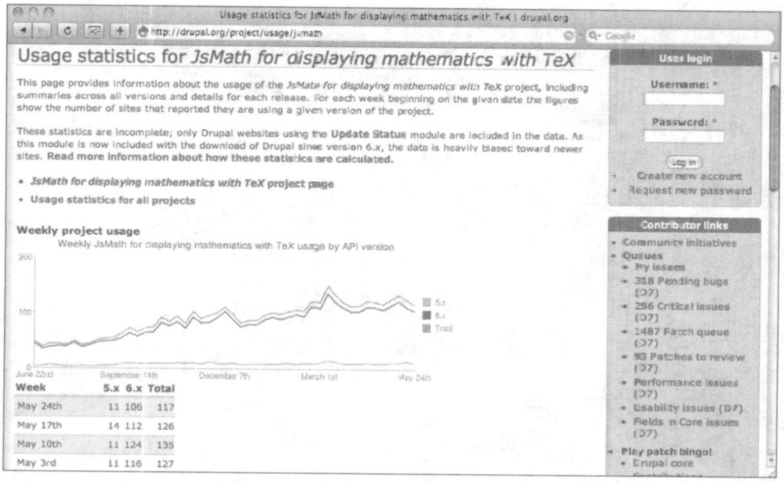

FIGURE 4.32
Check the usage statistics.

6. When you find a module you are interested in, download it to your computer.

Try It Yourself

Installing and Updating a Module

Once you have found a module and downloaded it, you need to install it.

1. Depending on your site and the module in question, you may want to have an entire Drupal site that you use only for testing. (This is the best choice.) It is prudent to take the site offline before installing the module if you are using your live site. The module will be packaged in a compressed tar.gz file. You can unpack it to a folder and then install it in Drupal in the appropriate modules folder. Do not install it in the modules folder located at the root level, as shown in Figure 4.33.

   Do install it in the modules folder inside the sites/all folder. If you want it to be available only for a specific subsite, create a folder for that site. The sites/all/modules folder starts out empty (you may even have to create it); it is shown in Figure 4.34.

   Installing modules in ./modules will work, but it is better to keep your downloaded modules separate from the modules that are part of the core Drupal distribution.

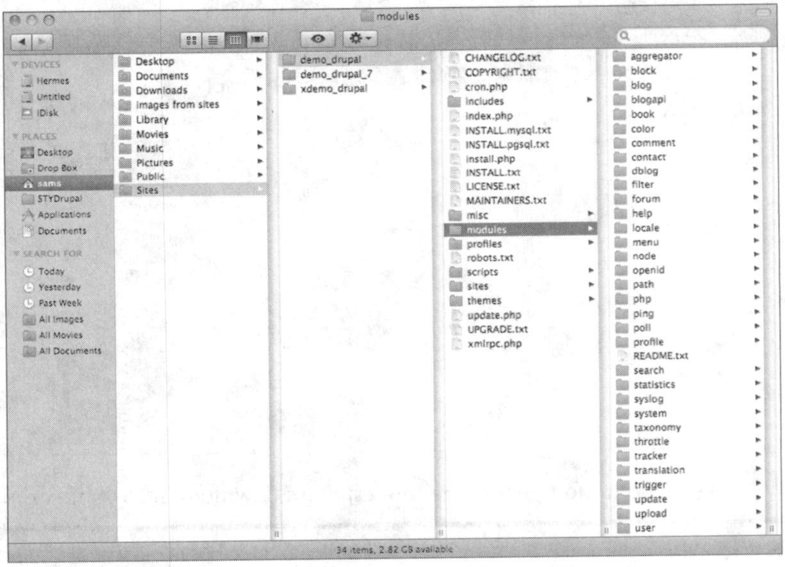

FIGURE 4.33
Do not install the modules in the modules folder at the root of your Drupal folder.

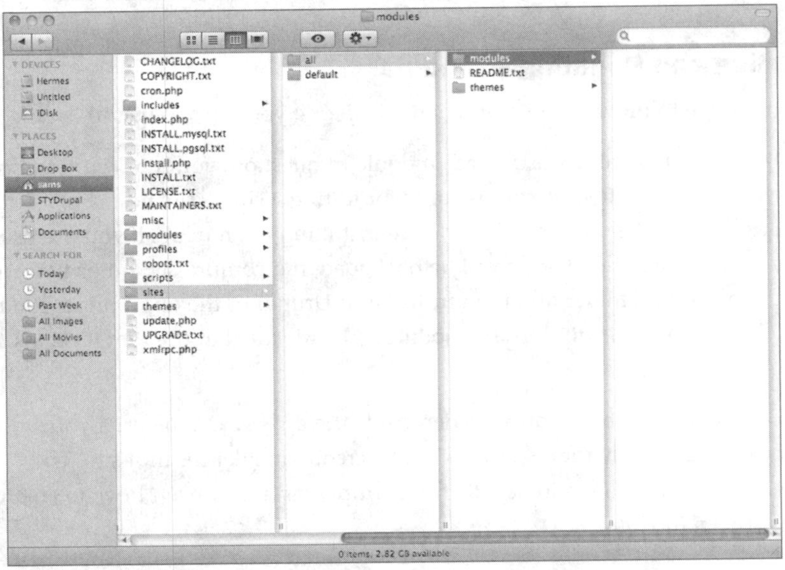

FIGURE 4.34
Install the module in the site/all/modules folder.

2. Once placed in the modules folder, all actual modules in the project module you have downloaded will appear in the list of projects in Site Configuration. You must enable them before you can use them.

3. If you have downloaded a previous version of the module, remove the old version and replace it with the new one. In that case, run `update.php` from `./update.php`. You will first be warned to back up your database, as shown in Figure 4.35.

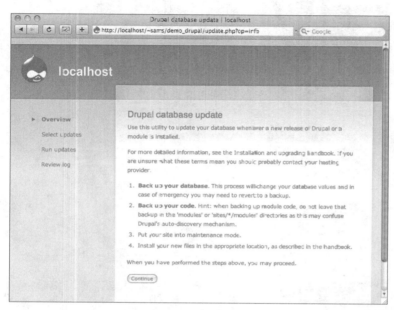

FIGURE 4.35
Back up your database before starting the update.

4. Before starting the update, you have an opportunity to change the copy of Drupal being updated, as shown in Figure 4.36. Most of the time, the default setting is fine.

5. The final step may not happen for a long time, if ever. If you decide to uninstall the module, use the Uninstall button of the modules list at Administer, Site Building, Modules, as shown in Figure 4.37. Not all modules support the uninstall mechanism, but more and more of them do. This makes it easier for Drupal to clean up loose ends that might be left by uninstalled modules.

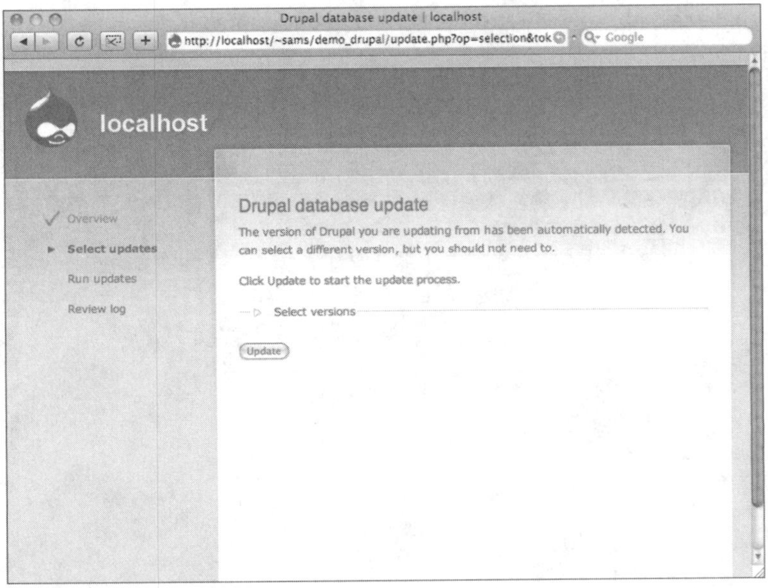

FIGURE 4.36
Complete the update.

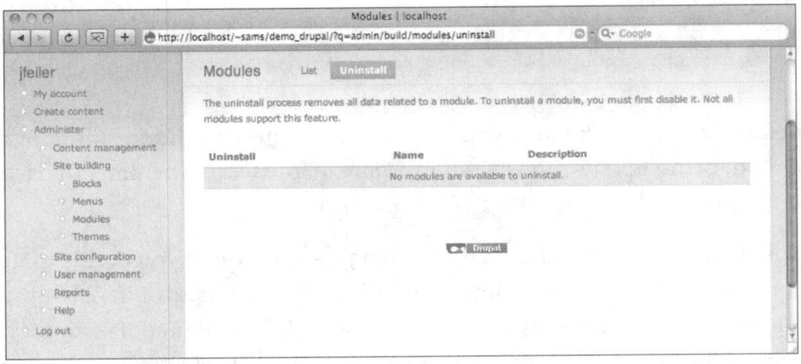

FIGURE 4.37
Use the Uninstall button when needed.

Summary

This hour showed you how to use Drupal's administration tools and how to find and install new modules to extend Drupal's functionality. By now, you should be familiar with the basic structure of administration and modules. You have also seen how to bring your site online and offline—a critical step in modifying the site.

Q&A

Q. *Are any modules essential to download?*

A. Over time, some contributed modules have been added to Drupal's core distribution. Someone starting with Drupal 6 may discover far fewer modules to be downloaded in Drupal 7 because many of the downloads for Drupal 6 are part of the Drupal 7 core. Among other things, this means that the lag time for contributed modules after a major Drupal release can be reduced because the modules are part of the core. The essentials vary by site. If you are building e-commerce sites, a module such as Ubercart might seem absolutely essential.

Q. *Are modules standalone plug-ins?*

A. You may have noticed in the modules list shown in Figure 4.27 that some modules are required by others or are used by others. Drupal keeps track of these dependencies as you store and enable modules. Thus, modules are not stand-alone plug-ins.

Q. *How do you evaluate modules?*

A. Read about them on the Drupal site, ask questions in Drupal groups, and for the best analysis, install the module on a test version of Drupal.

Workshop

Quiz

1. Where do you install modules?

2. What are common theme customizations that require no programming?

3. How do you take the site offline?

Quiz Answers

1. Use the `./sites/all/modules` folder, not `./modules`.

2. Changing colors, custom logos, and choosing to display specific site options (mission, for example) all require no programming.

3. Use Administer, Site Configuration, Site Maintenance.

Activities

As you start to think about your site, think about the functionality you might want. Explore the modules that might be useful by searching keywords at drupal.org/project/modules. Read the comments to track for other modules in the same area. Do not install new modules yet because you may find other ways of accomplishing your goals in the following hours. The point is to get familiar with the sorts of things people are doing with modules.

Using Drupal Nodes

What You'll Learn in This Hour:

▶ How to Build a Site from Scratch

▶ Explore Drupal's Node Structure

▶ Build Your Own Nodes

Introduction

Having explored the overall architecture of Drupal, it is time to get into the basics of Drupal's content architecture. The primary component of the content architecture is the node, the topic of this hour. In the world of computer science, a *node* is an abstract object that may contain data and may have relationships to other nodes. In Drupal, stories, articles, images, events, and just about every other type of content is a node. The abstraction comes about because it is possible to talk about nodes without having to specify "stories, images, events, and just about every other type of content." The main Drupal content types that are not nodes are users and comments.

You will also see how you can create a front page for your site automatically from recently created nodes. When that is done, you will know the basics you need to create a bare-bones site. Adding images, setting up security, and adding socialization are topics for the rest of this book.

Building a Site

There are two aspects to building a website whether it uses Drupal or not. Both are iterative processes, and they normally are done at the same time—at least at the start.

Designing the Site

Designing the site involves everything from the look-and-feel of the site to the logical layout of its content. You have already seen an overview of Drupal and learned how to administer the site. These are all primarily design tasks.

As you build the site, you may find that small or even major modifications are needed in the design; this is perfectly normal. Many designers, whether they are designing a website or a database, hew to the notion that "the data never lies." You can have the most wonderful design, but when you try to actually put data into the database or the website (or even into a cardboard carton!), it may not always fit. You can change the data or change the design. Fortunately, with Drupal, either choice is usually easy, but as time goes on, it becomes more difficult to make design changes because they may affect previously entered data in adverse ways.

That is why, at the beginning of building a site, you should watch carefully to see how it appears as you begin to enter data. Keep an open mind, and look for possible issues down the road.

One way to look for potential problems while they can still be easily corrected is to aggressively enter different types of data into the site. If you build a section of the site that contains all of your information about corporate policies, you will have completed an important component. But, by focusing on policies, you may discover after a while that some of your designs are awkward to use for e-commerce or user feedback.

Critique the design in meetings or in your head (for a one-person project). Do not be defensive, and, above all, do not assume that things will magically work out. Drupal supports many, many features, but magic is not one of them.

Building the Site

To test the design, you need content. Remembering that data does not lie, use real content. Far too many sites are built with entries consisting of placeholder text (sometimes called *lorem ipsum* because of the text that is often used) that breaks when real text for the site is inserted. Use content that has the features that you will need. It has to be your data with all of its complexities (or at least as many of them as you can find). With Drupal, there is a simple way to begin to create content for your site even before the design is complete. Assuming that you have followed the steps in this book so far, you will have an empty Drupal site, and you will be using the primary user account to enter data. Almost certainly, you will eventually choose to display at least some of the content on formatted pages, and you will want it to be reachable through menus.

Until you have a certain amount of content, it is impossible to create formatted pages and very difficult to create menus. The reason has to do with a strength of

Drupal's design: Drupal sites are often built from the bottom up. For example, you can create a node and then place it on a formatted page. If you create a formatted page and have no nodes to place on it, it will be blank. Likewise, you can create a node and then assign it to a menu. It is not easy to create a menu that has nothing in it, although it is possible. If you are used to designing a website by creating empty menus and pages, you may be somewhat frustrated. The easiest way to begin to build your site is to create some content—about a dozen nodes of various types. Then, you can experiment with assigning them to menus and formatted pages. (Remember to use real data wherever possible.)

Drupal's default settings for node creation make all of this easy. For each node, you must provide a title, and you usually provide content. If you leave the default settings, that is all you need to enter, but remember to scroll down to the bottom of the page to the Save button.

By default, Drupal will publish each node you create to the front page, just as blogs do. That lets you create your content and view it quickly.

Introducing Nodes

Almost all content in Drupal is contained in a node. Nodes can be stories, pages, polls, webforms, forum topics, blog entries, or images. Some of Drupal's content is not stored in nodes, and that list is shorter than the list of what is stored in nodes. Following is a list of primary non-node content in Drupal:

- ▶ Blocks that appear most often in the margins of pages.
- ▶ Users and their data, but nodes are always linked to a specific user.
- ▶ Comments, but they are always attached to a node.
- ▶ Files and images that are attached to nodes.

Although you should not touch Drupal core or its database in almost all cases, looking inside the database that Drupal creates for you is sometimes a good way to learn how Drupal does what it does and what you can do with it. (Remember: Look, but do not touch!)

The table that contains node data is called node. Its columns (as of Drupal 6) are shown in Figure 5.1.

In the next section, where you learn to create nodes, you will see the interface that lets you fill these columns. It is important to understand that the interface truly reflects the database, and that Drupal's node structure is sturdy, stable, and reliable (as well as an excellent example of relational database design. Remember that this information is available for every type of node that Drupal supports.

All of these fields are managed for you by Drupal, using appropriate data (the time-stamp for creation or changes) or default values that you can set (usually in the content type). The only ones you need to specify are the node type (which you specify by clicking a content type on Create Content) and the title for the node.

Node Identifications

A set of identifiers identify the node. These exist for every node:

▶ **nid**—This is a unique ID for each node. It is automatically assigned by the database. You can sometimes see it in a URL for a node. If you see . ?q=node/ 101 in the URL, that is node 101. You can use tools to clean up the URLs and hide the nid in most cases, but it is still there and is used internally by Drupal.

▶ **vid**—Version control is built into Drupal. Each node starts with version one. This is the current version. Version control is not something that is turned on or off. What is under your control is when a new version is created. You can enter and modify data as much as you want: no versions are saved. When you click the check box Create New Version on a node data entry page, the current content is frozen and your changes become the start of the next version. You also can and should type in a log entry explaining what the new version does or what has been achieved in the previous version.

▶ **uid**—This is the user ID of the user who owns the node. It is usually the ID of the creator.

Node Attributes

All these attributes are required for each node:

- **title**—This is a string of up to 255 characters for the title of the node.

- **type**—This is the type of node (at this point, you have only two types—stories and pages). It affects how a node is displayed.

- **status**—A node is either published or not. If it is not published, only administrators can see it. They can also edit it and change its status to published.

- **comment**—If 0, no comments are allowed. Values of 1 mean the comments are read-only, and values of 2 means they are read/write.

- **sticky**—You can specify that when a node appears in a list (such as the blog-like default front page), it appears at the top of the list. A value of 1 means yes, whereas a value of 0 means no.

- **promote**—This indicates that the node is to appear on the front page. It is often used in conjunction with sticky. Again, 0 means no and 1 means yes.

- **created** and **changed**—UNIX timestamps.

- **language, tnid,** and **translate**—Used for automatic translation.

Node Versions and Content

The content for a node is always contained in a specific version in node_revisions. Each version is linked to the node with using nid and vid. The node itself has the latest value of vid, so it can always find its content. There is also a uid column, which allows multiple users to revise nodes.

These are the other fields in node_revisions:

- **title**—This is the title of the revision (not the node). It is normally not displayed to end users.

- **body**—This is the content of the node.

- **teaser**—This is the brief part of the node that can appear in a summary; it generally is followed with a More link.

- **format**—This is the input format to use for the body text. The two usual choices are Filtered HTML and Full HTML. In both cases, links are automatically created from web and mail URLs; also, line and paragraph breaks are properly handled. Full HTML allows you to embed any HTML in the body that you want—it will be rendered appropriately when the end user sees the mode.

With the Filtered HTML format, all HTML elements are stripped out, except <a>, <em>, <strong>, <cite>, <code>, <ul>, <ol>, <li>, <dl>, <dt>, and <dd>. Note that <em> and <strong> are always available, but <i> and <b> are available only in Full HTML (and are discouraged today on the web).

▶ **log**—This is a description you can provide describing your changes from the previous version.

▶ **timestamp**—This is when the version was created.

Creating Nodes

To create a node, choose the Create Content link from the navigation menu at the left of most pages (when you are running as an administrator); in Drupal 7, click Add at the top. When you have just installed Drupal, your only choices are pages and stories (articles in Drupal 7). Figure 5.2 shows how you start to create a story.

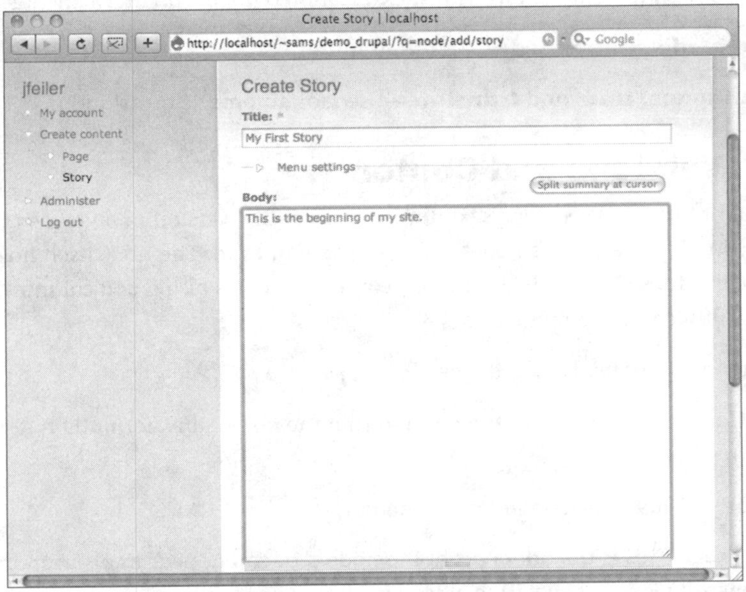

FIGURE 5.2
Start to create a story.

The Body of the node can contain HTML, so you can copy and paste all or part of an existing page into a node (a Page node is a good candidate for this). There is more on this in Hour 11, "Empowering User Input with Rich Text and Images."

As you scroll down the page, you can click to open a number of optional sections. None of them is required after you have set the title.

Setting the Menu

This is just below the title and above the content, as you can see in Figure 5.3. Remember that content (the nodes) have no *where* in Drupal. You can use this setting to set the menu for a node, but that information is menu information; it is not stored in the node.

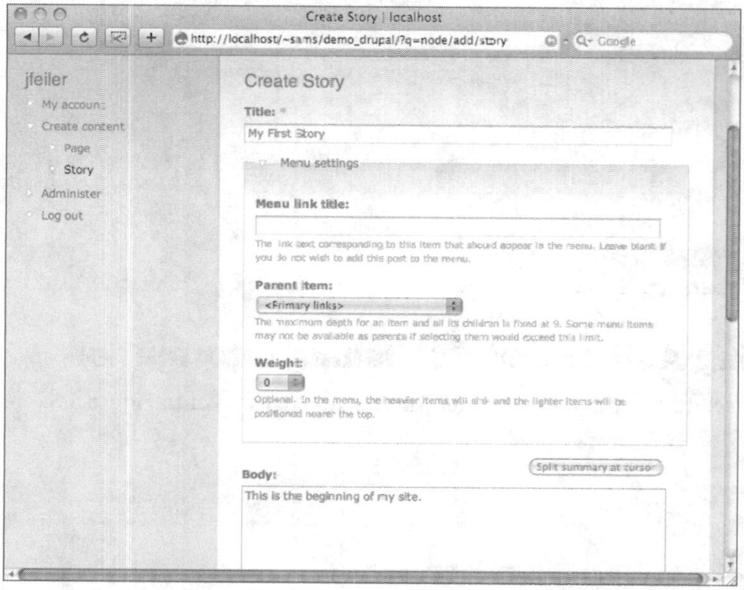

FIGURE 5.3
Set the menu.

Setting the Input Format and Version

Next, you can choose to set the input format, as shown in Figure 5.4. The default input format is set in Administer, Site Configuration, Input Formats (D6: admin/settings/filters D7: admin/config./formats content), as described in Hour 11, "Empowering User Input with Rich Text and Images."

The check box lets you create a new version; if you do not, you will make the change to the last version. Note that you can (and should) enter a log message describing what you have done.

Setting the Comment Controls

You can allow comments to be disabled, viewed, or both written and viewed. The default settings for these are controlled in Administer, Content Management, as described in Hour 4.

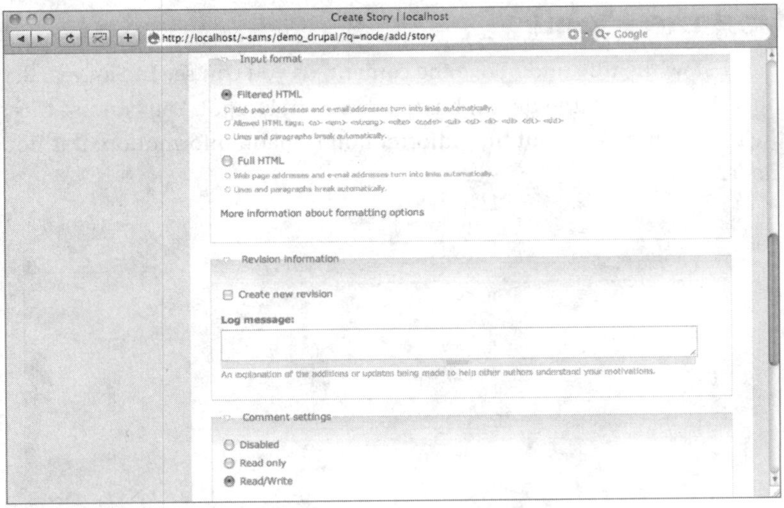

FIGURE 5.4
Set the input for-
mat and version
information.

Setting Author and Publishing Information

You can set authoring and publisher information, as shown in Figure 5.5.

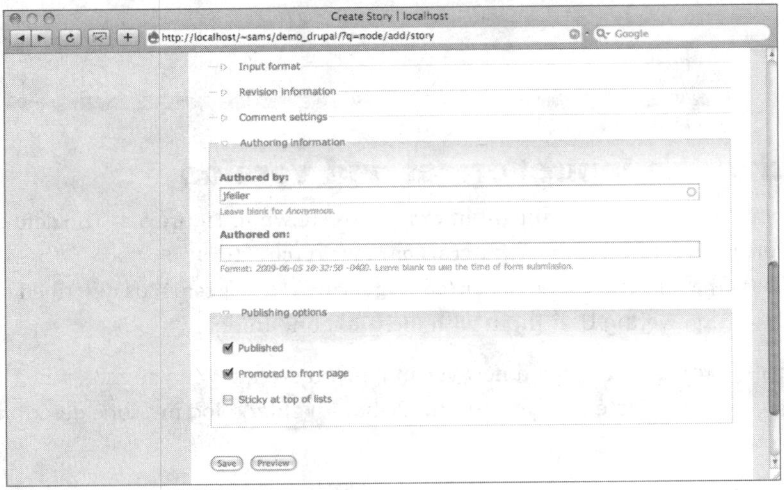

FIGURE 5.5
Set the author-
ing and publish-
ing information.

Publish the Node

Use the Save button to complete the process. You can also use the Preview button to see how the node will appear. This is particularly important if you have embedded HTML in the node body.

If you want to see exactly what has happened, you can use a query browser to look at the records in the node table. Figure 5.6 shows what it looks like after this story and a companion page have been published.

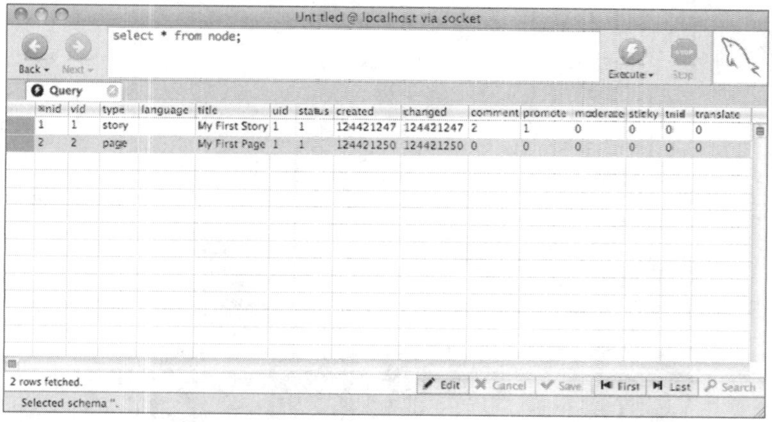

FIGURE 5.6
Drupal has stored your node in the node table.

Default values for publishing are set as described in Hour 4.

You can also look at node_revisions to see the body of these nodes, as shown in Figure 5.7.

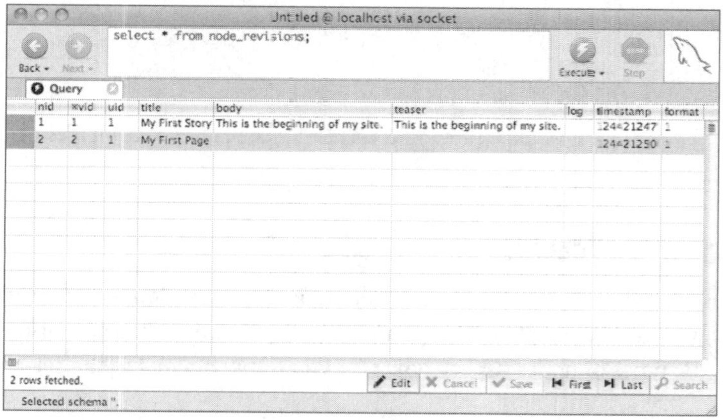

FIGURE 5.7
The content has been stored in the appropriate revision.

Using Alternate Input Pages

Your node editing page may look different for one of two reasons. First of all, the design has changed in Drupal 7. It has the same content, but it is presented in a more compact manner, as you can see in Figures 5.8 and 5.9.

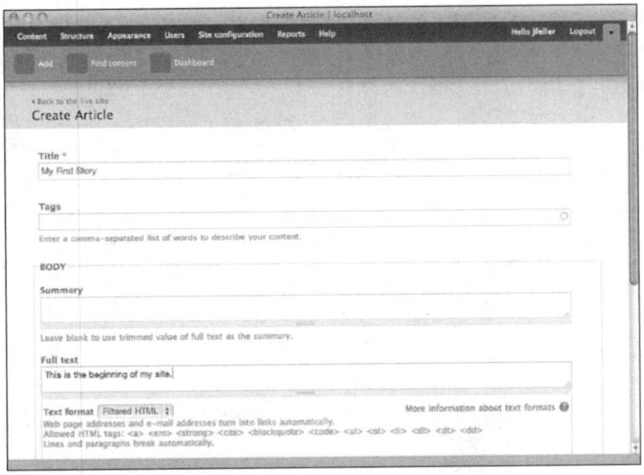

FIGURE 5.8
Create or edit a
node in Drupal 7.

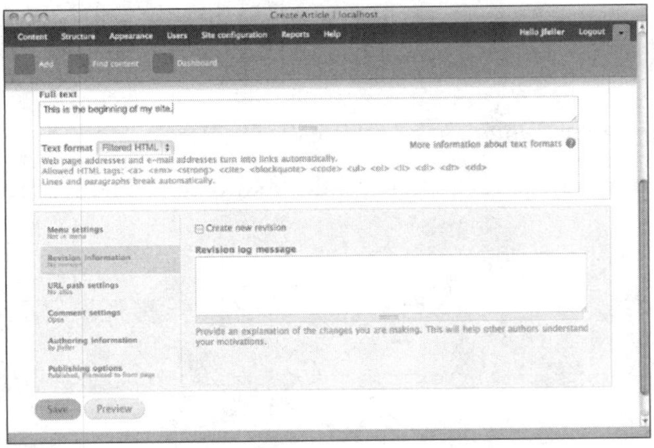

FIGURE 5.9
Bottom of the
create/edit page
in Drupal 7.

Editing a Node

You can use Administer, Content to edit nodes, as shown in Figure 5.10. With only a few nodes, you can scroll down the list and click the Edit link. You can also limit the list to specific types of nodes. Check boxes let you apply actions to the selected nodes.

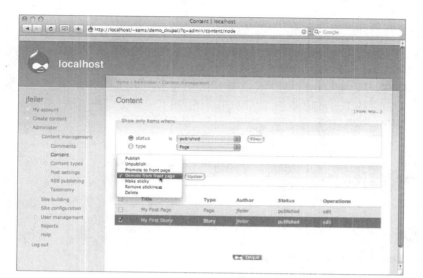

FIGURE 5.10
Select a node to edit.

Go To ▶

In addition, if you have the content construction kit (CCK) and panels 3 modules installed in Drupal 6 or if you are using Drupal 7, you can add fields to content types and rearrange the input pages. This is Described in Hour 7, "Using Content Construction Kit (cck) and Images," p. 107, Hour 20, "Laying Out Panels and Pages," p. 337 and Hour 23, "Using View Arguments and Modifying Built-in Pages," p. 395.

Summary

Nodes are the basic unit of content storage in Drupal. You have seen how their simple design incorporates version control and options for the behavior of comments, embedded HTML, and if and how the node is published.

Q&A

Q. *What are the best settings for all the options in a node?*

A. There is no one answer. Many people leave the installation defaults and never touch anything, with the possible exception of the menu See Hour 10, "Using Polls, Comments, Discussions, and Feed Aggregators" for suggestions on using comments effectively.

Q. *I thought Drupal could let you create polls and use images. Why do they not appear in Administer, Create Content?*

A. Many of these features are provided by modules—both user contributions and modules distributed as part of Drupal. The modules have to be installed and enabled before you can use them.

Q. *How do you turn version control on?*

A. You don't. Even if the body of a node is empty, a version is created when you click the Save button. What you can do is to determine when the *next* version starts. If you do not click the Create New Version check box before you publish a revision to a node, you will modify the information in the latest version rather than create a new version.

Workshop

Quiz

1. How do you store a draft of a node?

2. How many nodes can you have in a Drupal site?

3. Where are nodes displayed?

Quiz Answers

1. Change the publishing settings to unpublished.

2. In a practical sense, the number is limited only by the database resources. In MySQL, the maximum value that can be stored in an unsigned int(10) field, which is how nid is declared, is 4,294,967,295—so that is the theoretical maximum.

3. In the initial default Drupal installation, they are displayed on the front page just like a blog.

Activities

Create 10 to 20 stories in your new Drupal site. Make them of varying lengths, and experiment with stickiness and with turning the front page option on and off for each one. Make sure that you are comfortable with all the options.

HOUR 6

Managing URLs: Cleaning, Redirects, and Pathauto

What You'll Learn in This Hour:

▶ Using Clean URLs and Pathauto

▶ Redirecting URLs

Introduction

You have seen the basics of Drupal—its overall structure and how nodes are created. The extraordinary power of Drupal is built on its structure and its nodes, but there are many tools and features to explore. Among them are the issues related to the URLs that Drupal creates and uses. Some of these are Drupal-specific issues; others are issues related to any website (particularly large ones); and still others are Drupal responses to the issues that large websites have to contend with.

If you want to get busy with Drupal development, you can easily skip over this hour and come back to it later. However, URL issues on a website are often notoriously difficult to retrofit, particularly if you have publicly launched your site. As people visit your site, they bookmark pages in which they are interested. Similarly, search engines crawl your site collecting URLs for their databases, and helpful friends and colleagues can provide support for you and your site by adding your site and its key pages to their own site.

The web is fast moving, and its content spreads virally. If you have a choice, come up with your URL naming conventions before your site goes public.

GO TO ▶
For more information about moving an existing site to Drupal, see **HOUR 17, "BUILDING YOUR FIRST LIVE SITE,"** p 303.

Moving Your Existing Site to a Drupal Site

If you already have a website, your URLs are probably spread around the world in users' bookmarks and on other websites; they may be further disseminated by being printed in books and magazines, and perhaps they are displayed in television advertising. When you move to a new website, you need to decide what to do. (Note that this is not a Drupal issue, although Drupal has tools to help you.)

The first thing you may worry about is your domain name itself: mycompany.com. This is normally yours, and you can move it from one web hosting company to another, so you do not have to worry if your Drupal move will also involve a hosting move. For many people, moving an existing site to Drupal can be done in either of two ways. You can do a full conversion so that, at a certain time (2 A.M. on a Sunday morning is a popular time for this), the old site is replaced by the new Drupal site. The other way is to do a progressive conversion. In a progressive conversion, you address each area (sometimes even each page) with one of two approaches:

▶ **Redirection to Drupal**—If you know of specific URLs on your site other than your home page that are published or used commonly by visitors, you can use redirect statements to send them to pages with different naming conventions in your Drupal site.

▶ **Redirection from Drupal**—If there are sections of your existing site that need to be available but do not need to be updated for the Drupal conversion, you can leave them where they are and link or redirect to them from Drupal. Over time, you can move these pages into the actual Drupal site.

Using Clean URLs

When the web was first proposed, URLs were addresses of documents to be returned to the user. In most cases, they were HTML documents. Requests were handled by web servers that simply retrieved the given document and returned it to the user.

In short order, web servers morphed into more complex software that were capable not just of locating the requested document and returning it, but also of interpreting variable data in the URL request and assembling a dynamic HTML document to be returned to the user. Sometimes, these were called application servers, although that term is used less frequently today. As the web evolved, the format of URLs evolved and in their evolving complexity, URLs became divided into two categories: clean URLs and dirty URLs.

Dirty URLs

The format of a URL can incorporate a *query string*, in which dynamic information could be transmitted. The query string follows the address of the document; it is introduced by a question mark and continues to the end of the URL.

The query string consists of one or more name/value pairs of the form

```
width=17.3
season=winter
```

Name/value pairs are separated either by ampersands or semicolons, so that you could construct a URL with a query string as follows:

```
www.yourwebsite.com/home.html?width=17.3&season=winter
```

Inside the query string, some special coding may be required because URLs cannot have spaces and certain other characters within them. (For example, the query string is introduced by a question mark and its terms are separated by ampersands or semicolons, so those characters have special meaning.) Here are the encoding rules:

▶ Uppercase and lowercase characters remain intact.

▶ Underscores (_), dashes (–), tildes (~), and dots (.) remain intact.

▶ Each space is converted to a single + (thus, two spaces are converted to ++).

▶ All other characters are converted to a hexadecimal value and preceded by a per cent sign. An asterisk, for example, is %2A.

This process is supported in many programming languages, including PHP. The *urlencode* function accepts a string and returns the properly encoded value with the necessary replacements; the companion *urldecode* function does the reverse.

The presence of a query string in a URL may mean that the web server uses that information in retrieving the document to return; on the other hand, it may mean that the document is constructed completely dynamically. This, in fact, is what happens in Drupal. All requests to the Drupal directory are passed onto the admin.php file, and the query string is passed along so that Drupal can construct the HTML document to return.

For example, if you go to the Administration section of a Drupal site, your browser will show the following URL:

```
mycompanyname.com/~sams/demo_drupal/?q=admin
```

The demo_drupal directory exists and is visible if you look at the server, but that is as far as you can go. The query string q=admin determines what happens. For this reason, many search engines do not index URLs with query strings. If your website depends on search engines, it is important to make your URLs as search-engine-friendly as possible, and that may include minimizing or eliminating the use of URLs that create these *dynamic pages*.

A URL containing a query string is harder for people and search engines to immediately process. Over time, they have come to be known as *dirty URLs*.

Cleaning Your URLs

GO TO ▶
For more information on optimizing your site for search engines, go to a page such as www.google.com/support/webmasters.

Not surprisingly, the opposite of a dirty URL is a clean URL. Internally, Drupal uses dirty URLs with query strings in them. For example, this is a Drupal URL for the first node on the site:

```
localhost/~sams/?q=node/1
```

This is the same URL after it has been cleaned:

```
localhost/~sams/node/1
```

The difference is that the cleaned URL appears as a familiar sequence of pathnames separated by slashes rather than as a query string. People and search engine web crawlers can recognize them at a glance.

A query string, always introduced with a question mark, introduces information that is meaningful to the website and its developers. Syntactically, no difference exists between

```
localhost/~sams/?q=node/1
```

and

```
localhost/~sams/?width=17.3
```

In the first case, the name in the name/value pair is q, and in the second case, it is width. Although to your eye node/1 may seem like two items, it is a single value, just as 17.3 is single value. The specific web server will decide whether the slash or the dot is an internal delimiter. That is one of the reasons web crawlers have trouble and may even skip such a URL.

There is an option to turn on clean URLs; you can find it at Administer, Site Configuration, Clean URLs or at admin/settings/clean-urls. However, after the URLs are cleaned, you still have to take several steps to provide meaningful URLs (clean URLs can still be gibberish) and to handle issues such as redirection.

Clean URL Requirements on Apache and IIS

Turning on clean URLs requires mod_rewrite on Apache or as an extension to Microsoft IIS. Although you can run Drupal without clean URLs, it is increasingly becoming a de facto requirement. For example, the widely used ImageCache module is just one third-party module that requires clean URLs.

By the Way

Using the Path Module

Drupal allows you to construct meaningful path names. You can do so with the Path module, which is part of the core Drupal distribution; it is optional, so you need to enable it. This is a one-time task: After it is completed, it is not needed again.

Setting Up the Path Module

Install, enable, and set permissions for the Path module using the information provided in Table 6.1.

TABLE 6.1 Path Module Reference

Download from	Part of Core
Enable in section	Other
Permissions	
Path	Administer URL Aliases
Path	Create URL Aliases
Administration	
Administration, Site Building, URL Aliases (D6: admin/build/path; D7: admin/settings/path)	

GO TO ▶
For more on installing and enabling modules, see **HOUR 4, "ADMINISTERING DRUPAL, THEMES, AND MODULES,"** p. 47. For information on setting permissions, see **HOUR 8, "MANAGING USERS, ROLES, AND PERMISSIONS,"** p. 127.

Specifying a URL for Content

After the Path module is enabled, whenever you are creating or editing content, there will be a field to enter URL path settings, as shown in Figure 6.1. (If it is not there, the Path module has not been enabled.) The path is the relative path. Without a URL path that you specify, Drupal will construct a URL, such as yoursite.com?q=node/1.

For such a site, you could create an alternate URL path to use, such as welcome. You would enter **welcome** in the URL path field, and the user would be able to use yoursite.com/welcome to get to the content.

You can enter an alias when the Path module is enabled, as shown in Figure 6.1. (In Drupal 7, the URL Path Settings fieldset shown in Figure 6.1 is provided with a link at the left, as shown previously in Figure 5.9.) If the Pathauto module is enabled, this section will be changed; it is described later in this hour in the section, "Using the Pathauto Module."

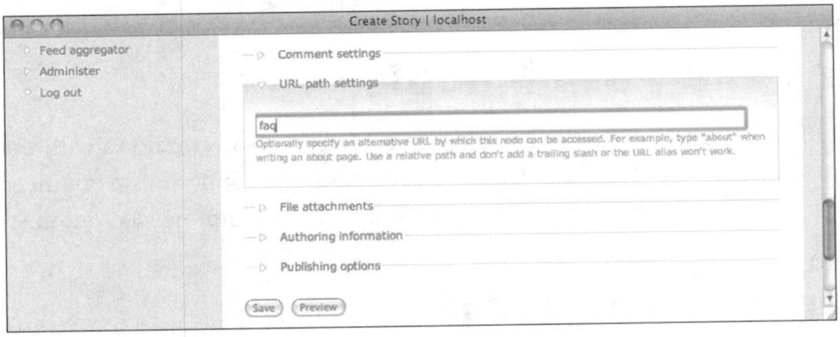

FIGURE 6.1
Enter a URL path for a node.

Managing Aliases for Content

Enabling the Path module also lets you create and manage aliases using Administer, Site Building, URL Aliases or D6: ./admin/build/path or D7:./admin/settings/path, as shown in Figure 6.2. Setting the URL alias from the list in this way is useful if you have a number of aliases you want to modify; otherwise, it is usually easier to create the aliases as you are creating or editing content.

But, for much easier creation of aliases, move on to Pathauto, and let Drupal take care of everything for you.

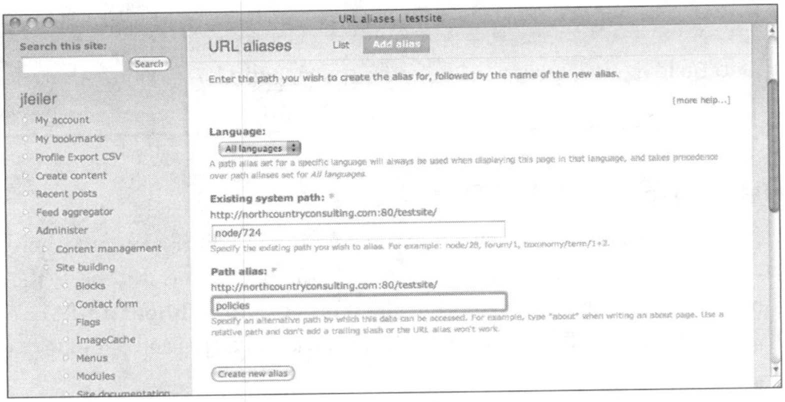

FIGURE 6.2
Manage URL aliases.

Using the Pathauto Module

Specifying a path for each module lets you avoid the dirty URL problems, but it means extra work for you. Not only do you have to manually enter the path you want to use, but you also have to come up with the names you will use. Users will see these, so from a user's point of view, little difference exists between a relatively meaningless path, such as a default Drupal path of node/24, and an equally relatively meaningless path that you have created, such as athena/sardbar.

There are two ways to address this matter:

▶ You can leave the Path field blank. Drupal will construct its own paths to those nodes, and you can specify meaningful paths to some of the nodes that you think need to be made more visible. Unfortunately, this adds a third task to the path process: you need to type in the path, decide what it will be, and decide whether to use a custom path or the default path.

▶ You can use the Pathauto module to created automated aliases. It involves some setup, but after that is done, you have nothing more to do. Every time you can set up a task or process for Drupal to do automatically, you save time; you also generally enforce standards and consistency.

Installing Token and Pathauto

Here is how to use Pathauto. It relies on the Token module, so you must install both modules. First, install, enable, and set permissions for the Token module using the information provided in Table 6.2.

TABLE 6.2 Token Module Reference

Download from	drupal.org/project/token
Enable in section	Other

Permissions

There are no permissions for the Token module.

Administration

You do not administer the Token module directly.

GO TO ▶
For more on installing and enabling modules, see Hour 4, p. 47. For information on setting permissions, see Hour 8, p 127.

Then, install, enable, and set permissions for the Pathauto module using the information provided in Table 6.3.

TABLE 6.3   Pathauto Module Reference

Download from	drupal.org/project/pahtauto
Enable in section	Other
Permissions	
Pathauto Module	Administer Pathauto
Pathauto Module	Notify of path changes
Administration	
Administration, Site Building, URL Aliases	Automated Alias Settings (admin/build/path/pathauto)

Permissions Using Pathauto

After Pathauto is installed and enabled, you see two new buttons on the URL aliases administration page: Delete Aliases and Automated Alias Settings. The second button lets you control how Pathauto works. If you are configuring Pathauto from the start of your website development, start here so that all the automatically generated paths are consistent.

By the Way

Dealing with Existing Aliases

If you already have aliases created for some or all of your content, you may want to delete them. It is easiest to look at what you can do with Pathauto and automated alias creation first and then decide what, if any, existing aliases you want to delete.

After you install Pathauto in a clean Drupal installation, the Automated Alias Settings section appears, as shown in Figure 6.3.

Pathauto will generate aliases according to the rules that you set up in this administration setting area. Those rules let you combine static text (such as forum or blog) with metadata, such as the date of a posting along with parts of the title or a node.

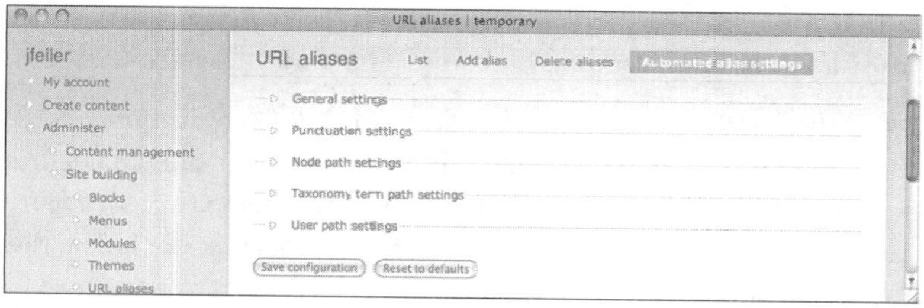

FIGURE 6.3
Manage auto-
mated alias set-
tings for
Pathauto and
various content
types.

After the rules are set up, you can forget about them. Your site's URLs will be clean and will present a user- and search-engine-friendly appearance beneath the aliases that are created.

Configuring these settings is not hard, and it is easy to experiment with them. The Delete Aliases button will let you come back and delete certain sets of aliases so that you can start over.

**Did you
Know?**

You Can Skip this Step

You can skip over this step and add content to your site without using aliases. Pathauto has the capability to come back and do bulk alias creation for your content. However, an operation like that will possibly change the address of every piece of content in your site. Obviously, back up the site and be prepared to restore it if something unfortunate occurs. In addition, you need to set aside time to carry out this maintenance and test that it has worked probably, and that probably means taking a production site offline. All in all, it is usually faster to at least experiment with automated aliases before much data is entered. When in doubt, accept the defaults.

Dealing with Content-Based URLs

Content-based URLs—that is, URLs that contain references to the content to which they point—have a problem that arises when the content changes. What happens to the content-based URL?

People who deal with databases already know about this problem, and they know that a field that uniquely identifies a record should be meaningless. As soon as you add a date or author's initials or product description in any manner to a unique iden-tifier, these problems occur. From a database standpoint, creating meaningless aliases or unaliased URLs is the best strategy. Unfortunately, you can wind up with gibberish that pleases database administrators and drives human beings nuts.

Many strategies exist for dealing with the issue. One of the most common is to identify major parts of the site that have known and absolutely unchanging addresses, whether or not they are aliases. Such common URLs are `yoursite.com/about_us` or `yoursite.com/todays_specials`. You want people to bookmark or link to these pages. You can then use dynamic naming for subsidiary pages. For example, `yoursite.com/todays_specials` can always be the daily specials; the previous days' specials can be found at `yoursite.com/daily_specials/04252010` or whatever date is desired. It takes more work to set up such a structure, but you can try to get external links and bookmarks to work effectively and productively. (There are two terms for the consequences of this problem: *Deep linking* refers to links into a website that may or may not still exist when they are used, and *link rot* refers to links that no longer work.)

This works for certain types of sites, but for others, it is impractical. An e-commerce site, for example, with hundreds or thousands of products can benefit from predictable URLs that people can generate on their own to find what they want. Search engines (both inside the site and products such as Google, Yahoo, and Bing) can help, but many people prefer to type in a URL that they think will work. In these cases, review the material cited previously at www.google.com/support/webmasters; you can also do a web search for search engine optimization (SEO), to find more ideas in this rapidly changing and important area. If you want to optimize your site for search engines and for users' ad hoc URLs, you can rethink the way in which you construct node titles to make them more search-engine friendly and to prepare for Pathauto's automated alias creation. Of course, this works only if you control the titles. For user-created content, you generally have to do your best with the Pathauto rules after the fact of title creation for an article, story, or other content. (It is the title that sets Pathauto in motion along with the rules that you provide.)

These are only Drupal issues to the extent that Drupal makes it so easy to build complex and large sites. These problems arise on those sites, more so than on a two-page site for a hot dog stand.

There are five major groups of settings. You can add others as you install additional modules. For example, if you have enabled blogs and forums, you will have settings for blog and forum paths.

> ▶ **General Settings**—Control the basic settings for automated alias creation, as you can see in Figure 6.4 and Figure 6.5. The basic strategy in producing these automated aliases is to use text from the title of the node

along with some strings and metadata that you can specify for each node type (the date of a blog entry, for example, or the string blog or forum to indicate the type of data that is behind the alias that is automatically created). You can adjust these settings as you experiment with Pathauto, but three settings really need to be decided on at the beginning.

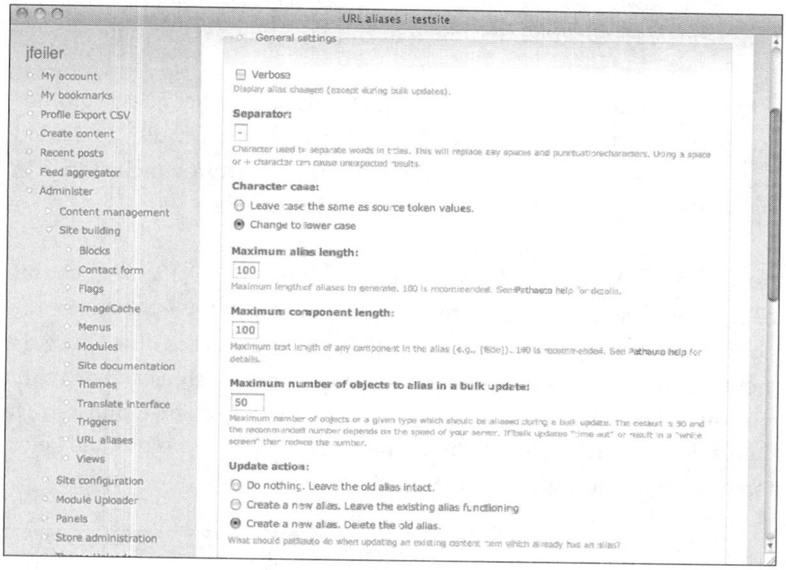

FIGURE 6.4
Review General Settings (top).

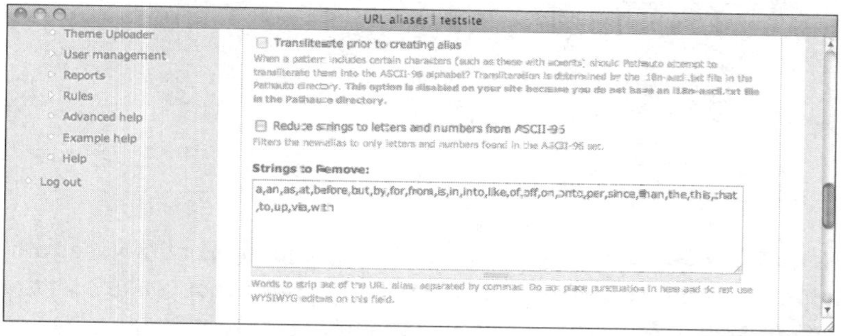

FIGURE 6.5
Review General Settings (bottom).

▶ The most important one is what to do with aliases that already exist. In the case of a blog posting where you are requesting that the date be made part of the alias, an update to the blog posting could create a new alias for the updated posting. Similarly, an alias that combines keywords from the title of a node can change if the title is changed. (Strings that become part of the URL, such as blog or forum, will not change, because after a node is created, you cannot change its type.)

▶ The default settings for the length of the URL and is components can be modified as you go along, but the default settings, along with the default setting for the separator, are usually best. In addition, many people prefer to use lowercase characters for the URL. This is a holdover from the days when capitalization mattered in URLs. It still does on some servers.

▶ Finally, you can add to the list of strings to remove. These common words can appear in a node title and clutter the automatically generated alias. (They are words that are commonly stripped from search strings in browsers.)

▶ **Punctuation Settings**—Shown in part in Figure 6.6. For special characters, the most common option is to remove them, but you have the choice of replacing them with a separator. (Later in this hour, you will see how to use the Taxonomy Terms Path Settings to drop common words, such as and or is, just as you can remove punctuation from the automatically created aliases.) The aliases that are created by Pathauto pass through the Path module before being stored; Path will handle illegal characters.

FIGURE 6.6
Manage punctuation substitutions.

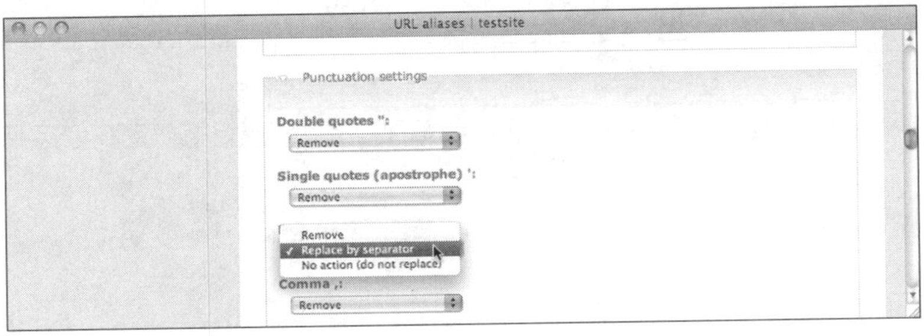

▶ **Node Path Settings**—Figure 6.7 shows the beginning of the Node Path Settings. You can set the default for all nodes; following that you can set the default settings for each content type you have created in your Drupal website. By default, you have a Story and a Page content type.

By the Way

> **Use Metadata in Paths**
>
> Drupal refers to replacement patterns that are the content-based strings inserted into the alias. These replacement patterns often are metadata—data about the data, such as the date of creation, but replacement patterns can also be data itself, such as a product number.

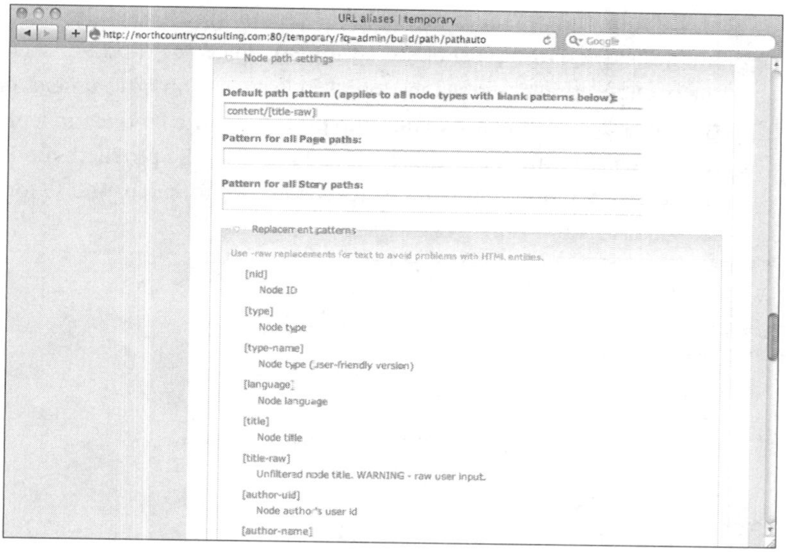

FIGURE 6.7
Use replacement patterns from the Token module in your aliases.

▶ The Replacement Patterns section shows you the fruits of the Token module's labors: metadata strings. Modules that you add to your Drupal installation can communication with the Token module and specify metadata that they can provide.

▶ The default setting shown in Figure 6.7 will create an alias for a node with the title Today's Specials, with the alias being content/todays-specials. This assumes the default settings for separators in General Settings (replace spaces with –), character case in General Settings (change to lowercase), and apostrophes in Punctuation Settings (remove).

▶ Pathauto allows you to specify a default pattern as shown here, but you can also specify a pattern for each content type that you create (or that is created during installation of a module such as the Ubercart e-commerce module). Figure 6.8 shows part of the Node Path Settings section for a Drupal installation with the blogs, forums, and books enabled (these are basic Drupal content types that you can enable in the Administer, Site Building, Modules section). In addition, some special types for a non-profit organization have been created with the Ubercart module (contributions and donations). Each of these could have its own path pattern, but there is often a benefit to using the default pattern so that the site as a whole has predictability to users.

▶ The list of replacement patterns is built by the Token module based on information that other modules provide to it. For example, a Drupal installation that includes the Ubercart shopping cart module, CCK, and ImageField contains a list of more than 80 replacement patterns! (This is the configuration described in Hour 16.) Because you have a field for each type of node, you can set a Pathauto pattern for the Product node that includes replacement patterns such as [model]—the product's model number, or replacement patterns for height, width, price, and so forth.

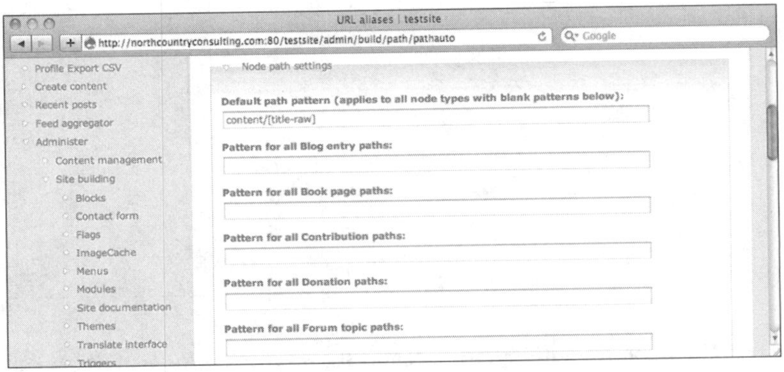

FIGURE 6.8
Pathauto lets you set patterns for each content type.

▶ For time-related nodes, you can construct patterns that include various date forms. One such pattern might be [yyyy]/[[month/[date], which would generate a string such as 2010/February/24. You will find many variations in the list of replacement patterns so that, for example, you could use [yy]/[mo]/[date] to construct 10/02/24.

▶ Notice that some of the replacement patterns are marked with warnings and contain the word *raw*. You can have Pathauto filter user input (raw data) to remove characters that are illegal in URLs. However, because the generated alias passes through the Path module, those characters will be stripped at that point, so you can safely use raw replacement patterns without running into problems.

▶ At the bottom of the Node Path Settings section, you can set an alias for RSS feeds, and, more important, you can check a box so that nodes that are not aliased will be aliased, as you can see in Figure 6.9.

▶ **Taxonomy Term Path Settings**—You can also set patterns for paths to taxonomy terms, as you can see in Figure 6.9. There, too, you have the choice to create aliases for terms that have not yet been aliased.

▶ **User Path Settings**—Finally, you can set patterns for users and do a bulk update for unaliased users. This, too, is shown at the bottom of Figure 6.9.

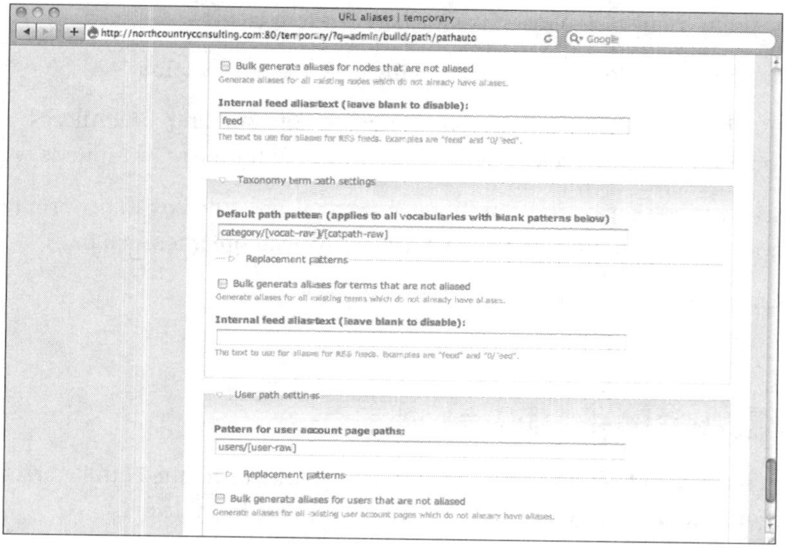

FIGURE 6.9
Create aliases
for unaliased
nodes.

The check boxes that let you create aliases for unaliased nodes of various types work
well with another set of check boxes that are installed along with Pathauto. The
Delete Aliases button, shown in Figure 6.10, lets you delete aliases for certain types of
nodes. (This list varies depending on the modules that you have installed and
enabled.)

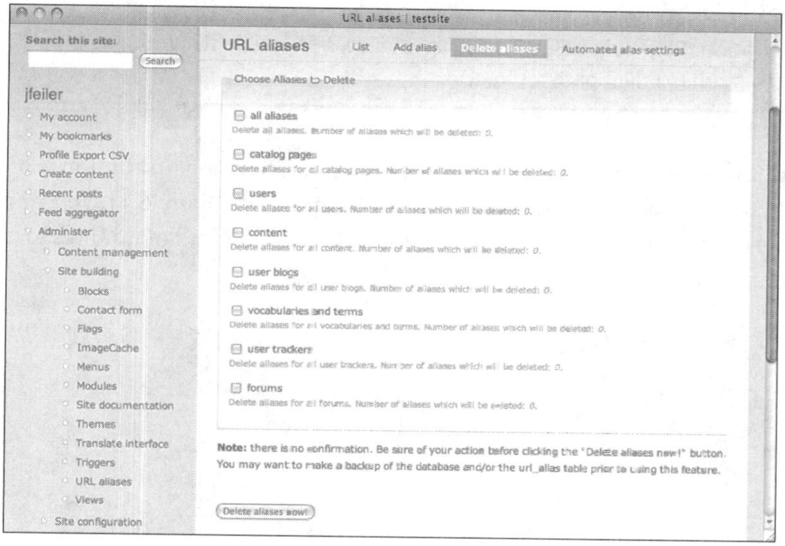

FIGURE 6.10
Delete aliases
by node type.

If you want to create new aliases, you can do it in four steps:

1. Back up the database and take it offline, as described in Hour 4.

2. Use the Delete Aliases button on Administer, Site Building, URL Aliases (admin/build/path/delete_bulk) to delete aliases for the relevant node types.

3. Set patterns, if necessary, for those nodes and check the box to perform batch updates for unaliased nodes of whatever type you are interested in.

4. Check the database, and bring it back online.

Redirecting URLs

You can set Drupal to redirect from one URL to another using the Path Redirect module. Install, enable, and set permissions for it, as shown in Table 6.4.

TABLE 6.4   Path Redirect Module Reference

Download from	drupal.org/project/path_redirect
Enable in section	Other
Permissions	
Path Redirect Module	Administer redirects
Administration	
Administration, Site Building, URL Redirects (admin/build/path-redirect)	List, Add-Redirect, Settings, Export

By now, the basic administration tools should be familiar. The first button is a list of the URL redirects that you have created. As you can see in Figure 6.11, you can edit or delete each one; you can also use the live links on the from and to URLs to check out what it is doing.

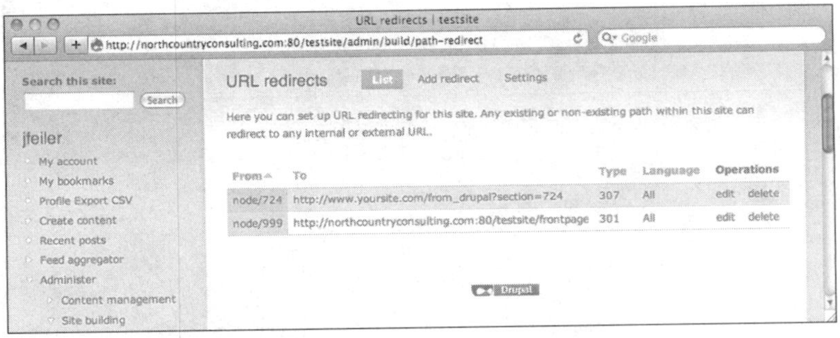

FIGURE 6.11
List, edit, and delete URL redirects.

If you choose to edit or add a URL redirect, you have the options shown in Figure 6.12.

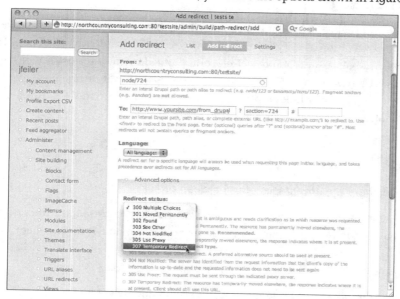

FIGURE 6.12
Add or edit a
URL redirect.

You can specify the path within your Drupal directory from which to redirect, and you specify the Drupal path or fully qualified path to which it should be redirected. Note that the redirection can include a query string.

You can also specify the status to be returned for this redirection. This is particularly important for helping search engines keep up with your site and its changing URLs.

The Settings section lets you set defaults for URL redirection, as shown in Figure 6.13. These are not Drupal-specific settings; they are the settings most people want to use to manage any reasonably complex website. You will normally not do any damage if you leave the default settings, at least while you are working to get your site up and running.

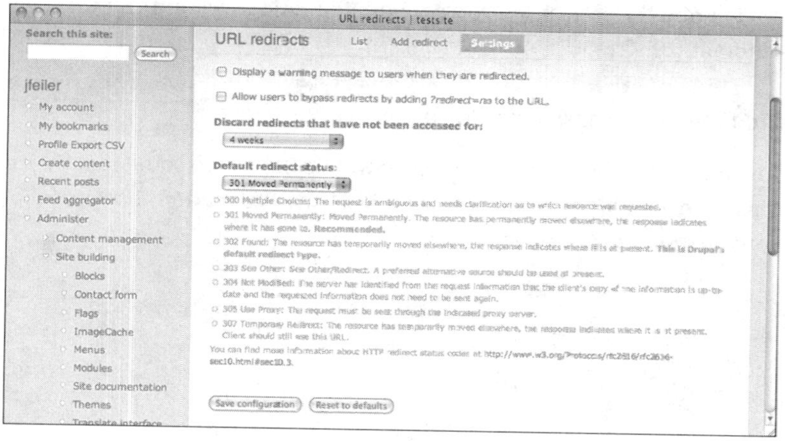

FIGURE 6.13
Configure default
settings for URL
redirection.

Summary

This hour showed you how to use Drupal's URL management tools to create aliases manually and automatically (with Pathauto), clean URLs, and use redirection. These are nuts-and-bolts issues for any website, and particularly as large as Drupal sites often are. Addressing these issues early in the process—ideally, before people have a chance to bookmark or link to specific pages on your site—can make future site maintenance easier than if you put off this work until later.

Q&A

Q. *What are the advantages of using clean URLs?*

A. Clean URLs are easier for people and web crawlers to parse than URLs with query strings. In addition, numerous contributed modules require them.

Q. *How can I start over with automatically created URLs?*

A. In Administer, Site Building, URL Aliases, use the Delete Aliases button to delete aliases of specific types. Then, use the bulk update check box for that alias type. Remember to back up the database and take the site offline during this process.

Q. *Should I have a different pattern for each type of node?*

A. You can, but it is not necessarily a good idea. The default setting prefixes all automatically created aliases with content/, and that is a good default. You can refine it if you want so that it is content/blog/ or content/forum/ as the case may be. But, you may choose to promote these apparent subdirectories so that the aliases start with either content/ or blog/ or forum/. It all depends on you and the type of site you are building (and how long you want your automatically created aliases to be).

Q. *Are there any aliases I should not change?*

A. Any alias or node URL that you know will be linked to should remain intact. This particularly applies to RSS feed URLs. Any RSS readers that are following your feed should not have to be reset.

Workshop

Quiz

1. Can users override a redirect?

2. How do I prevent people from deep linking to pages where the URL may change?

Quiz Answers

1. In the default settings for URL Redirects, enable the check box that lets people add ?redirect=no to a Drupal URL (and make certain that people know about it).

2. You can't, but you can provide other, more attractive pages to which to link. Make them more attractive by suggesting that people link to them (and that they not link to other pages).

Activities

If you have not done it already, review the webmaster guidelines on google.com, yahoo.com, and any other search engines that you or your users will likely use.

Think about your website and decide on the alias structure if you are going to use Pathauto. If you do not yet know the types of data you will have on your site, consider a generic alias structure, such as content/, user-input/, and reference/ (or other generic prefixes). Have something in place that you can use without changing it too much as your site grows.

Using Content Construction Kit (CCK) and Images

What You'll Learn in This Hour:

▶ How You Can Create New Content and Content Types with CCK

▶ Adding an Image Field to Any or All Content Types

▶ Using ImageCache to Automatically Resize Images

Introduction

In Hour 5, "Using Drupal Nodes," you saw the basics of how to create a node with a title and body. Hour 6, "Managing URLs: Cleaning, Redirects, and Pathauto," helped you prepare the site for supporting many nodes without running into addressing issues for users and search engines. Now, it is time to add more content to the site—more content and more types of content (polls, stories or articles, products for your e-commerce shopping cart, and so on), as well as more information within your content types (images for your products and articles, sophisticated data fields instead of your amorphous body text, and the like).

Although it is easy to add new content to Drupal, adding new content types and structures has not been a simple process. Until recently, there were two primary ways in which it can be done:

▶ You can get out your programming and database tools and extend Drupal with a new content type.

▶ You can install a new module that contains a new content type. You do not need any programming or database tools, but you must be able to find a module with the content type you need.

Today, there is a third way: Content Construction Kit (CCK) allows you to create your own content types and add fields to existing content types without writing code or delving into databases.

This hour shows you how to use CCK to add new content types and new fields within your existing content types (either those that are part of the standard Drupal distribution or those that you create or add through contributed modules). You can use these techniques for many data types, but the one that is shown here is *ImageField*, which allows you to use images with any content type. ImageField is powerfully expanded by Imagecache, which is also described in this hour. Imagecache provides powerful and automated manipulation of ImageField data. With these tools, you can easily add images to your website.

Using the CCK Structure

The node structure described in Hour 5 exists alongside CCK in Drupal 6 and, to a large extent, Drupal 7. One of the main problems with that structure has been that it is not easily extensible. If you want to have a node with an additional type of data in it, you need to get out the programming tools.

Like all Drupal data, node data is stored in the database for the site. That means that each data element has to be stored as a data type that is supported by the database. The challenge for Drupal or any other system that lets users create ad hoc database structures is how to let users specify those structures without writing SQL code. Over time, a fairly standard solution has evolved for these systems; this is Drupal's implementation of the solution.

The key is to create an intermediate level between the database itself and the user-visible structure (nodes, in Drupal's case). The structure described in Hour 5 has two basic components:

- ▶ The node contains data fields. These are given names in the node. The node provides some semantic guidance in the form of help text and, particularly if you are writing code, some error checking for data values.

- ▶ The data for these fields is stored in the database as one of the standard SQL data types.

With CCK, data storage is separated from nodes. An intermediate construct, a `CCK field`, is used. A field identifies a data element that is stored in the database, just as node data was. The field identifier and certain semantic rules that might have previously been part of a custom-written node now become part of the field.

Now, nodes no longer contain fields that map directly to SQL data cells. Instead, nodes contain references to CCK fields (this intermediate structure) and the CCK fields refer to the SQL data cells.

When you create a CCK field, you specify the SQL data type that it uses, but you also provide it with a name and a widget that facilitates data entry. The widget (such as a pop-up calendar) can be a critical part of the CCK field. A pop-up calendar, for example, is not just a tool to facilitate data entry: It limits the values that can be entered for the field. Thus, a data entry widget can make the CCK a more meaningful construct than a raw SQL data type, such as an integer.

You can create CCK fields with meanings that are relevant to your website: clothing size, school grade, package weight, or the temperature at noon. Down in the database, these are all numbers, but with CCK, you can create fields with meaningful names and widgets that help to keep the data clean.

More important, these semantically rich CCK fields can be used and reused through your Drupal installation. If you create a package weight field, you can use it in an e-commerce node and an in-store inventory node. You can also use it in a mailroom node to keep track of incoming packages. The field has the same meaning in all cases, but its uses vary.

An additional benefit of CCK fields is that each CCK field type can have its editing permissions set separately (more on this in Hour 8, "Managing Users, Roles, and Permissions"). As you will see, in addition to setting access controls for a specific content type, this feature allows you to block edit access to certain CCK fields within an otherwise-editable content type.

For many people, it is still the case that many extensions to Drupal's content structure are delivered through user-contributed modules. With CCK, however, those user-contributed modules do not just provide new functionality and, often, new node types. They sometimes provide new CCK fields. After you add a module with CCK fields, those fields are available to you in any other context where it makes sense.

Installing CCK and ImageField

The CCK structure has two primary sets of pieces:

▶ The basic infrastructure that handles storage and retrieval of data as well as use of CCK fields.

▶ A number of specific CCK fields. Some are installed with CCK, but they may need to be enabled. Others are available as part of other modules.

Download, install, and enable CCK with the settings shown in Table 7.1.

TABLE 7.1   CCK/ImageField Module Reference

Download from	project/cck (installed as part of Drupal 7)
Enable in section	CCK. Content and ImageField must be enabled.
Permissions	
ImageField	View ImageField uploads
Administration	
None	

Although ImageField is the only CCK field type required for this section, most people immediately enable all the field types that are part of the CCK module. They are as follows:

- ▶ **FileField**—Implements the ability to store files. (It is needed for ImageField.)
- ▶ **ImageField**
- ▶ **Node reference**—Can reference one node from another. There is more on this in Hour 23, "Using Arguments and Modifying Built-in Pages," p. 395.
- ▶ **Number**
- ▶ **Text**
- ▶ **User reference**—Can access a user's data.

Widgets that work with text and number fields can be enabled with Option Widgets in the CCK section of modules. These include check box, radio button, and selection widgets.

Adding an ImageField to a Story

Now, you are ready to add images to your nodes. This section walks you through two ways of doing that. You can create a new field for your story, or you can reuse an existing field with the right semantic meaning and appropriate widgets.

By the Way

Preserve Field Semantics

The importance of reusing fields with the right semantic meaning is that, unlike simple number fields, a field that is called weight and that contains the weight of an item is not logically interchangeable with another number field that contains a temperature. This has long been a problem with databases. When a new data element is needed, it gets shoe-horned into a field of the right data type regardless of its name or interface. This makes for database systems that are hard to maintain. In fact, much of the actual Y2K damage was caused by reuse of data fields without regard to their meaning. It was common to use year fields for the actual year, but also to indicate other information, such as missing data. Back in the 1960s, it was obvious that the two-digit year 00 could signify missing data. Sometime in 1998 or 1999, it dawned on even the dimmest bulb in the database chandelier that 00 might actually be the year that followed 1999 rather than the year that preceded 1901 (and that peculiar arithmetic was another part of the Y2K problem).

Managing CCK ImageFields

Now that you have ImageField set up (possibly along with other CCK field types), you can add those fields to any Drupal content type. Go to Administer, Content Management, Content Types (D6: admin/content/types; D7:admin/structure/types), as shown in Figure 7.1 For each content type, you can manage its fields. Editing the content type itself lets you change its name, description, and the like, but not the fields within it. In Drupal 6, these are links as you see in Figure 7.1; in Drupal 7, they are tabs for the individual content type you are editing.

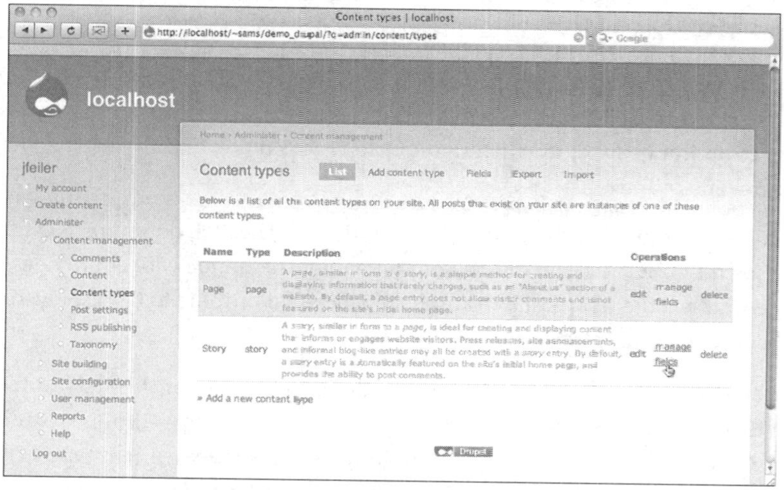

FIGURE 7.1
Manage fields for a content type.

Make Certain the Content Module is Enabled

If you do not see the Manage Fields links, the most likely explanation is that your Content module is not installed and enabled.

By the Way

As you can see in Figure 7.2, you can use the Manage Fields button to work with the fields in this content type. You can use the four-way arrows to drag fields up and down to control the order in which they are presented on the node editing page. (That is one reason why your data entry pages may differ from the figures shown in this hour.) Fields that are grayed out cannot be edited, but they can be moved up and down to change their order.

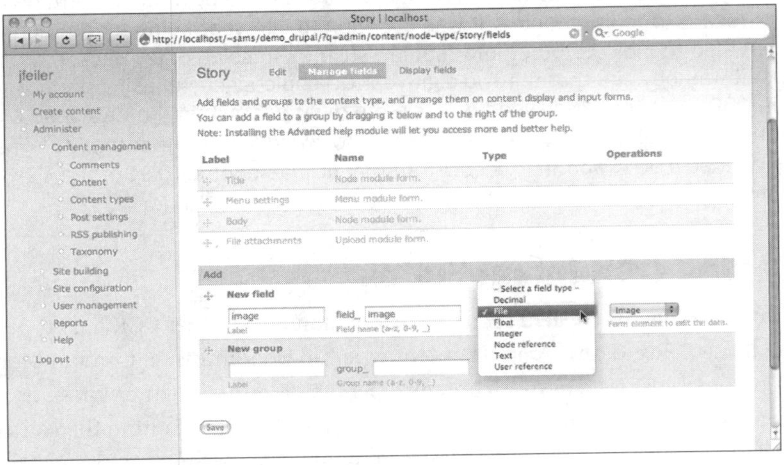

FIGURE 7.2
Create the image field.

At the bottom of the form, you can add a new field or a group. For now, add a new image field. (Groups will be described later in this hour.) You provide a label and a name; the name becomes part of the actual database column name. Thus, if you name the field image, the actual database column will be field_image.

As you can see from Figure 7.2, in addition to the label and name, you select the underlying field type. Selecting the field type controls your choices for the widget. In the case of an image field, the underlying field type is a file, and the two widget choices are File or Image.

This is a good example of the principles behind CCK. The SQL data type is a file, and it has to be a file: SQL has no image data type. But, the Image widget provides an interface that lets the user easily distinguish between a graphic to be displayed and a file to be treated as an attachment to the node.

When you click Save, you are prompted to enter information for this field as it will be used in this content type. (Note that the header is Story Settings—that is, settings for the new CCK field you have created in the context of the story content type.) Figure 7.3 shows this page. Note that the suffixes for file types have no punctuation—spaces (not commas) between them, and no dots before them.

You can scroll down the page shown in Figure 7.3 to supply additional settings for this field in the story content type context. The first item is Path settings, as shown in Figure 7.4. This enables you to create a subdirectory within the files directory for files uploaded for an image field.

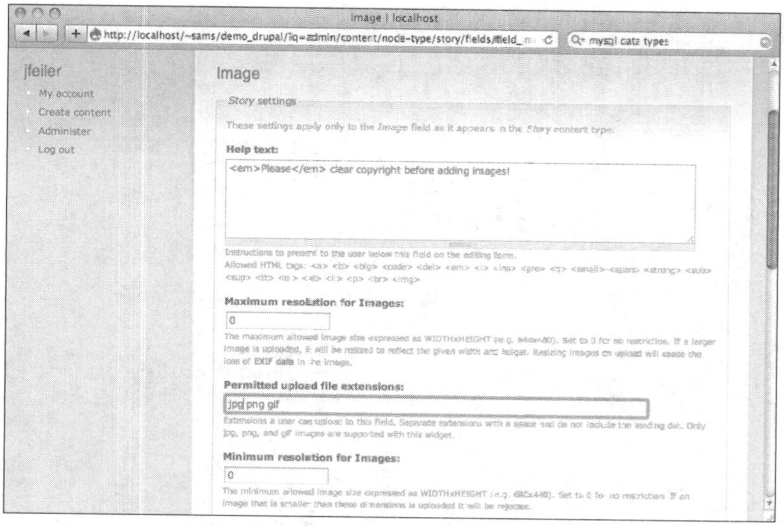

FIGURE 7.3
Provide interface
information for
the field.

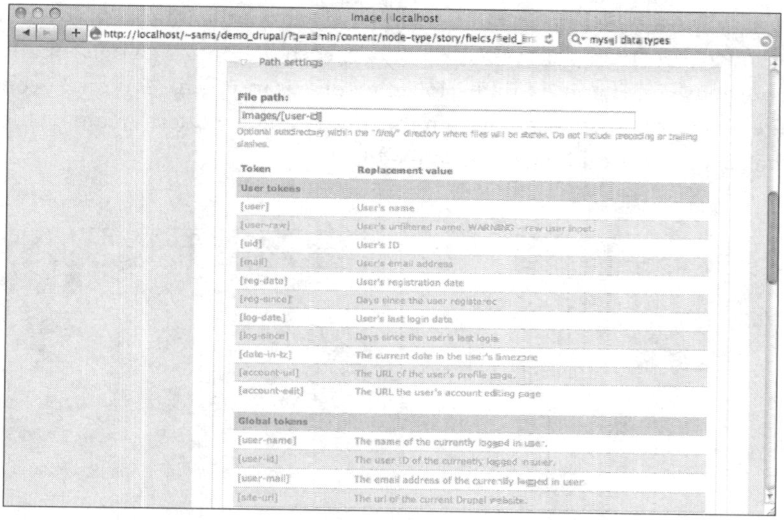

FIGURE 7.4
Specify the path
for uploaded
image files.

As you can see in Figure 7.4, if you have installed the Token module, your path can include token elements, such as the user's name or ID.

Below that, you specify the maximum size of each uploaded file and the maximum size of all uploaded files for the given node, as you can see in Figure 7.5. These settings are critically important when you allow user uploads.

Go To ▶

For more
information on
the Token
module, see
HOUR 6,
p. 87.

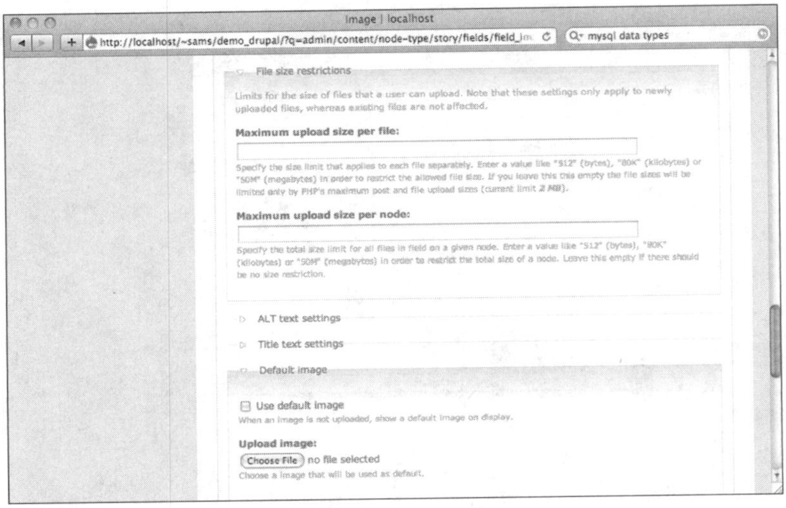

FIGURE 7.5
Specify file size limits for uploaded files.

You can also specify the default ALT text and title text for the image, as well as the default image (see Figure 7.6). When expanded, each area provides a list of tokens, as shown previously in Figure 7.4 (if the Token module is installed). You might consider using the user's name—[user-name]—in the title. A simple pattern might be the user's ID in the file directory and the name in the title.

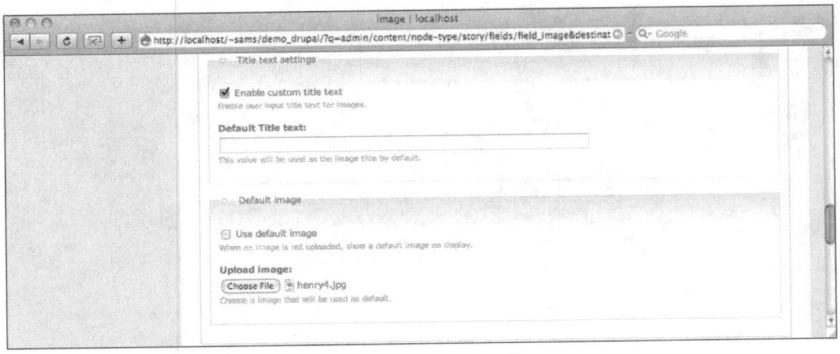

FIGURE 7.6
Provide default ALT, title text, and a default image.

Finally, the Global Settings shown in Figure 7.7 let you specify whether the field is required, the number of values it has, and whether the user can enter a text description. These global settings apply to this field everywhere it is used, not just in the context of the story content type.

When you save your changes, the listing of fields shown previously in Figure 7.2 is updated to show the new field, as shown in Figure 7.8. Later, you can come back to reconfigure the field. In this case, the Configure link lets you change these settings for the story context. You can switch to the basic settings; after you create a field, the only changes you can make are in its label and its widget. The field name and data type cannot be changed.

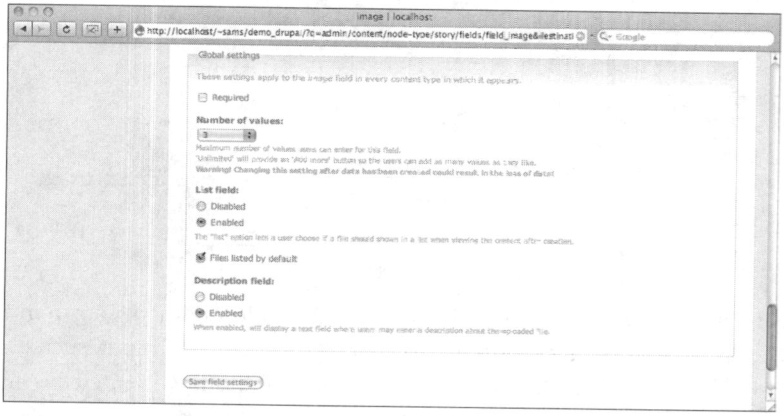

FIGURE 7.7
Add global settings for the field.

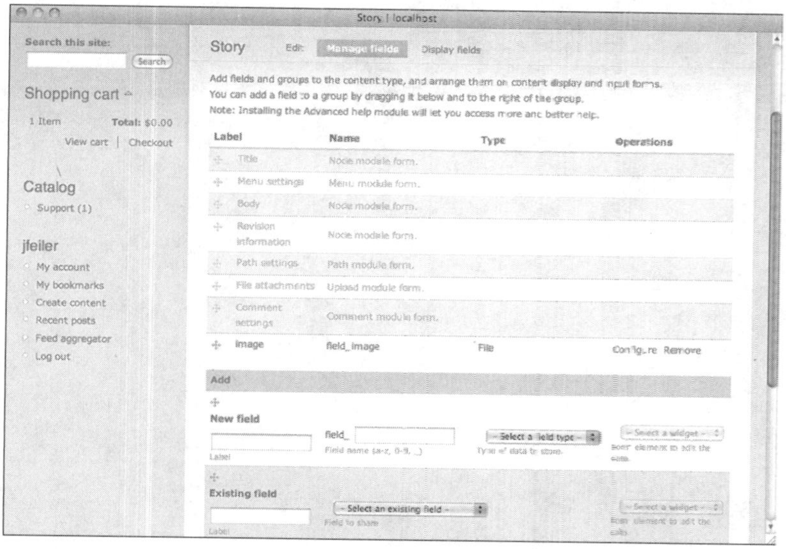

FIGURE 7.8
You can come back to configure or delete fields.

Managing Other CCK Fields

If you have installed and enabled the basic CCK data type modules, including Number and Text along with Option Widgets, you will see that you can create other fields in the same way. For example, Figure 7.9 shows how you can add a text field with choices to enter a color.

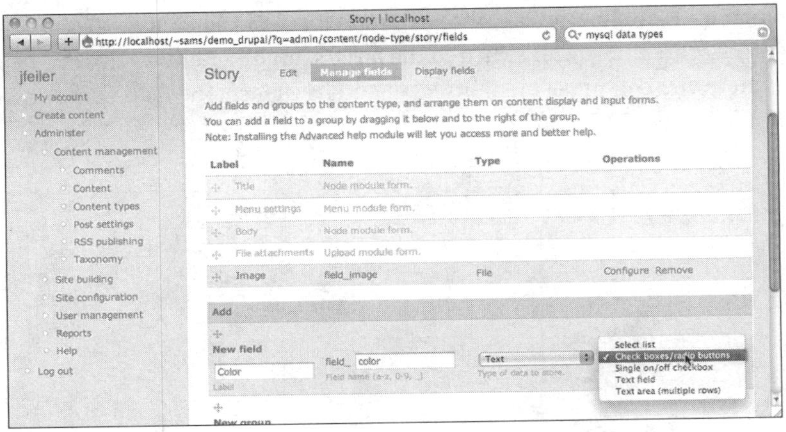

FIGURE 7.9
Create a text field with specified values for radio buttons.

After you create the field, you must provide the allowable values, as shown in Figure 7.10. This is not just a convenience for the user. By using filtered input, such as checkboxes or radio buttons, you know the range of values that may be entered. This lets you construct ad hoc queries without worrying about dirty data.

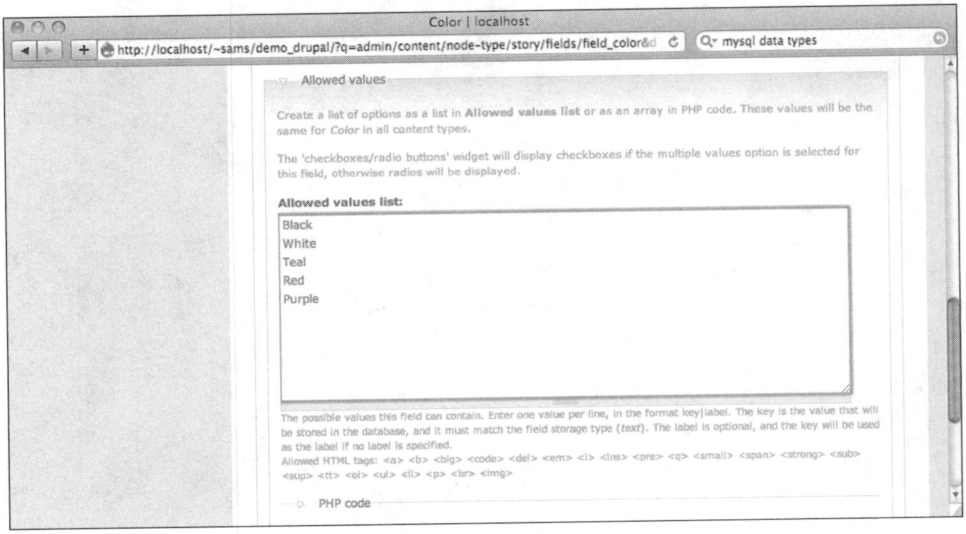

FIGURE 7.10
Specify the allowed values for a check box or radio button field.

Go To ▶

This will be important in **HOUR 14, "WORKING WITH VIEWS,"** p. 237.

After you create these fields, whenever someone tries to enter a new story, the appropriate fields will automatically be created for the user. All you may want to do is move fields up and down in the Manage Fields list. Figure 7.11 shows the input page that is created for you.

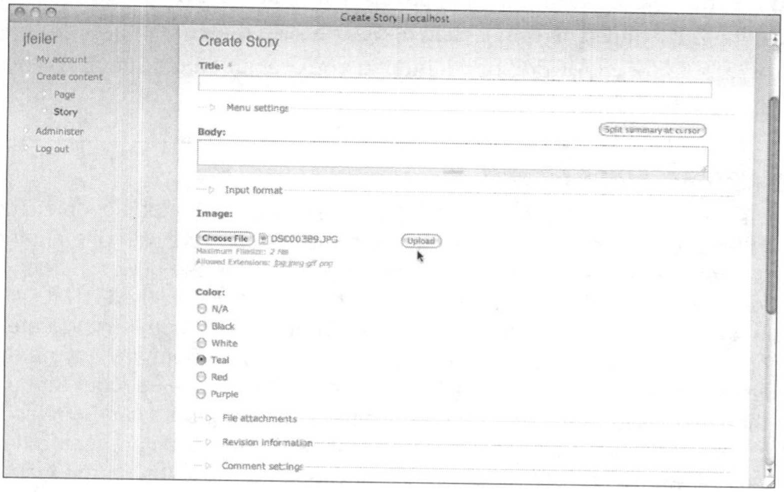

FIGURE 7.11
Drupal creates the user interface.

Optimize Create Content Forms

As you saw in Figure 7.2 earlier in this hour, you can move fields up and down. It is a good idea to use the Create Content command to check out the interface for the content type with which you are working. (As long as you do not click Save, nothing will be stored in the database.) When you look at the form that Drupal has created for you, you may want to rearrange the fields. Because Drupal adds new fields at the bottom, your own fields will, by default, follow sections, such as Publishing Options. Many people prefer to put all the content fields together—title, body, and added fields. Also, see the section on Groups later in this hour for other ways to organize the form.

Did you Know?

▼ **Try It Yourself**

Adding Data to a CCK ImageField

As shown in Figure 7.11, Drupal automatically creates the appropriate interface for data entry. This walks you through the process of adding an image to a content type to which you have added an image field as described in the preceding section. You can use it as a test of your work. In addition, if you are building a site that other people will update, this is a good handout.

By the Way

> ### Help People Add Content
>
> Drupal is terrific for building sites that will be assembled by various people. The security mechanism can be set up so that they do not interfere with one another or cause damage to the site. Such collaborative sites have the power to bring together people with web development skills (including old-fashioned HTML), domain specialists who know little if anything about creating websites, volunteers for nonprofit organizations, as well as interns or office staff from any organization. Although you may be comfortable with online documentation, a handout (of no more than ten pages) that covers the key points of entering data can be a big help. If you need more than a ten-page handout, or if you need more than a half-hour training session for these people, the site is too complicated or the instructions are too abstruse.

1. Have an image that is ready to add. It must be a JPG, PNG, or GIF file, unless some of those formats have not been enabled. (This is set in the field configuration, as shown in Figure 7.3.)

2. Use Create Content to create a new story or article, page, or other node.

3. Scroll to the image field setting (shown in Figure 7.11).

4. Click the Choose button to navigate to the file on your computer.

5. Click Upload to perform the upload.

6. Click Save at the bottom of the page.

If the image is not uploaded, chances are that you neglected either the Upload button or the Save button. The Choose button is only the start of the process.

After you upload a file, the Upload button becomes a Remove button. You can use it to remove the file from the node so that you can insert a different one.

By the Way

> ### Removing Images
>
> Removing the image from the node does not remove it from the website.

▲

Displaying CCK Fields

You can manage the display of CCK fields using the Display Fields tab, as shown in Figure 7.12.

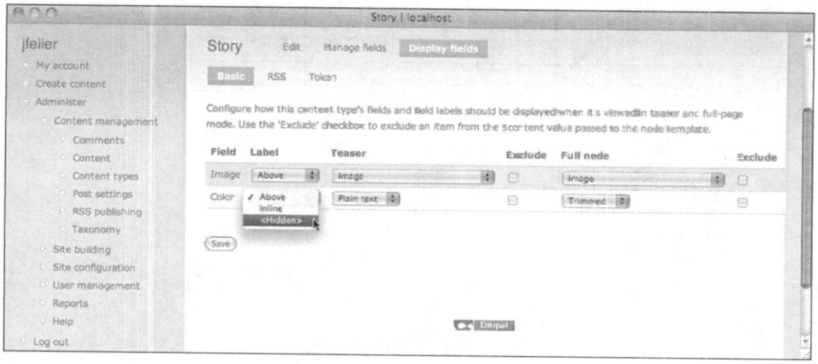

FIGURE 7.12
Display CCK fields in various displays.

As you can see, each CCK field in a node is listed, and you can control how each appears. Above the list of CCK fields, tabs let you specify the display options for different types of output. In this case, in addition to the Basic tab, you see settings for an RSS feed and for Tokens. Those modules are installed and enabled; if they were not, only Basic would appear. Other types of output may also appear if they are installed and enabled.

For each output type, you can set options for the label, as well as how the field appears in a teaser and in a full-node display; you also can use the check box to exclude the field from the specified output display. Because you know the data that each field will contain, you can make more informed choices than the defaults that simply deal with a generic number, text, or image field. (For example, you probably have an idea of the image size; if not, you will see how to control it later in this hour in the section, "Automatically Resizing ImageFields with ImageCache.")

Each type of data has its own display choices. For example, when it comes to images, you can display the image or the URL at which the image can be found (that is often a wise choice for an RSS feed). The full range of image options is shown in "Automatically Resizing ImageFields with ImageCache.")

Reusing Existing Fields

After you create a CCK field, it is available to any other content type in your Drupal environment. As you have seen, it can have global settings (for all content types in which it might occur) and content-type-sensitive settings (such as the path and default title or ALT text). For this reason, it makes sense to check to see if a field already exists that can be reused. After you have one or more CCK fields created in your Drupal environment, the bottom of the Add Fields page has a section for adding an existing field, as Figure 7.13 shows.

FIGURE 7.13
Reuse existing fields where appropriate.

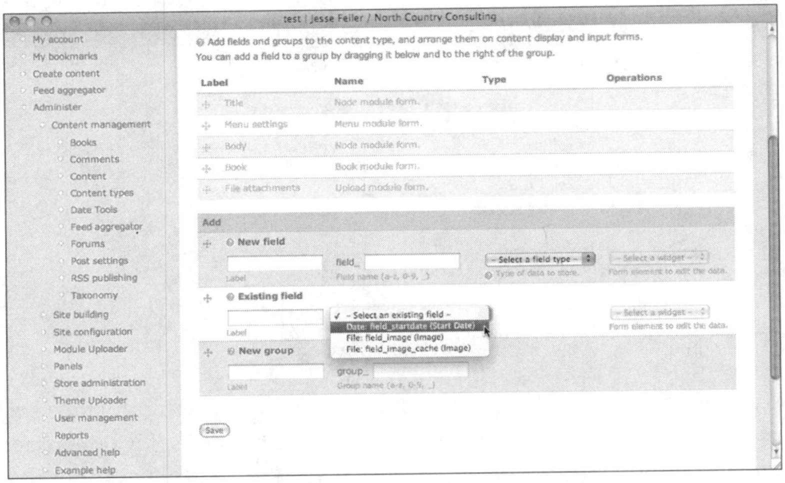

It is a good idea to reuse a field that has the same type of data element in it. The example shown in Figure 7.13 has three CCK fields that have been added to the Drupal environment, and it demonstrates how to make the most of field reusability.

Notice that, in the pop-up menu, you see the underlying data type (File or Date in these cases) and the field name that has been created. In parentheses, you see the default label for the field.

To make your fields reusable, make all these values as clear and specific as possible. In this case, a field based on the date type that is called Start Date is clearly just that. An image field called Image may be an absolutely generic image, but even that specificity might be made clearer if its default label is Generic Image and if the underlying field is called field_generic_image.

Take Care with Field Names

Your naming of the field and its label are largely irrelevant when you create a field for your own content type. However, the naming of the field and its label have everything to do with whether your work can be shared with others. Be clear and specific, but be careful not to be too specific. If the field is called Meeting Start Time, but it signifies only the start time of whatever node it is part of, its name should be Start Time. Try for the balance among specificity, clarity, and reusability. This is a question of judgment. When in doubt, set a timer for 15 minutes and sit down with the people involved. At the end of 15 minutes, either go with the consensus choice or draw straws. Deciding on names is a critical part of any project, but it can become a black hole of wasted time if carried to extremes.

Grouping Fields

At the bottom of Figure 7.13, you can see that, in addition to adding new or existing fields, you can add a group to the content type. A group is an interface element that lets you construct the form for data entry and editing. Figure 7.10 shows several such constructs, including the areas for Menu Settings, Input Format, and File Attachments. After you create a group, it appears in the list of fields with options for configuring it or deleting it. Among the configuration options is the name of the group; you can also choose whether it is always open, collapsed, or collapsible by default. Deleting a group deletes the group, but not the fields within it. (This requires that you enable the Field group module in the CCK section of your modules list if it is not already enabled.)

Automatically Resizing Image Fields with ImageCache

ImageCache provides automated image manipulation in conjunction with the image CCK field. To use it, you need to download, install, and enable the modules in ImageAPI and ImageCache, as shown in Tables 7.2 and 7.3.

ImageCache consists of a variety of *presets*, which are actions that are invoked as needed for image fields. When you go to Administer, Site Building, ImageCache (admin/build/imagecache), you see the list of your presets and can add new ones, as shown in Figure 7.14.

TABLE 7.2 ImageCache Module Reference

Download from	project/imagecache
Enable in section	ImageCache
Permissions	
ImageCache	Administer Imagecache
ImageCache	Flush Imagecache
ImageCache	View Imagecache basic
ImageCache	View Imagecache thumbnail
Administration	
Administer, Site Building, ImageCache (admin/build/Imagecache)	List, Add Preset

TABLE 7.3   ImageAPI Module Reference

Download from	project/imageapi (moving to core in Drupal 7)
Enable in section	ImageCache
Permissions	
none	
Administration	
none	

To the right of each preset are links that enable you to edit and delete them, as well as to export them for further use. The Flush link is an example of the benefits you get from using ImageCache. Drupal can cache the preset results for each preset that has been applied to an image. The Flush command will remove all those cached images; there will be a performance hit the first time they need to be recreated for any given image, but you may need to do this if you change the settings.

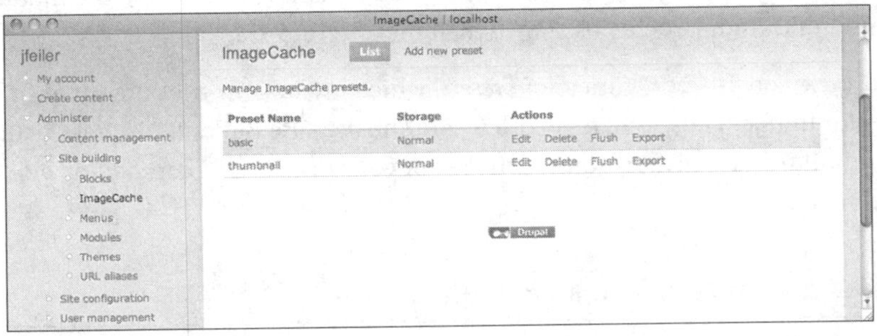

FIGURE 7.14
List and view ImageCache presets.

In Figure 7.15, you can see the actions that you can add to a preset. (You can add several to an individual preset.)

When you click an action to add it, you fill in the necessary values for that action, as shown in Figure 7.16.

The actions and transformations that you can choose are standard image manipulation ones. Most of the actions provide a check box that lets you specify whether the image can be upscaled—that is, if it can be made larger than the original. This can result in poor image quality. In general, it is better to downscale images, making them smaller than the original. (That is why multimegapixel cameras take photos that are more easily manipulated than low-resolution cameras.) The other action to watch out for is an action that changes an image's aspect ratio. Such actions cause distortions in the image. Each action has a brief description that provides information about its consequences. Also, the fact that this is not Drupal terminology, but image manipulation terminology, makes it easier for you to get more information if you want to study a book or article for further information.

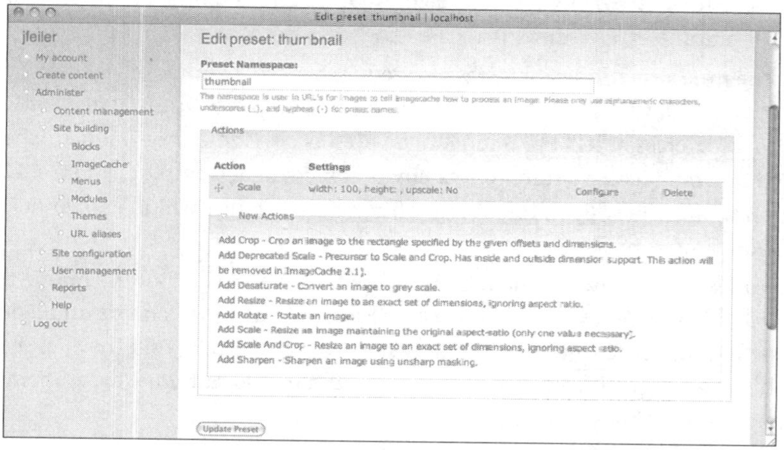

FIGURE 7.15
Add actions to a preset.

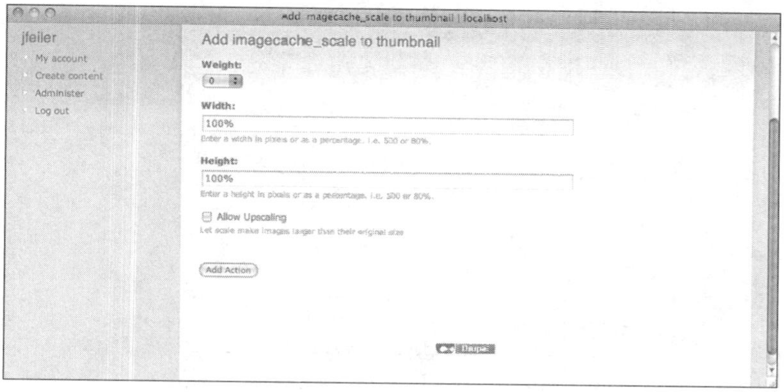

FIGURE 7.16
Specify values for a preset's action.

Bringing All the Image Pieces Together

Sometimes, people say that Drupal and other similarly powerful tools are "too difficult" to use. What they are noticing is that the work is moved around in the process. There may be more up-front preparation, but the payoff comes later on in the process.

As you have seen in this hour, there are a few steps involved in creating a field based on the CCK ImageField. After you create it, you can add it to any content type and use it as you see fit.

When you have a field based on the CCK ImageField, you can create ImageCache presets to be used on any CCK ImageField. Again, there is a little bit of setup here, but it will ultimately save time.

Now is the time when that savings is realized. As you saw earlier in Figure 7.12, you can specify how a CCK field is displayed in various output environments. For Image-Fields, those choices reflect the ImageCache presets providing that ImageCache is installed and enabled and that presets have been created. Compare Figure 7.12 to Figure 7.17, and you will see the wealth of transformations available to you after you have created a few presets.

As you can see, not only can the presets be used for the image, but the image that is displayed can be linked to the image itself or to the node to which it is attached. These settings apply to a specific field based on an ImageField, and they can be set for each content type in which that field appears. (You do not have to set them for each content type, but you can.)

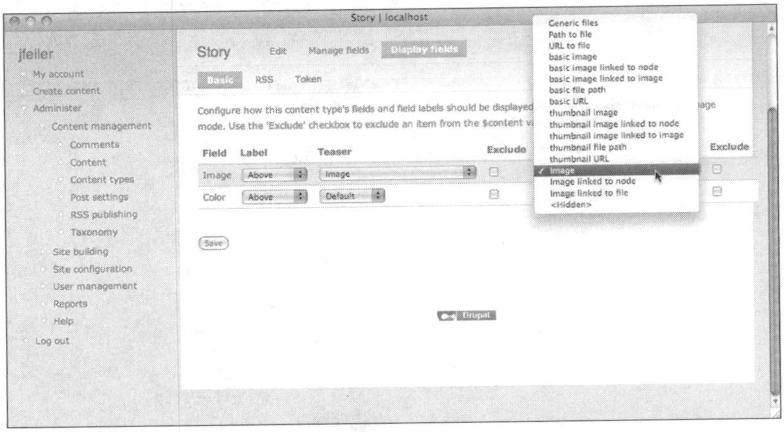

FIGURE 7.17
Use presets to display Image-Fields.

This means that, for a whole range of images (possibly all of them on your Drupal website), you can provide standardized resizing and reshaping so that it all just happens for you. This is where that setup work pays off.

There is still one more benefit, thanks to the Flush command. Should you decide to change the image settings on your website, just edit the preset, flush the cached images, and Drupal does the rest.

Summary

In this hour, you saw how to use CCK to create new types of fields. Although they are built on the basic data types stored in the database, their names and labels can indicate that they contain data with certain meanings. You can assign input widgets, such as radio buttons or selection lists to these fields, which not only makes the user interface easier to use, but it also limits the values that can be stored in the fields. In addition, you can control edit access at the field level (explored in Hour 8).

An example of a CCK field is a field to store an image. You saw how to create and manage such a field. By pairing it with ImageCache, you can define and automate transformations of the image when it is displayed in different output environments.

Q&A

Q. *I installed two user-contributed modules. Each of them defines a CCK field, and they appear to have the same meaning. What do I do?*

A. In most cases, nothing. This is a common problem in database environments where tables and modules from various sources are linked together. Unless you are able to control the data structures and naming conventions of every module you use, this will happen, and there is no reason to lose sleep over it. What you can do is to add CCK field analysis to your module selection process. For modules that are critical to your website, review CCK fields that they create to see if they duplicate fields you already have from other modules. If so, see whether modules share CCK field types. If the duplication is with fields that you have created, depending on the amount of data that has been entered, you might want to use the fields from your new modules and remove your old field (but you must reenter any data).

Q. *If I put an image in a CCK field, can I use it anywhere in my Drupal environment?*

A. The field with its label, name, and input widgets is available to any content type throughout Drupal. The data that you put into the field is specific to the node in which you have placed it (all data is stored in nodes). If you want to reuse images, use the IMCE module (discussed in Hour 11, "Empowering User Input with Rich Text and Images").

Q. *My node data entry page is becoming unmanageable. What do I do?*

A. By default, new fields are added at the bottom of the page. Your two management tools are the four-headed arrows that let you drag fields up and down, as well as groups that you can create and into which you can drag fields.

Workshop

Quiz

1. What are the performance impacts of having multiple ImageCache presets?

2. How many ImageCache presets can you have?

3. Can CCK fields have their own settings to allow or deny editing to the field type wherever it occurs?

Quiz Answers

1. They are used only when an image is to be displayed using a given preset, so there is generally none. The first time a preset is used, the result of the transformation is cached, so in fact, performance is as fast as possible. The only performance impact comes about if you have modified a preset and used the Flush command to flush the cache; in that case, each image for the preset will need to be recreated, but it is done only on demand.

2. There is no limit. However, make sure that you name them clearly so that you do not get confused. If you want to have two types of thumbnails, you can call them thumbnail_a and thumbnail_b, but you may be better off calling them thumbnail_cropped and thumbnail_uncropped (whatever the distinction is).

3. Yes—and this is an important tool for helping to implement your site's security.

Activities

With ImageCache and CCK enabled, create an image field as described in this hour. Create a set of presets where each one uses one of the installed actions. Place an image in the field and try out each action. If you are not familiar with graphic transformations, print them, label them, and staple them for future reference.

Managing Users, Roles, and Permissions

What You'll Learn in This Hour:

▶ How to Use the Security Structure

▶ Creating and Managing Users, Permissions, and Roles

▶ Exporting User Profile Data in CSV Format

Introduction

In 2000, Dries Buytaert and Hans Snijder set up a wireless bridge to share Hans's ADSL Internet connection. After graduation, they and their friends put their simple new site onto the web where, according to Drupal's own history (drupal.org/node/769), members began talking about new web technologies, such as moderation, syndication, ratings, and distributed authentication. Dries envisioned this as a small village, and attempted to register dorp.org as a domain name (*dorp* is Dutch for village). A typo resulted in the registration of drop.org. Drop.org slowly turned into a personal experimentation environment, driven by the discussions and flow of ideas. The discussions about these web technologies were tried out on drop.org itself as new additions to the software running the site. The software behind drop.org was released in 2001 as Drupal.

Over the past decade, Drupal has evolved, but its roots in what is now called social networking remain critical to its structure and its success. The original technologies of moderation, syndication, and ratings have been joined by formal constructs for user-contributed content, blogs, comments, and forums. This evolution has occurred for many reasons, including the rapid and successful rise of social networking in general.

In the first part of this book, you saw Drupal's basic structure, including the key building block (the node) and the more recent Content Construction Kit (CCK), which allows users to create new fields and content types without writing code or modifying database tables.

This part explores a wide range of Drupal features, including blogs, newsletters, calendars, discussions, and e-commerce. What ties all these features together is that they are inherently social: They cannot exist without more than one person, and often, it takes more than a few people to reach a critical mass in a forum discussion and various other social activities.

Drupal's social features build on its infrastructure and its history; they also are built on an extraordinarily robust set of security and other safety features. Security is one of the aspects of a system that is difficult to retrofit. (Version control is another such issue.) Without a secure environment in which people feel (and are) safe, no significant interaction can take place—at least not for long. It is much like planning a wonderful party: You may have the greatest music and the best refreshments, but without enough chairs, plates, and glasses, not even the finest herring will prevent your guests from wandering off.

Thus, this hour launches the socializing and communicating section of this book with what you need to do—and what Drupal has done for you—to create a secure, safe, and reliable environment for you and your guests.

Identifying the Security Components

Drupal implements a number of security components; you may not use all of them, but they are there if you want them. When you first start to think about your Drupal site (whether it is a new site or a conversion from another environment), security should be one of the first things you consider. The amount of time it takes to lay out your security strategy at the beginning is much less than the time it takes to devise it later on. (And the worst case is implementing security after the site is up and running.) There are three primary components to Drupal's security model:

▶ **Roles**—Like many security systems today, Drupal relies on a role-based model. This means that, instead of granting or denying access to specific areas of the site for specific users, you create *roles*. A role is identified by a name that you specify (such as webmaster), and you grant or deny access to that role and thereby to all the users assigned to that role.

▶ **Users**—User accounts are created with a user ID and a password. As you will see, Drupal implements state-of-the-art security protections at the user level. Users are assigned to one or more roles, sometimes automatically during the registration process. A user who is assigned to a role can use any of the resources available to that role. Users have an ID and password that they select; they also have an email address that can be automatically authenticated by Drupal.

▶ **Permissions**—The actual settings for what an individual role is allowed to access. Permissions generally apply to the ability to view, edit, or delete various types of content as well as to access certain commands.

Handling the Primary User

In addition to the security mechanism of roles, users, and permissions, there is the *primary user*, which is the user account that you created when you created the Drupal website. This cannot be deleted, and it has total access to the Drupal environment. As is the case with any superuser account, you should not use it in day-to-day work. As you will see, it is far better to create a highly privileged role, such as a webmaster that works within the Drupal security structure.

Creating Roles

Drupal has two built-in roles. You cannot delete them, but, as with all roles, if you do not grant permissions to them, they will not be able to do much of anything. Drupal implements a mechanism for letting users log in; these roles are related to that mechanism.

▶ **Anonymous**—Users who visit your website and do not log in. They are anonymous because you do not know who they are if they have not logged in. You can change the term for anonymous users in Admin, Site Configuration, Site Information (D6: admin/settings/site-information D7: admin/settings/user). Common replacements for "anonymous" are "visitors" and "guests."

▶ **Authenticated**—Users who have logged in with a password. You can use various options to confirm their authenticity, but the basic point is that you know who they are.

Roles interact with permissions. You may be tempted to mimic your organizational structure in roles, but that may not be the best solution. You need to create a role if people assigned to that role will have different permissions from people assigned to other roles. In a typical organization, managers and supervisors may occur in many different parts of the organization, and many of their roles are similar no matter where they work.

GO TO ▶
HOUR 17, "BUILDING YOUR FIRST LIVE SITE"
An additional security component is frequently used with Drupal. It is a module that can be installed to attempt to prevent robots from logging in to your website. One of the most common is CAPTCHA, p. 303.

One strategy is to add two new roles to your Drupal website. Together with the default roles, these allow you the flexibility to manage a large website with user contributions and distributed management. You can use any names you want for these roles; their functions are what matters. These are the additional roles:

▶ **Webmaster**—This role has access to almost everything. A few built-in permissions are dangerous to grant (such as the ability to insert PHP), and you may want to reserve these for the primary user. By creating a webmaster role in addition to the primary user, people in that role will go through the security mechanism rather than totally bypassing it as the primary user does.

▶ **Trusted user** or **Coordinator**—This role is for a user who has an intermediate privilege set between authenticated users and webmasters. For example, a webmaster may be able to create new menus, whereas a trusted user or coordinator may be able to edit and moderate comments and forum discussions. If you use Drupal's features that allow people to create accounts for themselves (thus becoming authenticated users), this role allows you to designate only specific people for this trusted status. The authenticated user can be self-authenticated, but a trusted user or coordinator is authenticated by someone else in the organization.

A single user can be assigned to multiple roles, with one exception. The anonymous role applies to people who are not logged in, so no one can simultaneously be assigned to the anonymous role and any other role (because the other roles are based on login information).

To create or edit a role, go to Administer, User Management, Roles (D6: admin/user/roles D7: admin/settings/roles), as shown in Figure 8.1.

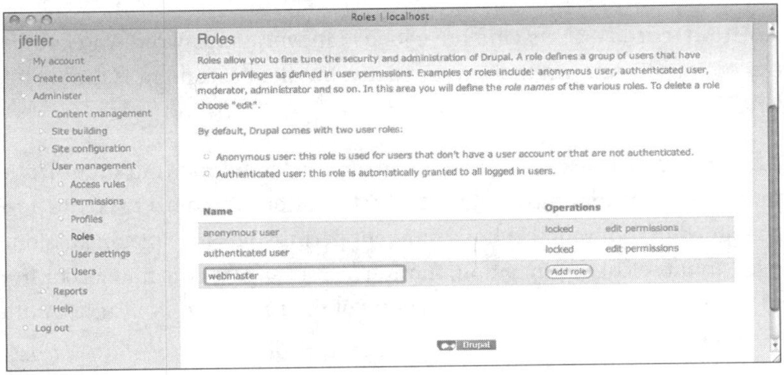

FIGURE 8.1
Create and edit roles.

Click Edit Permissions to set the permissions for that role. The two default roles are locked. The only editing you can do to them is to change their name. You cannot delete them, although you can delete roles you have created. There is always a blank line at the bottom; to create a new role, type a name for it and click Add Role.

Editing Permissions

Set permissions at Administer, User Management, Permissions (D6: admin/user/permissions D7: admin/settings/permissions), as shown in Figure 8.2.

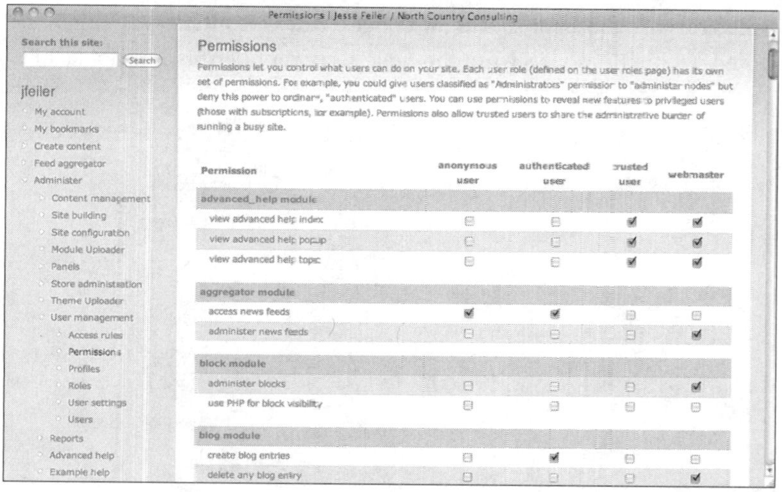

FIGURE 8.2
Set permissions.

If you have added the two roles described previously, your permissions may look something like the page shown in Figure 8.2. You can add or remove permissions with a check box for the permission and role.

Understanding Authenticated User Permissions

The role to which a user is assigned is based on that user's login information. This means that any user who is assigned to a role, with the exception of the anonymous (not logged in) role, is an authenticated user. In the example shown in Figure 8.2, every webmaster and every trusted user must, therefore, also be an authenticated user. (This is reflected more clearly in the Drupal 7 interface where checkboxes that are irrelevant are disabled.)

If any of a user's roles grant a permission, the user can use it. For example, the webmaster role may have permission to access news feeds because, although that permission is not granted to the webmaster role, it is granted to the authenticated role, and the webmaster automatically is authenticated as a result of having logged in.

Updating Permissions

After they are set up, roles are usually not updated often, although users can frequently be assigned and reassigned to different roles. However, permissions frequently are updated. They may be updated because of the needs of the website and the organization, but they also may need to be updated because new modules are added to the website. Often, when a module is added, it will add permissions.

Figure 8.3 shows how new content types that you create also add their own permissions. Remember that, in your basic Drupal installation, there are only story and page content types (story and article content types in Drupal 7). Thus, the only available permissions are those for stories and pages. After a content type titled test has been created, Figure 8.3 shows what the node section of permissions looks like.

FIGURE 8.3
New nodes create new permissions.

Permission	anonymous user	authenticated user	webmaster
node module			
access content	☑	☑	☐
administer content types	☐	☐	☐
administer nodes	☐	☐	☐
create page content	☐	☐	☐
create story content	☐	☐	☐
create test content	☐	☐	☐
delete any page content	☐	☐	☐
delete any story content	☐	☐	☐
delete any test content	☐	☐	☐
delete own page content	☐	☐	☐
delete own story content	☐	☐	☐
delete own test content	☐	☐	☐
delete revisions	☐	☐	☐
edit any page content	☐	☐	☐
edit any story content	☐	☐	☐
edit any test content	☐	☐	☐
edit own page content	☐	☐	☐
edit own story content	☐	☐	☐
edit own test content	☐	☐	☐
revert revisions	☐	☐	☐
view revisions	☐	☐	☐

Did you
Know?

Check Permissions as Your First Troubleshooting Strategy

If you add a new module to Drupal and it does not work, check permissions right away. It may need to be enabled on the Modules list and for permissions to be granted on the Permissions page.

For each node type, three basic sets of permissions refer to the actions involved:

- ▶ Create
- ▶ Delete
- ▶ Edit

Each one is further specified by ownership of the node:

► Own

► Any

As you can see in Figure 8.3, the permissions are grouped by actions in Drupal 6, so when you add a new node type (directly or as part of a module), you may have to jump around the node module section to find all the permissions you want to adjust. In Drupal 7, the permissions are grouped by content type.

If you are creating new CCK fields, you will find a section of permissions for each one of them, and that list is updated each time you add a CCK field.

Use Webmaster to Spot New Permissions

If you have a role such as webmaster, you can consider whether to enable all permissions (except the most dangerous ones) for that role. That way, when you add new permissions via new modules or in any other way, a quick scan down the webmaster column shows you the new permissions because they will be unchecked. This quickly lets you adjust those permissions for all roles.

Did you Know?

Working with Users

There are three aspects relating to users that you need to configure:

► Rules determining domains, hosts, and email addresses that will be allowed or denied access to the website.

► Settings for users, including automated emails to be sent on account creation, confirmation, and so forth.

► User accounts. You can let Drupal provide email authorization and screening of accounts based on the access rules so that most accounts can be created by the users themselves.

The user tools all rely on a user ID and password; the default interface, shown in Figure 8.4, allows users to enter their own ID and password, create a new account, or request a new password.

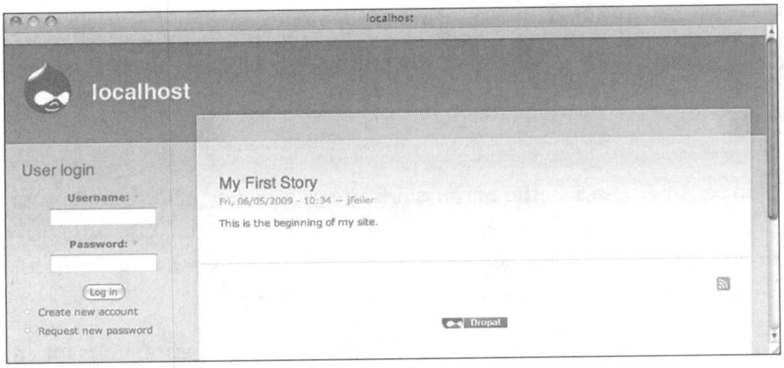

FIGURE 8.4
Users can log in
or create their
own account.

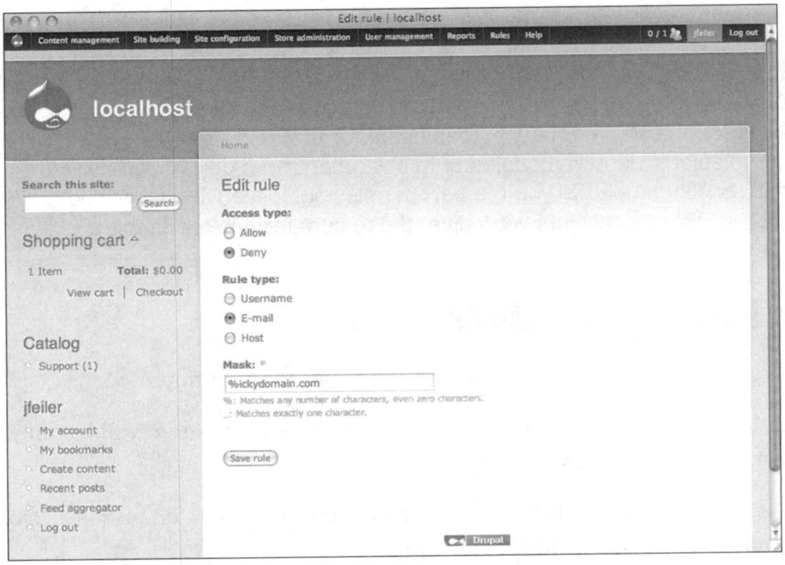

FIGURE 8.5
Set up access
rules.

Using Access Rules

Access rules can be managed at Administer, User Management, Access Rules
(admin/user/rules), as shown in Figure 8.5.

This is a powerful screening mechanism that is all the more powerful because, after it
is set up, you do not have to worry about it again.

The example shown in Figure 8.5 will deny access to anyone who attempts to register
with an email address from ickydomain.com. There are many examples of internal
websites where you want to reverse the process and allow access only from a specific
domain—your own company or school, for example.

After you save an access rule, you can test it with the Check Rules page, shown in Figure 8.6.

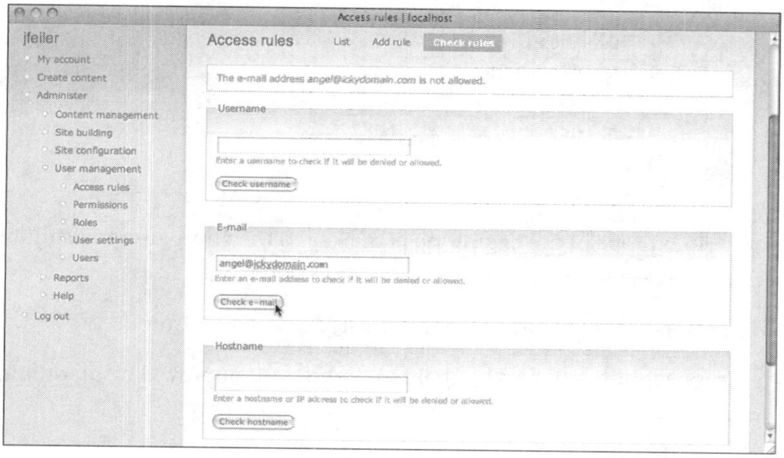

FIGURE 8.6
Test access rules.

By default, no access rules are created or enabled. Do not skip this step lightly: It can dramatically improve your site's security.

Creating User Registration Settings

As with so much of Drupal, spending a little time up front can save a great deal of time later. The user registration process can be completely automated, and to get the most out of it (for you and your users), set up the registration process thoroughly.

Make Sure You can Send Email

Much of Drupal's automated user management relies on email. If your Drupal installation cannot send email through an SMTP server, these tools will not work. Most hosting and shared hosting environments provide outgoing email. You are most likely to encounter difficulties on test installations using localhost.

Did you Know?

Begin by setting up Access Rules as described in the previous section. They will provide a basic filter for your users. Then, adjust the registration settings in Administer, User Management, User Settings (D6: admin/user/settings D7: admin/settings/user), as shown in Figure 8.7.

FIGURE 8.7
Set public regis-
tration options.

The set of radio buttons at the beginning is the key to the entire user registration system. You have to decide which of the three settings you want:

▶ No public registration—all accounts created by administrators.

▶ Public registration allowed but held in limbo until approved by an administrator.

▶ Public registration subject to the access rules.

Your choices obviously depend on your website and its sponsoring organization. One
way of eating your cake and having it is to use a role, such as the trusted user role
suggested earlier in this hour. You can allow public registration with only the access
rules limits, and an administrator can then manually move selected users to a new
role, such as trusted user.

It makes sense to check the box so that Drupal sends an email message that must be
responded to. This verifies the email address in a basic way—it exists and is somehow
associated with the person submitting it. (In other words, if someone registers with an
email address at the domain mickeymouse.gov, chances are that the required
response from the mickeymouse.gov domain will not be received and the user
account will not be created.)

The remaining options on this page are all designed to customize the user registration experience and answer many of the questions that new users may have. For
example, the guidelines you are asked to provide are shown on the registration page,
and they let users know that you will safeguard their data if you use text such as this.
You can also let people know that, after they have registered, they can apply for an
upgrade to another status level (if you provide that). Think of every question that
might be raised, and attempt to answer it in advance.

Reassure Users About Security

For example, you might mention that passwords can always be reset by the user, but they are stored in an unreadable (hashed) format so people need not worry that their passwords will be exposed through Drupal.

As you can see in Figure 8.8, you then provide the text for email messages that will be sent automatically when a new account is created by an administrator or when one is created by a user. Note that the message can contain placeholders, such as !username for the username that a user has selected or been given.

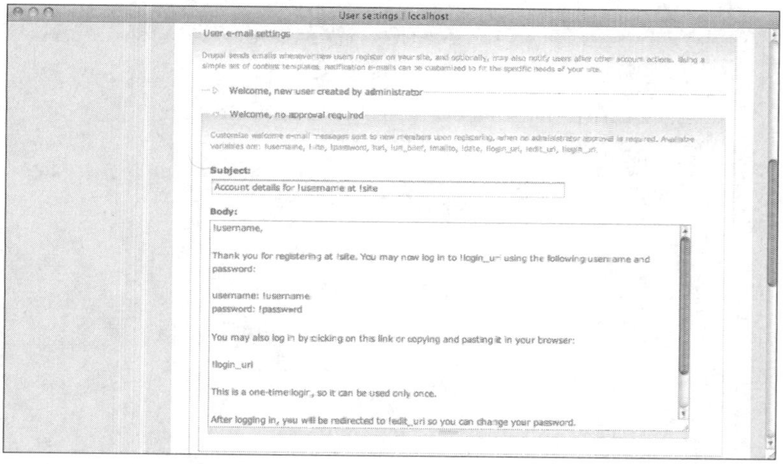

FIGURE 8.8
Provide text for automated registration emails.

Prepare for Future Messages

Although you can leave the defaults in place, it makes sense to go through every option on this page, even if you are not using it (for example, if you do not think you will use the option to block accounts). By reviewing the texts, you can make certain that if you do decide in the future to use additional functionality, the email messages that are sent will be appropriate.

Feel free to add whatever information is relevant and specific to your organization and website.

Further down the page, you can provide text for other messages, such as the message a user receives when attempting to reset a password or when a user's account has been blocked, as shown in Figure 8.9.

Finally, as shown in Figure 8.10, you can specify whether users can provide a signature and whether they can upload pictures.

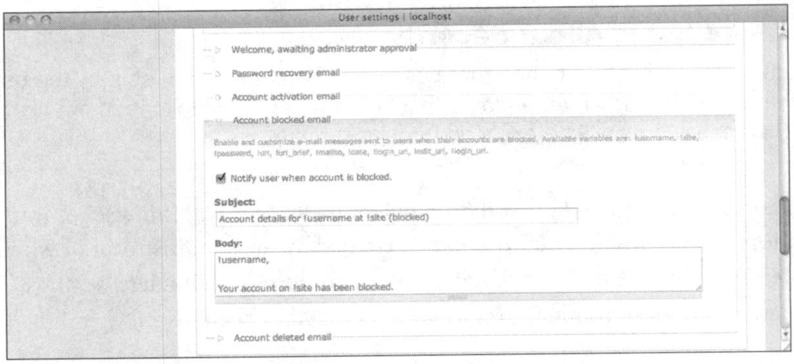

FIGURE 8.9
Provide additional email text.

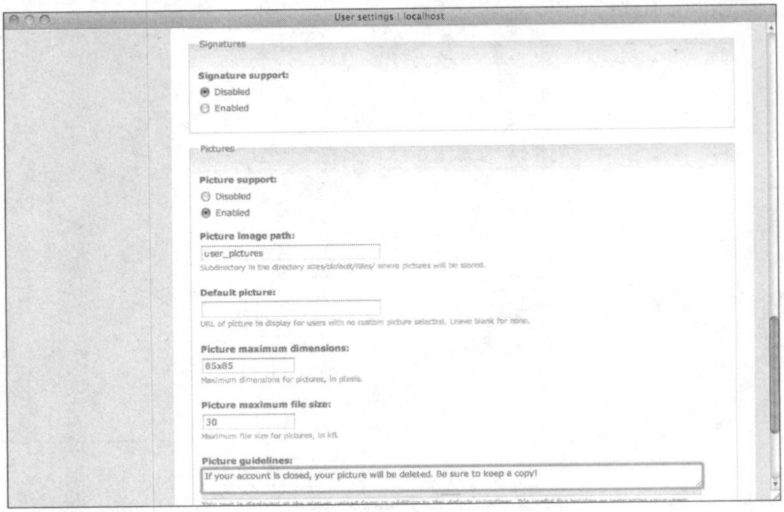

FIGURE 8.10
Provide settings for signatures and user image uploads.

Creating Users

Depending on how you have set up user registration settings, you may now be ready to add users to your site. If you allow self-registration, users can edit their own settings under My Account, as shown in Figure 8.11.

If you (or another administrator) create user accounts, a similar page is used under User Management, Users, with the Add User button (D6: admin/user/user/create D7: admin/people/create), as shown in Figure 8.12.

Note that this is where an administrator can assign a user to specific roles.

Using User Profiles

The Profile module, located in Core—Optional, lets you add fields to user profiles. After you enable it, a Profiles section is added to User Management, as you can see in Figure 8.13.

Because you are collecting verified email addresses for your users, you may want to use them for your bulk email database. If you do so, you may need to allow people to opt out of email messages. Depending on the laws that govern you, you may need to disclose with an opt-out choice that email addresses will be used. In the United

States, certain types of email messages are allowed without consent. If, for example, your users are customers or active students in your school, you can legitimately email them on those matters. For general websites open to the public, however, you may want to add the email opt-out option so that you can use the email addresses. (Even if you do not anticipate doing so now, you can set it up so that you can use it in the future.)

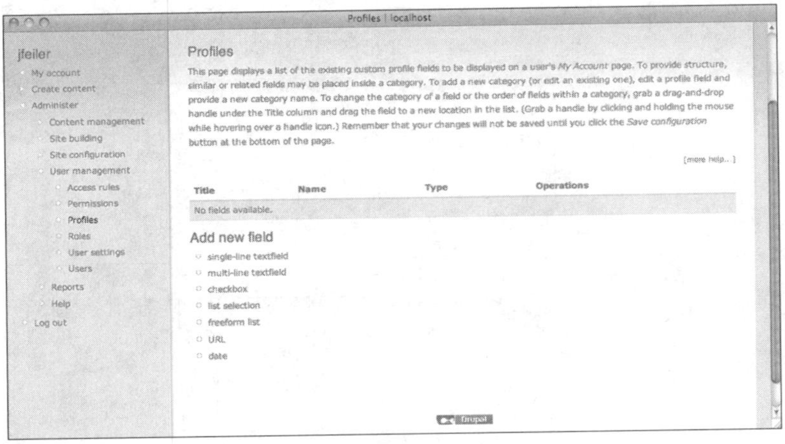

FIGURE 8.13
Enable the Profile module to customize profiles.

Figure 8.14 shows how you can add an email opt-out button to a user profile.

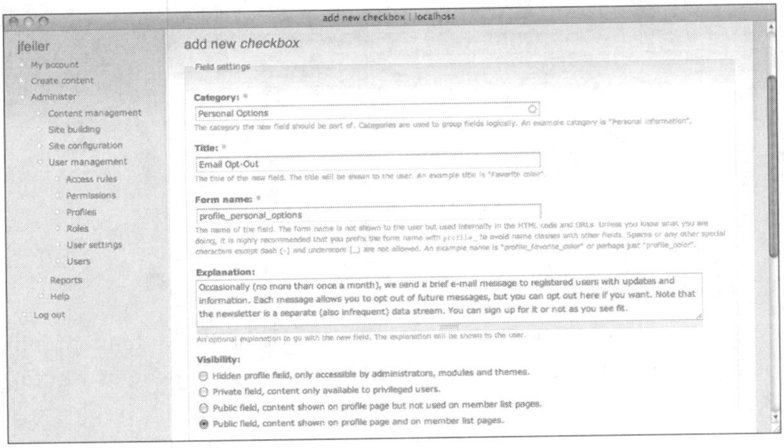

FIGURE 8.14
Add an email opt-out button to user profiles.

At the bottom of the page are more settings for the field you are adding as shown in Figure 8.15. Perhaps the most important is the check box that indicates whether the field is required.

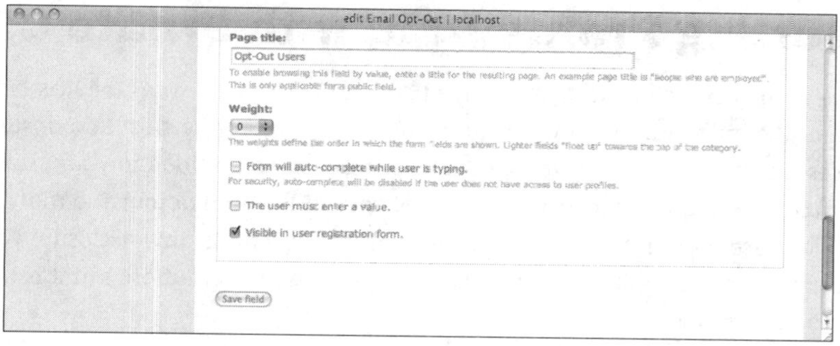

FIGURE 8.15
You can make profile fields required or not.

After you add the button, users who edit their accounts (using My Account from the Navigation menu) see the personal options shown in Figure 8.16.

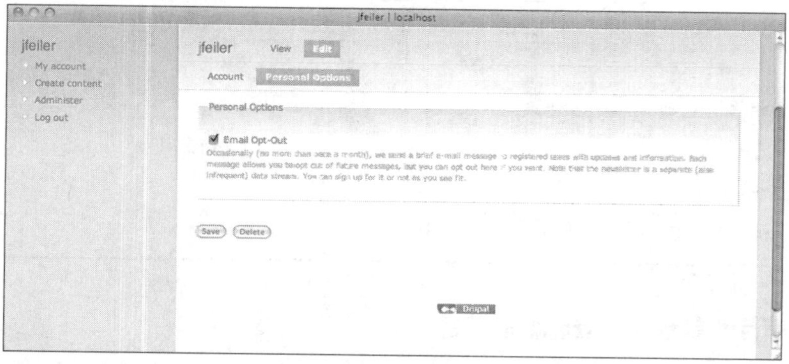

FIGURE 8.16
Users can set their options.

When a new user account is being created, these fields are displayed, and, if you have required them, Drupal will make sure that they are filled in before the account is accepted. Figure 8.17 shows the page for creating an account by an administrator; the self-creation field for users is similar.

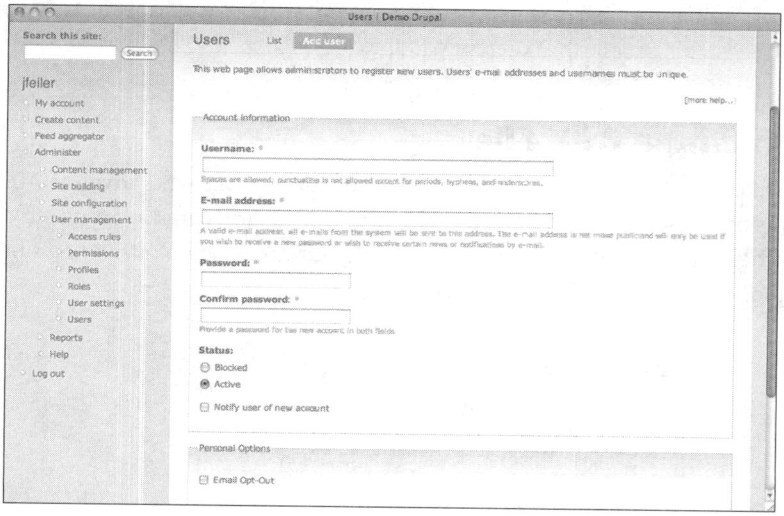

FIGURE 8.17
Profile fields appear on account creation pages.

Exporting Profile Data with Profile CSV

There is a small contributed module called Profile CSV that provides the link between Drupal and a bulk mail system, such as Constant Contact or Vertical Response. It produces a comma-separated-value (CSV) file that you can upload to your bulk email account. (You must review the terms of your bulk email account so that the text in your user account registration form and emails reflects any disclosure you must make. The email opt-out button is one type of implementation, but it is not correct for all situations.)

Download, install, and enable Profile CSV as described in Table 8.1.

TABLE 8.1   Profile CSV Module Reference

Download from	project/profile_csv
Enable in section	Other
Privileges	
Profile CSV	Download profiles
Administration	
Administer, Site Configuration, Profile CSV	

Setting Up Profile CSV

GO TO ▶
As you will see in **HOUR 12**, "**USING BLOGS AND NEWSLETTERS**," p. 197, you have various ways to communicate with your users.

You configure Profile CSV using Administer, Site Configuration, Profile CSV (admin/settings/profile_csv), as shown in Figure 8.18.

You do not select which records to export here. Everything will be exported; you will need to select the records to upload by selecting on the export opt-out field. If you are using the logic shown here, remember that opt-out will have a value of 1, so you want to select all records that are not equal to 1.

Producing a CSV File

Profile Export CSV appears in the Navigation menu for users who have the Administer Users permission. A file will be created and opened. You can import it into a spreadsheet to select the appropriate values of your check box or other fields before you upload it to your bulk email system.

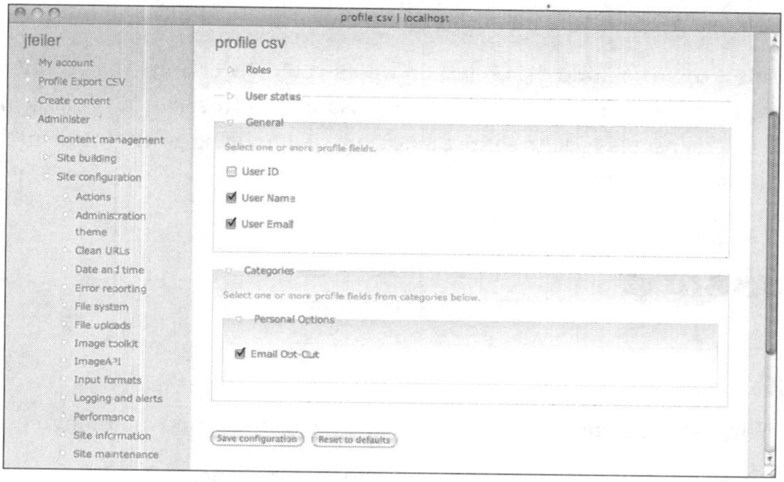

FIGURE 8.18
Select fields to
export.

Summary

This hour showed you Drupal's basic security mechanism, which is a role-based model in which users are assigned to roles, and the roles have (or do not have) permission to access various resources. The structure is simple yet powerful.

You can automate the entire process of user authentication with the default Drupal settings. Many sites augment the two default roles (anonymous and authenticated users) with one or two other roles that have more permissions than authenticated users but fewer than the primary user, who has total access to the site.

Q&A

Q. *Is it possible to create conditional permissions so that permission is contingent on content?*

A. Permissions are specified with check boxes and are assigned to roles. You can change the roles to which a user is assigned at runtime, but the structure is not designed for the conditional conditions described here.

Q. *Other than writing code, is there any way to extend Drupal's permissions structure?*

A. Permissions control access to functionality and content types. It is perfectly legitimate to create a content type that is identical to another content type and use one of them with different permissions. Just remember that they are different content types and the data is stored separately for each one.

Q. *Can two people share an account?*

A. This is up to you and the project on which you are working. An account is associated with a single email address; usually, it is associated with one person. If several people need to share an account, you may be describing something that should be a role.

Workshop

Quiz

1. What is the difference between an authenticated user and an anonymous user?

2. How can you remove the Create Account link in the login box?

3. How are passwords stored?

Quiz Answers

1. Authenticated users have logged in with a user ID and password. Anonymous users have not.

2. In Access Rules, use the No Public Registration radio button.

3. They are stored in an encrypted hash and are generally not readable. "Generally" is key because the hash used in Drupal 6 was considered secure at the time; it is being changed in Drupal 7 to another hash that is now considered secure (but it, too, in time, will fail).

Activities

After you start to define your roles and permissions, do some dry runs to see how you will implement them. A good way of testing security models is to see if they can be simplified. Can you get the same degree of control with fewer roles, for example?

Finding Information: Using Tags, Taxonomies, and Searches

What You'll Learn in This Hour:

▶ How to Set Up Cron and Poormanscron

▶ Configuring Site Search

▶ Building Taxonomy Structures with Vocabularies and Terms

Introduction

As a Content Management System, Drupal has a variety of tools to implement the basic management tasks. Internally, its physical storage is deep in its PHP code and its database. From the end user's point of view, this management focuses on the ability to locate needed information. So far, you have seen the basics of entering content and how you can view it when it is presented to you (for example, as an entry on the front page). In this hour, you will see how to enable the features that let you search for content. Furthermore, you will explore the Drupal features that allow users to categorize content so that it can easily be retrieved.

The difference between searching and categorization is fundamental: Searching examines the content for specific words or phrases. Categorization is a task that is manually done by the user—most often at the time of data entry. Both functions are essential for a fully searchable site. Categorization, for example, is required if you want to be able to search for content that includes a photograph of the Eiffel Tower. Unless those words are part of the image caption or part of the article's text, no automated tool can support searches to locate the image. (A great deal of work is going on now to implement this, but it is in its infancy, which is the stage it has been in for about 40 years.) At an even more basic level, a full text search that is looking for

Macbeth will skip over the line, "So foul and fair a day I have not seen." It does not contain the word "Macbeth," but it is *Macbeth's* first line at the top of the show.

Searching does not examine the text of every piece of content when you click the Search button. Rather, indexes are built behind the scenes as content is added to the site (and changed on the site).

Thus, searching is set up in the background after data entry, and categorization is set up in the foreground by the user at data entry time. Both types of preparation result in the ability to have almost instantaneous responses to a click of a Search button or a click that brings up content identified by a category.

For your website, you can choose to rely solely on searching, solely on categorization, or on both or neither. Most websites provide at least search capabilities; many provide both. This is not a technical decision; it reflects the purpose of your website and who your end users are.

In this hour, you will see how to prepare the search setup, which includes setting up a task that runs periodically to update the indexes. You will also see how to implement categorization so that users entering data can enter appropriate information.

Preparing for Search with Cron and Poormanscron

Like most websites, a Drupal website normally springs into action when it receives a request for a page. Like the web server and the database that support the site, it is idle for much of the time. (Even the busiest websites are idle for much of the time. To provide responsive service, the web server and network normally run well below 100% capacity to allow for temporary peaks of demand.)

Certain tasks, such as preparing indexes, need to be done in the background. Many systems have such tasks, ranging from periodic backups to checking for new versions of software, which Drupal does regularly. In many web environments, these tasks are managed by a job scheduler called *cron* (from chronograph). On Windows, there are versions of cron, but many people use the built-in scheduling of Windows.

As far as Drupal is concerned, a script that is installed as part of Drupal should be run periodically. It is accessible at www.mysite.com/cron.php in the standard Drupal installation. You can run it manually by going to that page in your browser, or you can schedule it to be run by cron or the Windows scheduler. As an alternative, you can use a contributed module, poormanscron.

When fired off by cron or the Windows scheduler, cron.php performs tasks such as indexing and checking for updates. Drupal manages this for you: All you have to do is start cron.php.

In some environments, cron is not available. Typically, these are shared hosting environments where several users share the same server. A few years ago, cron was not made available on shared servers. Today, as technology for sharing has improved, you are more likely to find cron available. If it is available, it is the best solution. Schedule it to run cron.php regularly. How regularly depends on your website and its demands. If it is a heavily trafficked site with a great deal of searchable content being added all the time, you may want cron.php to run once an hour so that it can keep the search indexes up to date. On the other hand, a heavily trafficked site that is not updated often may need cron.php to be run once a day or even once a week. Large sites may run it every few minutes.

The Poormanscron module is triggered whenever Drupal receives a page request. It checks to see if it would be appropriate to run cron.php, and, if so, it does so. It is not the time-dependent processing of a true cron job, but it works in many cases. In order not to degrade the user experience, the actual run of cron.php is started after the page has been sent to the user. Presumably, the user is looking at the page while the cron job is running.

Poormanscron and Newsletters

One of the tasks that cron.php performs is sending email newsletters if you have enabled them. There are reports that Poormanscron can send duplicate messages, so this is one case in which a true cron job is needed.

Watch Out!

If you are going to use Poormanscron, download, install, and enable it as described in Table 9.1.

TABLE 9.1   Poormanscron Module Reference

Download from	project/poormanscron
Enable in section	Other

Permissions

None

Administration

Administer, Site Configuration, Poormanscron (admin/settings/poormanscron)

The default settings shown in Figure 9.1 are a good place to start. As you build your website, you may want to periodically revisit these settings: The cron demands during development are likely to be very different from those during production.

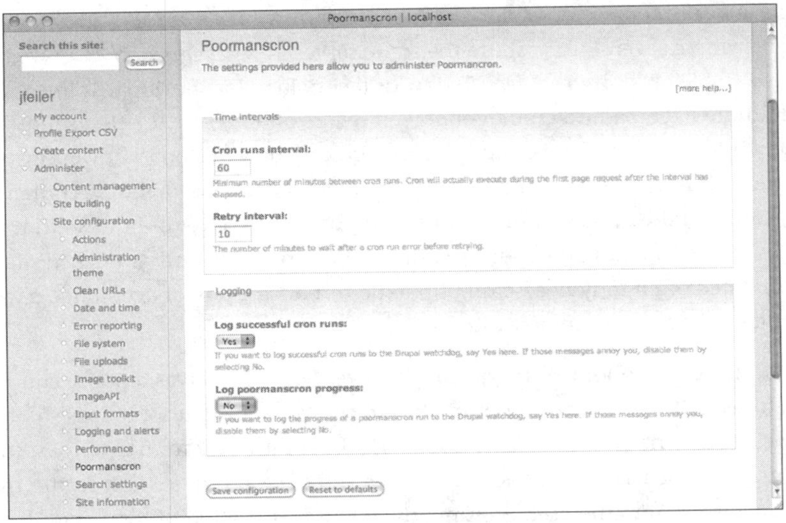

FIGURE 9.1
Configure Poor-
manscron.

The default settings simply list the fact of a Poormanscron run. You can review the most recent log entries at Administer, Reports, Recent Log Entries (admin/reports/dblog), as shown in Figure 9.2.

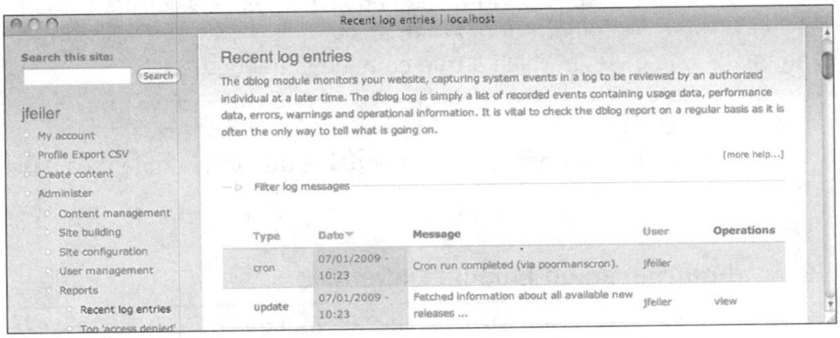

FIGURE 9.2
Periodically
review the log.

Setting Up Search

The Search module is part of Core, but by default, it is not enabled. Enable and configure Search as shown in Table 9.2.

TABLE 9.2 Profile CSV Module Reference

Download from	Core
Enable in section	Core—optional
Permissions	
Search Module	Administer search
Search Module	Search content
Search Module	User advanced search
Administration	
Administer, Site Configuration, Search Settings (admin/settings/search)	

The permissions for the Search module can be used as an example for how to set up roles for your site. It is common to allow anyone—authenticated or anonymous—to search the content of the site. Equally common is that only a webmaster or administrator can administer search. Whether you reserve advanced search for authenticated users is your choice. Most people are reluctant to go through a site-registration process. Providing added features can make registration more likely. By the same token, requiring registration for everything can discourage people from using the site at all.

The key to optimizing Search settings is shown in Figure 9.3, at Administer, Site Configuration, Search Settings (admin/settings/search).

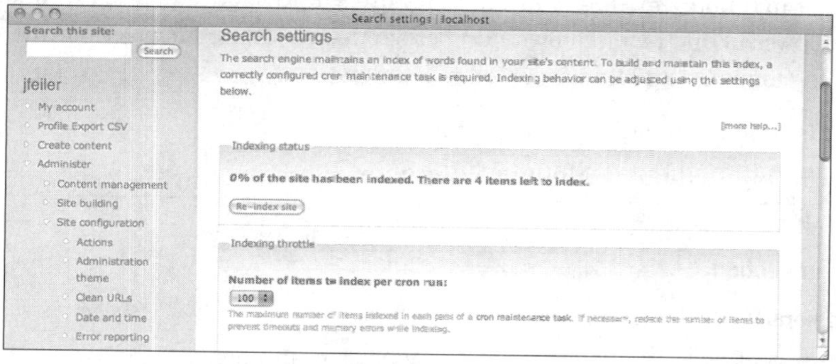

FIGURE 9.3
Configure Search settings.

As you can see, you can choose the number of items to index in each cron run. If you typically have a large number of items to index, you may get better site performance by doing fewer at a time, but doing them more frequently (that is, more frequent cron runs). Remember, the number of items to be indexed is basically the number of items added or edited since the last cron run. Even very large sites may have minimal indexing needs after the site has been indexed for the first time.

If your site is built with a lot of data that is not updated often, you may choose to index a large number of items in cron runs and do them in an off time (if there is an off time for your site).

Further down the page, you will find the settings shown in Figure 9.4. The most sensitive setting is the length of words to index. The content ranking settings adjust how the results are presented; they do not affect indexing itself.

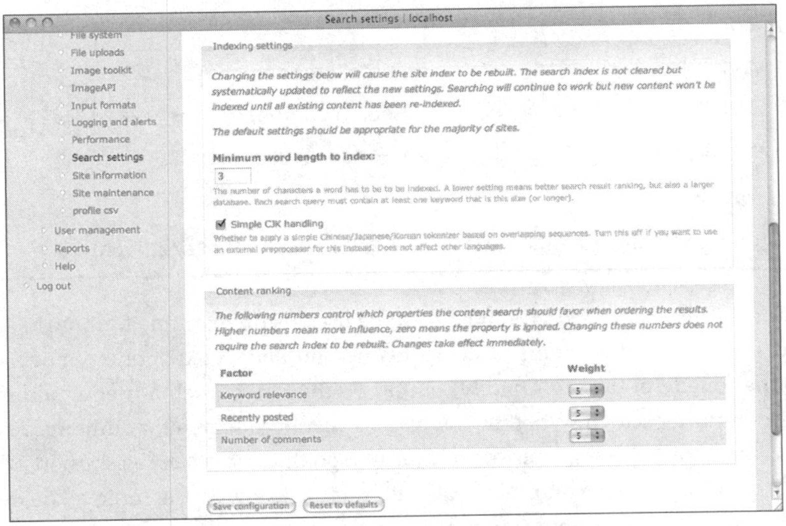

FIGURE 9.4
Choose minimum word length for indexing.

Setting Up Taxonomy

Using the Taxonomy module, you can allow users to categorize their data. Taxonomy is powerful and required by a number of other modules, such as Ubercart, discussed in Hour 16, "Building an E-Commerce Solution."

Enable Taxonomy as described in Table 9.3.

TABLE 9.3   Taxonomy Module Reference

Download from	Core
Enable in section	Other
Permissions	
Taxonomy Module	Administer taxonomy
Administration	
Administer, Content Management, Taxonomy (D6: administer/content/taxonomy D7: administer/structure/taxonomy)	

Taxonomy lets you build *vocabularies*, which consists of *terms* that can help categorize content on the site. Terms are unique within a vocabulary, but not within the entire taxonomy structure. For example, you can have a term *length* within a product vocabulary, but you can have a completely separate term *length* within a performance vocabulary.

You administer Taxonomy at Administer, Content Management, Taxonomy. This administration sets up how vocabularies will be structured; it may also create terms.

Vocabularies are normally associated with one or more content types. In addition, they are often automatically created. For example, the Forum module will create the Forums vocabulary shown in Figure 9.5.

The button at the top of the page lets you add a new vocabulary, as shown in Figure 9.6.

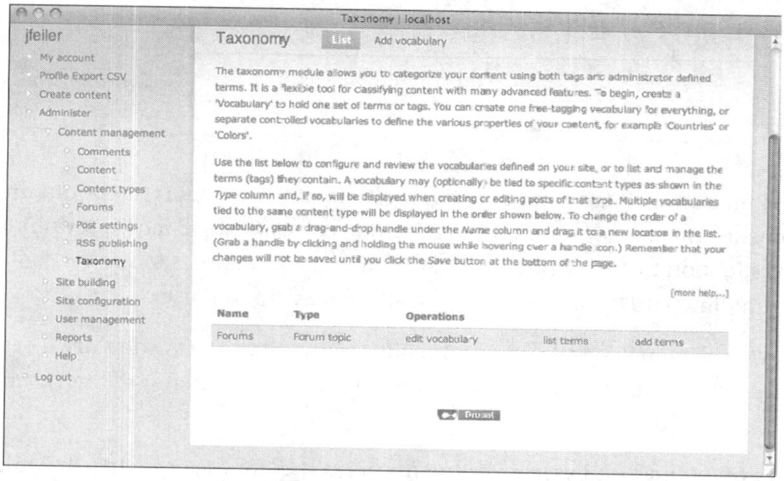

FIGURE 9.5
List vocabularies.

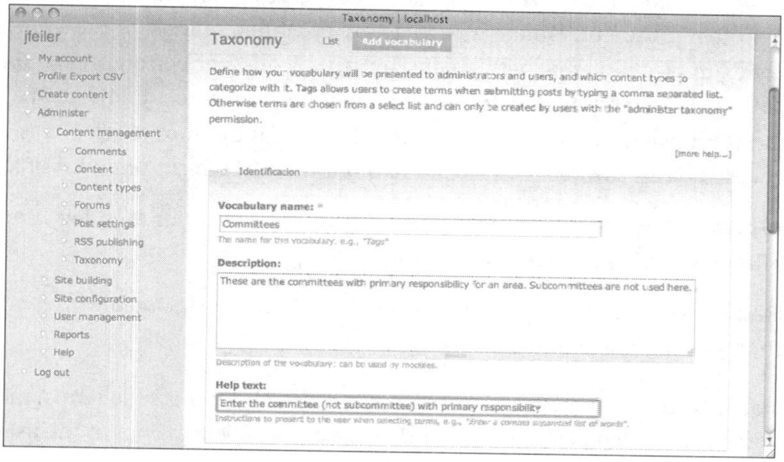

FIGURE 9.6
Add new vocabularies.

Each vocabulary can be associated with any content types you have created, as shown in Figure 9.7.

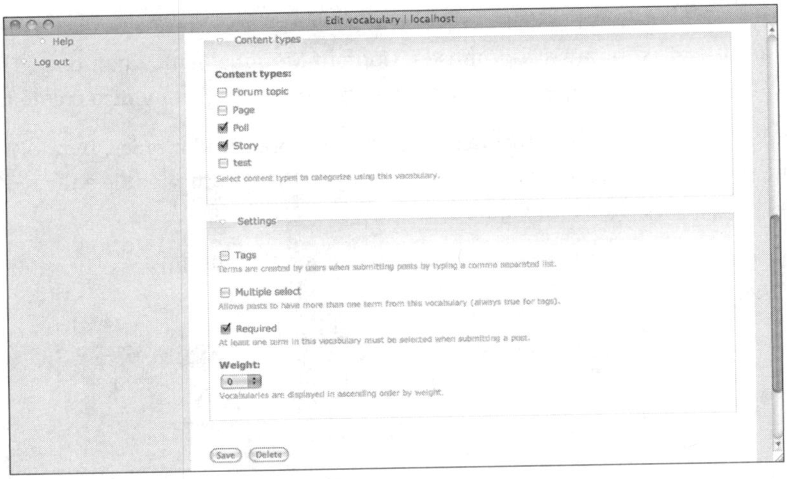

FIGURE 9.7
Assign vocabu-
laries to content
types.

The fact that a vocabulary can apply to multiple content types is important and useful. Someone looking for information related to a specific topic may not want to limit the investigation to one content type. By applying vocabularies to several content types, that limit can be done in Advanced Search by the end user.

As shown in Figure 9.6, you can also modify the settings for a vocabulary. These settings are reflected in the user interface of each content type that uses the vocabulary. These are the settings:

▶ **Tags**—Allows end users to create free-form tags for the data they are entering. It requires no previous setting up, so it is the easiest method to use. It is also not the most robust. Different people may use different tags for the same thing. For example, what one person considers *energy* another person might consider *power*. Tags are separated by commas when they are entered; this means that a tag can have space within it, as in *electric power*. If the Tags check box is not checked, users cannot enter free-form tags but must select from a list of terms.

▶ **Multiple Select**—This check box, which is always true for tags, lets users select more than one term from a list.

▶ **Required**—You can specify that at least one term is associated with a node that uses this vocabulary.

Not using tags (that is, making end users select from a list of possible terms) makes for a more robust categorization process. For example, if *power* is not in the list of terms, a user will probably be able to see that *energy* is available and can choose it if that is appropriate.

The content types for a vocabulary are shown in the list, as you can see in Figure 9.8.

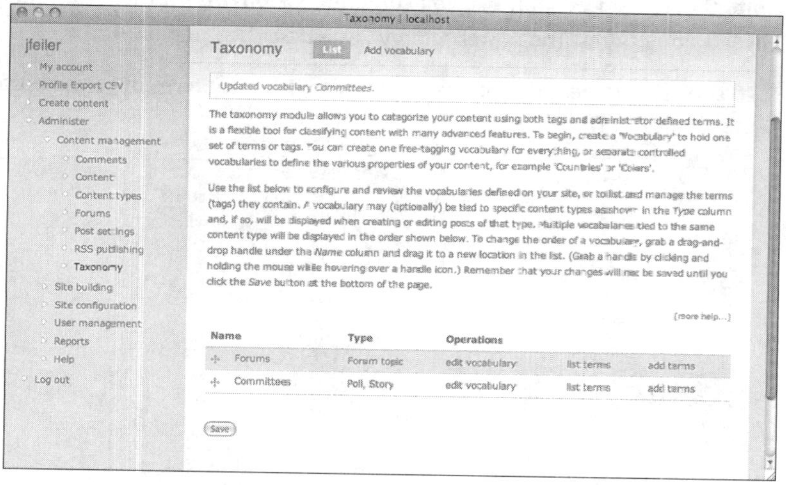

FIGURE 9.8
Content types
are shown in the
list.

Also in that list, you can choose to list or add terms to a vocabulary, as you can see in Figure 9.9.

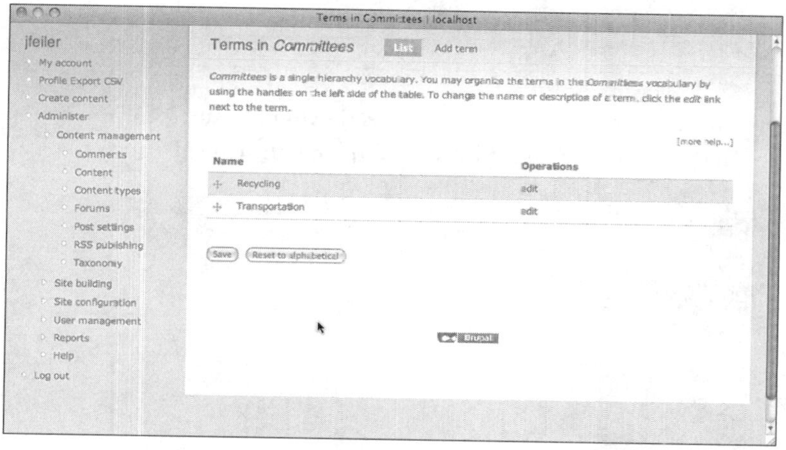

FIGURE 9.9
List and add
terms to a
vocabulary.

Because people may need to search a list of terms for the one(s) that is appropriate, there is a practical limit to the number of terms you can put into a vocabulary. This is not a technical limit; it is a human limit. The solution is to use subcategories, which can be set in Advanced Options when you create a term.

Advanced Options also allows you to specify related terms to create a "see-also" relationship. This is structurally implemented here; to use the see-also relationships, you need to install additional modules.

At the bottom of Advanced Options, you can enter synonyms for the term (one per line). This lets you address the power/energy issue described previously.

Figure 9.10 shows "Bicycles" created as a term with a parent term of "Transportation."

FIGURE 9.10
Create a hierarchy of terms.

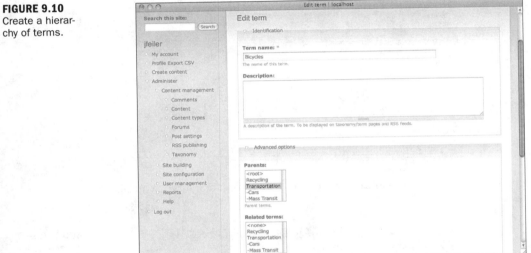

This hierarchy is shown in the list of terms, as shown in Figure 9.11. You can also rearrange the terms and subterms by dragging the four-headed arrows.

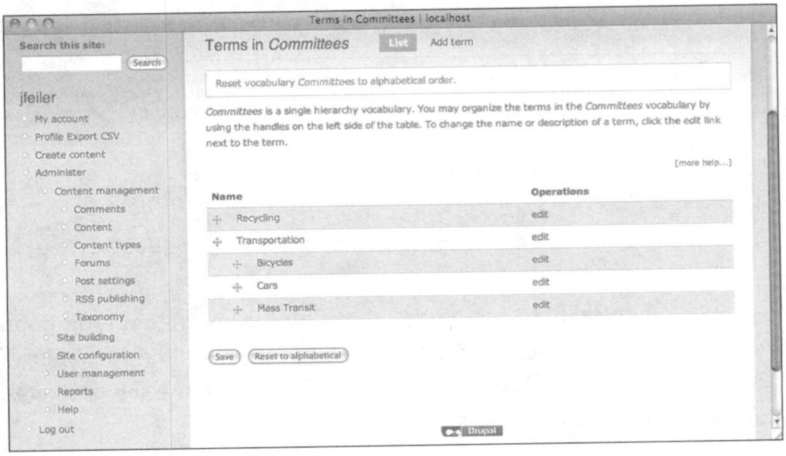

FIGURE 9.11
Rearrange subterms.

Permissions, content types, and vocabularies all interact. For example, Figure 9.12 shows a vocabulary that is assigned only to polls. On many websites, polls can be viewed and voted on by all sorts of users, but they can be created only by administrators or webmasters. In such a case, it is not a problem to create a vocabulary that uses tags, because the only people who could create entries would presumably know the issues involved.

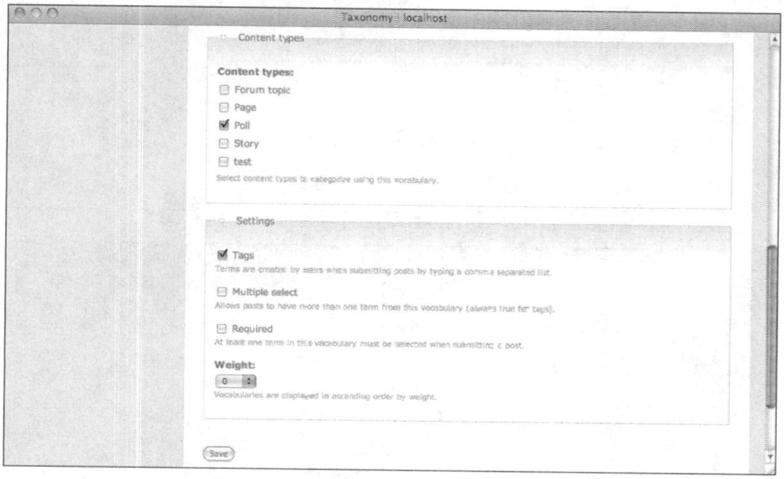

FIGURE 9.12
Who creates a content type can determine the type of term that is used.

Drupal presents you with a wide range of options. As in many cases, these options are not so much technical as practical—related to the website you want to create.

Using Taxonomy

When you combine these features and settings, Drupal modifies the data entry page for a content type, as you can see in Figure 9.13. The story content type has been designated to use the Committees vocabulary. An entry is required, and the Tags check box is not used, so the end user is required to select an existing term. This provides the most robust categorization. (Figure 9.13 shows an example of hierarchical terms.)

When viewing a node, the taxonomy settings may appear with the content, as shown in Figure 9.14.

Clicking the taxonomy setting automatically displays a list of similarly categorized nodes, as shown in Figure 9.15.

FIGURE 9.13
Enter data with a
vocabulary and
terms.

FIGURE 9.14
Taxonomy set-
tings can be dis-
played with the
content.

FIGURE 9.15
Use a single
click to find simi-
larly categorized
content.

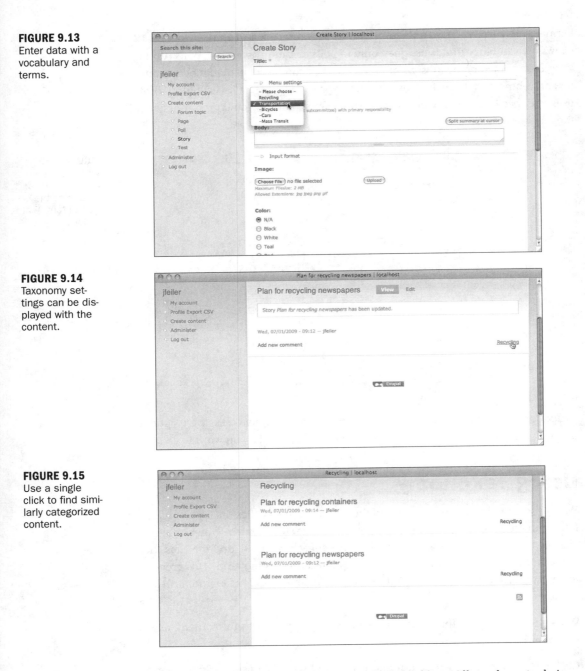

Drupal does all the work of maintaining these links and lists. All you have to do is
make sure that the content is categorized.

Summary

A website—particularly one built with Drupal's CMS—is a way to share content among many people. Tags, taxonomies, and searching are all ways of doing this. This hour explored the differences between searching and categorization. By configuring Search and Taxonomy, people entering data can easily set it up for speedy retrieval.

Q&A

Q. *I want to use the Taxonomy module for my Drupal site, but the site already exists. What do I do?*

A. It is not impossible to categorize existing data. If the volume of data is not large, you can do it manually (and carry on with Taxonomy settings as described in this hour). The other way is to use search to find a set of nodes and then assign them to a taxonomy term. You have to be careful that this semiautomated method works properly on your data. The best way to do this is to take your site offline, back up your database, and experiment. A number of modules are available for this because it is not an uncommon problem. The best way to find the current choices is to search for "Drupal taxonomy bulk update" or some variation thereof. You will find a variety of possibilities; to get the fullest range of choices, follow all links. Because these have often been built for specific data conversion projects, they may not be maintained for current Drupal releases. However, you should find several from which to choose.

Q. *I already categorized my site using menus. Is this duplication?*

A. Many people implement their site's taxonomy as a parallel structure to their menus. Certainly, the major divisions and subdivisions of the site are part of the menu structure and, usually, the taxonomy structure. However, taxonomy allows multiple paths and structures so that information is more readily findable. Also, as you will see in Hour 14, "Working with Views," taxonomy terms can function almost as menu items in creating dynamic lists of nodes based on their taxonomy.

Q. *How do I know I have the right taxonomy structure?*

A. The ideal structure lets every user find everything that is relevant on the first try. You can test out your taxonomy structure by using basic tools, such as pencil and paper. Although there theoretically can be a slight performance hit by using many synonyms, many people use synonyms as a key part of their taxonomy structure. For some websites, synonyms are not just true synonyms, but also misspellings. For example, in a practical sense, you might want to consider "`biodegradeable`" to be a synonym for "biodegradable."

Workshop

Quiz

1. How are tags different from other taxonomy terms?

2. How do you create a search index?

3. Where are related taxonomy terms displayed?

Quiz Answers

1. They can be created by users as they enter data. Thus, duplicative and inconsistent tags can be created.

2. You configure cron or Poormanscron to run periodically.

3. You can enter these terms in the main Drupal interface, but you need contributed modules to display them.

Activities

As you start to plan your site, keep a list of terms you come across. When you are constructing menus, you may debate the proper wording of a specific area's menu. Keep the notes from that discussion so that you can use the various versions as synonyms for taxonomy terms.

Periodically review the list of terms and share it with others. It is a good idea to periodically run it past people who are not heavily involved in the project, because they will have a fresh perspective.

Using Polls, Comments, Discussions, and Feed Aggregators

What You'll Learn in This Hour:

▶ How Interactivity Can Make Your Site More Interesting

▶ When and Where to Use Comments

▶ Using Feed Aggregators and Discussions to Easily Add Content to Your Site

Introduction

Now that you have seen how to manage security and access and how to set up methods for organizing content, it is time to start using the powerful built-in features of Drupal. Its socializing and communications tools are in the mainstream of modern website development. Whether yours is a personal website, commercial site, or a site for a nonprofit organization, most people today recognize that sites are most effective when visitors are involved and interested in the site. Most of the time, that means some form of interaction.

This hour focuses on the Drupal tools that you can use to allow users to add to your site by using polls, comments, or discussions. It also covers Drupal's feed aggregation technology that allows your site to be updated by RSS feeds from other sites. This means that your site's content can be created by others, but it does not mean that your work is lessened. In fact, in many ways, you have more work. Part of the work of maintaining a website consists of getting people to visit the site. Having more content and changeable content is one such strategy, and user contributions help mightily in that area. However, while some of your work may be lessened, you now have to add the challenge of attracting not just visitors but contributors to the site.

Go To ▶

For more on sidebar blocks, see **HOUR 19,** **"USING** **BLOCKS,"** p. 327.

Go To ▶

If you are soliciting user input, make sure that you have a statement of your policies on your site (perhaps in your About Us section). Furthermore, use the techniques described in **HOUR 13,** **"CREATING** **CONTACT** **FORMS AND** **WEBFORMS."** p. 215 to allow people to quickly contact you with complaints.

In addition, you need to set up the infrastructure that allows user contributions without compromising the security and integrity of the site. Fortunately, Drupal has done a lot of this work for you. In this hour, you will see how to set up and deploy the social networking tools of Drupal.

Using Polls

Internet polls are a popular way of sparking interest and interaction. The built-in Drupal poll module lets you create polls and, subject to your settings for roles and permissions, it will allow people to vote on polls and to revise their votes. It includes built-in controls to prevent multiple voting from the same account. Polls most often appear as blocks in sidebars on Drupal pages, as shown in Figure 10.1.

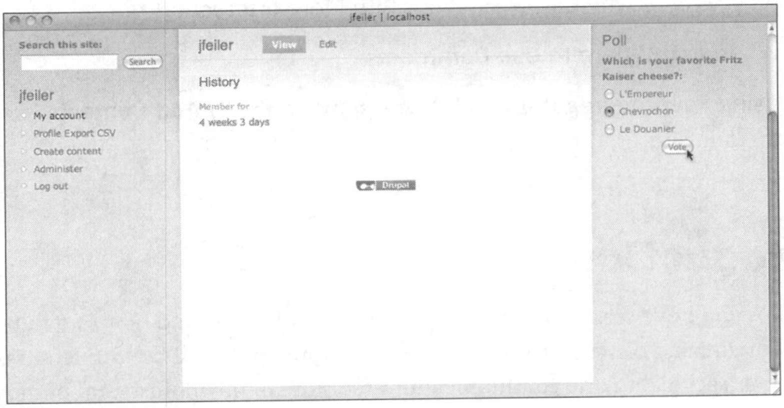

FIGURE 10.1
Drupal lets you create polls.

To begin using polls, install and enable the Poll module, as shown in Table 10.1.

TABLE 10.1   Poll Module Reference

Download from	Core
Enable in section	Core—optional
Permissions	
Poll Module	Vote on polls (generally do not allow anonymous users to vote)
Poll Module	Cancel own vote
Poll Module	Inspect all votes

TABLE 10.1   Poll Module Reference

Download from	Core
Poll Module	Create poll content
Poll Module	Cancel, celete, edit own poll content
Poll Module	Concel, celete, edit any poll content
Administration	
None	

Using Polls to Promote Your Site

Polls can range from trivia games to substantive (but nonscientific) surveys. You can integrate a poll into your site's promotional strategy, remembering that as you add social networking aspects to your site, you not only want to attract visitors but also contributors to your site. Anytime you can break out of your site's relatively closed world, and even out of the world of the Internet, you have a chance to bring in new users.

For example, you can construct a poll that is of interest to your users and people you want to have as users. For a site focusing on the environment, it might be a choice of the highest priority over the next year: recycling, energy, transportation, or local food. When the poll closes, you will have some nonscientific but interesting data that at least excludes multiple votes from an individual account. Writing an article on your website is a good use of that information, and using it in a newsletter or a bulk email letter is also a good idea. (Newsletters are discussed in Hour 12, "Using Blogs and Newsletters;" bulk email from your user list was discussed in Hour 8, "Managing Users, Roles, and Permissions.")

But you can and, in most cases, should go further. Let other people and media outlets know of your poll results. As part of your media release, you can provide information about your organization and your site. Do not forget to add information about the next poll—perhaps a follow-up to the priority identified in the first poll.

After you set it up, this process can be a routine event on a regular basis. If you limit voting to authenticated users, you can keep track of the poll participation over time, and you can track the numbers of new accounts created.

It is easy to implement this type of feature on a Drupal-built website. Because it is so easy, it is probably worth doing. And, because it is so easy and the resulting data is so simple to collect, if it turns out that if it is not beneficial, little is lost by dropping the idea.

Setting Up Polls In General

You can use admin/content/node-type/poll (D7: admin/structure/node-type/poll) to modify the settings for the Poll content type, as shown in Figure 10.2. Although the basic poll question is central, you can add additional fields (perhaps an image) to the poll's data.

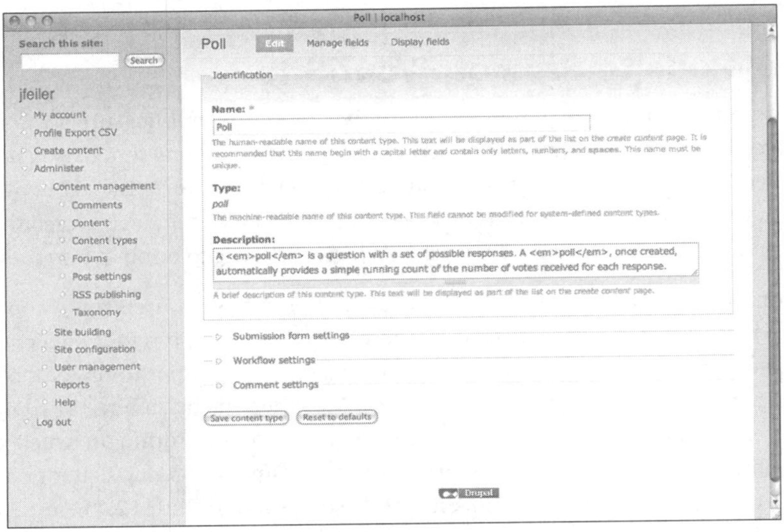

FIGURE 10.2
Modify settings for the Poll content type.

The submission form settings, shown in Figure 10.3, let you customize the form that users will see when they create a poll (not when they vote on it).

The workflow settings, shown in Figure 10.4, are commonly used for polls. You often do not want attachments, and you do not want a poll promoted to the front page because you may be displaying it in a block. However, if you are not using sidebar blocks, you might want a poll to be promoted to the front page and made sticky at the top. The choice is yours.

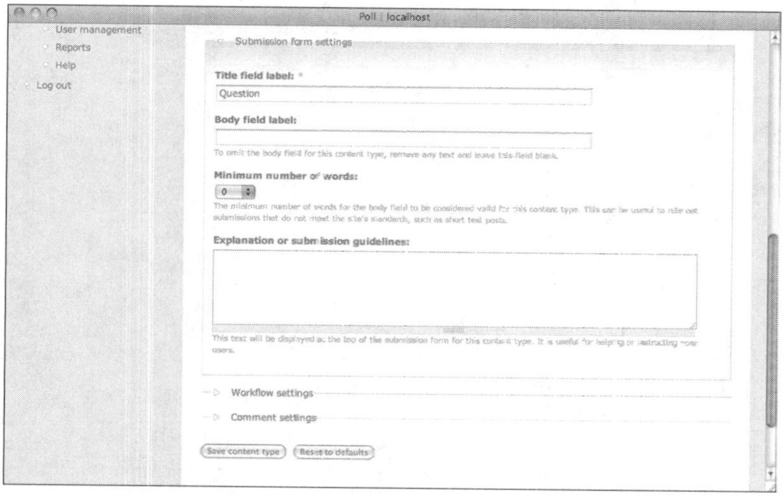

FIGURE 10.3
Modify submission form settings for a poll.

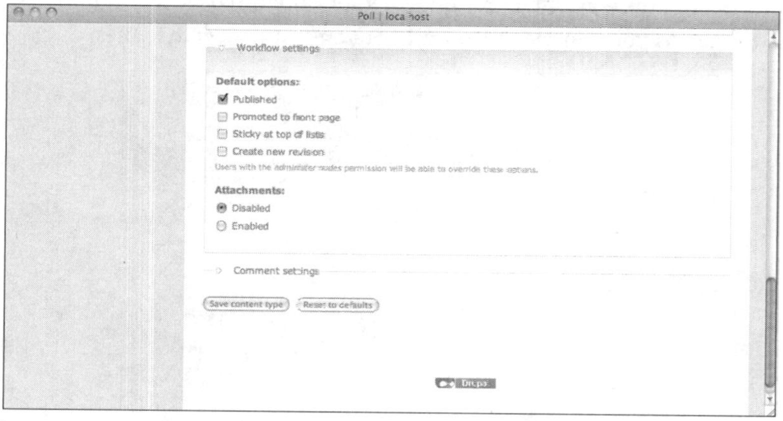

FIGURE 10.4
Set up the workflow for the poll.

Creating a Poll

After you set the Poll content type, you can create individual polls using Create Content, as shown in Figure 10.5.

If you marked the poll as active, it will appear immediately (subject to your roles and permissions settings). If you are publishing it on the front page (usually sticky at the top), that is where it will appear. If you as using the sidebar block for the most recent poll, it will appear there.

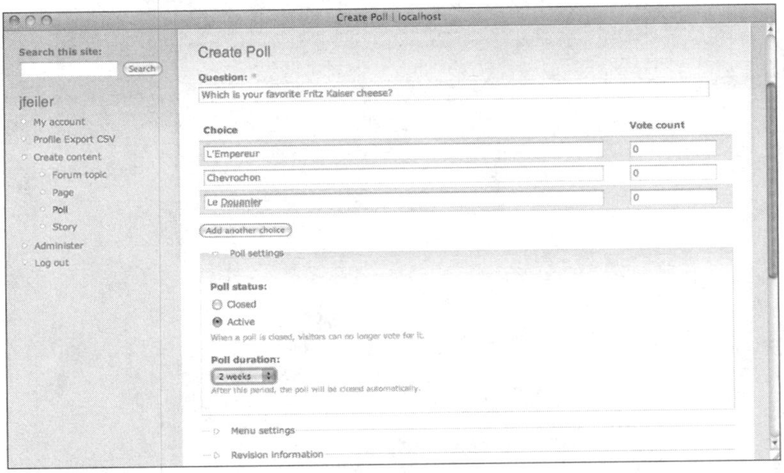

FIGURE 10.5
Create a poll.

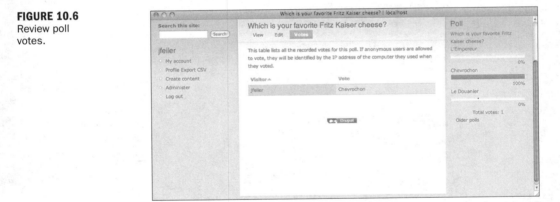

FIGURE 10.5
Create a poll.

You can use Administer, Content Management, Content (D7: Content button) to edit and view polls. As you can see in Figure 10.6, you can review the votes.

FIGURE 10.6
Review poll votes.

Using Comments

Comments can be enabled for any Drupal content. If you want to create a fully inter-active site, you may think that you should enable them across the board. Although that is the right choice in some cases, it is not always so.

For example, comments can be enabled on polls. Doing so may actually decrease voting in the poll as people register their preferences in comments rather than the poll.

When it comes to articles and other primary content types, comments may also be an unwise choice. The problem that you may encounter is that you wind up with one or two comments on several articles. A few comments scattered all over the site do not show activity and interaction; instead, they make your site look sedate or inactive.

When it comes to comments, consider these two strategies:

▶ You can enable comments only for major stories or for stories that you think will draw significant responses. You can also set a policy that stories themselves invite comments in their text if comments are allowed.

▶ Stories can direct people to a forum discussion. In this way, you may avoid the problem of scattered comments, because all comments on a specific issue are funneled to the forum discussion.

Whatever your choice, you probably want to have comments enabled in some places. Remember that you can create default comment settings for each content type on Administer, Content Management, Content Types (D6 admin/content/typesD7: admin/structure/types).

Install and enable the Comment module, as shown in Table 10.2.

TABLE 10.2   Comment Module Reference

Download from	Core
Enable in section	Core—optional
Permissions	
Comment Module	Access comments
Comment Module	Post comments
Comment Module	Post comments without approval
Comment Module	Administer comments
Administration	
Administer, Content Management, Comments (admin/content/comment)	

You can review comments at Administer, Content Management, Comments, as shown in Figure 10.7.

Did you Know?

Moderate Your Comments

Unless your site is very small, you will need a mechanism to deal with comments that should be deleted. You can use a contact form (as described in Hour 13) or you can provide an email address in a Contact Us section of the site. However you handle it, you should have a mechanism where people can report inappropriate comments and they can be dealt with quickly. Confining permission to post comments to authenticated users means that you will have a way of contacting the poster about inappropriate comments. If necessary, you can disable the account. Allowing anonymous comments is an invitation to chaos. But, allowing anonymous users to access (but not write) comments is generally a benefit. In fact, it may encourage anonymous users to open accounts so that they, too, can participate.

An approval queue is automatically created, as shown in Figure 10.8.

To keep the site running properly, configure automatic email messages to be sent when the approval queue needs to be reviewed. For more information, see Hour 22, "Managing the Site: Using Triggers and Workflows."

Using Forum Discussions

Forum discussions are a way to centralize discussions. They can augment or substitute for comments on individual articles. Drupal's taxonomy structure lets you create a discussion area for your website that is as simple or complex as you want it to be.

At the lowest level are *forum topics*. These are actually Drupal nodes, and as nodes, they can have comments enabled. A forum topic and its associated comments are a basic discussion.

Forum topics are part of a *forum*. A forum can have any number of topics within it. At a higher level, you can create *containers*, which are collections of forums (and of the topics and comments for those forums).

Did you Know?

Keep the Discussions Going

As is the case for real-life socializing, a little bit of crowding is productive. Given a choice between entering a room with one or two people in it or a room with a number of people chatting together in various groups, most people choose the more populated room. If you use the forum structure and taxonomy to devise a multitude of forums and forum topics in which the participants are widely scattered, your discussion area is likely to be a bit dull. Remember that it is always possible to split a crowded forum or forum topic after it gets too full (and too lively).

Install and enable the Forum module, as shown in Table 10.3.

TABLE 10.3 Forum Module Reference

Download from	Core
Enable in section	Core—optional
Permissions	
Forum Module	Create, edit, and delete forum topics
Forum Module	Create, edit, and delete own forum topics
Forum Module	Administer forums
Comment Module	Access, administer, and post comments
Administration	
Administer, Content Management, Forums (D6: admin/content/forum D7: admin/structure/forum)	

▼ **Try It Yourself**

Administering and Creating Forums

Creating forum topics is a task that is generally left to midlevel administrators. Administering forums is usually a task for a webmaster. You start from Administer, Content Management, Forums:

1. Create a container. If you want to use a container, create one, as shown in Figure 10.9. As is always the case in a taxonomy-based structure, the parent setting is key. This container is at the highest level, the root.

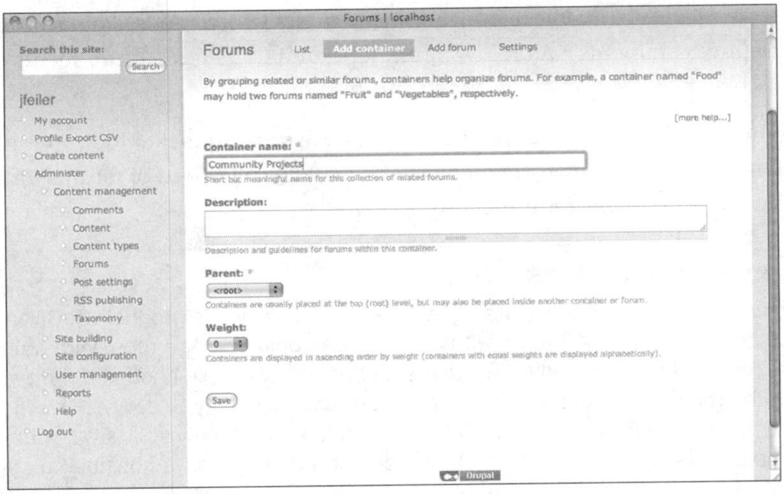

FIGURE 10.9
Create a container for forums.

Remember that you do not need a container; you can place your forums inside the root level itself rather than inside a container. Using a container may make future expansion easier.

2. Create a forum. You can add a forum either to the root level or to a container, as shown in Figure 10.10.

▼

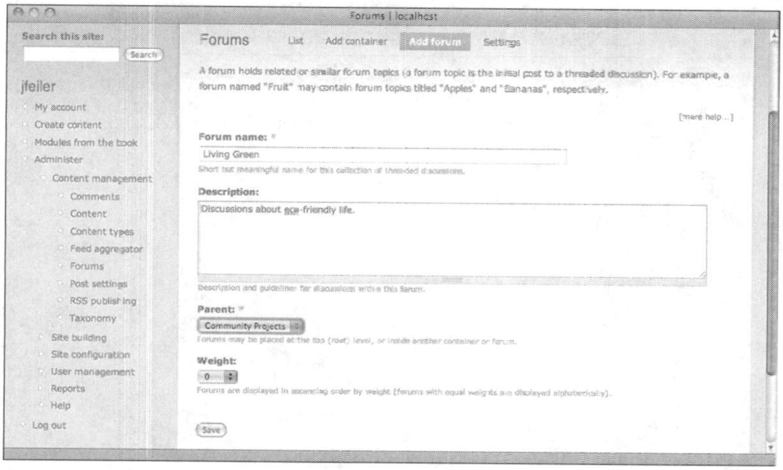

FIGURE 10.10
Add a forum.

3. Review your list of forums and containers. You can use the four-headed arrows to move items up and down and from one container to another, as shown in Figure 10.11.

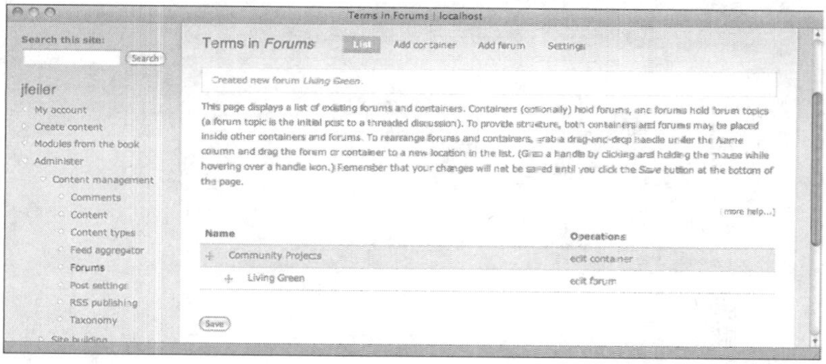

FIGURE 10.11
Work with the list of containers and forums.

4. Adjust forum topic settings. Use the Settings button shown in Figure 10.12 to adjust the settings. They apply to all forums.

Set forum content types. Use the link to the forum vocabulary page in the text at the top of Figure 10.12 to set content types for the forum, as shown in Figure 10.13. Forum topics are selected by default; in most cases, that is the only type of content you will use in the forum, so you can usually skip this step.

After the forum has been created and set up, anyone with permission to create a topic can do so by clicking Create Content and selecting Forum Topic. The entry page is shown in Figure 10.14. Double-check that comments are enabled so discussions can start.

FIGURE 10.12
Adjust forum settings.

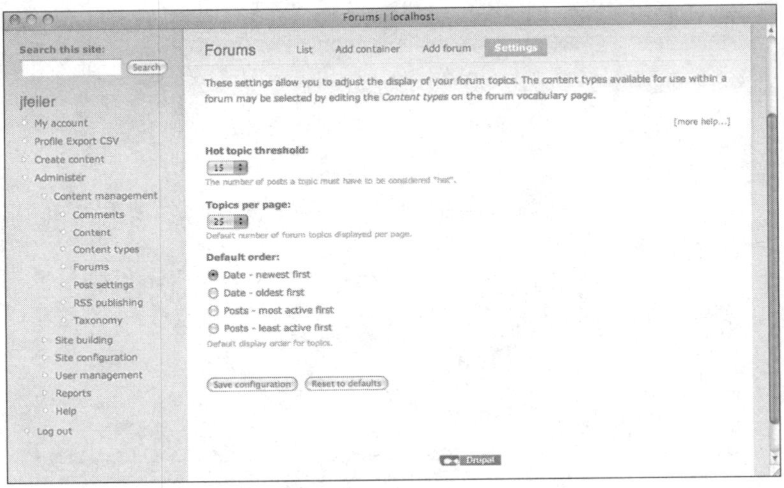

FIGURE 10.13
Set forum content types if necessary.

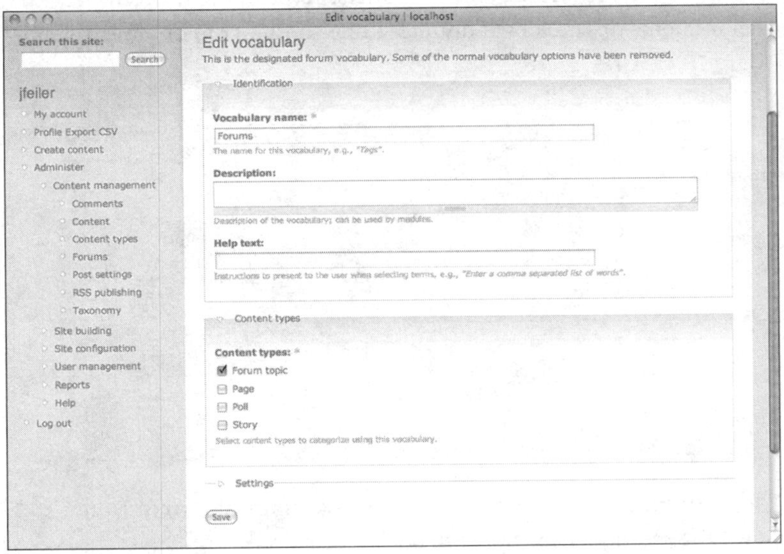

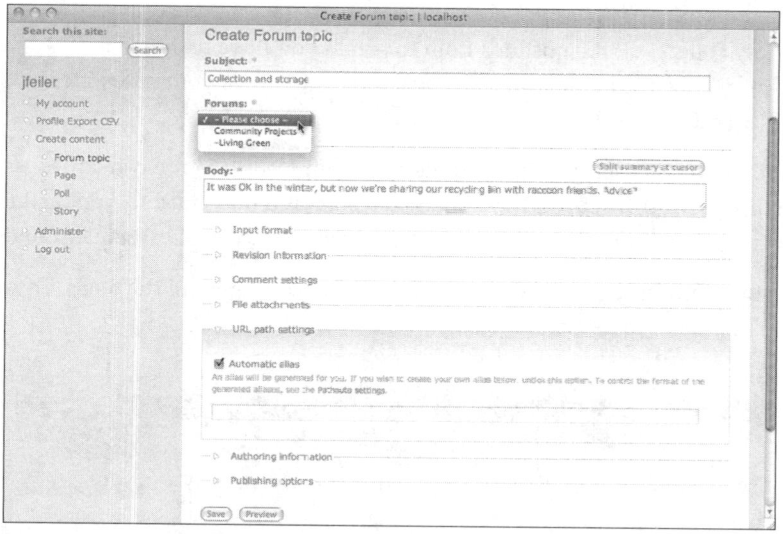

FIGURE 10.14
Create forum topics.

Using Feed Aggregation

Drupal lets users subscribe to RSS feeds from almost every page. The Aggregator module performs the reverse process: It lets you subscribe to feeds from within Drupal. This is a useful way to automatically add relevant content to your site.

The author's website, www.northcountryconsulting.com, provides an example of how this can work. This book refers to a number of modules from Drupal. The feed aggregator is used on the author's website to aggregate the feeds for the modules discussed in this book. Go to the Drupal area of northcountryconsulting.com to see the latest versions for the subset of Drupal modules discussed in this book.

To use the feed aggregator, install it as shown in Table 10.4.

TABLE 10.4 Aggregator Module Reference

Download from	Core
Enable in section	Core—optional
Permissions	
Aggregator Module	Administer news feeds
Aggregator Module	Access news feeds
Administration	
Administer, Content Management, Feed Aggregator (D6: admin/content/aggregator D7: admin/settings,aggregator)	

Add a feed, as shown in Figure 10.15, from Administer, Content Management, Feed Aggregator.

A category collects all the postings from the feeds you have assigned to it. As you will see in Hour 19, you can place any of your feeds and any of your categories in blocks—usually in a sidebar.

The Feed Aggregator lets you list and manage your feeds and the categories, as shown in Figure 10.16. If you have added a feed, it is a good idea to update it immediately to make certain that all is well. Dropal will take care of subsequent updates.

The Settings button shown in Figure 10.17 lets you configure all the feeds. These settings do not apply to individual feeds.

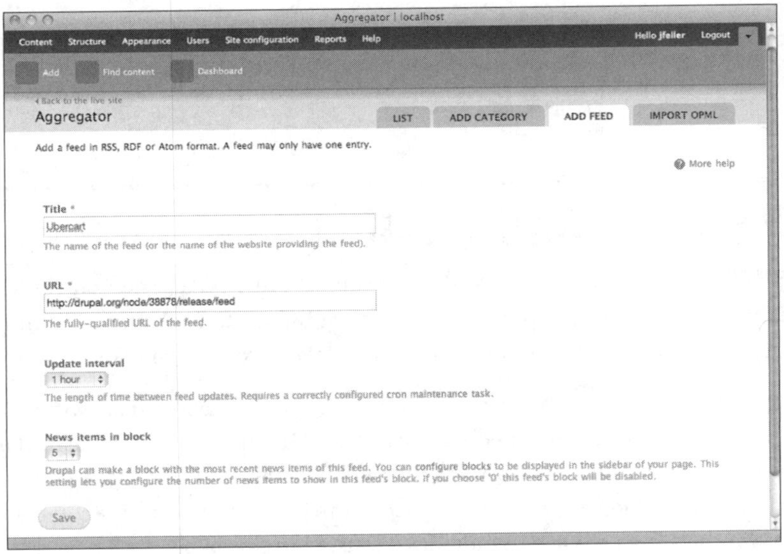

FIGURE 10.15
Add a feed.

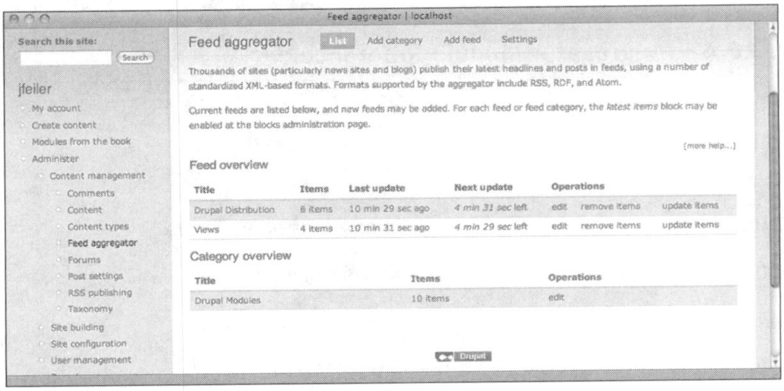

FIGURE 10.16
List your feeds and categories.

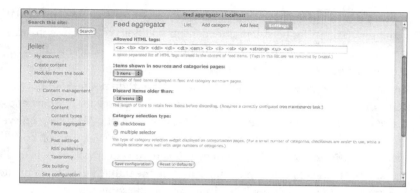

FIGURE 10.17
Adjust aggrega-
tor settings.

Summary

In this hour, you saw how to set up your Drupal website so that its content comes from external sources: users and RSS feeds. This makes the site more dynamic, but it means that, in addition to working to attract visitors to your site, you also have to think about attracting site contributors. All in all, that extra work is usually worth it, because sites that have a multitude of contributors and that support user discussions and comments usually are more involving to their visitors—whether the visitors are active or passive.

The next step in interaction is allowing users to directly update content on the site: that is the topic of the next hour.

Q&A

Q. *With comments and discussions enabled, my site is ready for social interaction. How do I get started?*

A. The challenge is not just building visitors, but building contributors. This obviously depends on your site and your expectations. In addition to the techniques discussed in this hour (such as funneling comments and discussions to a central area rather than letting them be scattered around), you can be proactive. End articles with a "What do you think?" closing. Encourage comments and discussions directly, just like a host of a party keeps an eye out for loners. If you receive email questions or comments from friends, colleagues, or even strangers, redirect them to your site's discussion area. The great majority of websites are low-volume sites; if you are providing a service or just having a good time while you learn Drupal, do not fret over the volume of traffic and contributions.

Q. *A very offensive comment was posted, and my boss wants all comments to be approved. Is this an overreaction?*

A. It depends on the site, the comment, and your boss. Chances are, this is going to happen at some point. If you are the website designer or developer, prepare your users and managers for this possibility. Remember that you can deactivate user accounts for persistent offenders. In addition, you can use the role structure to handle this. If you allow authenticated users to post without approval, consider setting the default to be that comments need to be approved. Add a new role for users whose comments do not need approval. You can manually move people into that group as you see fit. It all depends on the magnitude of the problem and on the size of your site. Also, keep an eye out for types of articles that generate problems. You can even turn off comments for articles that you know will be problematic. Most webmasters and managers are used to being in control. Inviting the public livens up your site, but you have to adjust to not being in control in the same way.

Workshop

Quiz

1. What is a feed collection?

2. Can you allow anonymous users to vote in a poll?

3. Can you turn off comments for an individual user?

Quiz Answers

1. Posts from any feed in the collection are shown together. You can place the collection as well as individual feeds in a sidebar.

2. Yes. Drupal will log the anonymous user's IP address to try to prevent double-voting. This is a bad choice if your website is an internal site (such as in a school where it is accessed from public computers in the library). It also is not reliable for IP addresses that change from day to day (such as many DSL or cable modem IP address leases).

3. No. You can turn comments on or off for a specific node or adjust permissions for a role. You can move users from a noncommenting role to another.

Activities

Start collecting feeds that you can aggregate for your site. If you just throw a clump of feeds together, you are not adding a great deal of value. Create a collection that is specific to your site. Because a collection can have any number of feeds in it, you can have low-volume feeds collected in an interesting group for your users. Continue interactivity by soliciting suggestions from your users.

Empowering User Input with Rich Text and Images

What You'll Learn in This Hour:

- ▶ How to Modify Input Formats

- ▶ How to Use Editors Such as FCKeditor and TinyMCE with the WYSIWYG Module

- ▶ How to Add Images with IMCE and WYSIWYG

Introduction

You have seen how Drupal works and how you (and others) can add all sorts of content: articles and stories, polls, comments, aggregated feeds from other sources, and discussions. With the robust and powerful taxonomy architectures, everything can be categorized, and, as you will see in Hour 14, "Working with Views," ad hoc queries and reports are easy to create.

At this point, most people point to an area in which traditional websites seem to function better than Drupal (that is, better until you have finished this hour!). The integration of images with text and the use of rich text seems easier using traditional HTML. As the Drupal community has expanded dramatically in the last few years, a number of people have implemented methods for dealing with these issues. These methods are largely based on common editors that use a word processing-like toolbar, as shown in Figure 11.1.

In this hour, you will see how to use one of the most popular architectures for managing rich text and image integration. Other sets of tools exist, but many people think that this architecture is the one that will move forward—in part, because it is the simplest.

In this hour, you will also see how to use images in conjunction with rich text. This means that you can place the image where you want within the text of a node (actually, within the HTML-based text of a node).

Whether you are doing this for your own convenience, for the convenience of your users (that is, the people developing and maintaining the site), or the convenience of end users who contribute content to the site, it is worthwhile and a major time-saver. In addition, it means that the skill set required of people who are entering text need not include even rudimentary HTML: a basic knowledge of simple word-processing interfaces is useful, but even that is not necessary.

FIGURE 11.1
Word processing-like editing is now available.

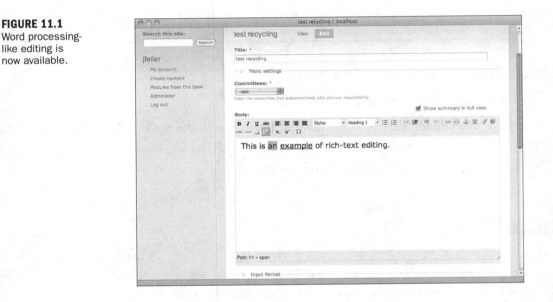

What "Rich Text" Means

Rich text is used here in its most general sense—text that can be styled with italics and other formatting.

Filtering HTML in Nodes

At this point, you may well have not pushed beyond the basics of input formatting as you have created nodes. Both filtered HTML and full HTML automatically sense URLs for web pages and email addresses; filtered HTML also provides you with the basic formatting tags for emphasis/italics, strong/bold, lists, and anchors. But you still need to know a bit of HTML to specify the tags at the start and end of each HTML element you want to use.

More important, the `<img>` tag is filtered out in filtered HTML, so there is no way to add images. You can modify the Filtered HTML filter to allow that tag; you will need it later in this hour.

This modification uses the Filter module; it is part of Core and is always enabled. Configure it as shown in Table 11.1.

TABLE 11.1   Filter Module Reference

Download from	Part of core
Enable in section	Always enabled
Permissions	
Filter Module	Administer filters
Administration	
Administer, Site Configuration, Input Formats (admin/settings/filters)	

Filtering works behind the scenes in most cases, so you may not give it a second thought. You may notice it in action in a few cases, so bear in mind the way that it is implemented. Filtering does not affect data entry at all. No matter what filters are enabled, you can type anything into the text area for a node. The filtering occurs when the node is about to be displayed. This means that you can type in HTML that is filtered out from the display today; if you change your filter tomorrow, it may appear.

Try It Yourself

Allowing `<img>` Tags in Filtered HTML

Follow these steps to implement `<img>` tags. You need to do it only once, so the details of what is going on are omitted:

1. Go to Administer, Site Configuration, Input Formats (admin/settings/filters), as shown in Figure 11.2.

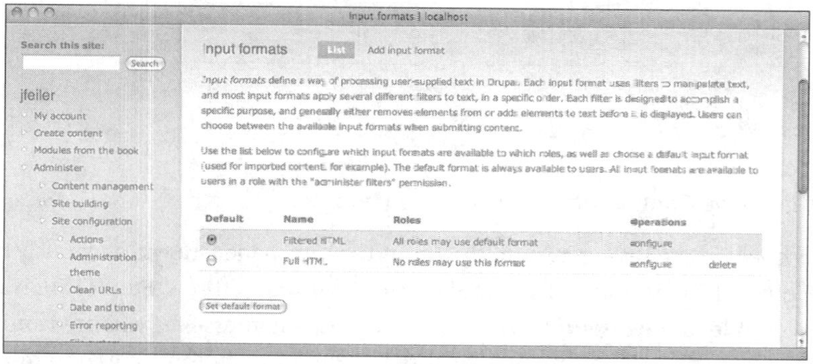

FIGURE 11.2
Start to configure Input Formats.

2. Click Configure next to the filter you want to use to open the page, shown in Figure 11.3, that lets you edit and configure the filter. Filtered HTML is the default filter, and you will see that all roles can use it and that you cannot change this. There is a Configure button at the top of this page; click it.

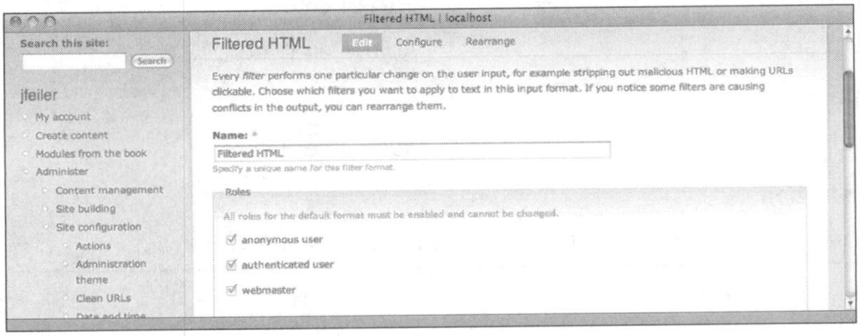

FIGURE 11.3
Go to the next configuration.

3. On the following page (shown in Figure 11.4) is a list of allowed tags. Add the following tags (separated by spaces) to that list. These are needed to insert images and support the rich text interfaces you may use.

```
<img> <h1> <h2> <h3> <h4> <h5> <h6> <address> <pre> <div>
```

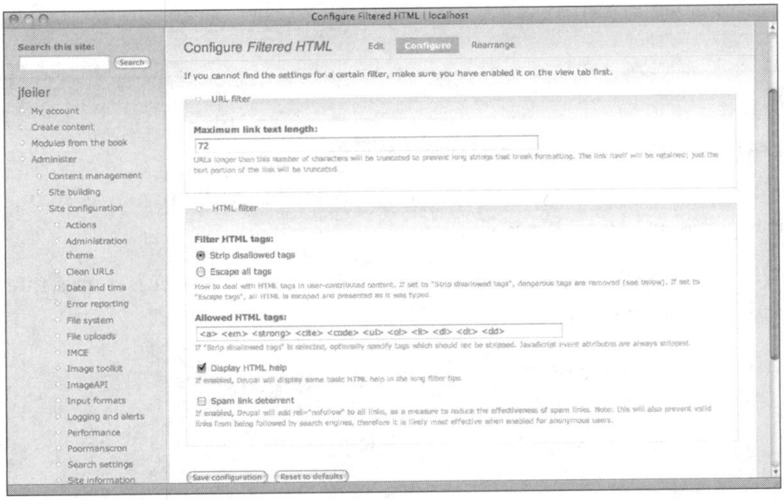

FIGURE 11.4
Add additional allowed tags.

4. Click Save Configuration to save your changes.

While you are here, return to the Input Formats page (shown previously in Figure 11.2). As you will see, in the default Drupal settings, Full HTML is not available to any user role. (You may have used it yourself if you are running as the primary user, because you bypass security.) To tidy things up and make the environment more secure and sustainable, click the Configure link for Full HTML to open the page shown in Figure 11.5. Add roles you have created, such as Webmaster. You do not want anonymous users or, in most cases, even authenticated users to have access to Full HTML.

FIGURE 11.5
Add roles to Full HTML.

Implementing Rich Text with WYSIWYG

You can use a variety of text editing tools with Drupal. The two most popular are FCKeditor and TinyMCE. Recently, an editor-agnostic module named WYSIWYG has been developed that lets you easily set up editing regardless of which module you use. As you will see in the following section, a bridge lets you work with images using IMCE and TinyMCE; you do not need a bridge to use IMCE with FCKeditor. Note that, in addition to the WYSIWYG module, you can find editor-specific modules, such as the FCKeditor.

Download, install, and configure WYSIWYG as described in Table 11.2.

TABLE 11.2 WYSIWYG Module Reference

Download from	project/wys wyg
Enable in section	User Interface
D7CX	

Permissions

Use WYSIWYG profiles and assign them to roles as described in this section.

Administration

Administer, Site Configuration, WYSIWYG (.admin/settings/wysiwyg)

WYSIWYG works with any of the most popular editing toolkits. When you have installed and enabled it, configure it at Administer, Site Configuration, WYSIWYG, as shown in Figure 11.6.

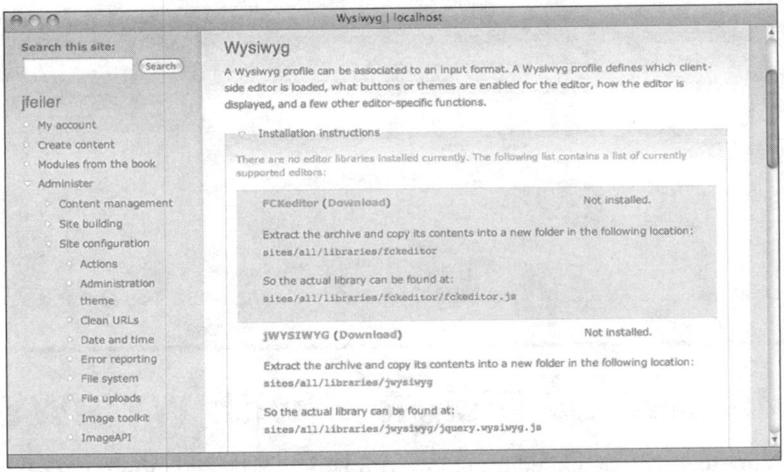

FIGURE 11.6
Start to configure WYSIWYG.

> ## Create WYSIWYG Profiles
> WYSIWYG lets you create a profile for each input format. Those profiles are what you are actually configuring.

By the Way

After you first install it, no editor is selected and, most likely, none will be installed. The supported editors are

- ▶ FCKeditor
- ▶ jWYSIWYG
- ▶ markItUp
- ▶ NicEdit
- ▶ openWYSIWYG
- ▶ TinyMCE
- ▶ Whizzywig
- ▶ WYMeditor
- ▶ YUI editor

Follow the download and installation instructions shown in Figure 11.6 for the editor you want to use. Note that they are installed in different places within the `./sites/all` Drupal directory. (You may have to create a libraries subdirectory.) You can install more than one of the editors, but you can use only one at a time for a given input format. After you install the editor, refresh this page, and you will see the version number of the installed editors rather than the text Not Installed. When you have at least one editor installed, the top part of this page lets you select an editor for each of the input formats, as shown in Figure 11.7.

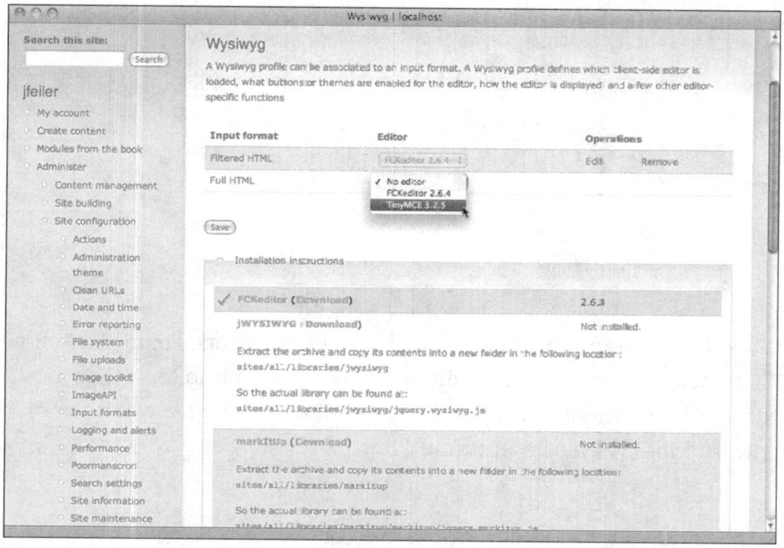

FIGURE 11.7
Select the editor you want to use for each input format.

You do not have to install an editor for each format. For example, the Full HTML input format is not yet available to anyone except the primary user; you could assign it to a special role (or perhaps one you have created, such as a supervisor, administrator, or webmaster). Because the Full HTML input format allows everything, you may choose not to put a WYSIWYG editor on it; that way, people who want to write HTML can write it without any distractions.

Click Edit to configure that editor for WYSIWYG. The basic settings are shown in Figure 11.8. These basic settings are usually fine, but do not relax: the next page will put you through your paces.

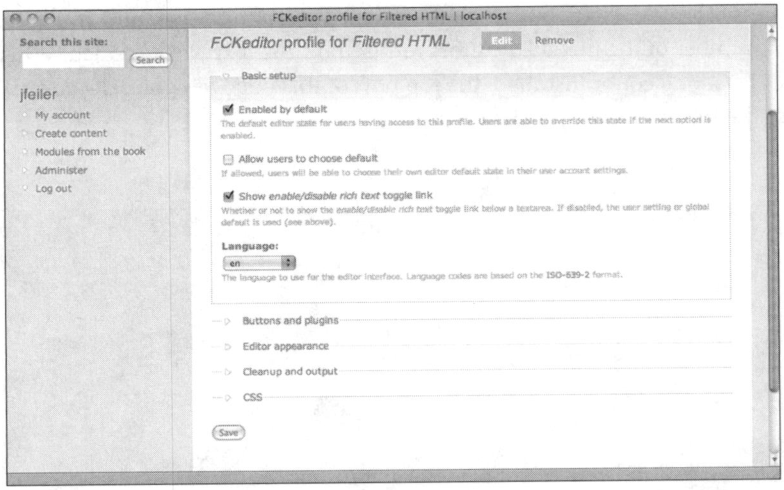

FIGURE 11.8
Configure basic
settings.

You are about to confront an issue shared by all these editors. Figure 11.1 showed TinyMCE in action; it implements a limited number of editing tools. The most popular editor, FCKeditor, implements far more. Installing it can give you a remarkably unfriendly interface, as shown in Figure 11.9.

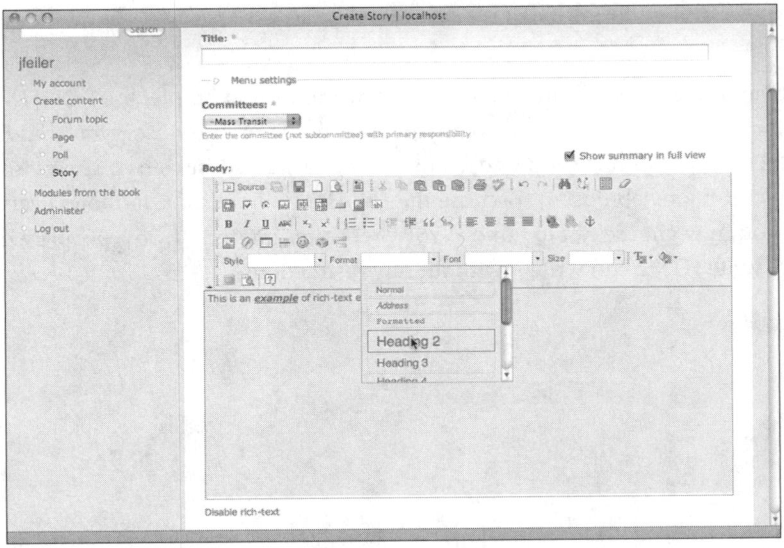

FIGURE 11.9
FCKeditor pro-
vides a multi-
tude of editing
features.

You can tidy this up in the Buttons and Plugins section of WYSIWYG configuration, as shown in Figure 11.10. Depending on who your users are and what kind of text they are working with, you may be able to eliminate a large number of these buttons. Of course, you may have users who want every last button (and perhaps will swear that it is a simple and elegant interface).

There is a simple way to handle this: Just create a new input format and assign a different set of buttons to it.

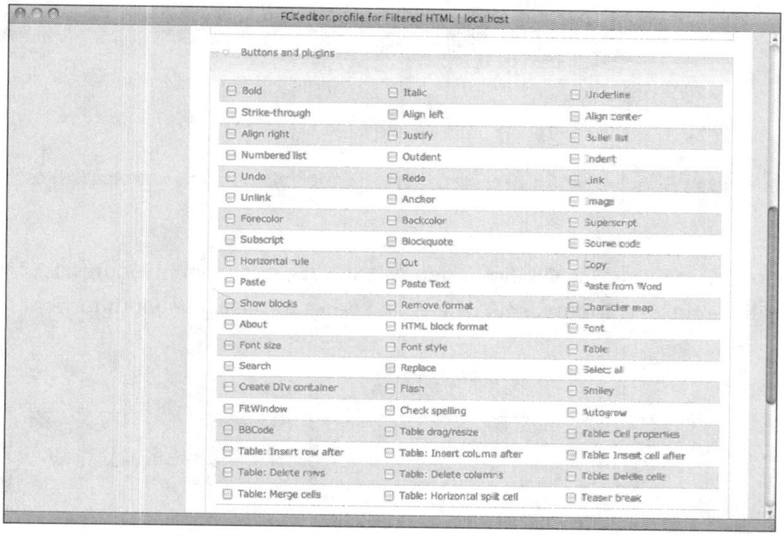

FIGURE 11.10
Enable editing buttons you want to use.

Try It Yourself

Create a New Input Format with Its Own Editing Buttons

Here is how you create a new input format with its own editing buttons:

1. Go to Configure, Site Configuration, Input Formats (shown previously in Figure 11.2). Click Add Input Format at the top of the page.

2. On the next page (shown in Figure 11.11), name the new input format. You can assign it to one or more roles, and you can choose whether to base it on the filters from Full HTML or Filtered HTML. (The difference is whether the HTML Filter box is checked; if it is, you are using the Filtered HTML settings.)

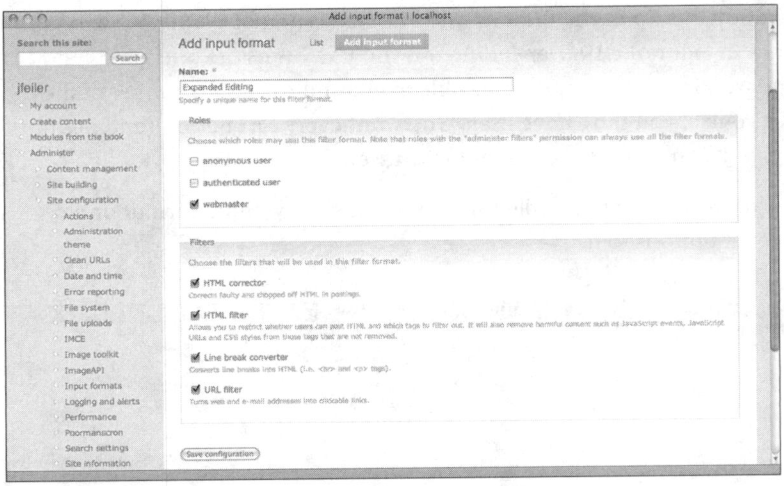

FIGURE 11.11
Name the new input format.

3. Go to Configure, Site Configuration, WYSIWYG, as shown in Figure 11.12. You will see the new input format there, and you can select the editor for that format.

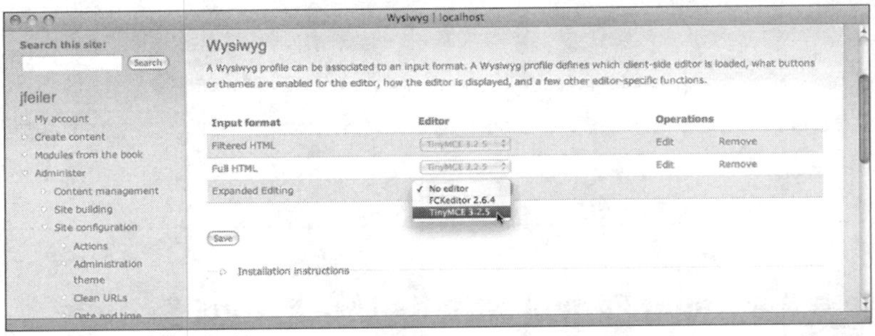

FIGURE 11.12
Select the editor for the new input format.

4. Save your choice. What you have created is a WYSIWYG *profile* for the selected input format. You can edit it if you want to select a smaller or larger set of buttons (or even a different editor). If you click Remove in the WYSIWYG page shown in Figure 11.12, you will remove the WYSIWYG profile, not the associated input format. (Double-check that the title of the page is WYSIWYG, not Input Formats, just to be safe.)

5. Subject to the roles you have selected, users can now choose from the two out-of-the-box input formats and the new one you have just created, as shown in Figure 11.13.

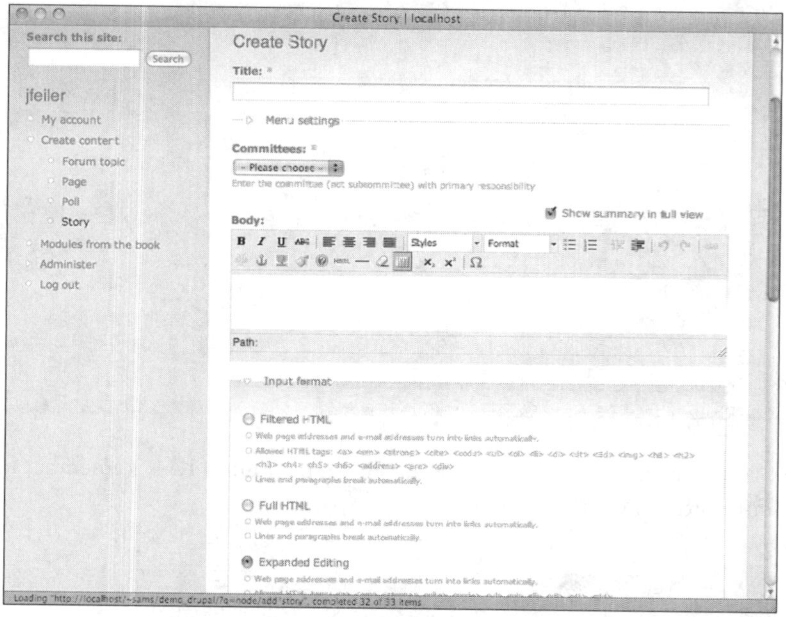

FIGURE 11.13
Users with the appropriate roles can use the new input format.

Complete the configuration of the WYSIWYG profile with settings such as the Editor Appearance settings, shown in Figure 11.14, which determine where the toolbar is placed in relation to the text area.

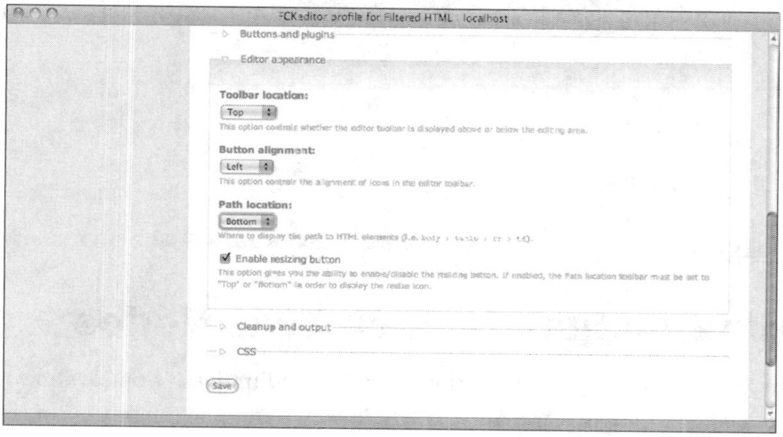

FIGURE 11.14
Set Editor Appearance options.

The cleanup options shown in Figure 11.15 are usually satisfactory, but you can change them.

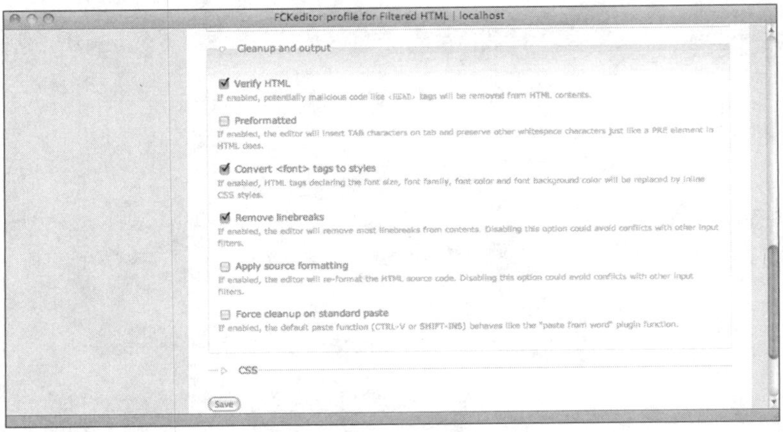

FIGURE 11.15
Adjust cleanup
settings.

Finally, you can customize CSS settings, as shown in Figure 11.16. Remember to save all of your hard work before you navigate away from the page.

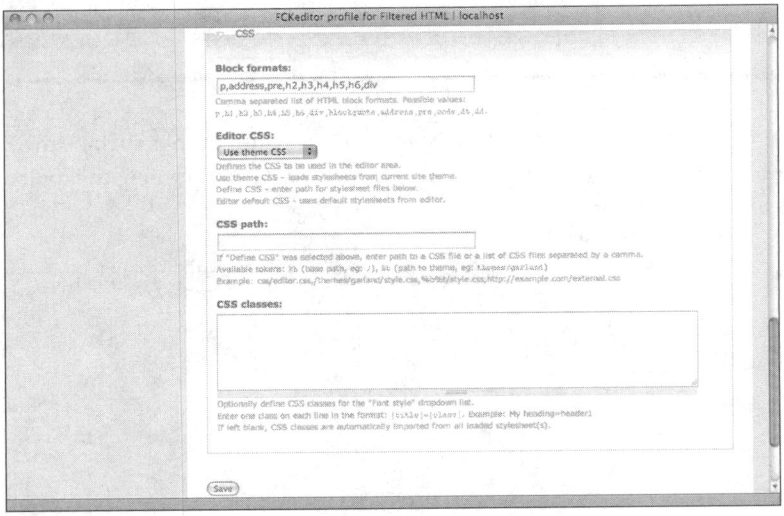

FIGURE 11.16
Customize CSS
settings if you
want and save
the WYSIWYG
profile.

Adding Images to Rich Text Nodes

In Hour 7, "Using Content Construction Kit (CCK) and Images," you saw how to add CCK image fields to nodes. You also learned how to automate the process of creating thumbnails and specify which versions of images should be displayed in specific environments, such as RSS feeds. That addresses a host of issues related to images, but it does not solve one of the most basic—how to include an image in the body text of a node. (In all fairness, that is not one of the objectives.)

In some contexts, the addition of image fields to nodes is exactly what is needed. For example, in an e-commerce solution, such as Ubercart (described in Hour 16), it is a definite advantage to have an image field for each product. Placing images inside a text field of the product description might be useful for a discussion, but not for an image that must appear in a shopping cart in a specific place on the page for each product. Perhaps most important, creating a separate image field in a content type means that you can make it a required field.

Other contexts, such as blogs, articles, and stories, benefit from user-defined image placement. In fact, you may need both types of image placement. This section shows you how to integrate images with the WYSIWYG module.

Setting Up WYSIWYG and IMCE

WYSIWYG can work with IMCE; other image modules are in the works. IMCE is discussed in this hour because of its widespread use. IMCE lets you upload image files and then use them; along the way you can create thumbnails in addition to the original image file.

To begin, download, install, and enable IMCE, as described in Table 11.3.

TABLE 11.3 IMCE Module Reference

Download from	project/imce
Enable in section	Other
D7CX	
Permissions	
Set up IMCE profiles as in the following section.	
Administration	
Administer, Site Configuration, IMCE admin/settings/imce)	

If you are using IMCE with WYSIWYG and the TinyMCE editor, you also need to download, install, and enable WYSIWYG IMCE API Bridge, as described in Table 11.4.

TABLE 11.4   WYSIWYG IMCE API BRIDGE Module Reference

Download from	project/imce_wysiwyg
Enable in section	User Interface
Permissions	
None	
Administration	
None	

Like WYSIWYG, IMCE lets you set up profiles; you then assign profiles to specific roles rather than using the permissions structure in User Management.

This is done at Administer, Site Configuration, IMCE (.admin/settings/imce), as shown in Figure 11.17.

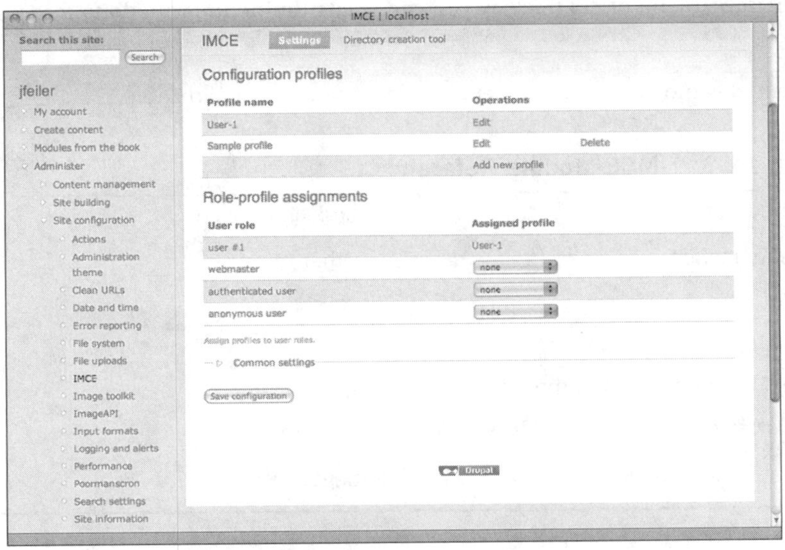

FIGURE 11.17
Configure IMCE profiles.

The common settings in the lower part of this page let you control uploads and thumbnails, as shown in Figure 11.18. More customization is possible in individual profiles.

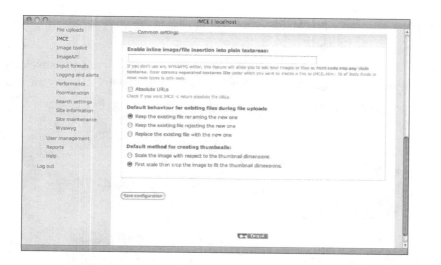

FIGURE 11.18
Review common settings.

Because the profiles can allow users to upload image files to your server, you probably want to review the profile settings carefully so that people do not abuse the server. Figure 11.19 shows the sample profile being edited.

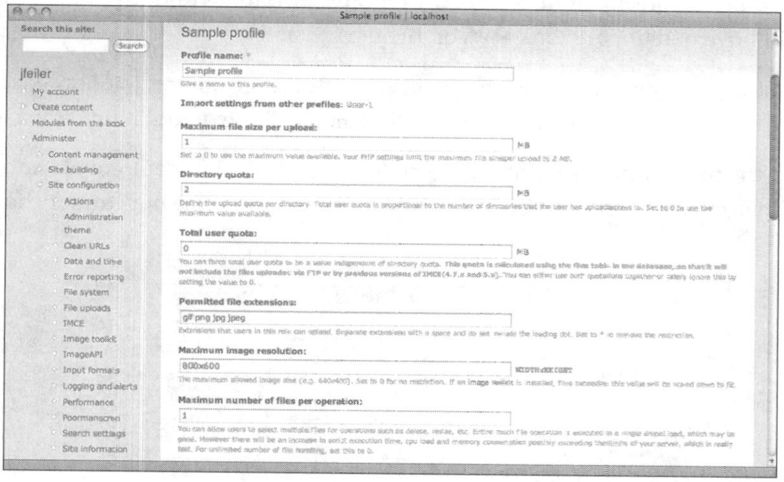

FIGURE 11.19
Review profile settings.

Notice that you can import settings from another profile so that you can then change one or two settings. Remember that the profiles will be associated with user roles (not individual users), so your settings must map to a profile such as webmaster.

The most important settings for most people are those shown in Figure 11.19. These are fairly restrictive in terms of the size of files and the numbers of files that can be uploaded. The User-1 profile, which initially applies to the primary user, is much less restrictive.

Figure 11.20 shows where you specify the directories to which your users have access. You can specify three directories, each with different permissions and with the choice

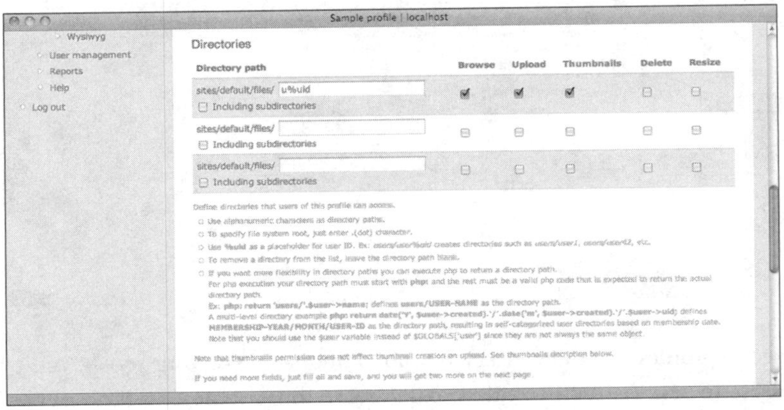

FIGURE 11.20
Set directories and permissions.

of including subdirectories. If you specify all three directories and save the profile, you will have additional blank rows on the next page.

You can use %uid for the user ID in a directory path. It is common to allow each user to have a directory and for users working together to share an additional directory.

Finally, the thumbnail information shown in Figure 11.21 lets you provide names and dimensions for thumbnails. Users can choose among these but cannot change them.

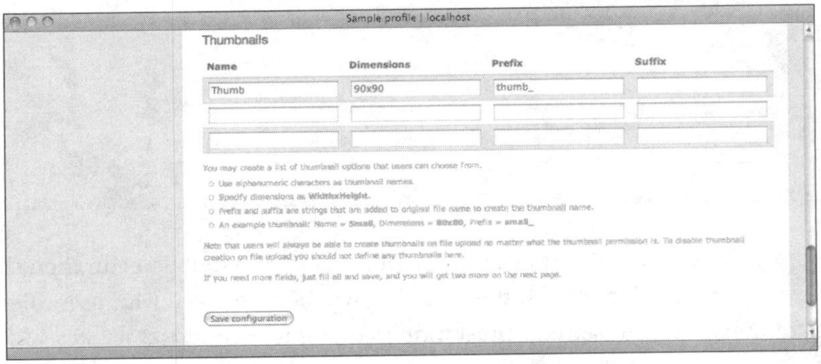

FIGURE 11.21
Configure thumbnails.

With IMCE and its profiles configured, you have one last step before you are ready to use images yourself and let your users use images. The Buttons and Plugins section of WYSIWYG profiles has a new check box for IMCE, which is shown at the lower right of Figure 11.22.

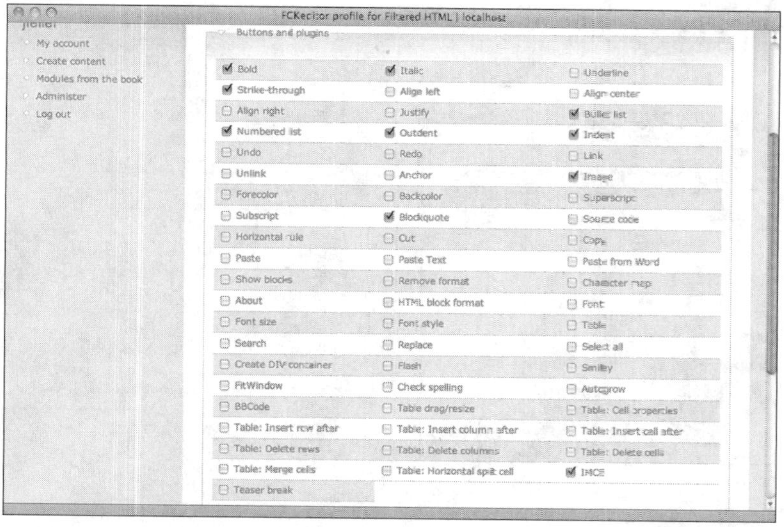

FIGURE 11.22
Enable IMCE in
WYSIWYG.

You need to check both the Image check box and the IMCE check box. The Image check box puts the image button into the toolbar; the IMCE check box enables IMCE itself, as you will see in the following section.

Using Images

Now that you have set up input formats to allow <img> tags, WYSIWYG, your editor of choice, and an image module such as IMCE, you are ready to use them.

Create a new node using Create Content. You should see a toolbar above the body text area. You can experiment to see the interplay between the Image and IMCE check boxes. If you enable Image but not IMCE, clicking the image button in the toolbar lets you specify a URL for the image, as shown in Figure 11.23.

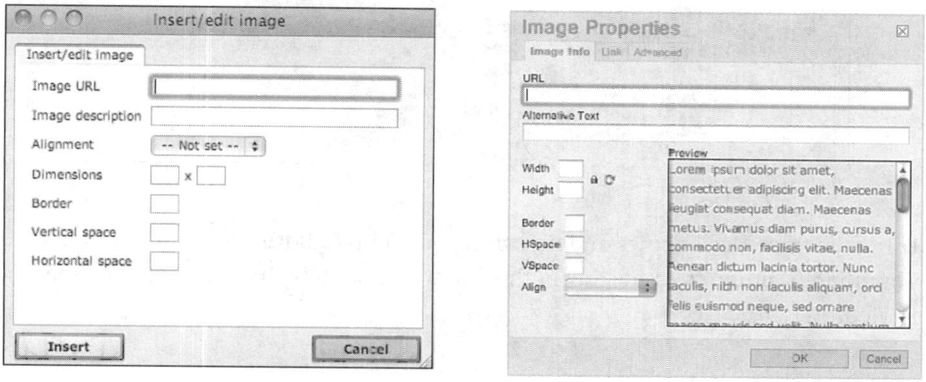

FIGURE 11.23
Use the Image button with IMCE not enabled (TinyMCE editor left, FCKeditor right).

Compare Figure 11.23 with Figure 11.24, in which IMCE is enabled.

With IMCE enabled, a new window opens that lets you view images on your server. You can click the Upload button at the top to upload an image from your computer to the server, as shown in Figure 11.25.

Using the thumbnail names and sizes that you set up in IMCE, you can now use the Thumbnails button to create any of them that you select with check boxes, as shown in Figure 11.26.

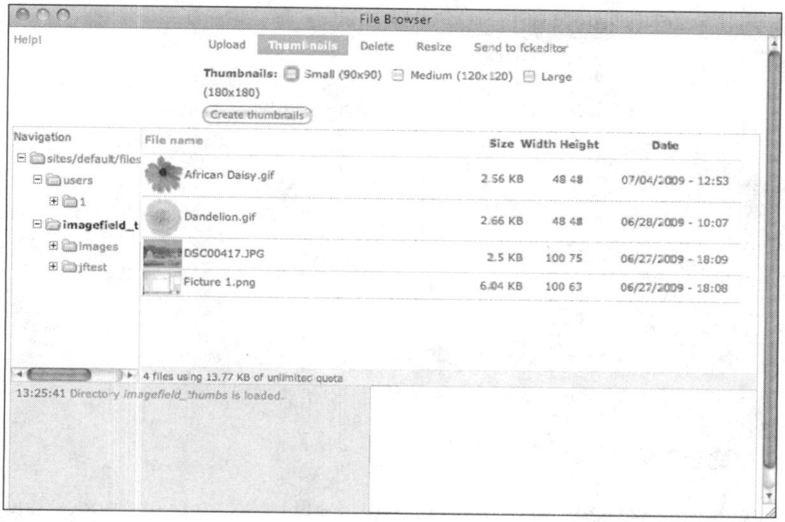

FIGURE 11.26
Create
thumbnails.

If you do not want to use a thumbnail, you can resize the image—either the original or by creating a new image, as shown in Figure 11.27.

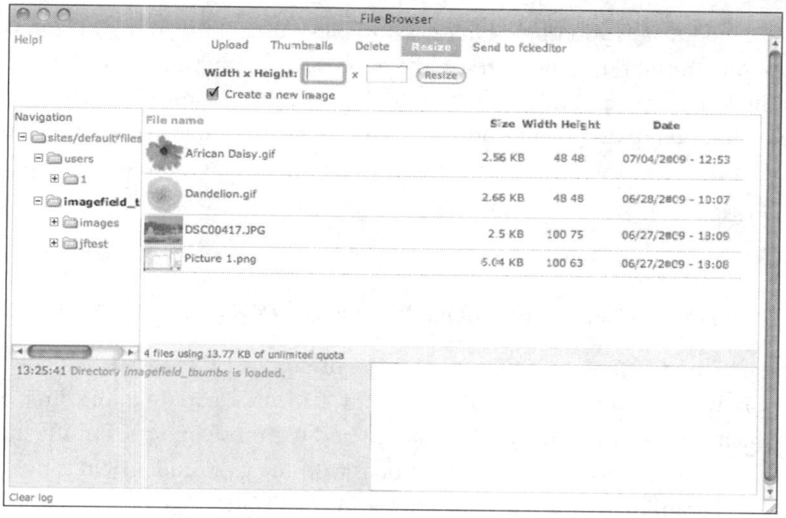

FIGURE 11.27
You can also
resize images.

The last button lets you select an image and send it back to your editor as shown in Figure 11.28. FCKeditor has a preview that lets you see the image and how text will wrap. Many people choose left alignment because that is the way that most images look best. (They are at the left of the text, and the top of the image is aligned with the first line of text, which then flows down and under the image.)

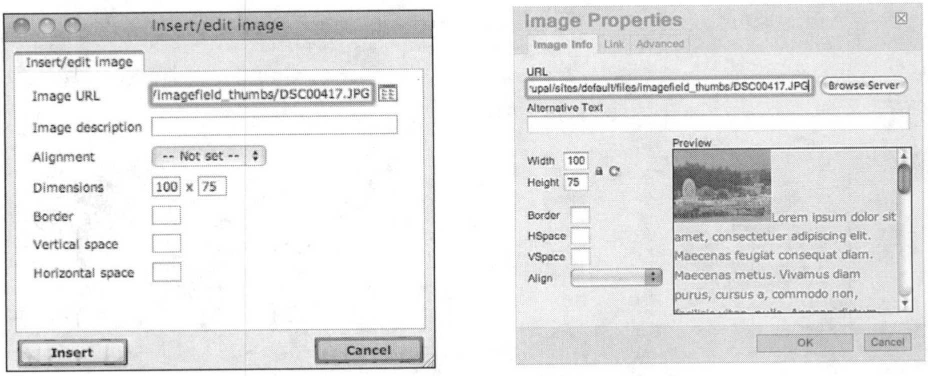

FIGURE 11.28
Send a selected image back to your editor enabled (TinyMCE editor left, FCKeditor right).

Summary

This hour showed you how to add modules and editors so that your nodes' body text functions like a word processor or the way many input areas on the web work. You can style text with italics and boldface, as well as using numbered and bulleted lists. Although the editors will be generating HTML, you just type the text and style it with buttons.

The IMCE module lets you upload images and place them into your text. You can use it to generate thumbnails and to resize the image. For many people, it is automatic to add the WYSIWYG and IMCE modules to their Drupal environment. Doing so is not difficult, and it pays off enormously in end-user satisfaction. This can be one of the moments in a website's development when things click for end users.

Q&A

Q. *What is the difference between IMCE and the CCK ImageField?*

A. The biggest difference is that, as of this writing, the CCK ImageField does not work with the WYSIWYG module directly. You can navigate to the directories in which images are stored for ImageField and use those images, but the automatic processing and caching of images with the CCK ImageField is not available. For inline image place in text, the WYSIWYG/IMCE combination is the most usable for many people. The advantages of the CCK ImageField are its caching and automation along with the fact that a separate CCK field can be made required for a specific content type. You may use both of these image architectures.

Q. *I've edited some text with WYSIWYG, and it is not formatting properly when it is displayed. What happened?*

A. The basic problem is that what is stored in the body text of the node is HTML; the WYSIWYG editor that you use provides an interface to the creation and editing of that text. Input formats that filter HTML do their filtering just when it is about to be displayed, so that is one time when a problem could occur. More often, the problem arises when you paste formatted text into the body text area. The constructs that often appear to cause problems are lists and indents. This can be because they are fairly complex HTML structures (a numbered list, for example, is a `<nl>...</nl>` element that contains individual `<li>...</li>` elements. One missing `</nl>` or `</li>` can throw everything off.

If you want to diagnose the problem, display the page with the bad formatting and use your browser's View Source command to look at the HTML. Find the text that is formatted incorrectly and see if you can find the misaligned HTML.

Rather than diagnosing the problem, you can often solve it by copying the text you want to paste into a text editor that does not support HTML or that has HTML turned off. This will remove all the formatting. Then, copy and paste the plain text into the WYSIWYG editor and reapply the formatting you want. There are no guarantees, but this often solves the problem.

Workshop

Quiz

1. How do you control which editor is used by WYSIWYG?

2. What is the difference between the Image and the IMCE check boxes for WYSIWYG buttons and profiles?

3. When is filtered HTML stripped out?

Quiz Answers

1. You configure WYSIWYG to use a specific editor for a given input format, such as Filtered HTML. You can create additional input formats so that people can use different editors. (This is commonly the case when you have several people devoting a lot of time to text data entry and each of them has different and strong preferences.)

2. Image gives you a pop-up dialog in which you can provide the URL for the `<img>` element. With IMCE enabled, you can upload a file and browse the server to find the file to use. Without IMCE, you have to type in the address.

3. HTML is never stripped from the actual node body text. It is temporarily removed when the text is about to be displayed.

Activities

If you have a number of people who will be entering and editing text, survey them to see what editor they want to have installed in the WYSIWYG module. This may seem like a small thing, but heavy users of editing software have strong preferences in many cases, and it is easy to accommodate them.

Similarly, decide together on the thumbnail sizes that you will use on the site. Having several sizes to choose from—but only those sizes—can make the site more attractive and consistent.

Using Blogs and Newsletters

What You'll Learn in This Hour:

▶ Difference Between Drupal Blogs and Other Nodes

▶ How to Use the Blog API to Post From a Smart Phone or Browser Plug-In, Such as ScribeFire

▶ How to Set Up a Newsletter with Simplenews

Introduction

You saw how to add socializing and communications tools to your site with discussions, polls, and comments from your site's end users. In this hour, you will explore the other direction—communicating to your site's end users.

Blogging software is the fastest way to publish information to the web. By now, users expect their blogging software to support the inclusion of images and other attachments, as well as areas for comments and discussions. All of these are built into Drupal itself; the Drupal blog content type adds some additional functionality.

Further functionality can be provided by the Blog API module that is part of Drupal's Core. This is the same type of API that many dedicated blogging software packages support; it allows you to create blog entries without logging into a specific site or program (such as Blogger). Many applications support one or more variations of the blogging APIs; as a result, you can update a blog from your desktop computer or from your smart phone.

Email newsletters, along with bulk email, are a tried-and-true way to stay in touch with your site's users. Information published on a website or in a blog is noticed only when someone explores the site or uses a newsreader to keep up with new postings. Email messages can get more attention when they land in someone's Inbox (but there are spam filters to evade along the way).

Every component of interaction that your site provides can add to its attractiveness to end users and, ultimately, to its success.

Using Drupal Blogs

Subject to permissions, every user on your site can have a blog. Many sites have only a single sitewide blog or separate blogs for each administrator or manager. The choice depends on your site, its purpose, and your users.

Using Drupal's Blog Content Type

By default, Drupal has a number of blog-like behaviors for its content:

▶ In every node's publishing options, you can choose to publish the node, promote it to the site's front page, or make it sticky at the top of the front page list. If you use the Promote to Front Page option (either as a default in the content type's configuration in Administer, Content Management, Content Types or in a specific node), and if you use the default front page (Administer, Site Configuration, Site Information), your site looks and behaves like a blog with postings presented in reverse chronological order (newest first).

▶ All nodes can be configured to allow comments and discussions.

▶ A blog page has an icon you can use to subscribe to that blog (at the bottom of the page by default).

▶ You can tag any node. The Tags taxonomy type is a traditional blog-like tagging structure in which free-form tags are separated by commas. Tags can be shown in each node listing; they are clickable to bring up all nodes with that tag. Allow tags (or any other taxonomy) for specific node types in Adminster, Content Management, Taxonomy. Many people allow free-format tags only for the blog content type; they prefer the more structured taxonomy for articles and stories.

Thus, you can use articles and stories for content and set their behaviors so they look exactly like a blog. But, you can also use the Drupal blog content type to achieve some specific goals. Your website and your preferences (along with those of your users) will help you decide whether to use the Drupal blog content type. Here are some of the features of the blog content type:

▶ Subject to permissions, blogs will be among the choices for a user's Create Content page. They will automatically be tagged with that user's name.

► Sidebar blocks can let you display recent blog posts from any users that have blogs on your site. (For more on blocks, see Hour 19, "Using Blocks," p. 327.)

► Whether you choose to promote individual blog postings to your front page or not, the address www.yoursite.com/blog presents the most recent blog postings from all site users, as you can see in Figure 12.1. This allows you to use the front page for a more formal and structured welcome and the dynamically created blog page for a view of what is on the minds of the administrators.

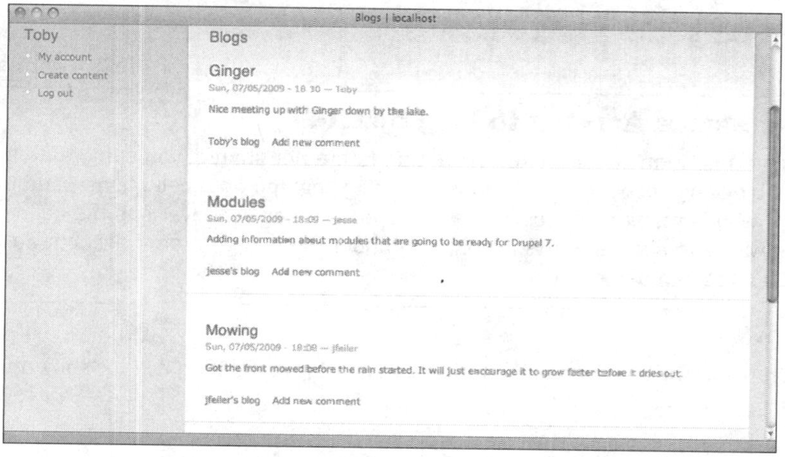

FIGURE 12.1
View recent postings from all blogs on the site.

To use blogs, enable and configure the Blog module (part of Core), as shown in Table 12.1.

TABLE 12.1 Blog Module Reference

Download from	Core
Enable in section	Core—optional
Permissions	
Blog Module	Create blog entries
Blog Module	Delete and edit own blog entries
Blog Module	Delete and edit any blog entries
Administration	
None	

Blogging From Your Phone and Browser

Drupal supports blogging APIs that let you create blog posts from a browser plug-in, a smart phone, or a desktop application. This can be an incredibly useful feature for websites that use blogs to update statuses. If you use the default front page (or make the blog page your front page), the most recent postings will automatically be there. A school principal, theater house manager, restaurant maitre d', or traffic coordinator can create blog postings from a cell phone to keep people updated. In the case of a specific person's need to know—your table is ready now—this is not efficient. But, in the more general case—there is a 10 minutes wait for a table—it can be enormously helpful.

Use a Shared Account to Blog Updates

Although it is normally the case that accounts are not shared, you can create a status blogging account and even install a blogging app on a cell phone used by a person who is monitoring a changeable situation. Then, whoever has the cell phone will have access to the Drupal blog under the shared status account so that updates can be posted.

To begin using the blogging API, enable and configure the Blog API, as shown in Table 12.2.

TABLE 12.2   Blog API Module Reference

Download from	Core
Enable in section	Core—optional
Permissions	
Blog API Module	Administer content with Blog API
Administration	
Administer, Site Configuration, Blog API	

Configure the Blog API, as shown in Figure 12.2.

Posting from a smart phone is different from posting from an application on a desktop or from a browser plug-in. In the case of smart phones, you may want to limit Blog API posting simply to blogs. Stories and articles, by contrast, often have lengthy text that is difficult to enter on a smart phone.

After you have Drupal configured, configure your smart phone, browser plug-in, or other software to post to the blog. ScribeFire is a plug-in for Firefox that lets you use the blogging API. (You can find more information at www.scribefire.com; you can download it at addons.mozilla.org/en-US/firefox/addon/1730.) This section shows you how to configure ScribeFire. Other products are set up in the same way. iPhone (and other smart phone) blogging apps use the same procedure.

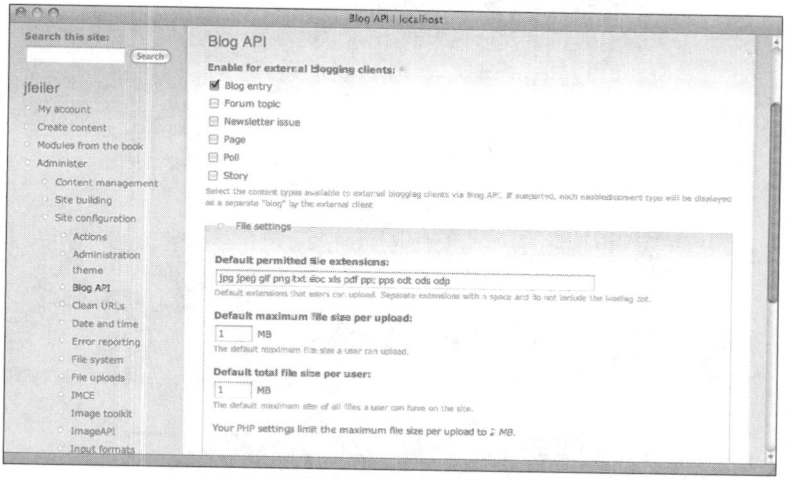

FIGURE 12.2
Configure Blog API.

Try It Yourself

Set Up ScribeFire (or a Smartphone App) to Post to Your Drupal Site

Follow these steps to configure ScribeFire, a smart phone app, or a desktop blogging application:

1. Install and configure the Blog API as described in the previous section.

2. Install ScribeFire (or another blogging app) on your computer, as a browser plug-in or on your smart phone.

3. Launch Firefox and choose ScribeFire from the Tools menu.

4. Click Add in the lower right of the window to create a new blog account, as shown in Figure 12.3. It may open for you automatically the first time you launch ScribeFire if you have no accounts.

5. In the Introduction window, enter your blog name as shown in Figure 12.4. For Drupal, it is the site name followed by /blog/n, where n is the number of the blog. ScribeFire then attempts to connect to the blog. Unless you get an error message, click Continue. If you do get an error message (which might happen if you do not know the blog number), click the option to configure manually.

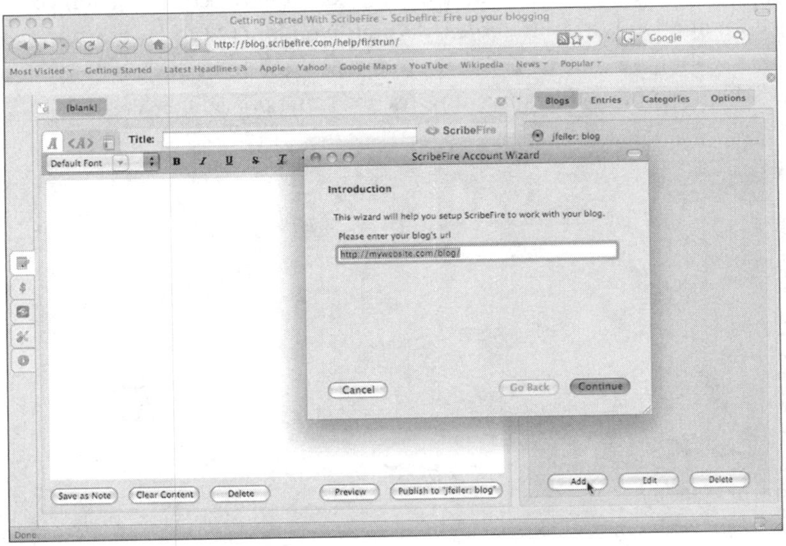

FIGURE 12.3
Add a new blog.

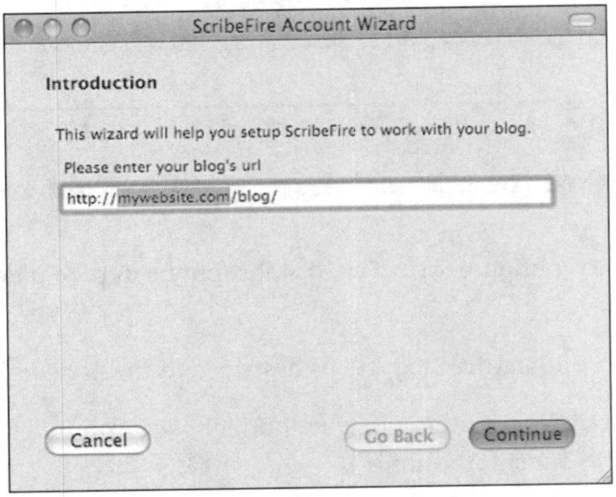

FIGURE 12.4
Enter your blog name.

6. After you click Continue, you are asked to choose your blogging service. For Drupal, you want Custom Blogging Service, as shown in Figure 12.5. (You may have to click a button to manually specify the provider for the blog with this dialog.)

7. On the next dialog, select Drupal as your system type, as shown in Figure 12.6. You normally can leave the API URL as it is: your site name followed by /xmlrpc.php.

8. The next dialog asks for your Drupal username and password. Enter them and click Continue.

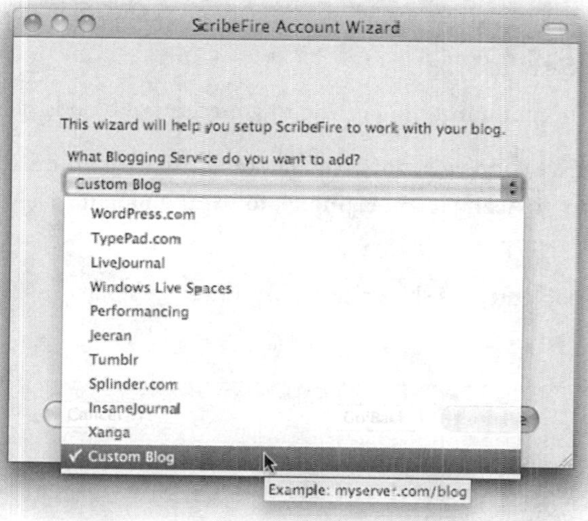

FIGURE 12.5
Select your blogging service.

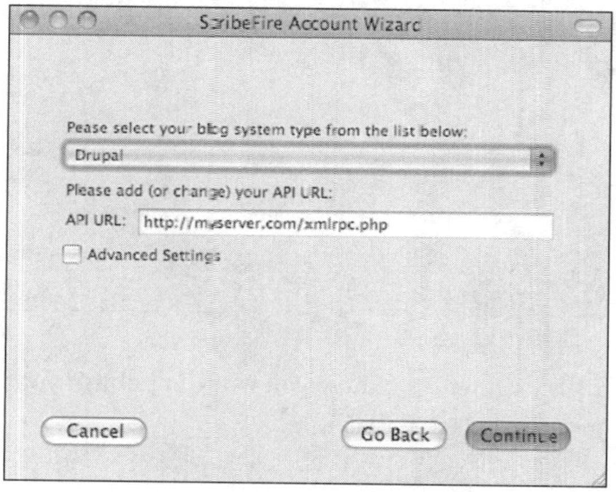

FIGURE 12.6
Select your system type.

9. If the log in is successful, you receive a confirmation, as shown in Figure 12.7. If it is OK, click Continue. If it is not OK, click Go Back and try again.

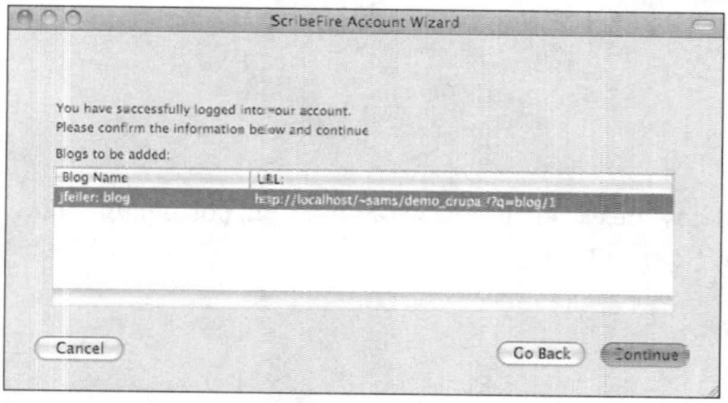

FIGURE 12.7
ScribeFire connects to your blog.

▼   **Try It Yourself**

Posting from ScribeFire

After you set up the configuration, posting to your Drupal blog is simple:

1. If the ScribeFire window is not open, choose ScribeFire from the Firefox Tools menu. If you are using a smart phone, touch the Blog (or New Blog) button in your blogging app.

2. Type your blog entry, as shown in Figure 12.8.

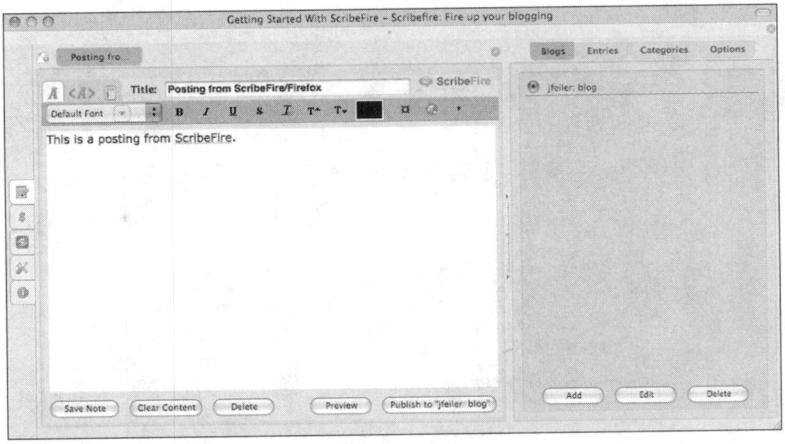

FIGURE 12.8
Type in your post.

3. You may be asked for details of how you want to publish your posting, as shown in Figure 12.9. Click Publish.

FIGURE 12.9
Select your posting options.

4. You (and anyone else) can now view your blog posting on your Drupal site, as shown in Figure 12.10.

▼

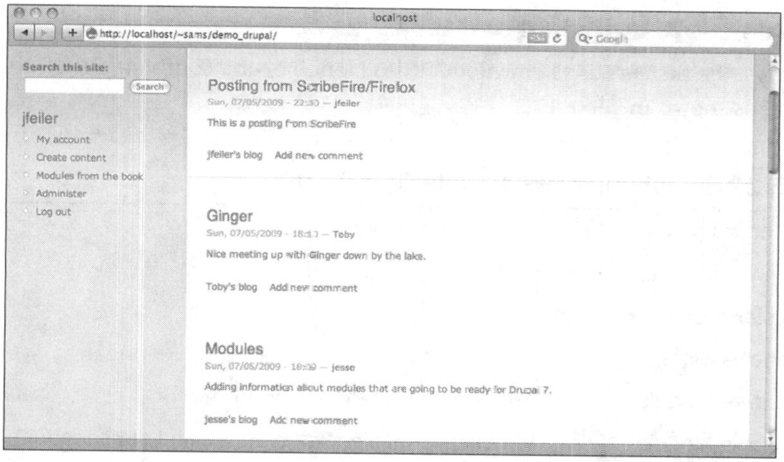

FIGURE 12.10
View your post in Drupal.

Creating Newsletters with Simplenews

Do not let the word newsletter mislead you: A *newsletter* in the Simplenews sense, is an email message sent to a list of people (the *subscribers*). A newsletter can be a one-sentence message reminding people of an upcoming event. It can also be a pages-long message with various topics covered. Also, if you add the MimeMail contributed module, a Simplenews newsletter can include styled text and images.

People can subscribe to RSS feeds for blogs and other pages on Drupal, but newsletters represent a different type of communicating (generally referred to as *push*). Simplenews is a contributed module that makes newsletters easy to produce and manage.

There are three major components to Simplenews:

▶ **Setup**—You do this once (with occasional updates) to configure your newsletter environment.

▶ **Managing subscriptions**—This process lets people sign up or cancel their subscriptions. From your point of view, it is a mostly invisible process—it is highly automated, and the work involved in signing up or canceling a subscription is done by end users.

▶ **Managing newsletters**—A newsletter is a single mailing to subscribers. Simplenews lets you create new newsletters (they are a content type); you can also review old newsletters and newsletters that are pending.

Setting Up Simplenews

As always, the first step is to download, install, enable, and configure the Simplenews module, as shown in Table 12.3.

TABLE 12.3 Simplenews Module Reference

Download from	project/simplenews
Enable in section	Mail
Permissions	
Simplenews Module	Subscribe to newsletters (for recipients)
Simplenews Module	Send newsletter (for authors)
Simplenews Module	Administer Simplenews settings and subscriptions
Simplenews Module	Administer newsletters
Administration	
Administer, Site Configuration, Simplenews (admin/settings/simplenews)	

Begin with Administer, Site Configuration, Simplenews (admin/settings/simplenews), as shown in Figure 12.11.

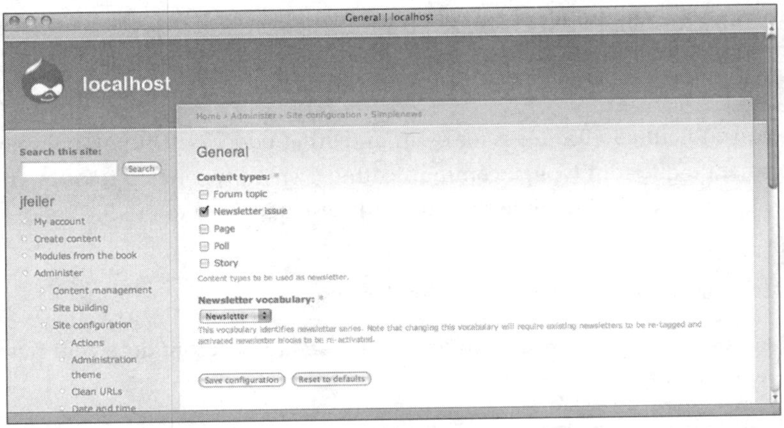

FIGURE 12.11
Configure general settings.

These settings apply to all newsletter issues. Because Simplenews relies on the Taxonomy module, it needs its own vocabulary, which it manages. Changing the vocabulary can cause problems with Simplenews.

Also, as shown in Figure 12.11, Simplenews can send nodes of various types as newsletters. Blog, stories, and polls, for example, can all be sent as newsletters.

Bear in mind that Simplenews uses this terminology:

▶ **Newsletter**—This is a newsletter that is sent out occasionally. People can subscribe to it. It may have a name such as "Latest News" or "Recent Events." You can have as many newsletters as you want.

▶ **Newsletter issue**—This is one issue of a newsletter, the February issue, for example.

You use Create Content to create and send newsletters.

The next set of settings is the default newsletter settings shown in Figure 12.12. These are defaults for all the newsletters that you will be creating. Here is where you can set the default content type (Mime Mail must be installed to use it) and the priority. Perhaps most useful is the default settings for sending a newsletter; sending a test newsletter is a good choice.

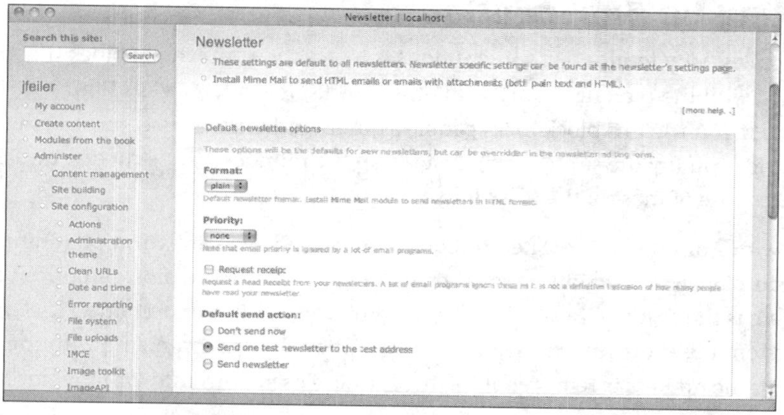

FIGURE 12.12
Set defaults for newsletters.

Further down the page are the settings for test accounts (separate the addresses with commas). You also provide default return addresses, as shown in Figure 12.13.

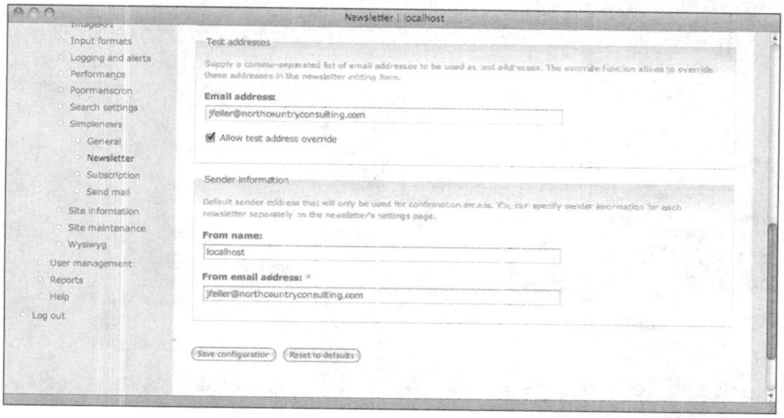

FIGURE 12.13
Set default for test addresses and return addresses.

> **Do Not Send Spam**
>
> In general, newsletters are considered unsolicited commercial email (UCE), more commonly known as spam if it is not desired. The laws make it clear what unsolicited means in each case. For example, for a period of time after someone has transacted business with you (even if that is only a query), you can follow up with email that is considered solicited as a result of the transaction. Simplenews makes it easy for people to sign up for subscriptions, and that is obviously a form of solicitation for email. However, you must quickly honor unsubscribe requests; if you do not, you may be accused of sending unsolicited commercial email. Some people believe that these laws do not apply to nonprofit organizations. In the United States, that is not true. The laws come into force based on the content of the email, not on the status of the organization sending the email. For further information in the United States, visit the Federal Trade Commission site at www.ftc.gov.

Setting Up Subscriptions

The simplest way to manage subscriptions is to use the Simplenews block that is installed with the module. Along with other blocks, it is discussed in Hour 19, "Using Blocks." If you use this block to let people sign up and unsubscribe, most of the work is done for you (by the subscribers). Just set up the management structure and Drupal takes care of most of the work for you.

Begin with Administration, Site Configuration, Simplenews Subscription (admin/settings/simplenews/subscription), as shown in Figure 12.14. The most important setting here is the first one to synchronize subscriptions with user accounts. The email address on a user account is used for a subscription; by synchronizing with the user account, the address is removed if the account is closed. This may or may not be the behavior you want.

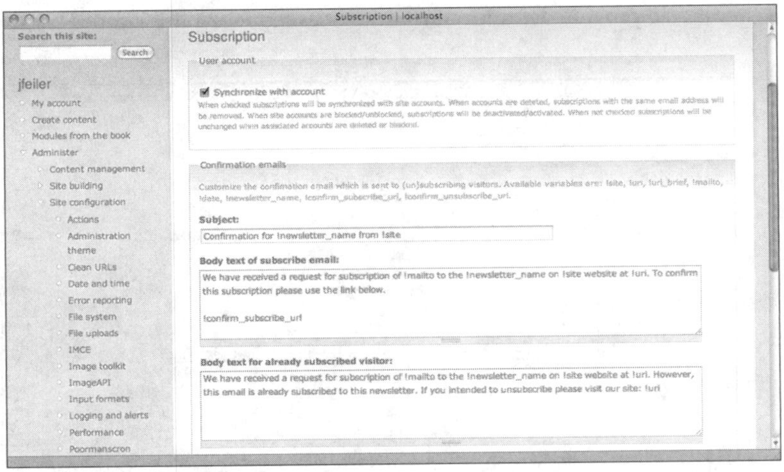

FIGURE 12.14
Set defaults for subscriptions.

Further down the page are fields of text with placeholders for usernames and the like. You can configure these for customized email messages confirming subscriptions and unsubscribing as you see in Figure 12.15. As with the customizing of the user registration emails, it pays to take some time to review these. After you save the settings, Drupal takes care of everything for you. You do not want news subscribers to be welcomed to your "newslitter" or some other typographical error.

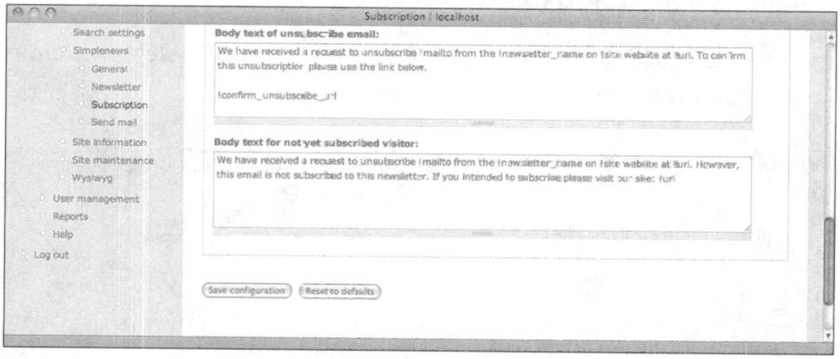

FIGURE 12.15
Set the email confirmation message texts.

The final group of settings in Administration, Site Configuration, SimpleNews, Send Mail (admin/settings/simplenews/mail) is shown in Figure 12.16. This configures how Simplenews will send the message.

Sending newsletters is a perfect job for cron. Use these settings to configure how many messages are sent at a time. (Test messages are sent immediately without going through cron.)

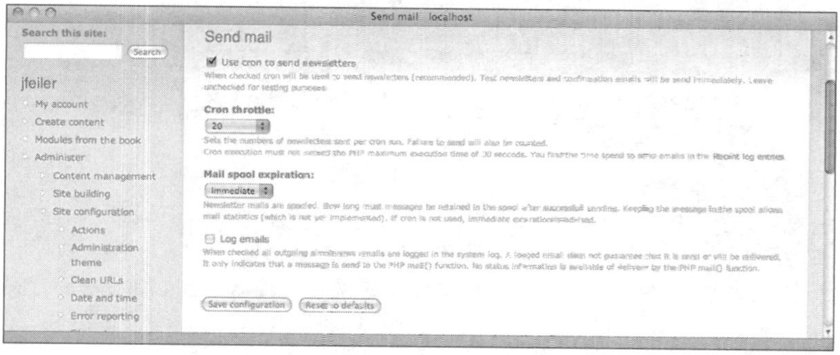

FIGURE 12.16
Configure sending mail.

The Poormanscron module can be used if you do not have access to cron on your web server. In most cases, it is a satisfactory replacement. However, be aware that it is not recommended for sending newsletters with Simplenews. It can send duplicate messages. If you cannot gain access to cron on your own server, investigate other servers and other possibilities.

Creating and Sending Newsletters and Newsletter Issues

Now that you have set up Simplenews, you will want to create content: newsletters and newsletter issues.

To create a newsletter, select use Administer, Content Management, Newsletters, Newsletters to open the page shown in Figure 12.17.

In addition to the basic information, specify how plain-text newsletters handle hyperlinks, as shown in Figure 12.18.

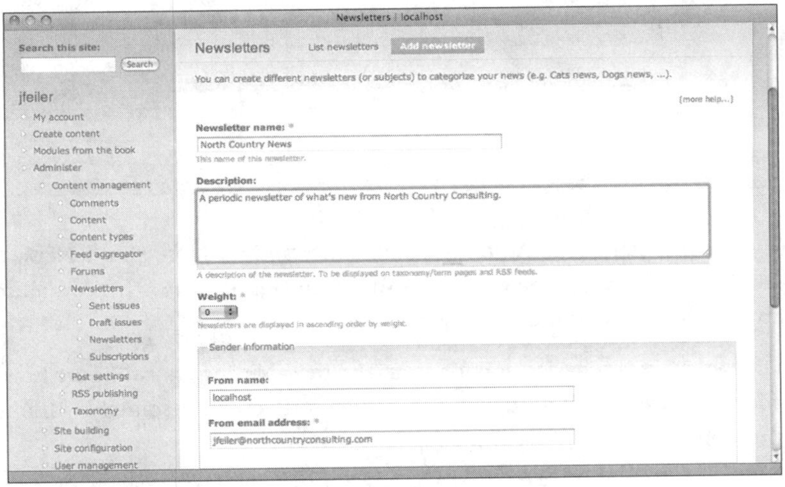

FIGURE 12.17
Create a
newsletter.

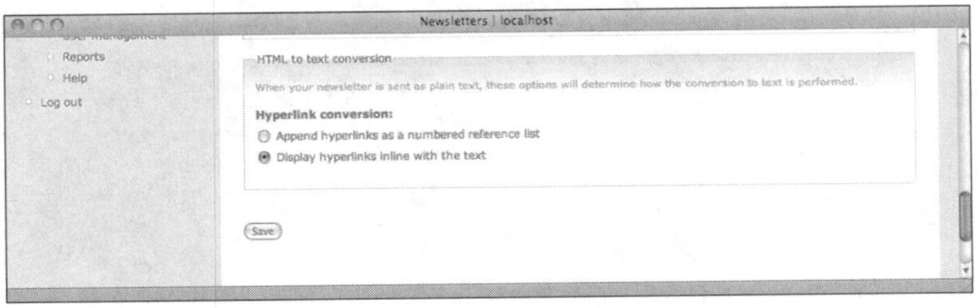

FIGURE 12.18
Set return
addresses for
the newsletter.

To create a newsletter issue, you use Create Content and choose Newsletter Issue. You must give it a title and select a newsletter of which it is part. (The newsletter determines the subscription list.) Add your content, as shown in Figure 12.19.

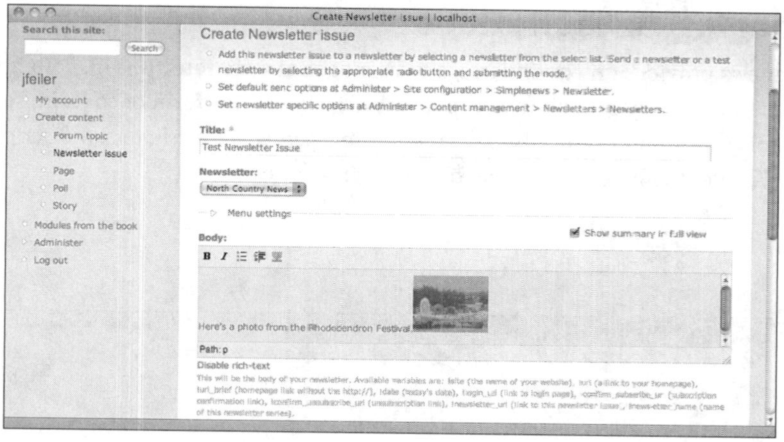

FIGURE 12.19
Create a
newsletter issue.

At the bottom of the page, you can send the newsletter issue or a test, as shown
in Figure 12.20. Remember that the test addresses were set in Administer, Site
Configuration, Simplenews, Newsletter (admin/settings/simplenews/newsletter) and
were possibly overridden in Administer, Content Management, Newsletters,
Newsletters (admin/content/simplenews/types) as described previously.

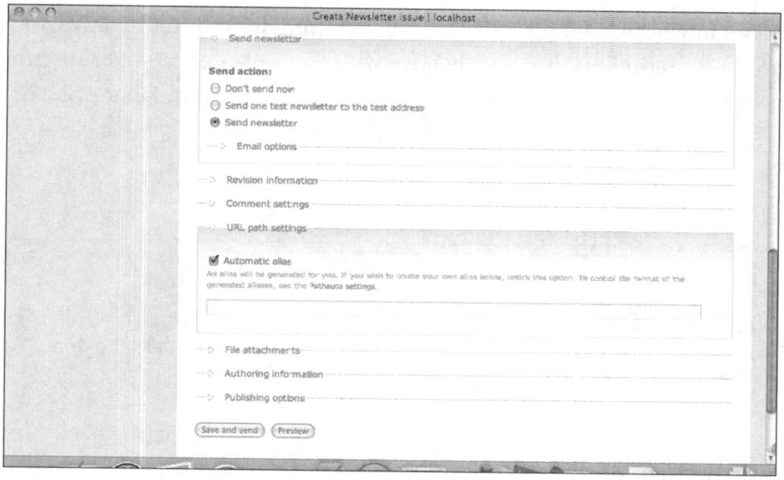

FIGURE 12.20
Create a
newsletter.

Managing Subscriptions

Simplenews provides an easy interface to manage subscriptions. It is like other interfaces you have seen throughout Drupal. Subscriptions are a form of content, so they are managed through Administer, Content Management, Newsletters, Subscriptions (admin/content/simplenews/users), as shown in Figure 12.21.

FIGURE 12.21
Administer sub-scriptions.

You select the subscriptions you want to manage, click the check boxes, and then select an action to be applied to the chosen subscriptions.

Simplenews integrates well into the Drupal environment so that not only can you manage the subscriptions that people have with your newsletters, but subscriptions are shown to individuals on the My Account pages, as shown in Figure 12.22.

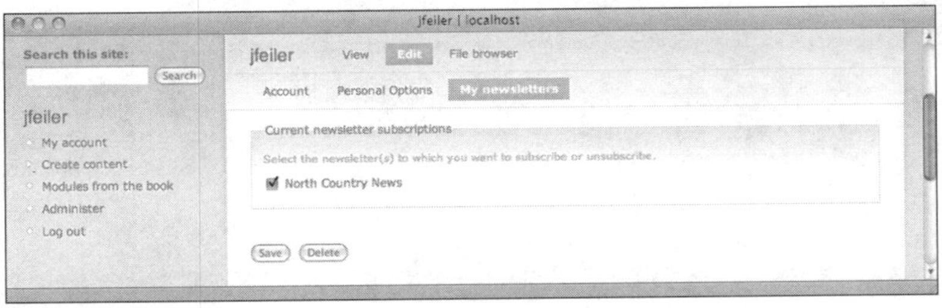

FIGURE 12.22
Individuals can see their sub-scriptions.

Summary

Blogs are remarkably efficient communication tools. Creating a blog posting is a simple process—made even simpler with Drupal's Blog API module so that you can create a Drupal blog posting from a smart phone or a browser's plug-in. Users can subscribe to blogs to get the latest and greatest news.

You can also use the contributed Simplenews module to push information to users. Simplenews lets users subscribe and unsubscribe to any number of newsletters. After you set up Simplenews, everything is taken care of for you—subscriptions, unsubscribing, and even mass imports and exports.

Q&A

Q. *Is there guidance on what types of information belong in blogs and what types belong in newsletters?*

A. You can construct summary newsletters and summary blog postings. One strategy is to have a summary newsletter that contains summaries of recent blog postings and a separate newsletter for full text. It is not a great deal more effort, but it allows end users to be in control.

Q. *What are the privacy rules for mailing lists?*

A. They vary from country to country. In the United States, consult the Federal Trade Commission's site at www.ftc.gov. Best practices include a clear statement on your website of how you will use information that users provide. In addition, for unsolicited email, an opt-out link in each message is a good idea and may even be a legal requirement. In addition to the power of the law, if you send out messages that are considered spam, many ISPs will block your mail in the future.

Workshop

Quiz

1. How many newsletters can I have?

2. What is the benefit of allowing Blog API postings?

3. How does Simplenews send newsletter issues?

Quiz Answers

1. There is no real limit except for the amount of effort required to write them.

2. You can get fast, on-the-spot postings from smart phones.

3. It uses cron. Poormanscron is reported to have sending problems, so be careful with it.

Activities

The decisions on blogs and newsletters are not technical: Involve your users in the choices. As is often the case with Drupal, plan for how you will handle large volumes of transactions. From the point of view of your Drupal system, whether you have one newsletter or 50 does not matter. Knowing that you can manage such large quantities of communication is reassuring, but begin by setting up blogs and newsletters on a scale that you and your colleagues can manage. People who subscribe to a monthly newsletter that appears twice a year are likely not to form a positive impression.

You might want to think about an alternative meaning for CMS: Communication Management System. Drupal and its tools help you think about content in action rather than just sitting in a database.

HOUR 13

Creating Contact Forms and Webforms

What You'll Learn in This Hour:

▶ Use Personal Contact Forms

▶ Create and Manage Webforms

▶ Use Webform Components

▶ Analyze and Export Webform Data

Introduction

This hour continues to explore the socializing and communicating tools of Drupal. You have seen how to communicate to your end users with newsletters and blogs. You have also seen how end users can communicate to the world at large, or at least your Drupal-based site's part of it, using comments and forum discussions. Now, the emphasis is on inbound communications—messages to you from your end users.

These inbound communications are basically one-to-one communications. For example, a user sends a message to you. Although it is fundamentally a one-to-one conversation, the message may automatically be routed to more than one email address (perhaps a webmaster and a coordinator). Likewise, when you place a webform on your website and users fill it out, each submission is basically a one-to-one message, even if thousands of your website users take the opportunity to submit their own forms.

You can post an email address for comments or questions on your site, but forms are more practical. By designing them carefully, you can collect the information that you will need to properly handle the input from your end users.

Drupal supports two types of forms:

► The Contact module (part of core) lets you set up contact forms. These can be used to contact individual users through their accounts; you can also configure them to be delivered based on a category (Contact Jesse, Ask a Question, and so forth). In both cases, the underlying email addresses are not shown to the end user who is submitting the form.

► Contributed modules, such as Webform, allow you to construct forms for your users to submit.

GO TO ►
Anytime you allow forms to be submitted, you may get some garbage submissions generated by spambots. This can particularly be a problem if you allow anonymous users to submit forms. For information on using CAPTCHA to prevent this, see **HOUR 17**, **"BUILDING YOUR FIRST LIVE SITE,"** p. 303.

Note that both of these types of forms allow users to contact you; you can specify form fields that they can (or must) fill in. Information about the form submission is stored in the database, but the form data is not stored in nodes.

Using the Contact Form

Contact forms are created with the Contact module that is part of Drupal core. Enable it and set permissions, as shown in Table 13.1. The Contact module is used both for personal contact forms (that is, contacting a user) and for sitewide contacts to sections of the site.

TABLE 13.1   Contact Module Reference

Download from	Core
Enable in section *Drupal 7 Status*	Core—optional (Drupal 6)/Core (Drupal 7)
Core	
Permissions	
Contact Module	Access sitewide contact form
Contact Module	Administer sitewide contact form
User Module	Access user profiles

TABLE 13.1   Continued

Administration

Administer, Site Building, Contact Form (D6: admin/build/contact D7: admin/structure/contact)	List
Administer, Site Building, Contact Form (D6: admin/build/contact/add D7: admin/structure/contact/add)	Add Category
Administer, Site Building, Contact Form (D6:admin/build/contact/settings D7: admin/settings/contact)	Settings

Working with Personal Contact Forms

The personal contact form is available from a user's account page. In addition to having the Contact module enabled, the person sending the form needs permission to access user profiles. The recipient also has to have enabled the personal contact form so that others can use it to contact them

Figure 13.1 shows a user account with the personal contact form enabled.

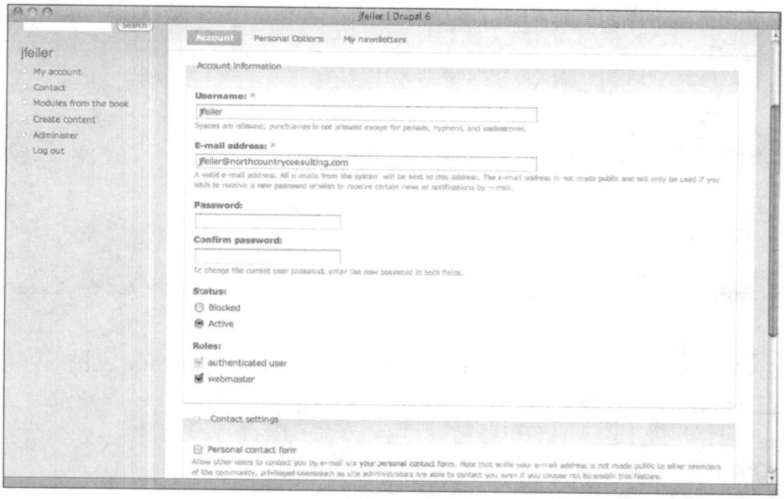

FIGURE 13.1
Enable the personal contact form.

You can make the process a little easier by setting the personal contact form to be enabled by default for all new users, as shown in Figure 13.2. Note that in Drupal 6, this is available from Administer, Site Building, Contact Form, Settings, whereas in Drupal 7, this is available in Administer, Site Configuration, Contact Form (D6:admin/build/contact/settings D7: admin/settings/contact).

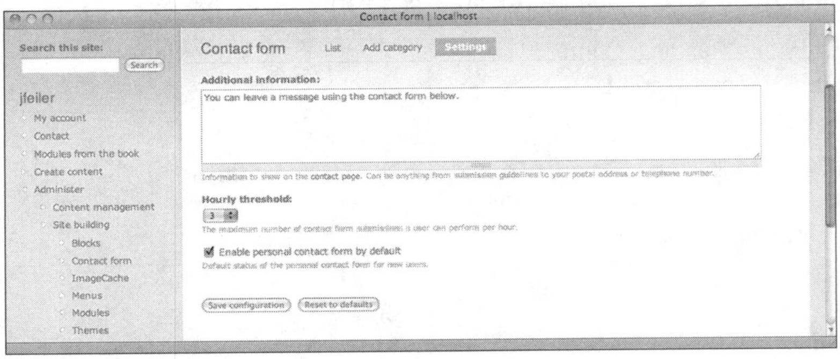

FIGURE 13.2
Enable the personal contact form by default for new users.

Try It Yourself

Contact a User with a Personal Contact Form

Assuming that the personal contact form is set up for the user you want to contact as described in the previous section, here is how you actually contact that user:

1. Go to the account page for the user you want to contact. The easiest way to do that is to use the Search box to find the user, as shown in Figure 13.3. You will need permission to search content and permission to access user profiles to do this.

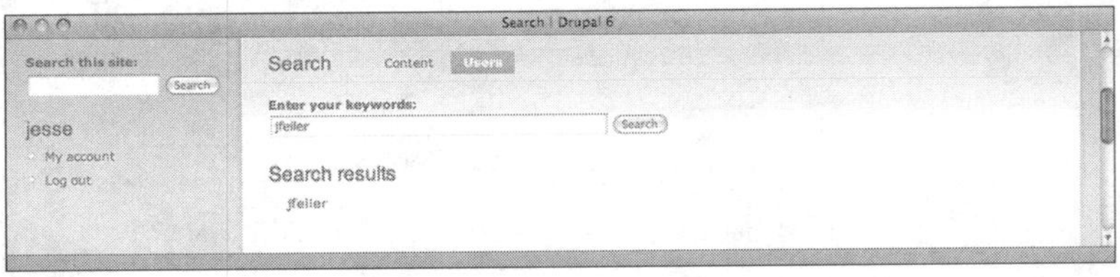

FIGURE 13.3
Search for a user.

2. Click Contact on the user's account page to open the personal contact form, as shown in Figure 13.4.

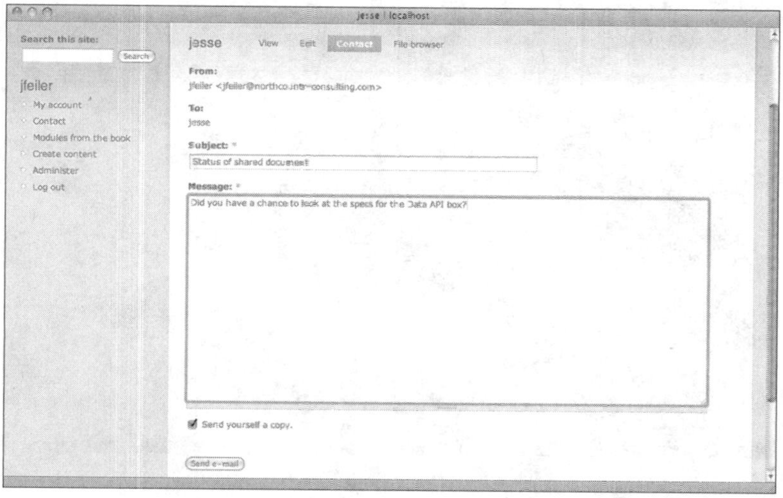

FIGURE 13.4
Contact a user.

Working with the Sitewide Contact Form

Drupal supports a sitewide contact form; it is shown in Figure 13.5. Its key is a category that identifies how the contact form should be routed. As with personal contact forms, recipient email addresses are not visible to the sender.

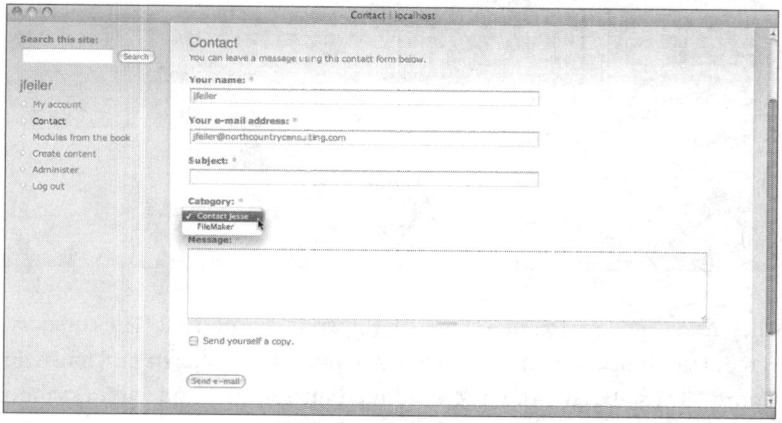

FIGURE 13.5
Use the sitewide contact form.

When you enable the Contact module, a Contact menu item is added to the Navigation menu, but it is disabled. Normally, you want to enable it right away, as shown in Figure 13.6. The only circumstance in which you would not want to do so is if you have an interface that eschews menus and relies solely on links and buttons.

FIGURE 13.6
Enable the Con-
tact menu item.

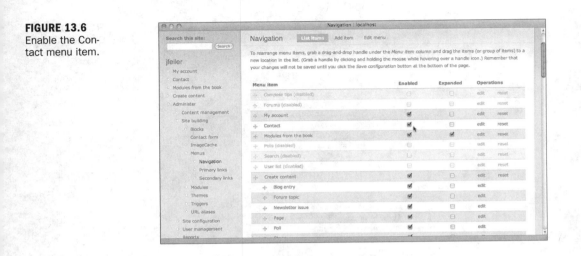

▼   **Try It Yourself**

Creating a New Category for a Sitewide Contact Form

The sitewide contact form is available after the Contact module is enabled. For end
users to be able to access it, you must add one or more categories to it:

1. Go to Administer, Site Building, Contact Form as shown in Figure 13.7 (D6:
admin/build/contact D7: admin/structure/contact).

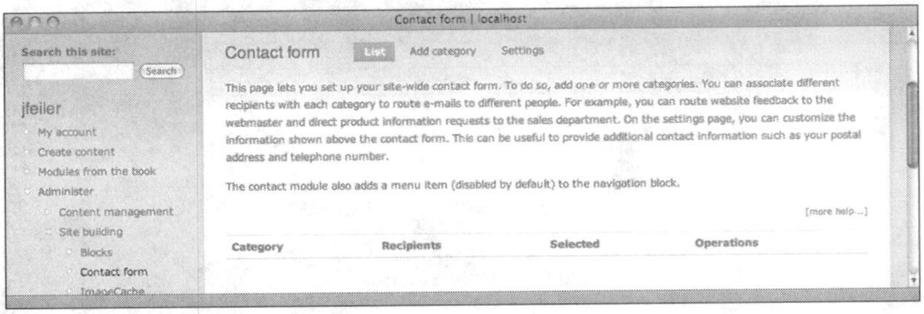

FIGURE 13.7
Administer con-
tact forms.

2. Click Add Category to open the page shown in Figure 13.8. The category name
is required. It appears in the Category pop-up menu shown previously in
Figure 13.5, so be sure that the wording, punctuation, and capitalization is
what you want to be shown to the user. (Note that the Category pop-up menu
only appears if there is more than one category. There is no reason to display it
if you only have one category.)

▼

3. Provide the email addresses to which the form submissions for this category should be routed. Separate multiple addresses with commas.

4. Although an auto-reply message is not required, it is a good idea to provide one to let the user know that the form has been submitted.

5. Indicate whether this category should be selected by default in the pop-up menu.

6. When you save the category, you return to the contact form administration page, as shown in Figure 13.9. In the future, you will be able to edit or delete each of the categories.

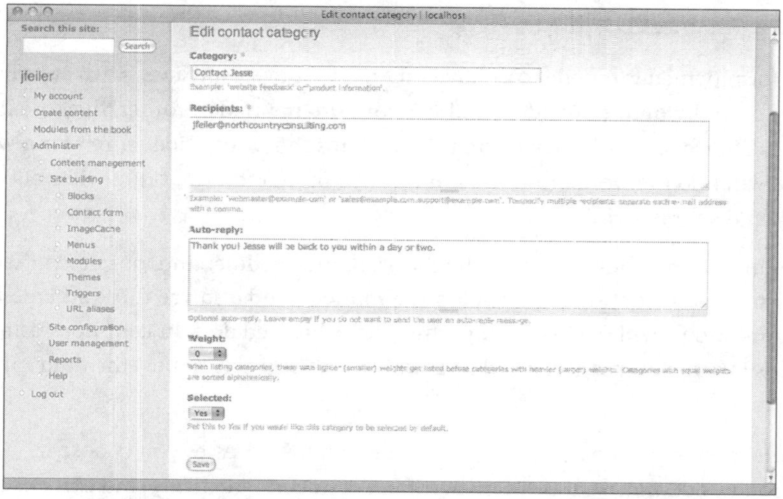

FIGURE 13.8
Add the category for the form.

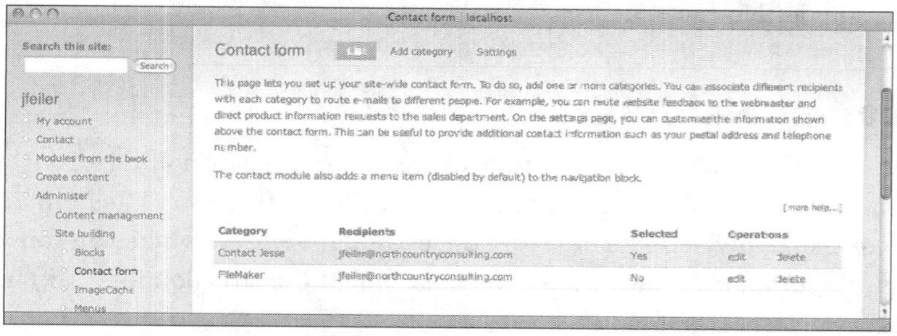

FIGURE 13.9
The category is added to the contact form list.

Using Webforms

Personal and sitewide contact forms provide a simple way to allow end users to communicate with you or with other end users. The contributed Webform module implements a more general webform.

Contact forms are their own type of database entity (they are stored in a table called `contact`), but webforms are true nodes. This means that they have titles, a body, and they conform to all the conventions of nodes. A webform can be published or not; it can be promoted to the front page; and it can be sticky in lists in which it appears. This last point is particularly useful in building webforms: By publishing them, promoting them to the front page, and making them sticky, you have a webform that can be made available to end users without further action on your part.

Also, in common with all other nodes, webforms can have comments enabled. This is often a feature you want to turn off. If you allow comments on webforms, you can wind up with webform information that should be submitted on forms that is submitted in comments.

A webform (which is a node) can have any number of *submissions*. Each submission is from an individual respondent. Submissions are not nodes; rather, they are linked to the webform to which they belong. This means that a sitewide search for a word or phrase will find the word or phrase if it appears on a webform, but it will not be found on a submission.

Managing submissions is handled by the Webform module, and, as you will see in this section, you can use variety of tools to manage and analyze those submissions. Webform also provides tools for exporting the submitted data in common formats (such as tab- or comma-delimited formats) so that you can import the data into other applications.

You can specify that webforms are sent via email to addresses you choose in advance. In addition, you can view webform results interactively and can export them in standard formats.

Exploring Webforms

Webforms can have a variety of input fields, as you can see in Figure 13.10. This webform will serve as the example that is constructed in this hour. The form and its fields look like many Drupal data entry pages, and the way in which you construct them is also familiar. However, these are not Content Construction Kit (CCK) fields. These are webform *components*.

There are four types of components:

▶ **Data entry components**—These are standard form and data entry fields: date, textarea, textfield, and time. The *select* component implements radio buttons, a menu, and check boxes, just as its comparable HTML element does. The *hidden* component is a standard HTML-type field that is not visible to the user.

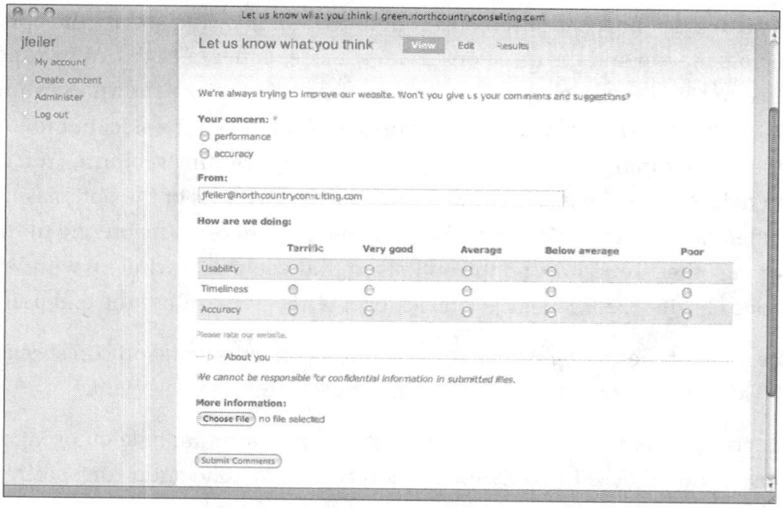

FIGURE 13.10
Use webforms to
collect data.

▶ **Webform formatting components**—These let you format the form that you are constructing. Pagebreak splits the form at the place where you place it; markup provides some HTML that is displayed but not submitted as part of the form. (Both are shown in the following section.) The fieldset component lets you group components together for an improved user interface. It, too, is not submitted, although the components within it are submitted.

▶ **File**—This allows submission of a file from the end user's computer.

▶ **Email**—This field is automatically set to the email address of the end user; its value is submitted.

As you will see in the following section, an individual webform can implement some dynamic processing so that, for example, the address to which it will be sent can vary depending on a select component.

The components shown in Figure 13.10 look like any webform, and that is what they are. Here are the webform names and options that you see in Figure 13.10.

▶ Your concern is a select component, and it is required (note the asterisk). A select component can be allowed to have multiple selections; if it does not have that option enabled, it is rendered as a set of radio buttons.

▶ From is an email component that is set to the end user's email address as a default value. Although you cannot see from Figure 13.10, this field has been marked as not changeable so that the only way to not submit the email address is to not submit the form at all.

▶ How are we doing is a webform component—a *grid*. You specify the options across the top and the questions down the side. Either or both can be randomized to try to reduce survey bias. In a case such as the one shown in Figure 13.10, it makes sense to randomize the questions down the side, but to leave the options in the same order for every user who sees the webform. (You can try to reduce survey bias somewhat by having two versions of the options on two different webforms, with better being at the right in one version and at the left in the other. Randomizing the options so that you might wind up with Very good, Terrific, Poor, Average, and so forth is likely to confuse the end users.)

▶ We cannot be responsible... is a markup component. You can specify HTML markup with text and elements, such as the <em> element.

▶ More information is a file component. The Webform module automatically inserts the Choose File button and manages the upload. (You can specify the allowed file types and maximum size, as you will see.)

▶ Submit Comments is a standard Submit button; the Webform module lets you customize the text, or you can leave it as *Submit*.

Figure 13.11 shows the About You section of the webform expanded. (You can specify the initial state and whether the end user can collapse or expand the section.) Industry is another select component that allows multiple choices. This time, instead of check boxes it uses a list box; What do you do uses check boxes for its multiple choices.

Finally, the Comments component is a text field.

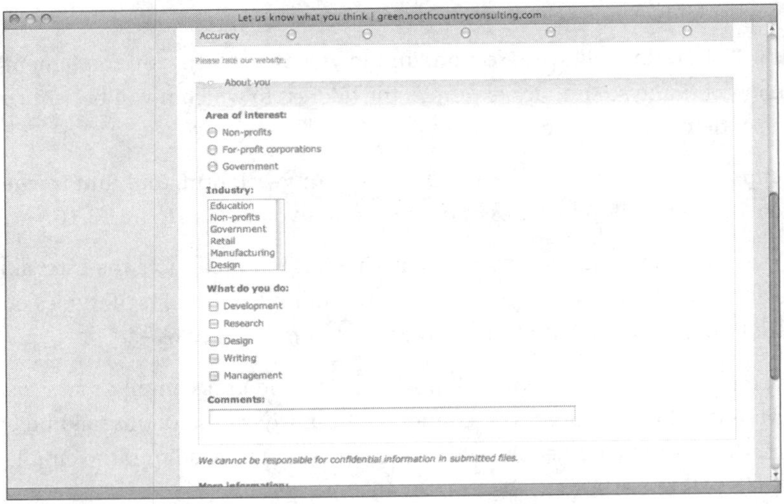

FIGURE 13.11
Webform fieldsets can be collapsed or expanded.

Getting Started with Webforms

As is often the case, the first step is to download, install, and enable the relevant module—in this case, the Webform module, as shown in Table 13.2.

After you install the Webform module, you can configure the global Webform settings and then move on to create and manage your own webforms.

TABLE 13.2 Webform Module Reference

Download from	project/webform
Enable in section	Other
Drupal 7 Status	
D7CX	
Permissions	
Webform Module	Access, edit own webforms
Webform Module	Edit own webforms
Webform Module	Create, edit own webforms
Webform Module	Access, clear webform results
Administration	
Administer, Content Management, Webforms (admin/content/webform)	Individual webforms
Administer, Site Configuration, Webform (admin/settings/webform)	Global webform settings

---

Start with Default Values

You can always come back to configure the global settings. The default values are usually fine to start out with.

Configuring Global Webform Settings

Begin the configuration at Administration, Site Configuration, Webform (admin/settings/webform), as shown in Figure 13.12.

The first section of the configuration settings lets you choose which components are available to your webforms. If you disable a component here, you will not be able to add it to the new webforms that you create. The default setting is to enable all the components.

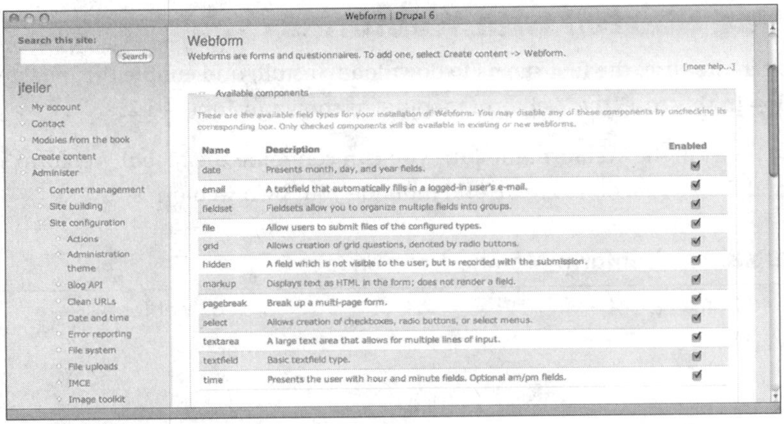

FIGURE 13.12
Set available
components.

The default email values, shown in Figure 13.13, can save time when you create web-forms. If you normally use the same email values for a number of forms (perhaps even all of them), enter those values here and skip the individual webform data entry fields.

Finally, the advanced settings shown in Figure 13.14 let you configure defaults that apply to all webforms unless they are changed. Usually, the settings that are installed with the Webform module can be used without changes.

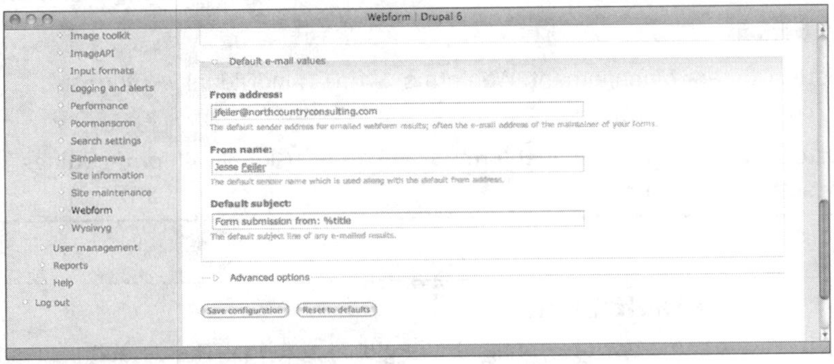

FIGURE 13.13
Set default email
values.

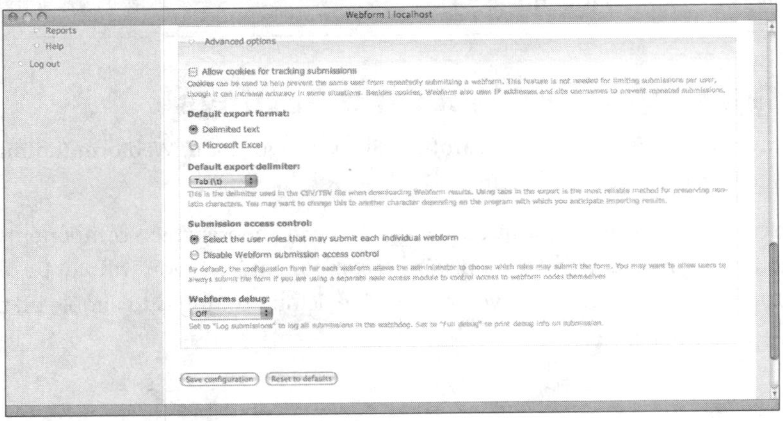

FIGURE 13.14
Configure
advanced set-
tings.

Creating a Webform

With your global default webform settings configured, you are ready to create your own webforms. The first step is to decide what you want to collect on the webform. The possibilities for using webforms are almost endless, but most of them fall into these broad categories:

▶ **Requests for information**—These typically let end users choose among various topics of interest. In many cases, you can fill in the email address of the end user, possibly allowing it to be changed to another address. You can use text fields to collect a street address.

▶ **Surveys and questionnaires**—Drupal polls are great ways to get an informal reading of opinions on a single question; webforms let you conduct more complex research. The fact that you can easily export the data for further analysis makes them an ideal tool. These webforms may not be sent automatically to email addresses; rather, you can download the results for analysis.

▶ **E-commerce orders**—The Ubercart module (described in Hour 16, "Building an E-Commerce Solution") is a more robust choice, but if your needs are very simple, a webform may serve.

▶ **Support and assistance**—Using the feature that allows a file to be sent with the webform, you can easily provide support to end users.

▶ **User management**—If you have several roles on your site, end users can request that they be moved to another role with a webform. For example, you can let people register for accounts using Drupal's standard registration process, which includes verification of their email. If some of the end users qualify for status as a moderator, a supervisor, a member, or some other specific role in your organization, they can request that role change using a webform.

Test Your Webform

Whenever you are creating a form, try it out on people as you develop it.

Did you Know?

Try It Yourself ▼

Creating a Webform

Creating a webform falls into two tasks. First, you create the webform itself and configure it with a title and other attributes. Then, you create and edit form components.

▼

You can always switch back and forth between these two tasks, but the basic creation task has to come first:

1. Create a new webform using the Create Content command in the menu. This opens the page shown in Figure 13.15. As with all nodes, you must provide a title (Remember that the webform itself is a node; the submissions from end users are linked to the node.) Although you do not have to provide the description and the confirmation message now, it is a good idea to do so before you forget.

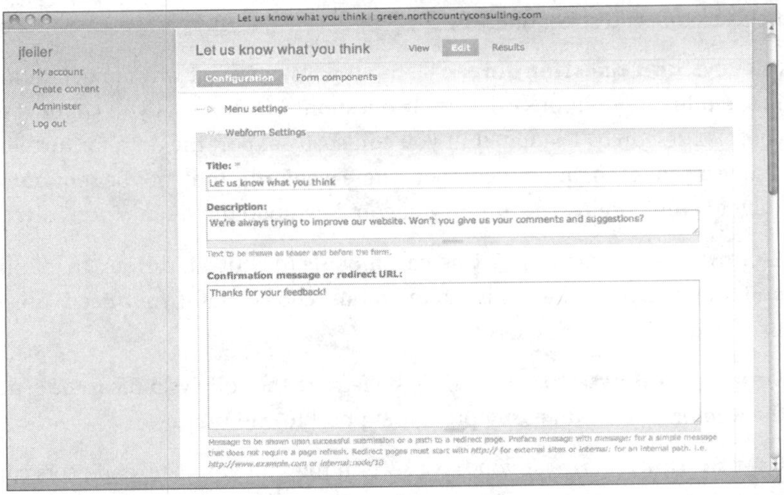
Let us know what you think | green.northcountryconsulting.com
jfeiler
My account
Create content
Administer
Log out
Let us know what you think
View
Edit
Results
Configuration
Form components
Menu settings
Webform Settings
Title:
Let us know what you think
Description:
We're always trying to improve our website. Won't you give us your comments and suggestions?
Confirmation message or redirect URL:
Thanks for your feedback!

FIGURE 13.15
Create a new webform.

2. Further down the page, you specify the access control for the webform, as shown in Figure 13.16. In many cases, you do not want to allow anonymous users to submit the webform. The exception might be in a "send me information" form, where you want to cast the widest possible net for prospective customers or clients.

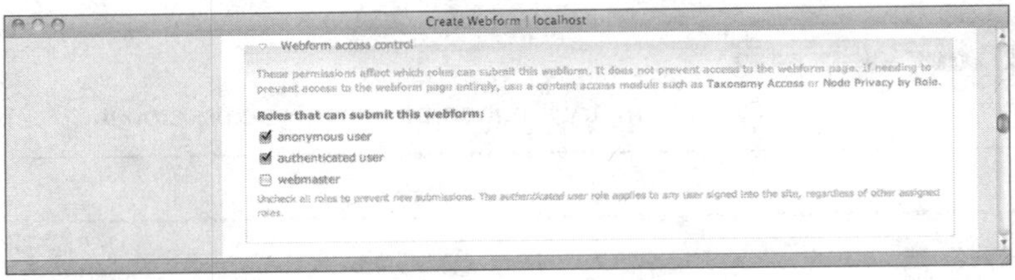
Create Webform | localhost
Webform access control
Roles that can submit this webform:
anonymous user
authenticated user
webmaster

FIGURE 13.16
Set access to the webform.

3. Configure the webform email settings further down the page, as shown in Figure 13.17. You can use the default values, or you can type in custom values. After you create components, you can use them for email settings. For example,

you can create a field into which end users can type the subject of their query and then use that field's contents as the email subject.

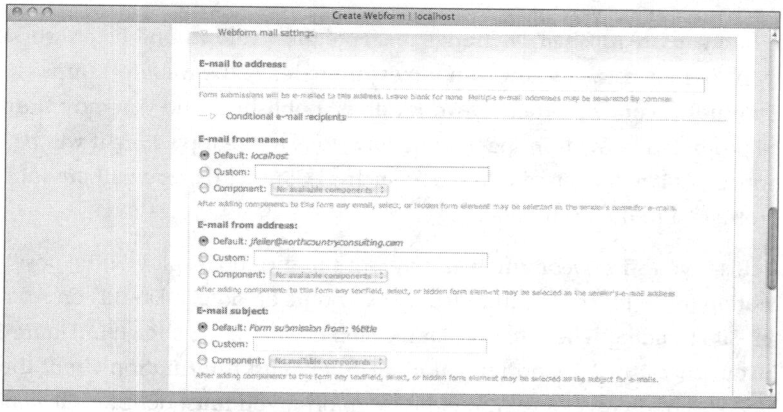

FIGURE 13.17
Configure email settings.

4. The advanced settings, shown in Figure 13.18, let you enter PHP code for additional validation (but as always, be careful with adding PHP code). The most common settings you need to consider are the number of submissions and whether to rename the Submit button. Webform uses username and the IP address to check for duplicate submissions. (In the global configuration settings, you can also let it use cookies, but that option does not add a great deal of refinement to the existing username/IP address checking, so you are usually better off to leave the defalt settings.)

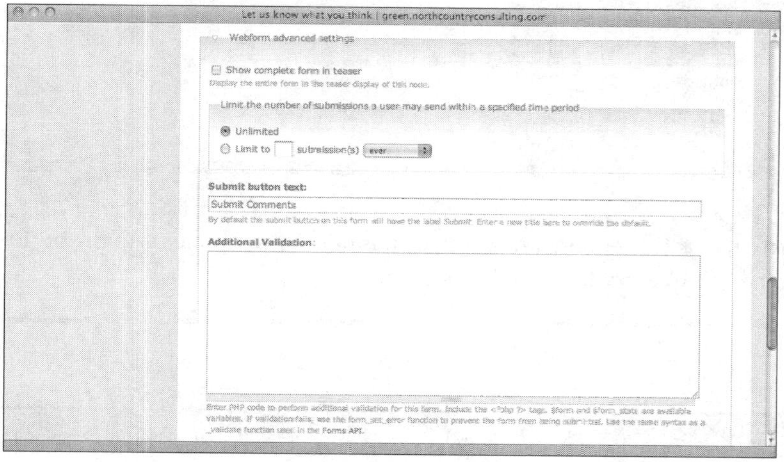

FIGURE 13.18
Configure advanced settings.

GO TO ▶
HOUR 19,
USING BLOCKS,
for more on
blocks.

5. Most of the time, you should disable comments for the webform. You want comments and other input to come in through the webform itself. (But, do make sure to have a free-format field where people can add their thoughts.)

6. When you are finished, click Save to create the webform and begin working with components. For now, you may want to leave the webform unpublished. Eventually, you will probably want it to be published, and you may want it to be promoted to the front page—possibly stuck to the top where it will be noticed. If it will be used in a block, such as Contact Us, you will probably not promote it to the front page.

7. If this is your first webform, you may want to turn off display of the post information for webforms ("submitted by username on date"). Do this on Administer, Site Building, Themes, Configure, Global Settings, as shown in Figure 13.19. Just uncheck the Webform box under Display Post Information On at the right. You cannot do this for an individual webform; you must do it for all webforms, but that is usually the correct choice.

FIGURE 13.19
Turn off post display.

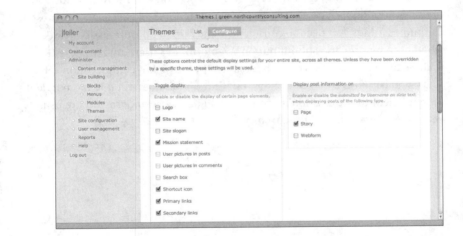

The second task in creating a new webform is adding components to the basic webform. These data entry fields make up the form.

Try It Yourself

Adding Webform Components

After you create a webform, you can add components. After you submit the webform configuration information, go the components page shown in Figure 13.20.

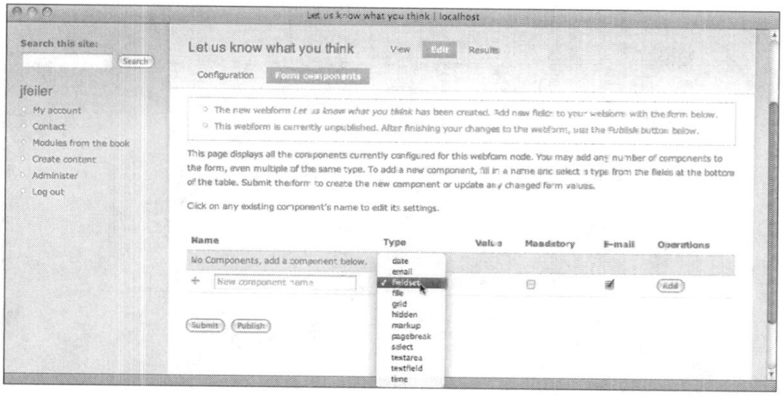

FIGURE 13.20
Begin to enter
components.

The process of adding a component is simple:

1. Enter the name of the new component, as shown in Figure 13.21.

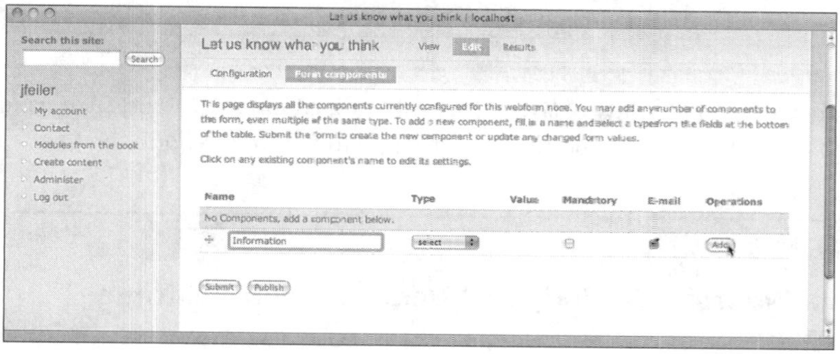

FIGURE 13.21
Create a new
component.

2. Select the component type from the list. After you add the component, you can change everything except the component type.

3. Click Add to add the component. If you click Submit before you add the component, you will lose the data you have just entered (the name and the component type).

4. All components are stored in the submissions table. In addition, you can automatically generate email messages with the submitted data. In the form components section, you can use the Advanced Setting area to include a specific component in the emails that are generated, as shown in Figure 13.22. The default setting is to include all components, but in the case of lengthy forms, you may want to make the email messages more compact.

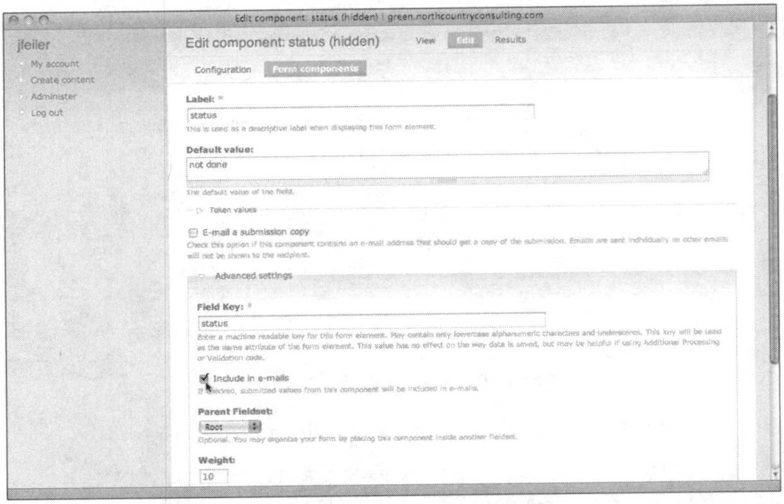

FIGURE 13.22
Include hidden
fields in email
messages if you
want.

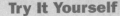

Webforms are an ideal way of structuring inbound communications, such as requests for help or information, suggestions for changes to the website, and the like.

Try It Yourself

Build a Webform for Help and Requests with Multiple Addressees

These forms are stored as submissions, but you usually also want to use the option to deliver them via email. If you have multiple addressees depending on an option, you can have the Webform module manage them. As always, the actual email addresses will not be visible to the end user.

1. Create a select component that lets users choose the subject of the webform; this determines the addressee. Make sure that the select component does not allow multiple selections. It should appear as an option button set like the Your Concern button set, shown previously in Figure 13.10.

2. In the Options field for the components, provide both the selection name and the email address, as shown in Figure 13.23. The email address comes first; it is followed by a pipe character (vertical line) and then by the selection option that will be visible to the end user. (Under some circumstances, the e-mail address can be discovered by savvy users.)

3. In the main configuration section, use Webform Mail Settings to configure the recipients, as shown in Figure 13.24. The Conditional Email Recipients fieldset

will let you choose the select element that you created in the first step. It also is a good idea to additionally send email to an account that is always monitored.

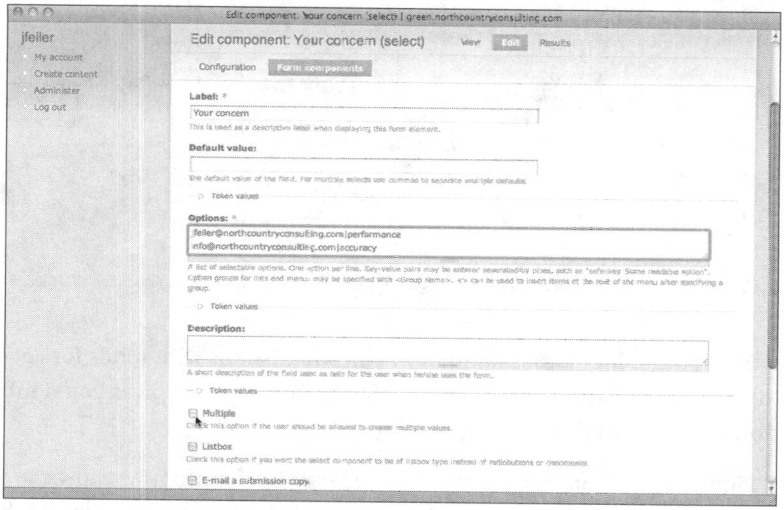

FIGURE 13.23
FIGURE 13.23
Create a select component containing the email address and the visible option for the end user.

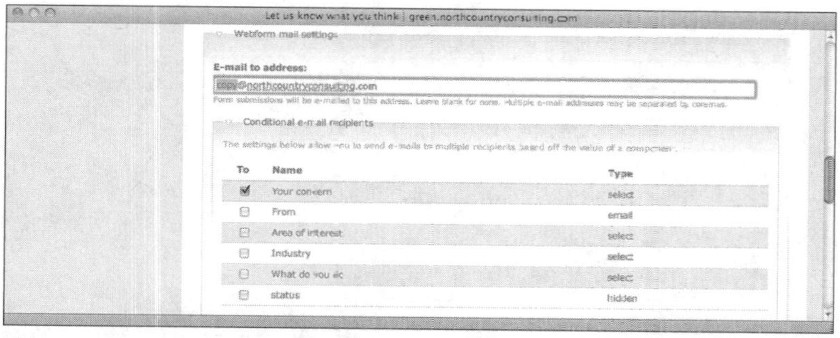

FIGURE 13.24
Use conditional email recipients.

4. If you want to monitor the status of requests, add a hidden component to the form (you can call it status). You can provide it with a default value of not done. When you export the data into a spreadsheet or database, that field will be exported; it will serve as a reminder to act on the request until you change its value in the spreadsheet or database to done or some other value.

Managing Webform Results

If webforms are automatically emailed to recipients, there may be no need for further analysis. However, the Webform module provides significant tools for such work.

You will find your webforms under Administer, Content Management, Webforms. When you go to a webform from Content Management or by going to the form with permission to edit it, you will find links to Submissions, Analysis, Table, and Download, as shown in Figure 13.25.

The Analysis button provides a summary of all submissions with totals for each choice as well as average length of text fields. The Table button gives you a tabular view of all submissions with one entry per line.

For any kind of serious analysis, you want the Download button. As shown in Figure 13.26, it exports the data in a format that you can then import into a spreadsheet or database program.

FIGURE 13.26
Download submissions for a single webform.

Summary

Forms are integral parts of most websites. They let you collect information from users in a structured fashion; you can even block submission of a form that is incomplete. Contact forms and webforms allow you to construct forms for the user to submit without revealing the email address to which they may be sent. In the case of webforms, in addition to sending them via email, you can review submitted data either in reports or by exporting that data to a spreadsheet or database.

Q&A

Q. *A user wants a guarantee of privacy and no unwanted messages. How do I do this?*

A. Anonymous users are private. Authenticated users generally have an email address that has been confirmed and that can be visible to administrators. They can turn off their personal contact form by editing their user account so that other users cannot contact them.

Q. *How can I test webform submissions? Every time I try, I am blocked because I have already submitted the form.*

A. First, allow unlimited form submissions in the configuration of the webform. Then, make sure you have permission to edit your own webform submissions (or all webform submissions). Go into the most recent submission, edit it, and then delete it. You are ready to resubmit it. A better solution is to have a set of three accounts for test: a webmaster account (that is a new role you can create, but it is a common one for many Drupal websites), an authenticated account, and, for emergencies, access to the primary user account. You should experiment from time to time with anonymous access to the site.

Workshop

Quiz

1. How many sitewide contact forms can you have in Drupal?

2. You can close a Drupal poll. How do you close a webform that some people may have bookmarked?

3. I want to use CCK widgets with webform components, but can't figure out how.

Quiz Answers

1. There is only a single site contact form. It allows for multiple categories, each of which can be routed to a different recipient.

2. Mark it as unpublished. Deleting it will delete the submissions. That is okay if you have downloaded them to a spreadsheet or database

3. Webform components are not CCK fields. You cannot use CCK widgets with them.

Activities

If you are planning a new database, start thinking about implementing feedback forms from the beginning. Think about the questions you want to ask users about their experiences on the site. If this is a group project, discuss the feedback form with your colleagues. As many people have discovered, the discussion of the feedback form can help you in the design of the site, so it is a good idea not to postpone the feedback form to the end of the project (after you may have implemented the site in an awkward way).

HOUR 14

Working with Views

What You'll Learn in This Hour:

- ▶ Explore Built-In Views for the Front Page
- ▶ Build Views for Database Queries
- ▶ Explore View Interfaces, Such as Pagers
- ▶ Let Users Control View Selections

Introduction

Drupal is built on the very stable and flexible base of a modern relational database (most frequently, it is MySQL, but others are also supported). Relational databases store, retrieve, and manipulate data with remarkable speed and efficiency. However, a challenge for the nearly half-century of database use has been how to make the creation and manipulation of database structures (*schemas*) accessible to nonprogrammer types. A companion challenge over the same span of decades has been how to make it easy for end users to construct queries and reports from these powerful data engines.

Along with other Content Management Systems (CMS), Drupal has been addressing these issues aggressively. The Content Construction Kit (CCK) in effect implements a mechanism that allows users to create fields in the database that support their content. (From the user's point of view, that is what happens; the reality is more complex and is not of concern to the user who is building a Drupal site.)

GO TO ▶
HOUR 7, "USING CONTENT CONSTRUCTION KIT (CCK) AND IMAGES" p. 107 for an overview of CCK.

Over the last few releases of Drupal, the Views module has been developed and refined. Whereas CCK makes it possible for users to create fields that can be reused from node to node, the Views module implements a combined query and display mechanism to complement CCK. You need not use the combination of Views and CCK, but that is common practice today, and it is increasingly evident that it will be even more common in the future.

This hour introduces you to the Views module and its basic features. As you will see during this hour and in those that follow (particularly Hour 15, "Using Events and Calendars"), the basic features of the Views module are often hidden from end users because sophisticated displays are driven by the Views module and the underlying database.

Introducing Views

The best place to start is with out-of-the-box Drupal. With the default settings, new content is published to the front page; it is displayed in reverse chronological order (newest first), as shown in Figure 14.1.

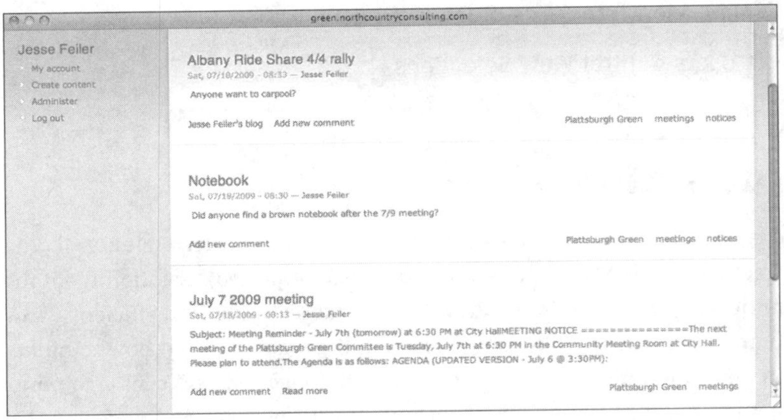

FIGURE 14.1
New content is added to the front page by default.

If you have used tags or other taxonomy features to categorize your content, the taxonomy terms are shown in the lower right of each node. As you can see in Figure 14.2, clicking a taxonomy term retrieves the entries for that term and displays them, too, in reverse chronological order. On these dynamically constructed pages, an RSS feed icon is provided so that users can subscribe to the feed of new content for the specified term.

The Views module can provide much more specific selection of data. As you can see in Figure 14.3, it can allow the end user to select from various categories. Furthermore, its visualization features allow you to customize the display of data, to number or otherwise organize the various items retrieved, and to use a pager (you have a choice of two) so that lengthy lists of results are manageable by users. (The pager in Figure 14.3 is in the lower-right; it displays information ["1 of 2"], and provides relevant controls to go forward and back.)

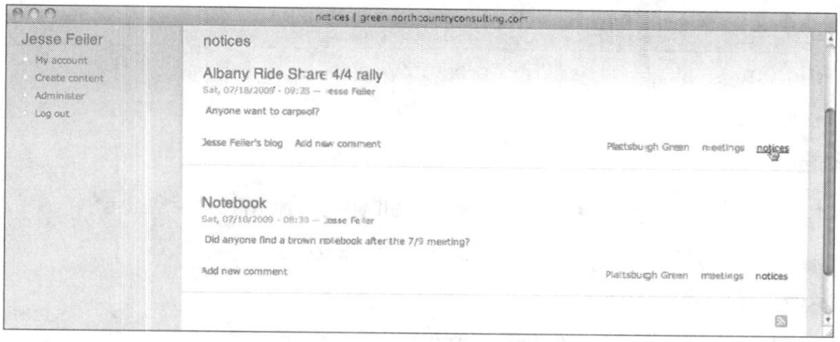

FIGURE 14.2
Dynamically create a list of content tagged with a specific term.

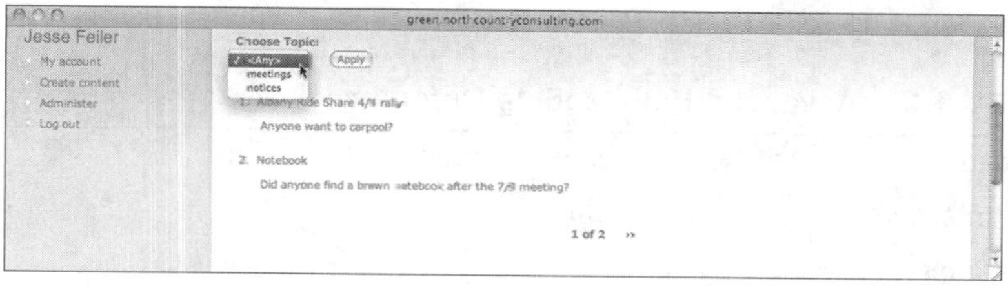

FIGURE 14.3
Use the Views module to retrieve and display data.

Explore the Riches of Views

The Views module is incredibly powerful. This hour provides an overview of its features and functionality. There is more to the module that will be explored in other hours and that you can experiment with on your own. This hour just gets you started with some of the most frequently used aspects of the Views module.

By the Way

Getting Started with Views

The Views module has had two major incarnations, and with Drupal 7 a third one is approaching. In old documentation and discussions, you will find references to Views 1 and Views 2. The current version for Drupal 6 is Views 2.

The documentation for Views is provided with the Advanced Help Module. To get started with views, you need to download, install, and enable both Views and the Advanced Help module, as shown in Tables 14.1 and 14.2. (The Views module will function without Advanced Help, but it will be more difficult to use.)

Take Your Time

The Views module is large. If you need to download it from the Drupal site and then upload it to your server, you may need to set aside as much as an hour, depending on the speed of your connection.

By the Way

TABLE 14.1   Views Module Reference

Download from	project/views
Enable in section	Views
Permissions	
Views Module	Access all views, administer views
Views Export Module	Use Views Exporter
Administration	
Administer, Site Building, Views (D6: admin/build/views)	

TABLE 14.2   Advanced Help Module Reference

Download from	project/advanced_help
Enable in section	Other
Permissions	
Advanced Help Module	View advanced help index, topic, pop-up
Administration	

Out of the box, the Views module provides a number of default views that you can use. Every view can be enabled or disabled; the default views are disabled until you enable them. Most of them simulate standard Drupal displays such as the front page or recent comments. You can use enable and use the views so that you can customize the displays in ways that previously would have required code.

View the list of view at Administer, Site Building, Views (admin/build/views), as shown in Figure 14.4.

This is the page you use to manage your views. If the Advanced Help module is not installed, instead of the link to the Getting Started page, you will have a link to the Advanced Help module page. In addition, the Help links next to each default view will go to Advanced Help documentation if that module is installed.

The format of each view's entry is consistent. The only differences among entries are for enabled or disabled views: enabled views give you links at the right to Edit, Export, Clone, or Disable the view, whereas disabled views simply give you an Enable link. Exporting, cloning, and importing views are discussed later in this hour; this section is devoted to editing views.

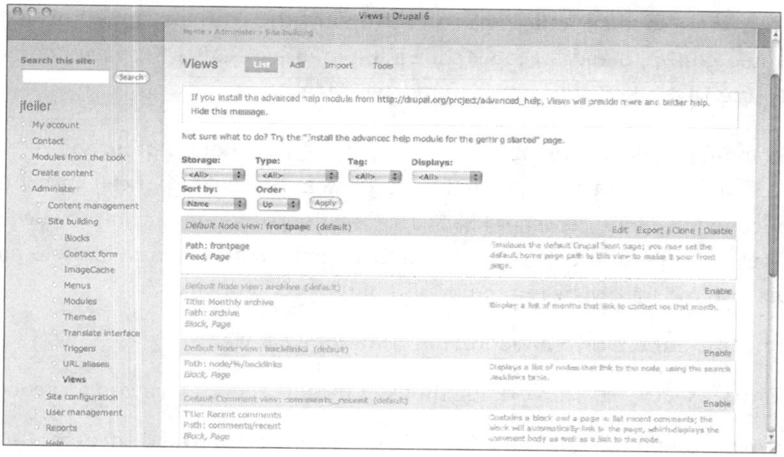

FIGURE 14.4
Review the list of
views.

Exploring a View Listing

Each view listing has a title bar followed by several descriptive fields. These are the components that are shown in the title bar for each view. At the top of the list are four pop-up menus that let you select values for one or more of the view components. Below them, two other pop-up menus let you sort the list in ascending or descending order. Click the Apply button to perform the selection and the sort. If your list of views is not lengthy, you need not worry about selecting or sorting your list of views.

▶ **Storage**—Views can be implemented in code; these are *default* views. You can also create views using the Add button at the top of the Views list shown in Figure 14.4. Views that you create in this way are *Normal* views; they are stored in your Drupal database. You can also create *Overridden* views that are based on default views; overridden views are stored in the database. You can revert an overridden view; if you do so, the database version is removed and the view implemented in code is used again.

▶ **Type**—A view contains data drawn from a specific type of Drupal data, such as nodes or comments (more on this in the section, "Adding Views"). You set a view's type when you create it; you cannot change it thereafter.

▶ **Name**—Each view must have a name that consists of alphanumeric characters and underscores. In Figure 14.4, the name of the first three views are frontpage, archive, backlinks, and comments_recent.

▶ **Tag**—Like so many other objects in Drupal, views can have tags. This helps you organize them. The tag is shown in parentheses after the view's name. In Figure 14.4, the first four views have the `default` tag.

Views combine a query with one or more displays for the data that has been retrieved. Displays can be full pages, blocks, content panes (for panels), attachments (which let you combine views) or RSS feeds. Contributed modules can provide you with other displays for the data types that they implement. The capability to have multiple displays for a view is a major part of the power of views.

Below the title bar are several additional fields for each view:

▶ **Title**—A view may have a title that can include spaces; it is used for readability.

▶ **Path**—If present, this is the Drupal path to a page or feed display for this view.

▶ **Displays**—Below the title and path, you will find a list of the types of displays supported by each view.

▶ **Description**—The description of the view that is shown at the right of each listing. As always, it is a good idea to document your work and describe what you have done (or what you intend to do) with a view. This description applies to the entire view and not just to an individual display of the view. The description is entered in the tag section of the view.

Editing View Settings

Most of your work with views consists of editing them. After a view is created or enabled, you can click Edit at the right of its title bar to open the editor, as shown in Figure 14.5.

FIGURE 14.5
Edit a view.

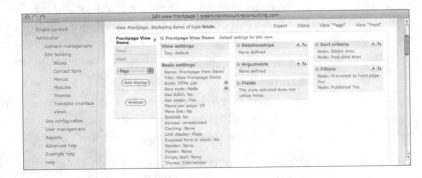

Experiment Safely with the Front Page View

This section uses the front page view that is distributed with the Views module. It mimics the behavior of the default front page in Drupal; however, because it is a view, you can build on it and modify that behavior. Although it is distributed with the Views module, as you can see from the list of views it is disabled by default. Enable it to begin editing.

This editor has three major sections. At the left are the various displays. You always have a set of default settings, but you can choose from the pop-up menu to add a display. In Figure 14.5, in addition to the default settings, you see that a Page and a Feed have been created.

The second column contains the major settings for the view. These settings change depending on whether you are editing the default settings or a specific display; the default settings carry through to each display, but additional settings may exist for specific displays. Click a highlighted link to edit a setting. For example, in Figure 14.5, the first links in the second column are default (for Tag settings), Defaults (for Name settings), and None (for Title settings). When you click a link, data entry fields appear below the main section of the view, as shown in Figure 14.6.

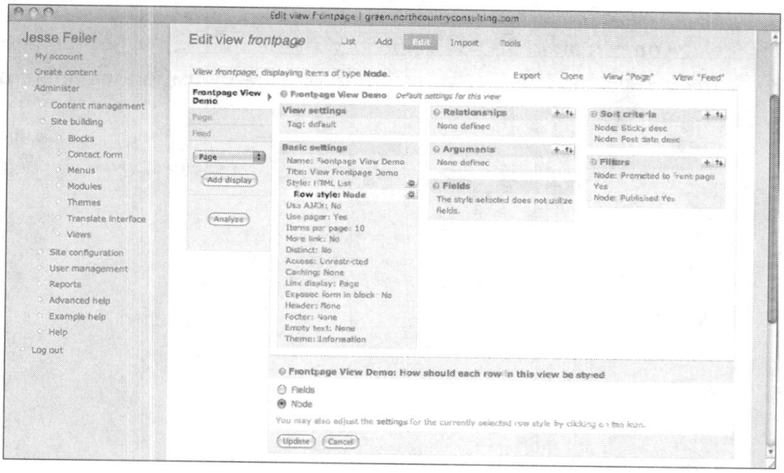

FIGURE 14.6
Enter values.

When you enter the value you want, click Update (or Cancel if you do not want to set the value). Some of the items in the view editor require not just values, but settings that are dependent on the selected value. For example, choosing the Node option button in Figure 14.6 and then clicking Update opens the settings shown in Figure 14.7. (The icons next to some settings also open these displays.)

Remember to click the Update button when you have finished.

As you work with the view editor, you will soon get into the swing of things:

▶ Update the various settings in the view editor as you go along.

FIGURE 14.7
Update settings.

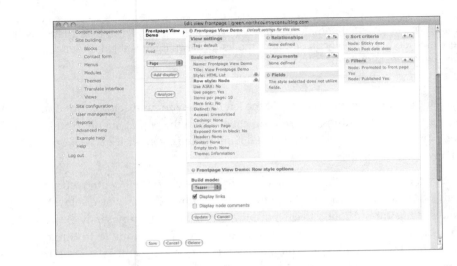

▶ Save all of your changes with the Save button after you have done the individual updates.

As you proceed, you will often find a live preview of the view at the bottom of the page. You can choose which display you want to preview by using the pop-up menu, as shown in Figure 14.8.

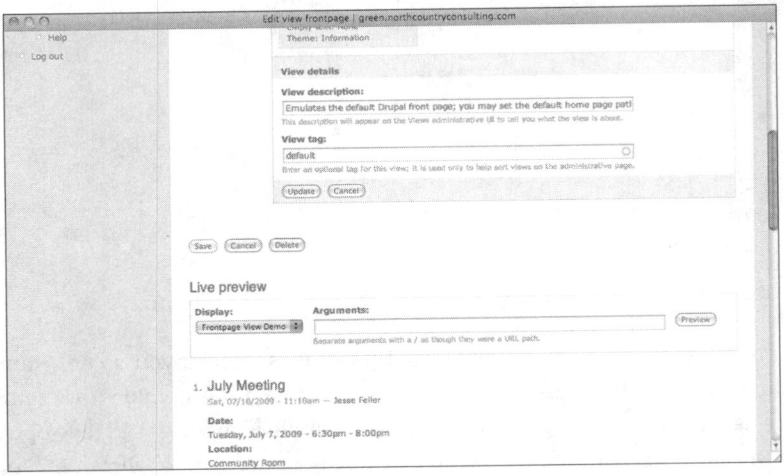

FIGURE 14.8
Save a view and use the preview.

GO TO ▶
Relationships
and arguments
are described in
**HOUR 23, "USING
CONTEXTS AND
MODIFYING
BUILT-IN PAGES,"**
p. 395. The
other settings
are discussed in
this hour.

Building a View Query

Remember that a Drupal view combines a database query with the displays that present the data. The two columns at the left of the view editor help you build the displays; the two columns at the right are devoted to building the query.

There are five sets of inputs for the query: Relationships, Arguments, Fields, Sort Criteria, and Filters. Each starts out with nothing defined for it. Two icons next to the section name let you add to the query that you are building. The plus icon lets you add to the section so that, for example, clicking the plus icon in the Fields section lets you add a field. The companion icon with up- and down-pointing arrows lets you rearrange the items in the list.

Anatomy of a Database Query

If you are familiar with relational databases and their access language (SQL), you are used to the structure of queries, and you can map the view editor to an SQL query. If you are not familiar with SQL, do not think that you need to study up on SQL syntax, and you can skip this sidebar.

The basic form of an SQL query is

```
SELECT data FROM table WHERE condition ORDER BY sort-data
```

Capitalization can vary by SQL implementation. However, in Drupal the db abstraction commands that insulate Drupal itself from the idiosyncrasies of the supported databases require that SQL reserved words be capitalized (drupal.org/node/2497). That convention is adopted in this book as it is in many other places.

The sections of the view editor that map to the query are the following:

SELECT data	Fields
WHERE condition	Filters
ORDER BY sort-data	Sort Criteria

Creating a View

As is the case with most Drupal objects, you first create a view. That process includes setting basic values (such as an internal name) that cannot be changed. After you create the view, you customize it by editing it. Editing a new view (or any Drupal object) is the same whether you have just created the view or if you or someone else created it several months ago.

From Administer, Site Building, Views (admin/build/views), click Add at the top of the views list to open the page shown in Figure 14.9.

The view name contains alphanumeric characters and, possibly, an underscore. No spaces are allowed. You will be able to create and change the title of the view to a more accessible title for users. The view name cannot be changed.

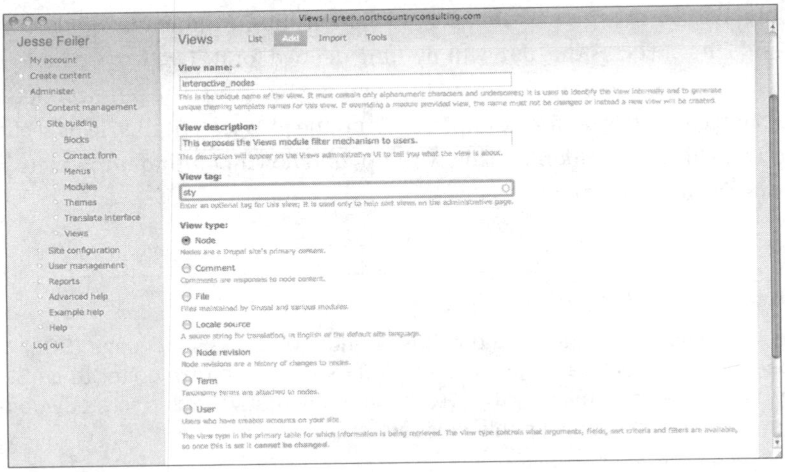

FIGURE 14.9
Add a view.

You also must specify what the data for the view will be—this is the *view type*. The view type cannot be changed after you have created the view. Some of the possible view types are listed here. You might have other view types if you have installed and enabled various modules; for example, enabling the Aggregator module in Core - optional will add the Aggregator Item view type to the list. Some of the views are used in default and disabled views that are installed as part of the Views module.

▶ **Node**—As noted in Hour 5, "Using Drupal Nodes," almost everything in Drupal is a node. Selecting this view type means that articles and stories, blog entries, forum discussion topics, and custom content types can all be displayed in the view. This is the most common view type. You can filter certain node types in or out of the view so that if you want only blog entries, for example, you select the Node view type and then apply a filter so that blog entries are omitted or included.

▶ **Comment**—Lets you view comments regardless of the node to which they are attached. A default but disabled view that is part of the Views module installation demonstrates this view type in the comments_recent view.

▶ **File**—Files managed by Drupal.

▶ **Locale source**—Helps support language translation if the Core-optional module Locale is enabled.

▶ **Node revision**—Lets you access revisions to nodes directly (rather than just the most recent revision by going to the node itself).

▶ **Term**—Use this view type if the content of the view is to consist of taxonomy terms as in the taxonomy_term default view. The most common use of taxonomy terms with views is to use them as filters; thus, in the example shown in this section, you will see a view that displays nodes tagged with taxonomy terms. At runtime, the end user can select which taxonomy term is used.

▶ **User**—Drupal users.

The tag and description for the view are useful for organizing your views. Fill them in when you create the view so that you do not forget. Both fields can be modified later, so you lose nothing by setting them now.

Editing a View

Having created a new view (or choosing to edit an existing view), proceed to the view editor, as shown in Figure 14.10.

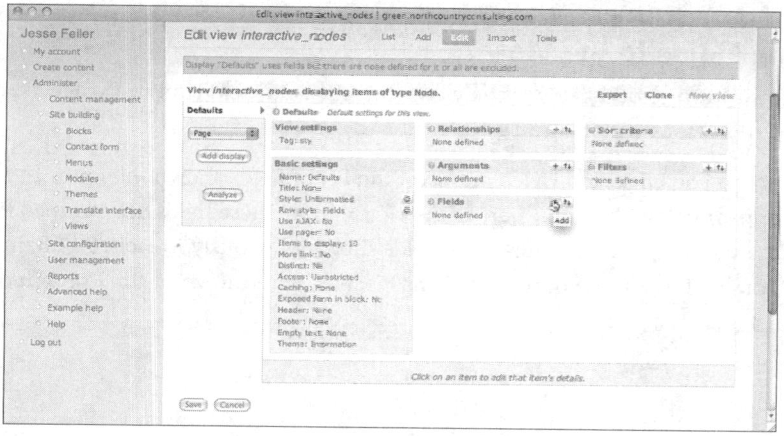

FIGURE 14.10
Edit the view.

The view that is created here is the view shown at the beginning of this hour. It displays fields from nodes, and it filters the data based on criteria. The criteria are taxonomy terms; you can do this filtering by specifying it in the view, but you can also expose the filtering to make the view dynamic. This example uses dynamic filtering by the end user to demonstrate how the view works. The first three tasks are those identified in the sidebar "Anatomy of a Database Query:"

▶ **Adding fields**—The SELECT part of the query

▶ **Filtering data**—The WHERE part of the query

▶ **Sorting data**—The ORDER BY part of the query

A final task is to refine the interface to the view. You can perform these tasks in any order that you want; you can also modify them as you go along so that you do part of one task, part of another, and so forth. Until you have added at least one field, Drupal warns you that no data will be displayed in the view, as shown in the error message at the top of Figure 14.10. As long as you add fields before you finish, there is no urgency to add them.

It is common as you develop view and work with the data that you get a better understanding of the data that you are working with. You, and your users, should stop periodically and review the view-in-progress. New presentation techniques and new ways of sorting and filtering data may come up as you work with the data; fortunately, Drupal makes it easy to change views as you go along.

▼   **Try It Yourself**

Adding Fields to the View

When you want to add fields to the view, click the Add Field icon in the Fields section, as shown previously in Figure 14.10.

1. When you click Add Fields, the scrolling list of fields shown in Figure 14.11 will appear below the main part of the view editor. These fields are grouped into the same types as the view type fields shown previously in Figure 14.8; in addition, CCK fields are part of the list. CCK fields are shown in the Content group.

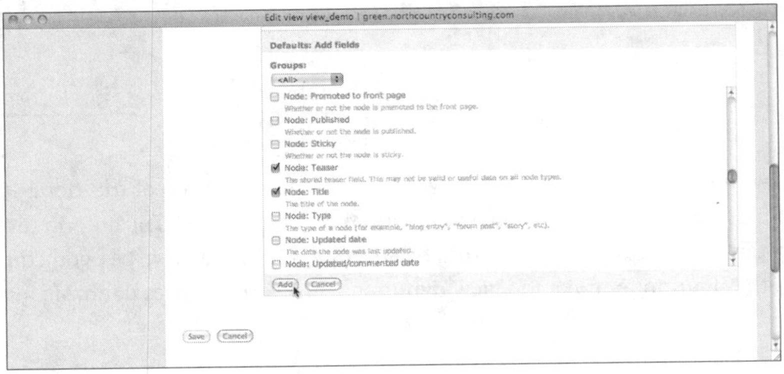

FIGURE 14.11
Add fields.

If a field is chosen that does not happen to exist in a given node that is selected for a view, no error occurs. There is no field, no data, and no problem. But, if you select a field that is part of a selected content type, it will be displayed where appropriate. Click Add when you have selected your fields.

2. The view editor will then cycle through the selected fields. For each one, you can specify the title and various display options, as shown in Figure 14.12. Many people immediately remove the default field label. The reason is that a number of common fields require no labels. A node teaser, for example, simply presents information and does not need to be identified as a teaser, so you can remove its label. Remember to click Update.

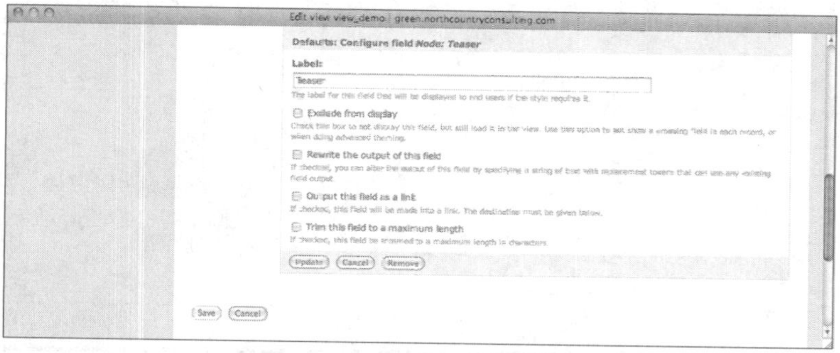

FIGURE 14.12
Configure each field's display.

3. You can configure links for any field; the most common is to turn the title of an entry into a link to the node itself, as shown in Figure 14.13.

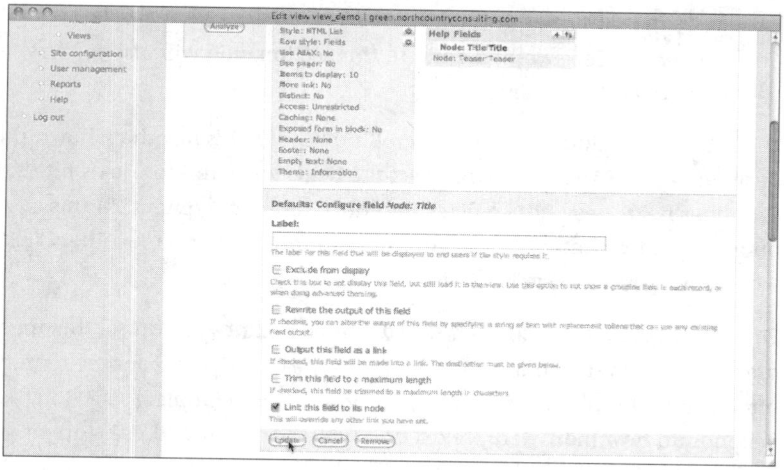

FIGURE 14.13
Make data displays "hot."

4. If you want, you can use the up- and down-pointing arrows to rearrange the order of the fields in the view. The arrows open the section shown in Figure 14.14.

You can drag fields up and down or you can use the icon at the far right to remove a field. Remember to click Update when you are finished with the rearrangement and to click Save when you are finished editing the view. (If your Internet connection is unreliable, click Save periodically so that you do not lose a great deal of work if the connection fails.)

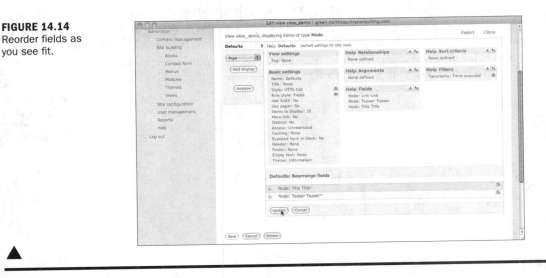

Try It Yourself

Adding Filters

Add a filter to only retrieve wanted data. In this section, you will also see how to allow end users to modify the filter.

1. Click Add in the Filters section. A scrolling list of fields like that shown previously in Figure 14.11 is shown; select the fields you want to use as filters. Note that filter fields need not be fields that are chosen for content. In this case, Taxonomy: Term is chosen so that you can filter on a taxonomy value. Click Add when you have made your choice.

2. Drupal will cycle through each selected filter so that you can set the appropriate interface, as shown in Figure 14.15. In the case of a taxonomy term, you often want a drop-down menu rather than an autocomplete selection, but it depends on how many terms exist and how good your end users are at spelling. Click Update when you are finished.

3. After you click Update, Drupal prompts you to configure the filter, as shown in Figure 14.16. For each filter, you can decide to expose its inner workings to end users. If you decide not to expose the filter, the choices that you make here are

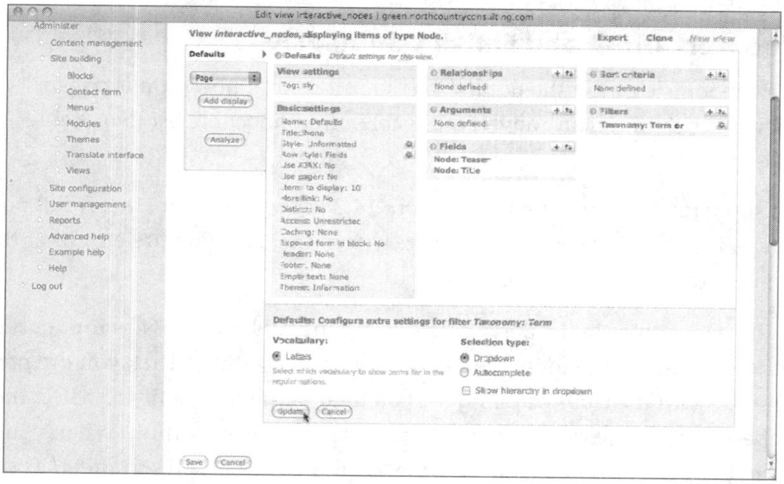

FIGURE 14.15
Set up a filter.

applied when the view is run, and the lower portion of this area (five check boxes and three text fields) is not shown.

If you do expose the choices, your settings are used as the default settings, but end users can change them. You can also choose the Limit List to Selected Items check box. In that case, if you have a dropdown list of choices, as is the case in Figure 14.16, you can select one or more of the choices. The drop-down list that the user sees will consist only of your selections. Also, note that you can change the label of the choice. As shown previously in Figure 14.3, Choose Topic is a more user-friendly label than the default Taxonomy: Term. Figure 14.3 also shows how the end-user drop-down menu consists only of the choices made in this step.

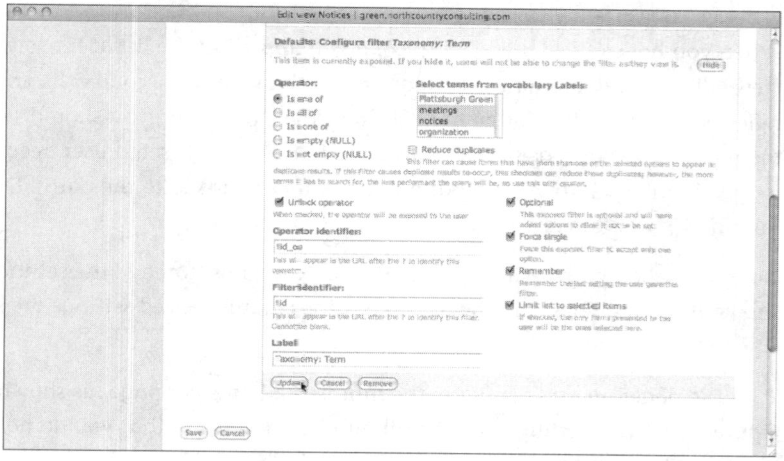

FIGURE 14.16
Configure the filter.

Set the Sort Order and Finish the Display

The View module can sort the data. You also can control how data is paged. Together, these settings can convert a possibly unmanageable list to a usable resource for end users.

Drupal supports two types of pagers. Figure 14.3 showed a minipager. A full pager lets you go to specific pages forward or back from the page you are on rather than just the next and previous page.

1. Add a sort order to the Sort Criteria using the Add button. New input areas are shown beneath the main view editor, like other settings. First, you are presented with the same scrolling list you used for fields and filters. Select the check box (or boxes) for the fields you want to use for sorting. When you finish, Drupal cycles through each one, asking you to pick a sort order, as shown in Figure 14.17. Click Update.

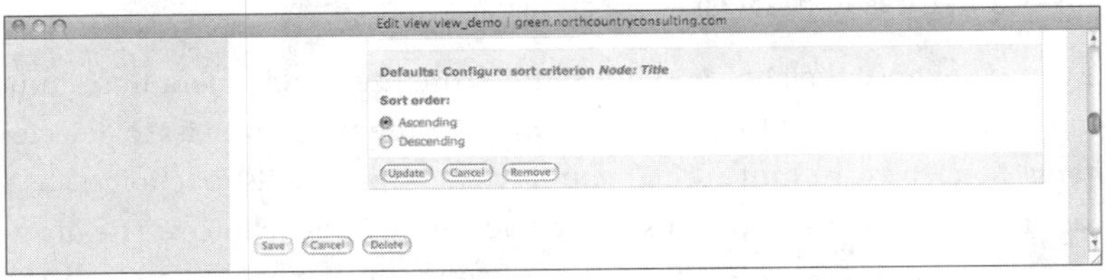

FIGURE 14.17
Choose the sort order.

2. So far, the view settings have been for the default display rather than for any specific display. To finish, add a Page display by selecting Page from the pop-up menu at the left and clicking Add Display. You can add other displays, but for now, it is a good idea to do them one at a time so that you can troubleshoot any issues.

When you have added a Page display, it will appear in the list at the left of the view editor. In addition, new settings are available in the second column that reflect settings specifically for the Page display. One setting you should set is the path to the page, as shown in Figure 14.18. After it is set, a user needs only to type in the path (or click a button or menu item linked to the path). Drupal and the view do the rest.

Note that when you are in a specific display's settings, some of the settings are shown in italics. These are the default settings; nonitalicized settings are specific to the display.

3. Turn the pager on and configure the number of items per page, as shown in Figure 14.19. (For testing, use a small number of items so that you do not have to enter a lot of data.)

▼

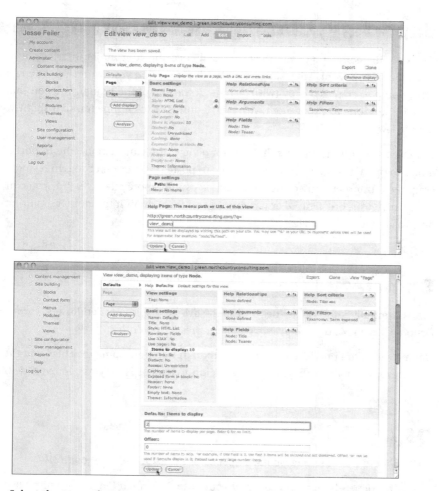

FIGURE 14.18
Create and configure a Page display.

FIGURE 14.19
Set the number of items per page.

4. Select the type of pager you want to use, as shown in Figure 14.20.

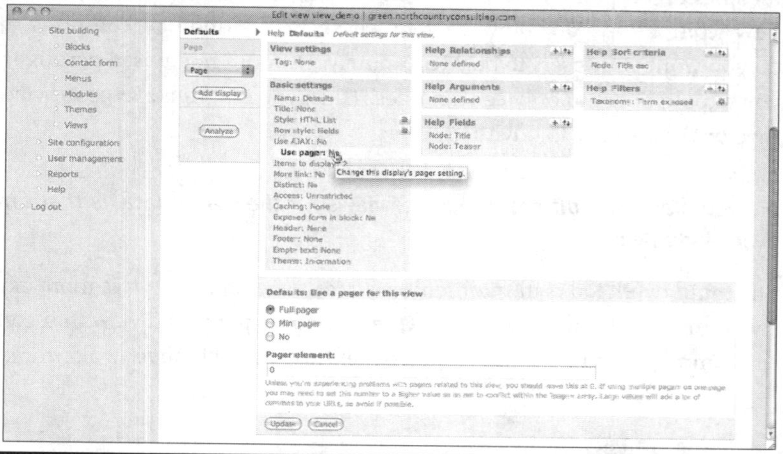

FIGURE 14.20
Choose the type of pager.

Exporting, Cloning, and Importing Views

Views are incredibly powerful; they can easily become your major interface development tool if you want. They support methods for reusing your work. You can clone a view; doing so creates a copy (with _clone at the end of the name). You can then work in the clone to experiment with new features or to change it into a slightly different view.

The Export command exports the code for a view. You can then use the Import command to open a window into which you can paste the exported code. In a single Drupal environment, the clone command is usually more effective. But, you can export a view in one Drupal environment and then email it to another environment and paste it into a new view.

Summary

Views combine database queries and sophisticated displays for end users. For many Drupal sites, views are the primary tool for presenting data.

Default views are provided as part of Drupal; in addition, some modules add their own views to the list. You can use these default views as-is, or you can override them.

Q&A

Q. Should the user always have access to the exposed view controls?

A. This depends on your users and your data. It is not a Drupal question, because it comes up on every database-driven website. The fundamental question is how "computer-y" do you want your website to be (and how computer savvy do you want your users to be)? Fortunately, Drupal's role-based permissions let you expose pages to only certain roles. Thus, you can make exposed view controls available only to advanced users.

Q. My users all want different types of views for the same data. Is there much overhead in views?

A. The main overhead is in maintenance: Maintaining 20 views is more expensive than maintaining two views. One strategy is to build a view that combines the common features of the requests. (Perhaps you will have two or three basic views.) Then, put them aside and create clones; the clones can be simple variations (perhaps a change of title or a different type of pager for navigation). This may make your users happy, but may not create a maintenance nightmare. Just remember that a change to the underlying view will require that you recreate the clones.

Q. *What is a good way to test views?*

A. Because views combine a database query with a display of the returned data, you have to be careful that you know what should be displayed (and what should not be). If you are using a field as a filter for the view, you do not have to display that field. But, for testing, it makes sense to display all the filters as regular fields—as well as just about anything else to which you have access. Make certain that you know what is in the database so that you can verify that nothing is missing from the view's display.

Workshop

Quiz

1. Are there limits on the number of fields or filters in a view?

2. How do you access a view?

Quiz Answers

1. No.

2. Page displays always have a path. You can type it in or make it a link in a menu. to display the view.

Activities

Experiment with views and show the options to your users. Discuss what the choices are. For many websites, it is easier for the users and designers (not to mention the end users) to limit the options and features to a constrained set. Use and reuse familiar components rather than throwing a whole range of options at your users (and yourself).

Designing the interface (which is what views are), is not really a technical or even aesthetic activity. Many database and interface designers believe in the adage that "the data doesn't lie." Do not use test data, and avoid making up data. Use real data to experience firsthand the oddities that users may have gotten used to. If you do not understand the data, you are well on the road to being able to develop a usable interface, not least so that you can make sense of the data.

HOUR 15

Using Events and Calendars

What You'll Learn in This Hour:

▶ Use the Contributed Date and Calendar Modules

▶ Implement an Event-Driven Calendar

▶ Create a Calendar to Organize Nodes by Date

▶ Modify Calendar Views

Introduction

Many websites need to manage a variety of dates and events. They can be websites for organizations that have meetings or other gatherings, or they can be community websites that consolidate events from a variety of sources. Managing events and calendars can be remarkably difficult. Many tools exist that accomplish parts of the task, but many of them have limitations.

Drupal provides sophisticated calendar and date management through its own structure, the Views module, the Content Construction Kit (CCK), and a contributed module, Date. Together, they provide almost everything most people need in a calendar. In this hour, you will see how to put them together and use them on your site.

Because of the complexity of calendaring operations, it is strongly suggested that you use the Date module and its companion modules as they are, out of the box. Install them and use them at least in a test environment. Walk through them, and see if they serve your purpose. If they need modification, you can create your own derivative fields from the Date field that is part of the Date module.

You can also create your own views or clone the views that are part of the Date module and make modifications to them. If you start by modifying the Date module's fields and views before having explored them, you may do unnecessary work.

Introducing the Date and Calendar Modules' Calendar and Upcoming Events

For most people, the fact that the Date module implements a CCK date type is not terribly important. What they want is a calendar or a list of upcoming events. They want functionality that is built on top of the Date and Calendar modules. In this section, you will see what it can do out of the box.

Within the Calendar module are two different calendars you can use:

▶ An event-based calendar displays events. These are a content type that you can create with a wizard that is built in to the Date module. You can add your own fields to this content type, but it starts with a Date field built in to it (along with the title, body, menu settings, and file attachments fields that are part of content types). Built-in views show a monthly calendar with links to days that have events scheduled for them.

▶ A second calendar also displays links, but these are not for events. These are the days on which Drupal nodes were last revised. This calendar is a useful way to see what entries were made when.

Figure 15.1 shows the calendar view.

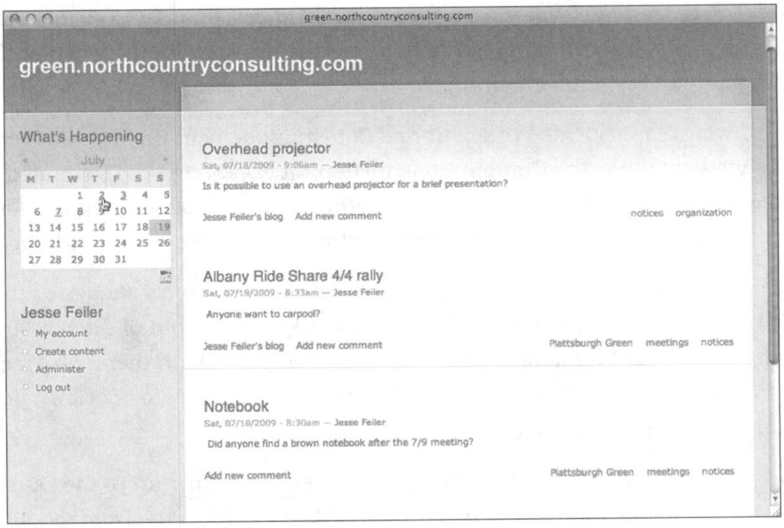

FIGURE 15.1
View dates on the Date module's calendar.

Clicking a day in the calendar opens the view shown in Figure 15.2. You can switch among the various views at the top (year, month, day, and week); you also can add a new event for whatever day you have chosen.

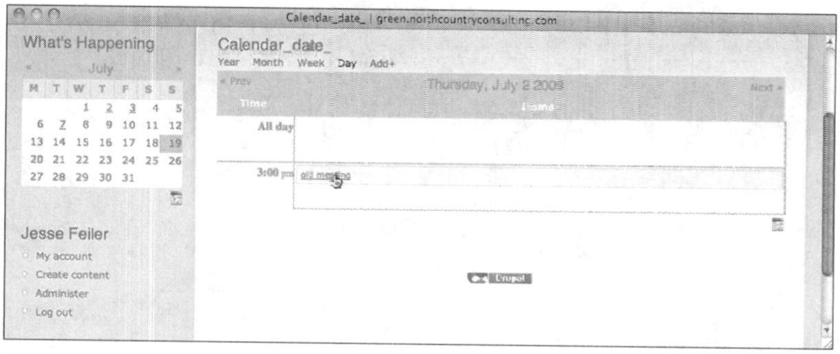

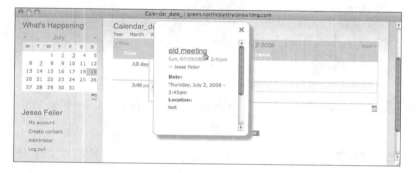

FIGURE 15.2
Go to a specific month, day, year, or week.

Events on the larger view are clickable. Figure 15.3 shows the small pop-up summary view that a single event mouse click displays.

FIGURE 15.3
Click to see an event summary.

From the summary, you can go to the full event listing to edit it, as shown in Figure 15.4.

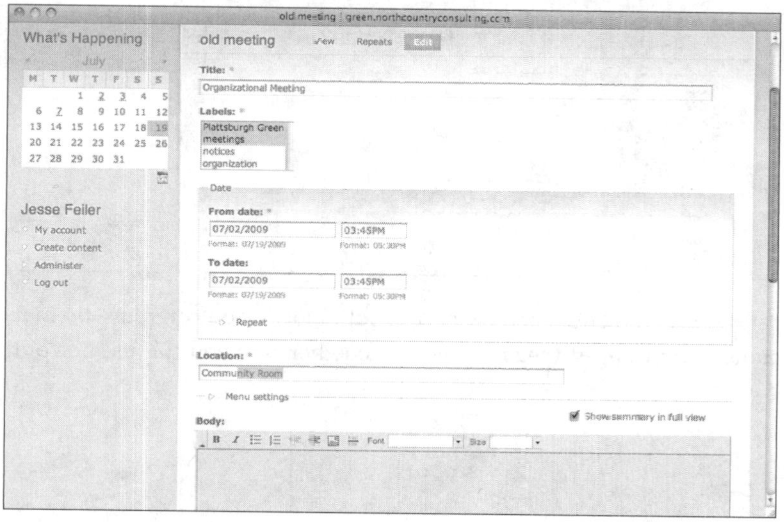

FIGURE 15.4
Edit an event.

Date entry is made easier with the Date module using pop-up calendars, as shown in Figure 15.5. Events usually have both a start and finish date and time.

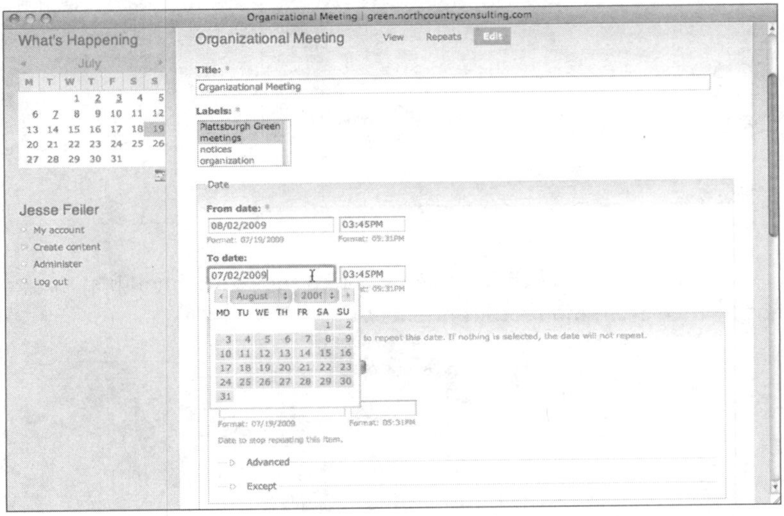

FIGURE 15.5
Enter dates with pop-up calen-dars.

If you change the date of an event to a date in the future, it will show up in the list of Upcoming Events, as shown in Figure 15.6.

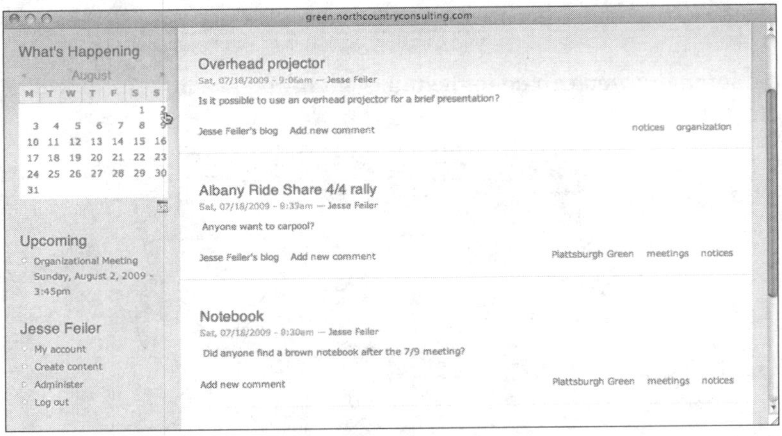

FIGURE 15.6
Upcoming events are listed auto-matically.

The calendar and the upcoming events are both blocks. You can place them in various regions of your pages; they need not be together, and you can use one or the other if you want.

Keep Upcoming Events Visible

The upcoming events view appears only if there are upcoming events to display. Some people are nervous about a component appearing and disappearing, even though it is a logical behavior in this case. You can place a far-off event into the calendar so that the upcoming events always appear.

Did you Know?

Finally, the calendar has a small icon in the lower right of the view. This exports events to iCal or another desktop-calendaring application, as shown in Figure 15.7.

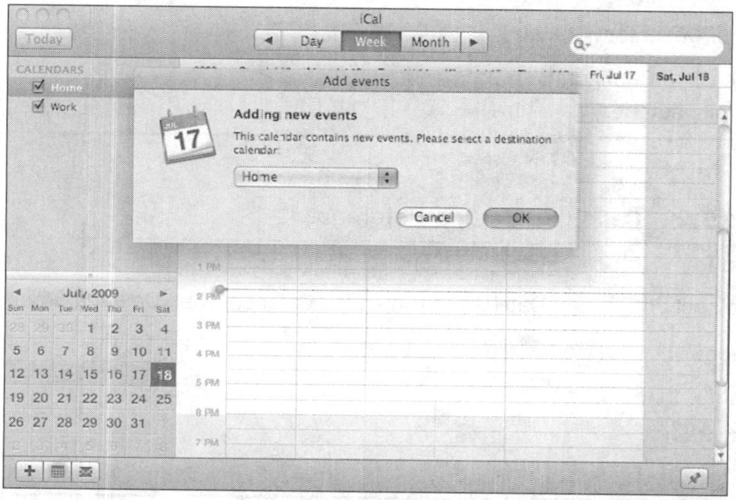

FIGURE 15.7
Export events to a calendaring application.

GO TO ▶
Blocks are described in **HOUR 19, "USING BLOCKS,"** p. 327.

Getting Started with the Date and Calendar Modules

Download, install, and enable the Date module, as shown in Table 15.1, along with the Calendar module shown in Table 15.2.

TABLE 15.1   Date Module Reference

Download from	project/date
Enable in section	Date/Time (enable all except Date PHP4 unless you are not using PHP5)
Drupal 7 Status	
D7CX	
Permissions	
Date Module	View repeats
Date Tools Module	Use date tools

TABLE 15.1   Continued

Content Permissions Module	Edit, view field_date (or any other field you create based on the Date module)

Administration

Administer, Content Management, Date Tools (admin/content/date/tools)	List, wizard, import
Administer, Site Configuration, Date Popup (admin/settings/date_popup)	
First day of week, formats, etc.	
Administer, Site Configuration, Date and Time (admin/settings/date-time)	

TABLE 15.2   Calendar Module Reference

Download from	project/calendar
Enable in section	Date/Time (Calendar, Calendar iCal, Calendar Popup)

Permissions

None

Administration

None

Configuring Date and Time Settings

Adjust Drupal's date and time settings at Administer, Site Configuration, Date and Time (admin/settings/date-time), as shown in Figure 15.8. These settings are not part of the Date module, but they are used by it. Before using the Date module, you may have used dates simply by typing them into text fields. Now that you actually will have fields that have dates in them, your settings may need to be updated.

One of the most important settings is shown in Figure 15.8: the first day of the week. (Be prepared: Discussions of whether the first day of the week is Sunday or Monday can become unexpectedly heated.)

The settings for various types of date formats, shown in Figure 15.9, are also used repeatedly throughout Drupal. You can override them for the date field type that you create with the Date module.

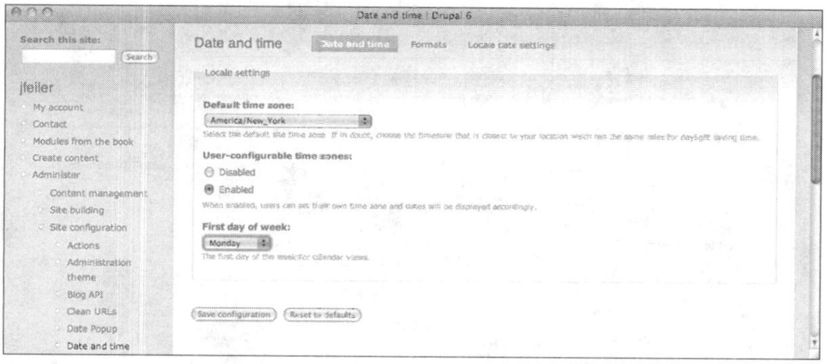

FIGURE 15.8
Set the first day of the week.

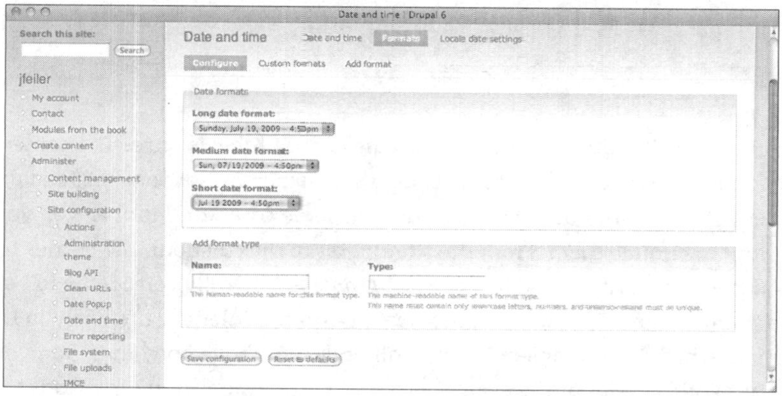

FIGURE 15.9
Set formats for dates.

Using the Date Wizard

After you install the Date and Calendar modules, the next step for most people is to go to Administer, Content Management, Date Tools (admin/content/date/tools) to use the wizard, as shown in Figure 15.10. This creates a new content type and a calendar to which it is linked.

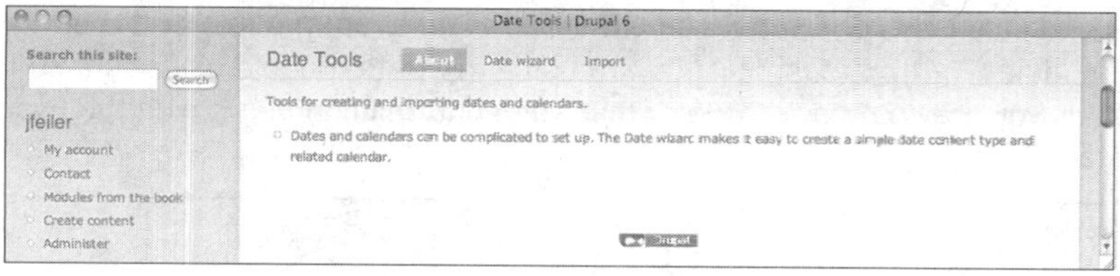

FIGURE 15.10
Use the date wizard.

After you click to start the date wizard, the wizard walks you through the process of creating a new content type and the calendar to which it is linked. The first step is shown in Figure 15.11, and it is here that a customization will make your life easier.

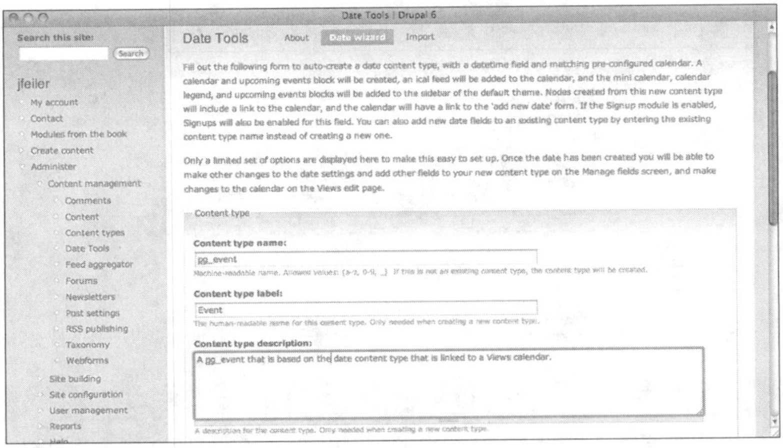

FIGURE 15.11
Name the new
content type.

The default name for the field is date, and the default label is Date. The content type description is A date content type that is linked to a Views calendar. The default entries can turn out to be misleading in some cases, and that is why you might want to change them. From the standpoint of the calendar, the entries that are made on it are usually referred to as *events*. A *date* is generally considered to be just that—a point in time. The events that you place on the calendar are likely to have a description, which is no problem because all nodes can have body text. But, you may also want to add a field for the event's location. Furthermore, you may want to bring your taxonomy settings to the events allowing a vocabulary to be used for the new content type. (You will see how to do this later in this hour.)

By the Way

About the Event Module

There is an Event module contributed to Drupal, so naming this entity an event might cause confusion in some cases. However, most people who are handling dates and calendars on Drupal use either the older Event module or the newer Date module. For that reason, if you are using the Date module as described in this hour, you may not have to worry that someone will confuse it with the Event module.

Adjusting the name and description (and possibly the label) will let you indicate not only that this is an event rather than just a date; you also can prefix the name with an identifier that will remind everyone who is using the field that it is not a generic field. Because the content type you create here is linked to a calendar, if someone accidentally uses it in a more general way, the fact that it shows up in a calendar may be a bit of a surprise.

When you scroll down the page shown in Figure 15.11, you will find the settings for the date field that will automatically be placed into the new content type, as shown in Figure 15.12. The settings that are important for you are whether to use the pop-up calendar and whether to allow repeating date options, as for a regular monthly or weekly meeting.

The content type you are creating (pg_event Event in this case) is linked to the calendar using a filter on the node type in the calendar view. For that reason, you do not have to worry about field_date being accidentally shown in a calendar. In fact, it makes sense not to create a special date field that appears only in a calendar. The only concern about possible ambiguity is over the name of the content type—that is why something like pg_event is suggested.

To get the full experience of the Date module, answer Yes to the three questions at the bottom of the page shown in Figure 15.12:

▶ Create a calendar for this content type and this date field.

▶ Add calendar blocks to the current themes (but you will need to use Administer, Site Building, Blocks to place them, as described in Hour 19, "Using Blocks").

▶ Turn on signups.

The advanced settings shown in Figure 15.13 can be accepted as is. The only change you might make is in the granularity for the time component. If you want anything less than an hour, you must go down to minutes unless you need finer control and must go down to seconds. (There is no quarter-hour granularity.)

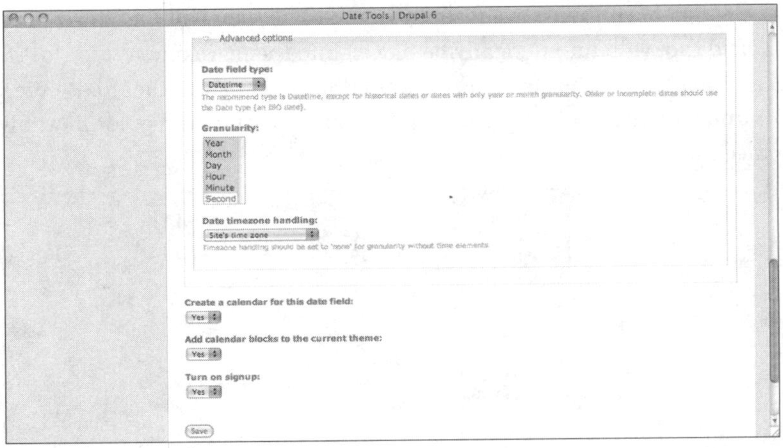

FIGURE 15.13
Configure
Advanced Set-
tings.

Adjusting the Calendar Views and Content Type

When you click Save, the wizard will complete its work of creating the calendar view. Save it when you have made any changes you want. (But, at this point, it is probably best not to make changes because the default calendar will probably serve your purpose.) You still have a few steps to finish your work.

First, go to Administer, Content Management, Content Types, and choose to edit the fields for the Event content type that you just created. Add a Location field for the event, as shown in Figure 15.14. Save the new field. You will then have a chance to adjust the settings for the Location field. You can just save the default values unless you want to make it a required field in this context.

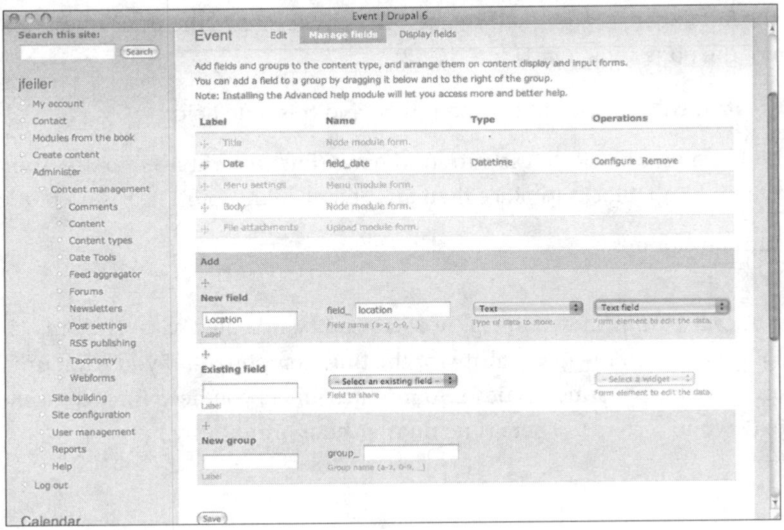

FIGURE 15.14
Add a location
field.

As noted previously, CCK lets you create, use, and reuse CCK fields. They are the same field type, but in each context, they can have separate settings. Thus, a Location field that is part of an event might not be required, but a Location field that is part of a different context such as a face-to-face-event might be required. (Presumably, a generic event would include virtual events and events for which a location is specified.)

You may want to rearrange the fields so that the Date and Location fields are just below the body rather than all the way at the bottom of the page.

Use Fields Properly

You may wonder why it is not sufficient to put the location information in the body of the event node. Whenever you have a specific data element, such as a location, that is a part of one or more content types, it makes sense to use a separate CCK field. You can then use that field in views and reports, knowing that it is not just undifferentiated body text but that it is a specific data element. In that vein, consider that you should never use a field for something other than what it is labeled as containing. Using the new Location field for a data value, such as "bring a dessert," is an invitation to data management disaster.

By the Way

While you are in the content management section of the new event content type, click Manage Fields to edit the CCK fields that you have added: Date and Location.

Figure 15.15 shows the additional settings for the Date field.

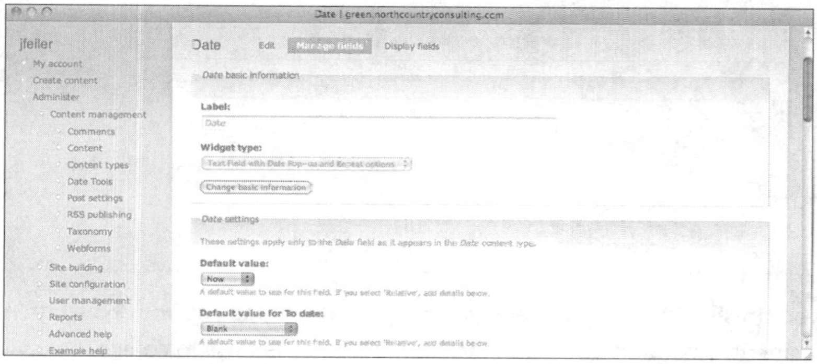

FIGURE 15.15
Configure the Date field.

Here is where you can set default values for the field's start and end date. As Figure 15.16 shows, you can also set formats here. Unless you know that you want a special setting, the Custom Input Format field should be blank. For example, the default setting shown in Figure 15.16 specifies a format with the hour shown as H. In PHP, that is a 24-hour value, and thus, regardless of other format settings, you will be required to enter 24-hour values rather than AM and PM 12-hour values.

You have additional settings, as shown in Figure 15.17.

After you finish with the Date field, you may want to go to Administer, Content Management, Taxonomy. Select the vocabulary that you use to categorize articles and stories. Edit it to allow it to be used with the new Event content type that you have created. (Reusing the vocabulary that you use for articles and stories means that related events will show up in taxonomy lists.)

You may also want to change the default comment settings for the event content type. If you have comments enabled, you are likely to get comments such as, "I will be there," and "Sorry, I have a conflict." Use the Signups or Flag modules to manage attendance and reservations; eliminating comments will also help.

The final step is to rename the default calendar views that have been created. Go to Administer, Site Building, Views. The list of views will vary depending on your other Drupal settings, but you should find two calendar views, as shown in Figure 15.18.

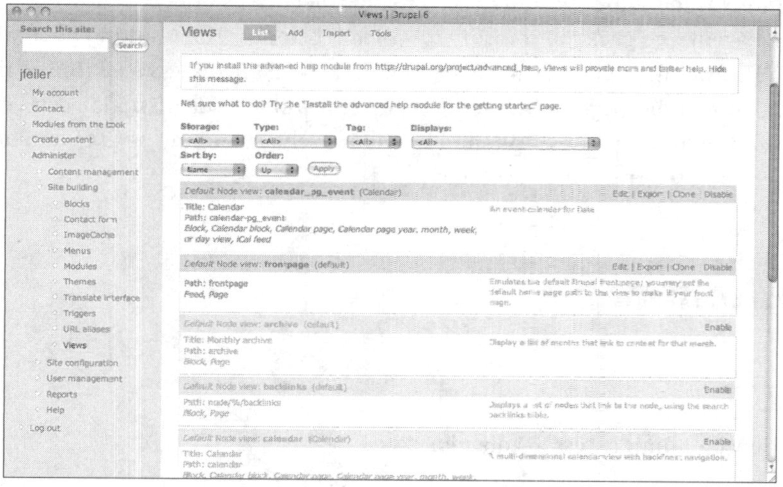

FIGURE 15.18
Edit the calendar views.

Change the title of the calendar based on the event type that you just created. It is initially set to `Calendar`, but if you rename it something like `What's Happening`, you will not confuse it with the calendar that displays nodes based on their last revision date.

You have finished creating your calendar and the upcoming events section. In Hour 19, "Using Blocks," you will see how to position them on your site pages.

Summary

Calendars are one of the most frequently requested features of websites. The combination of the Date and Calendar modules lets you implement a powerful calendar environment for your users. Using the out-of-the-box settings is a good way to start. If you want to customize your calendars, you can delve into the views that construct them.

Q&A

Q. *Can I have multiple calendars?*

A. Yes, but each calendar is linked to a specific content type (such as pg_event in this hour's example).

Q. *Someone wants to subscribe to an RSS feed of a calendar. Is that possible?*

A. The easiest way to do this is at the event level, not at the calendar level. As suggested in this hour, add a taxonomy vocabulary for your events (it normally is the same vocabulary you use to categorize stories and articles). Go to an event and click the category to which it belongs. The resulting page will be all entries with that vocabulary term, and you'll see an RSS feed icon at the bottom of the page. Subscribing to the term will provide all updates. If you want to limit the subscription to calendar events, you may need to add an additional term to the vocabulary

Workshop

Quiz

1. How do I limit access to calendar data?

2. Where do you set the first day of the week?

3. I've set all the options, but do I still have to enter 24-hour time?

Quiz Answers

1. Calendar data is implemented in a CCK date type that is created by the wizard. Limit access to the field in Content Permissions. (The default date field is field_date.).

2. Administer, Site Configuration, Date and Time.

3. The Custom Input Format on the date field's settings for the event content type overrides all other settings. The default value is 24-hour time.

Activities

The toughest part of keeping a calendar up to date is maintaining changes. Make sure that you and your colleagues know who is responsible for adding (and correcting) calendar events.

If you website has public input, make sure that you have a policy as to what items can be listed in your calendar.

Building an E-Commerce Solution

What You'll Learn in This Hour:

▶ How to Install Ubercart

▶ Setting Up Product Classes and Catalogs

▶ Handling Money

▶ Selling Downloads

▶ Shipping Products and Keeping Track of Stock

▶ Offering Paid Memberships

Introduction

This hour completes the socializing and communicating section of this book. Commerce is impossible without socializing and communicating, and commerce (in its broadest sense) makes those aspects of life possible. In a relatively brief period of time, the world of e-commerce has come into being. Ubercart, a major contributed module to Drupal, has nearly 10,000 websites using it, and it is the topic of this hour.

Out of the box, Ubercart supports most of what you expect from an e-commerce plug-in. In Figure 16.1, for example, you can see that Ubercart provides a shopping cart and a catalog, both of which are provided as blocks that you can place wherever you want on your pages. (Many sites keep their catalog and current shopping cart visible on all pages; it increases sales.)

For some people, e-commerce is the main reason for creating a website, and Drupal together with Ubercart can be the simplest way of reaching this goal. Other people have websites that are based on a community or joint project; they may be interested in creating a website that provides information that can be updated. For these people, e-commerce may be the furthest thing from their mind.

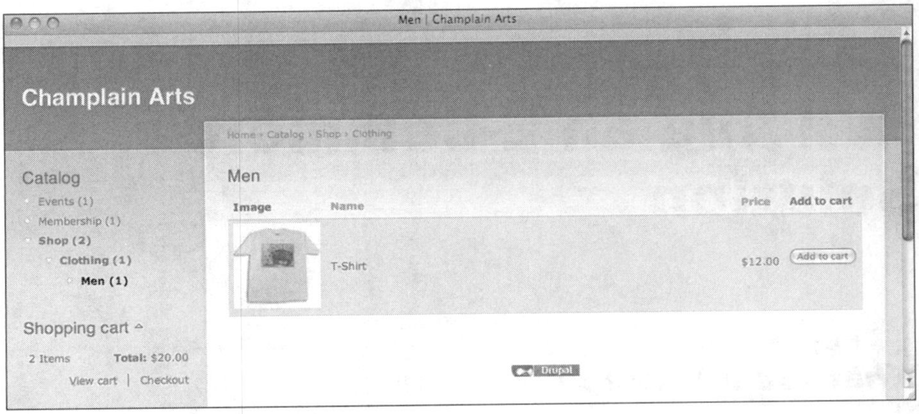

FIGURE 16.1
Ubercart provides a catalog and shopping cart.

If you think you are in this second group of people, you may want to think again. As you will see in this hour, e-commerce in general—and Ubercart in particular—let you manage numerous types of operations. The examples in this hour will demonstrate them:

▶ **Downloadable sales**—Drupal and Ubercart work together very well to allow you to sell downloads of software, music, or anything else that is delivered as a downloadable file. In most cases, neither shipping nor inventory needs to be tracked, and that is why many businesses have discovered how much more profitable downloadable sales can be than deliveries of physical objects.

▶ **Reservation sales**—Whether you are selling tickets to a concert or rooms at a hotel, these sales are a combination of physical and downloadable sales. In most cases, no physical object is delivered. However, you need to keep track of how many tickets or rooms have been sold, so in a sense, you need to track inventory stock.

▶ **Physical sales**—These are sales of physical objects that need to be delivered. They may be books, jars of your special marmalade, or anything else you can think of. Ubercart can manage two particular aspects of these sales: It can manage shipping and keep track of inventory. These are optional features; many people manage one or both of these tasks manually.

▶ **Membership sales**—This may be the most interesting integration point with Drupal. You allow access to various Drupal resources and functions based on roles that you create. (There is more on this in Hour 8, "Managing Users, Roles, and Permissions.") You can set up a role such as Member and assign to that role access to certain parts of your website. Ubercart can then let you sell access to that role, and the access can even be configured for a specific period of time.

Ubercart is probably bigger than other modules you use. (In fact, it has five sections of modules to be enabled in your modules list.) Although Ubercart is big, it mostly builds on existing Drupal concepts and functionality, such as taxonomy, roles, and file downloads. For that reason, you will probably not find many challenges on the Drupal technology side in this hour. However, if you are new to e-commerce (or even to commerce in general), those aspects of Ubercart may be unfamiliar to you.

This hour can serve as review of the various components of Drupal that you have already seen. Drupal pulls them together. Most people find it easiest to work through this hour using the defaults and suggestions made here. Then, feel free to go back and experiment with other settings.

SilverGraphics Product Images

Product images in this hour courtesy of SilverGraphics Studios Inc., art-based fundraising, www.silvergraphics.com.

By the Way

Getting Started with Ubercart

Ubercart has a variety of modules you can install. You need to have an overall roadmap so that you can make your installation choices.

Finding Your Way Around Ubercart

Here are the sections of Ubercart modules:

▶ **Ubercart-core**—As with Drupal core, these modules need to be installed and enabled.

▶ **Ubercart-core (optional)**—You can enable or disable these. One of the most commonly enabled modules is Payment; if it is not enabled, you cannot use any of the Ubercart-payment modules. Also, Taxes and Tax Reports are needed for sales tax processing. Of the other modules, the most commonly used are Attribute, Catalog, and Reports. You will not get in trouble if you enable those three. If you will be shipping physical objects, enable Shipping and Shipping Quotes. Finally, enable File Downloads and Roles to be able to sell file downloads and memberships or other role-based products.

▶ **Ubercart-extra**—In this section are optional modules. Many people use GoogleAnalytics to manage their sites. There is a GoogleAnalytics Drupal module (downloadable from drupal.org/project/google_analytics); if you have it installed and enabled, you can enable Google Analytics for Ubercart. The Stock module automatically handles inventory. Use it for managing inventory of physical objects or reservations (such as room or ticket sales). The Product Kit lets you group several products together; it is useful for creating a cost-saving package in which users can buy several products together for less than their individual prices. (Product Kits do not have to be cheaper than their individual product prices, but they often are.)

▶ **Ubercart-fulfillment**—These modules calculate shipping expenses. Flat Rate and Weight Quote can be used by anyone. UPS requires a UPS account; there is more information at www.ups.com. USPS requires a Web Tools User ID, which is available at www.usps.com/webtools.

▶ **Ubercart-payment**—Ubercart incorporates a number of payment modules. All require Payment in Ubercart-core (optional) to be enabled. Most people enable Test Gateway, which lets you test processing without actually charging credit cards. (You disable it after you are finished testing.) Payment Method Pack handles non-credit-card transactions, such as checks and CODs. The Credit Card module must be enabled for all credit card purchases. You generally use a specific service for processing credit cards. Your choices in Ubercart are Authorize.net, CyberSource Silent Payment, and Google Checkout. You normally enable only one of these. To complete the roster, you have a PayPal module. Because of the structure of payment modules, additional ones can be added.

Installing and Enabling Ubercart

As usual, you begin by downloading and enabling Ubercart. The downloaded project contains a number of modules that will be installed in five new sections it will create in your module list.

Ubercart and Drupal 7
Ubercart 2 is the current version of this complex set of modules as of the time of this writing. It is targeted for Drupal 6. For that reason, no Drupal 7 links are provided in this hour. See ubercart.org and the author's website for additional information as it becomes available.

Table 16.1 shows the modules you should enable to work through this chapter.

TABLE 16.1 Ubercart Module Reference

Download from	project/ubercart.
Enable Ubercart-core	All.
Enable Ubercart-core (optional)	All.
Enable Ubercart-extra	Product Kit, Stock.
Enable Ubercart-fulfillment	Flat-rate, U.S. Postal Service, Weight Quote. If you have a UPS account, you can enable UPS as well.
Enable Ubercart-payment	Credit Card, Payment Method Pack, Test Gateway. For production add other modules such as PayPal, Authorize.net, and Google Checkout if you have the relevant accounts.

Permissions

Permissions are defined for Ubercart modules; all of the r names begin with uc_. Permissions are indicated for you (or another site admin strator) and for customers.

uc_attribute module	You: all
uc_catalog module	You: all; customers: view catalog
uc_credit module	You: all
uc_file module	You: all; customers: download file (if you want that feature)
uc_order	You: all; customers: create, delete, and edit orders; view own orders
uc_payment	You: all
uc_product	You: all
uc_product_kit	You: all
uc_quote	You: all
uc_reports	You: all
uc_roles	You: all
uc_shipping	You: all
uc_stock	You: all
uc_store	You: all
uc_taxes	You: all

TABLE 16.1   Continued

Administration

Administer, Store Administration

(admin/store)

By the
Way

> ### Try Ubercart in Its Own Environment
>
> Ubercart is big, but it is not particularly complicated (unless you have to learn the basics of e-commerce). However, because it is so big and has many moving pieces, and particularly if you are new to e-commerce, you might want to create your first Ubercart e-store in its own Drupal environment.

Store Administration (admin/store) is shown in Figure 16.2. You can show or hide links for each module.

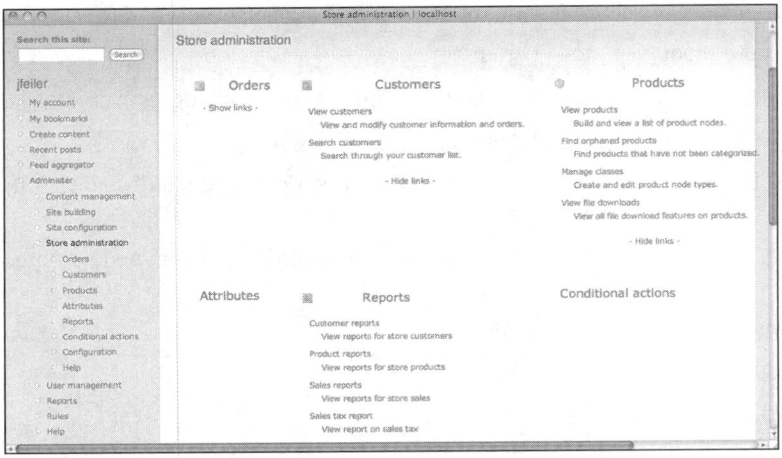

FIGURE 16.2
Store Administration gives you an Ubercart overview.

If you scroll to the bottom of the page, you will find the status report shown in Figure 16.3.

This is a high-level overview; you should either correct or explain each anomaly. For example, in Figure 16.3, you can see that credit card encryption has not been set. You cannot accept credit cards until you do this, but that is OK for testing. The Images error is much more serious. Although you can have an e-commerce store without images, it is almost always a mistake, so the inability to post images is a showstopper for many people. If you see this error message, track down the problem. This problem arises sometimes on test installations of Drupal: It is generated by not having Clean

URLs turned on, and that, in turn, is often caused by the .htaccess file being improperly configured. List your .htaccess file and look for the comments about configuration. The file is short, but remember that it is a hidden file so you must configure your FTP client to list hidden files.

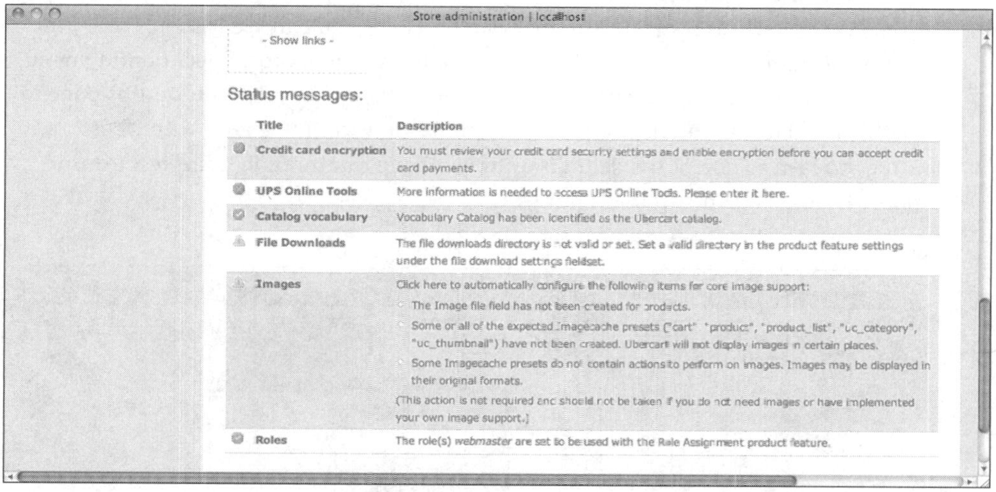

FIGURE 16.3
Check store status.

Using Drupal Integration

Ubercart is very well integrated with Drupal. You will see the familiar buttons that let you add images to nodes, whether they are product nodes or any other nodes. When you see them, use them. Some people spend a great deal of time and money customizing their Drupal site's look and feel when the use of simple icons for nodes and inventory items can be much more effective (and much less expensive).

Working with Money

To test your Ubercart store, you need to be able to complete sales without actually charging a credit card. To do that, you can set up Test Gateway to process a credit card without actually charging it. You can also enable COD and check payments.

Go To ▶

APPENDIX A, "INSTALLING DRUPAL," for more on clean URLs and the htaccess file.

These are not automated, so you can process them as if you had received the check or consigned the shipment for COD. If you will ultimately accept checks and handle COD orders, this is a useful leg up. If you will only accept credit cards, use the Test Gateway. Nothing prevents you from setting all of them up in your test environment.

In the module list, enable Payment in Ubercart-Other in the Ubercart-Payment section. Go to admin/store/settings/payment/edit. As you can see in Figure 16.4, the Administration Menu module (downloadable from drupal.org/project/admin_menu) is worth its weight in gold when you are using Ubercart. The defaults on this page (all enabled and a standard message) are fine to begin with. In general with Ubercart, it is a good idea to accept the defaults until you have run through a few test transactions. Then, you can customize things.

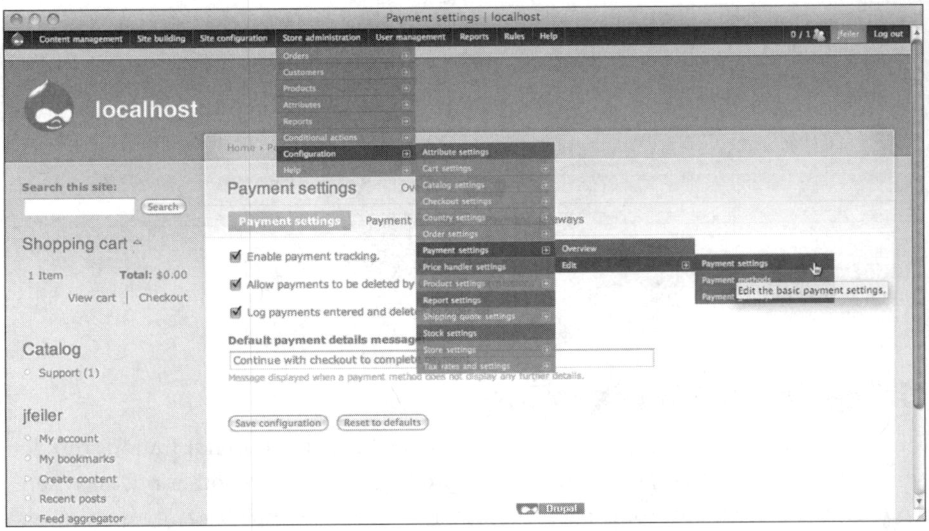

FIGURE 16.4
The Administration Menu module helps you navigate Ubercart's complexity.

The default payment settings shown in Figure 16.5 are fine to start with.

Enabling COD and Check Payments

Click Payment Methods or go to admin/store/settings/payment/edit/methods to continue, as shown in Figure 16.5.

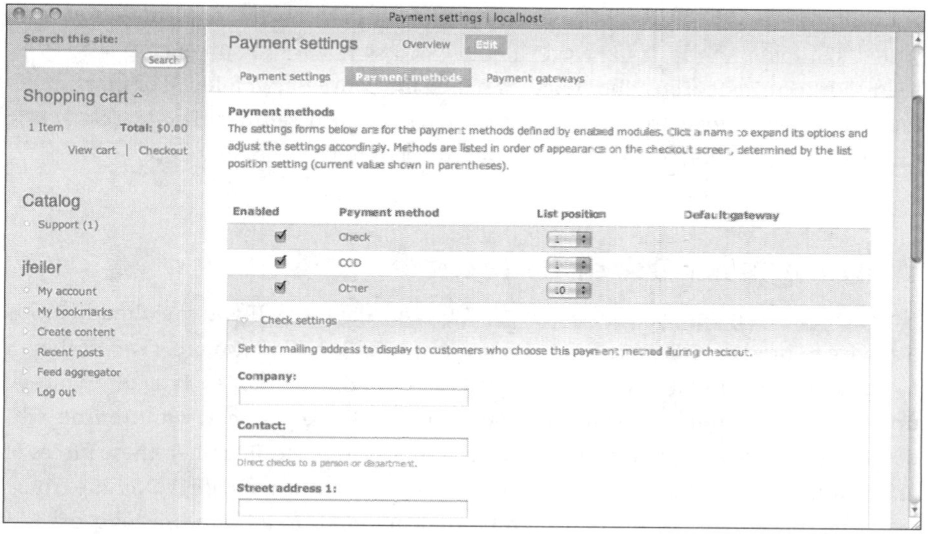

FIGURE 16.5
Enable checks, COD, and other payment methods.

If you want to use COD and check payments, enable the Payment Method Pack module in Ubercart-Payment. Enable them in the Payment Methods section, as shown in Figure 16.5. You need to provide additional information for checks, COD, credit cards, and other payment methods, as you see at the bottom of Figure 16.5.

Save your Payment Methods configuration.

Among the settings at the bottom of the page are those for credit cards. If you are using Test Gateway, turn on Operate in Credit Card Debug Mode and turn off Validate Credit Card Numbers at Checkout. (By turning off credit card number validation, you can use a card number, such as 12345, that does not conform to the standards for credit card numbers.)

Enabling Credit Cards and Test Gateway

If you want to test with credit cards, enable Credit Card and Test Gateway in Ubercart-Payment.

When you have enabled Credit Card and Test Gateway, you will see that you can add credit cards as a payment method; you will need to select the Test Gateway as the Default Gateway for their processing. When you start to actually use the site, you will use one of the other gateways to provide credit card authorization and charging. All you will need to do is to enable the appropriate gateway in your Ubercart modules and select it in the Default Gateway column here.

You will also need to set up encryption for credit card processing. This consists of constructing a folder to which Ubercart will have access; it will store an encryption key there. For security reasons, that folder is not inside your Drupal folder. For more information, see www.ubercart.org/docs/user/2731/credit_card_settings. The process of setting up the encryption folder is simple, and it needs to be done only once.

Working with Other Gateways

Normally, other gateways are installed in Ubercart-Payment. If you are already using a service to process online credit card sales, you will likely find it there. (Two of the most commonly used, PayPal and Google Checkout, are available.) Typically, you set up an account with the gateway provider; you receive a key to send with transactions, and you let the gateway know the location of your site. Together, these pieces of information inform the gateway that the submitted transactions are legitimate. You can generally enter keys and other similar information through Administer, Store Administration, Configuration, Payment Settings (`admin/store/settings/payment`).

Receiving Money

After a customer moves to check out a cart, the sale is ready to be completed. Minor differences exist, depending on the type of payment (credit cards, for example, are automated), as well as on what is delivered and how the delivery is made. Here is the general scenario.

What the Customer Does

The customer is shown a page with the order total, including tax and shipping if necessary. (This is like any other e-commerce system.) At the bottom of the page, the user chooses the payment type, as shown in Figure 16.6.

If the customer is paying with a credit card, the information is entered at this time.

SSL Security
You should use HTTPS to transmit this page via SSL. This may require coordination with your hosting provider, but it is necessary to maintain your credibility and to safeguard your customers' data. Most hosting providers have add-on products that support SSL. Look at drupal.org/project/securepages for a Drupal module to handle this.

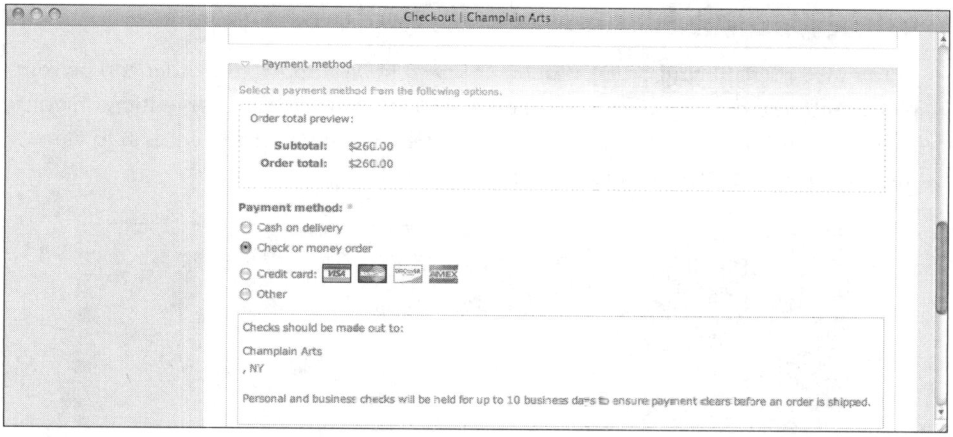

FIGURE 16.6
The customer chooses a payment type.

After the payment is made, the order is reviewed for the user, as shown in Figure 16.7.

Confirmed orders result in an email being sent to you.

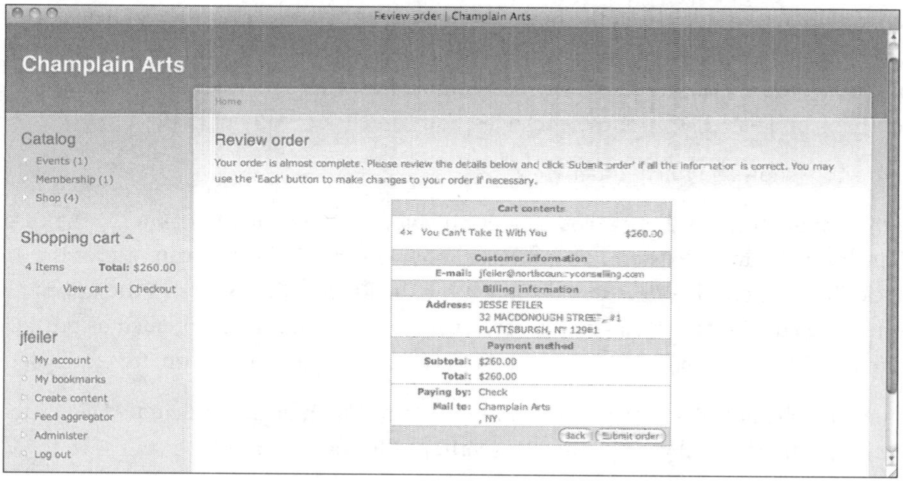

FIGURE 16.7
The customer confirms or changes the order.

What You Do

In the case of credit card orders that do not need to be shipped, the order can be completed automatically by Ubercart. All other orders require some intervention on your part. Go to Administer, Store Administration, Orders (`admin/store/orders`) to view the list of orders shown in Figure 16.8.

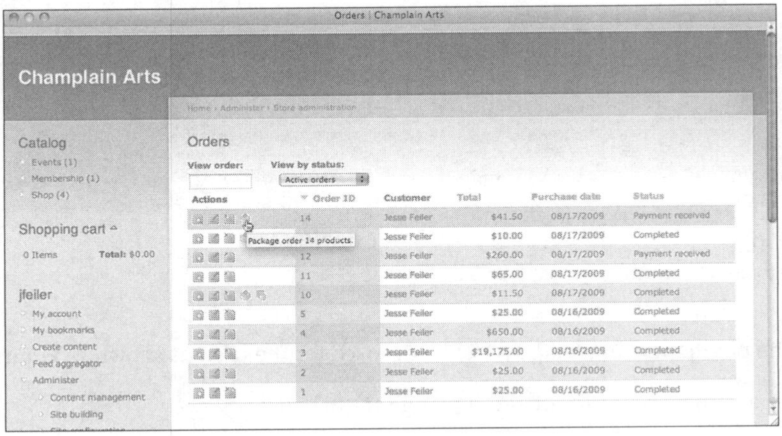

FIGURE 16.8
View the list of orders.

Depending on the status and the type of order, you may have a number of icons at the left of each order. For all orders, the first three icons are View, Edit, and Delete. For shippable orders, another icon lets you assemble the order's products into packages. Another icon lets you ship those packages. You can click on any of these.

Figure 16.9 shows a typical order view.

At the top are buttons that let you produce invoices and receive payments. In the case of an order where the customer has selected payment by check, you can receive the check directly from the View icon display (note the Receive Check link in the upper right). The Payments button lets you receive more complex payments, such as partial payments and multimodal payments (check combined with credit card, for example).

When you click Receive Check, you fill in the details, such as the anticipated clearing date, the amount, and your comments (perhaps the check number).

Finally, update the status of the order to Complete at the bottom of the order page shown previously in Figure 16.9. The bottom of that page is shown in Figure 16.10.

Remember that these instructions apply only to non-credit-card orders or orders with some physical processing. Credit card orders for virtual delivery are totally automated.

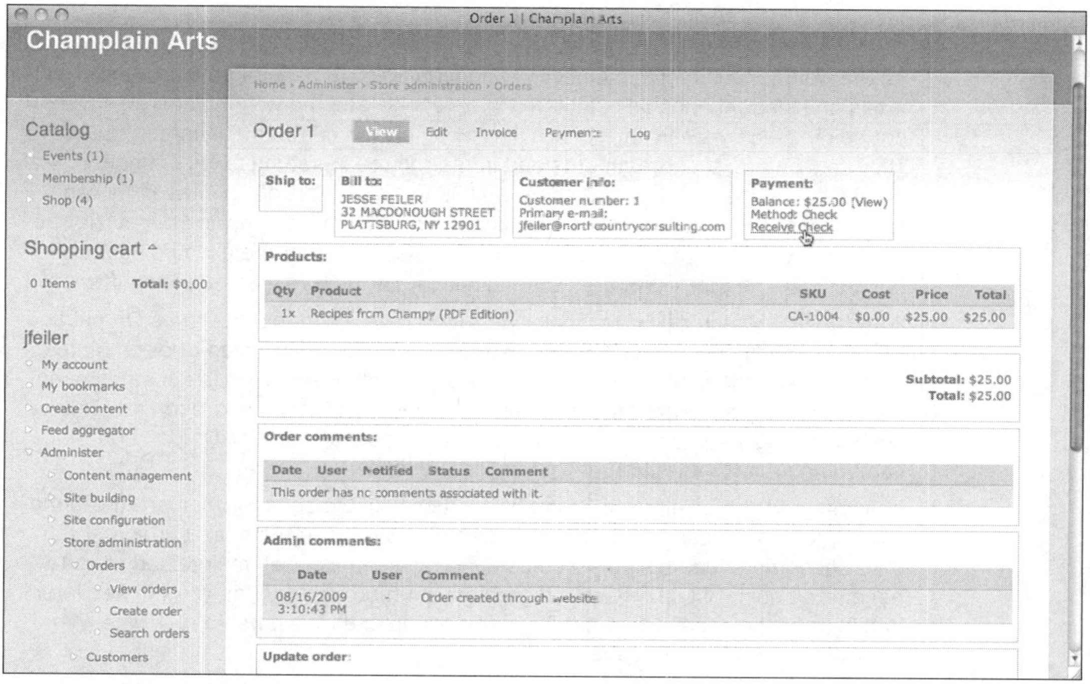

FIGURE 16.9
View the order.

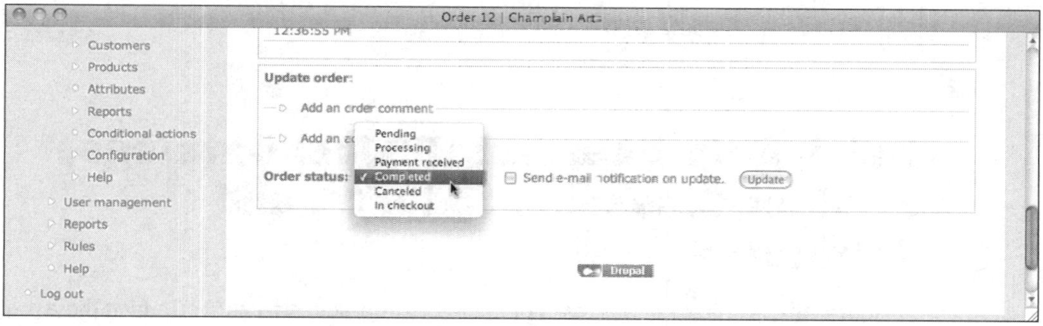

FIGURE 16.10
Mark the order complete.

The Small Business Approach to Web Sales

As the world of e-commerce has grown and matured, the role of small businesses in it has changed. Although e-commerce in particular, and the web in general, started out being used by small enterprises, large companies came to dominate the scene. They could afford the investments and infrastructure in setting up e-commerce, although in many cases, it took them a while to do so. Part of the reason for the long delay in the maturation of e-commerce was that it was a moving target. (It was not many years ago that the insane and wild prediction that there would be a billion dollars in online sales over the year-end holiday period was greeted with guffaws.)

With the maturation of the technology of e-commerce and tools such as Drupal and Ubercart, small businesses can take advantage of the efficiencies of e-commerce. In many ways, the distinctive features of many small businesses (such as personal attention and great expertise) dovetail very nicely with Drupal and Ubercart. This section has focused on the social aspects of websites built with Drupal, and that can be an important feature of your online presence.

In addition to the small business opportunities with Drupal and Ubercart, the world of nonprofit organizations likewise can benefit from these tools. In a nonprofit run on a shoestring, fundraising becomes difficult. An almost self-maintained shop to benefit the nonprofit can make a significant contribution. And, as you will see later in this hour, the capability to handle membership and membership renewals with Ubercart is extremely valuable.

For people who have spent a week (or more!) every year folding and stuffing envelopes for an annual appeal, Ubercart and Drupal appear almost unbelievable. True, the day when youngsters will ask, "Granny, what's an envelope?" is not quite here yet, but it is certainly conceivable.

Setting Up Ubercart Basics: Catalogs, Product Classes, Products, and Attributes

In Figure 16.1, you can see the basics of the Ubercart product structure. (In fact, these are the basics of most e-commerce sites.) A catalog lists categories of products. In Figure 16.1, those categories are Events, Membership, and Shop. Next to each category name, a number in parentheses indicates the number of products in that category. (This number is never zero; if there are no products in a category, the category is not listed.)

If you click a category, you can see its products. You then can click an Add to Cart button, as shown in the center of Figure 16.1.

As with so much of Ubercart, understanding how to use categories, products, and attributes is more about the e-commerce side of things than the technology. Following are some of the issues to consider.

Using Categories and Product Classes

Categories and classes are related but different concepts in Ubercart. Categories are simple taxonomy entries. Ubercart automatically creates a *Catalog* vocabulary when you install it. You can add terms to that vocabulary just as you would to any other taxonomy vocabulary (go to admin/content/taxonomy/list and click Add Terms for the Catalog vocabulary). Because this is a simple taxonomy vocabulary, all the rules apply. In particular, you can create hierarchies of entries. For example, you can have a Shop term, and you can create a Clothing term with Shop as its parent. You can go further to create a Women term with Clothing as a parent (and, therefore, Shop as a grand-parent).

After you have created catalog entries, you can assign them to the products that you create. Any product can have multiple catalog entries. For example, a nonprofit organization might place T-shirts under Clothing as well as under Support Us.

Deciding where to place products and how to structure your catalog is more an art than a science. There is a delicate balance to be struck between listing products in several places and thereby increasing their sales and, on the other hand, annoying people because no matter what category they are looking at, those dratted T-shirts are showing up again.

Product classes are Ubercart's variation on the content types such as pages, stories and articles, blogs, and polls that you use in other areas of Drupal. You manage them through Administer, Store Administration, Products, Manage Classes, as shown in Figure 16.11.

As you can see in Figure 16.11, an existing Shop product class exists; a new one, Support, is being added. The catalog shown at the left of the window helps to illustrate the difference between product classes and catalog entries. The Shop product class has been used to create products tagged as Events, Shop, and Membership. Until the Support product class is saved, all products that have been created have been Shop products. From now on, both Shop and Support products can be created.

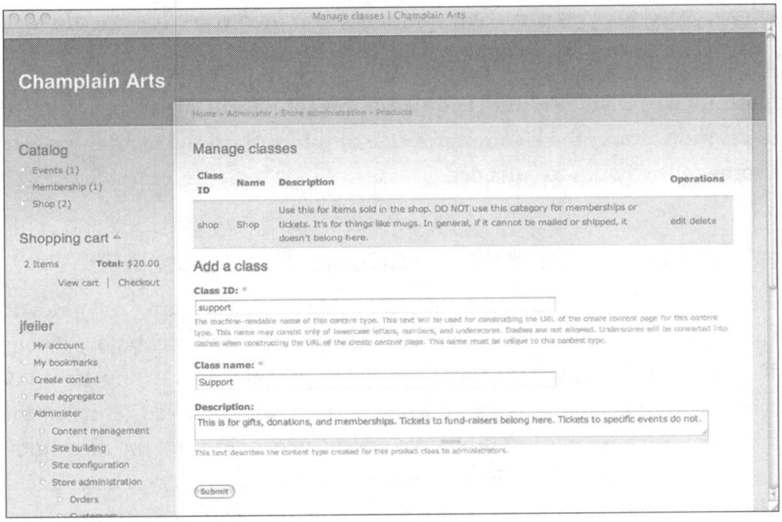

FIGURE 16.11
Manage product
classes.

After you create a product class, Ubercart creates it as a content type and adds some product-specific fields. Thereafter, it is, to all intents and purposes, just another content class.

Creating Products

Figure 16.12 shows how you create a product. After the product class has been created as described in the previous section, the name and description show up in the list of available content types, as shown in Figure 16.12. (Look for Shop and Support at the bottom of the list.)

When you create a product, remember to select its catalog category so that it will show up in the catalog.

Using Attributes and Options

In addition to categories and products, Ubercart supports attributes and options. An *attribute* is a characteristic of a product, such as its color. An *option* is a specific value for an attribute; thus, the color attribute might have options of green, blue, and yellow. Options may have incremental costs associated with them. In many cases, different colors for a product do not have different prices. However, different finishes for products may have different prices; a gold leaf picture frame is likely to cost more than a cardboard frame. Ubercart handles these issues for you.

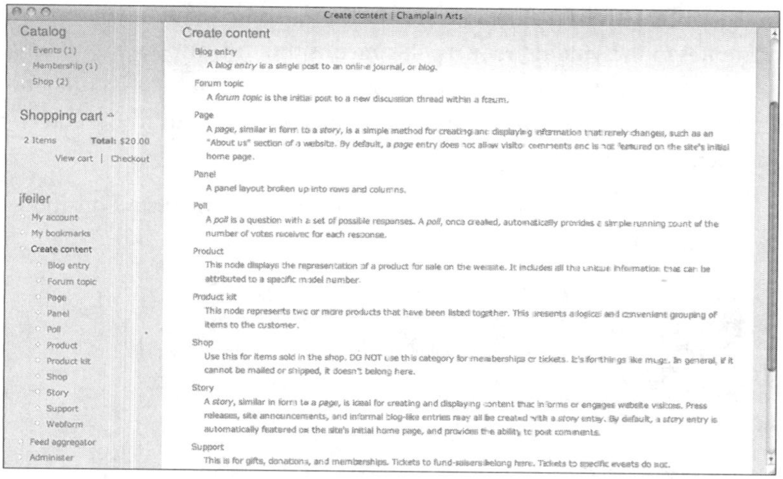

FIGURE 16.12
Create new products with the Create Content command.

Although attributes are assigned to products, you can choose which specific options for each attribute are available for each product. (You can also assign attributes and options to product classes.)

Attributes and options live in the general Ubercart environment. You assign specific ones to specific product classes and products. Create an attribute, such as Color, from Administer, Store Administration, Attributes, as shown in Figure 16.13.

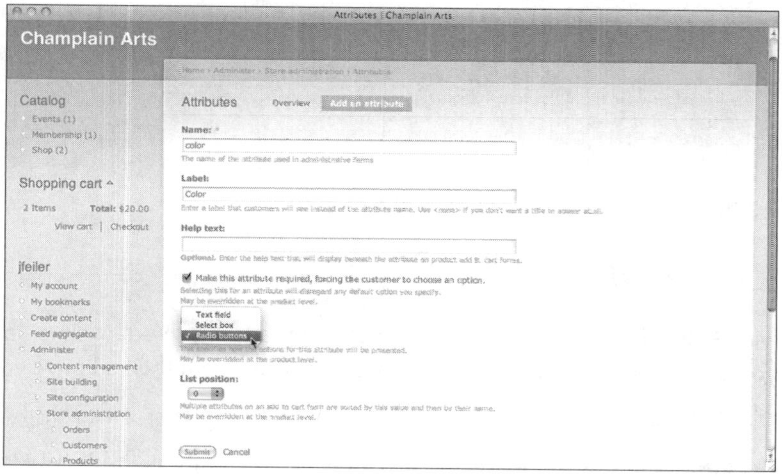

FIGURE 16.13
Create an attribute.

Notice in Figure 16.13 that the attribute is marked as being required. Because you assign attributes to individual products, this means that the attribute is required only if it is assigned to a product. You might assign the color attribute to T-shirts and mugs but not to ice scrapers. In addition, the options assigned to the attribute can be over-ridden for each product.

After you create the attribute and save it, it will be added to the list of attributes shown in Figure 16.14.

FIGURE 16.14
Add an attribute to the list.

Click Options at the right of the list to configure its options, as shown in Figure 16.15.

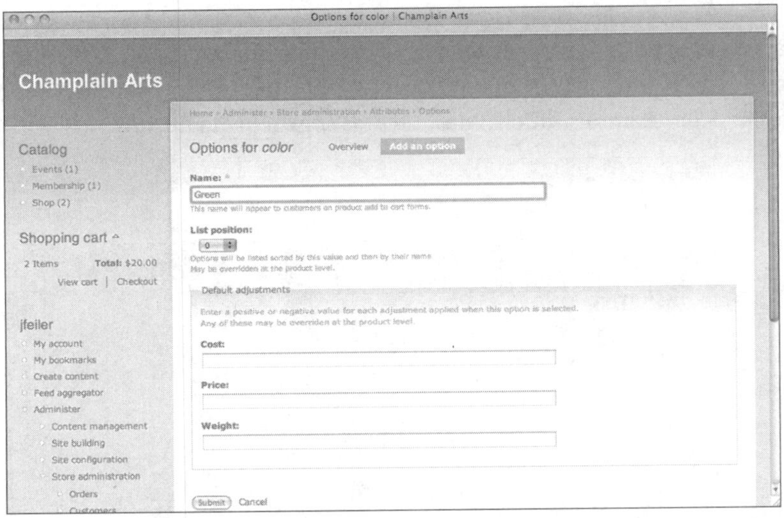

FIGURE 16.15
Configure options for an attribute.

After you create an attribute, you can assign it to a product or product class. In both cases, you go to a list—either products or product classes—and then edit it. Here is how you proceed:

▶ **Product Classes**—Go to Administer, Store Administration, Products, Manage Classes (admin/store/products/classes) and click Edit for the class you want to edit. Then, click Attributes to choose an attribute and, from there, Options to set options.

▶ **Products**—Go to Administer, Store Administration, Products, View Products (admin/store/products/view). Select the product and click Edit. From there, click Attributes and Options as you did for product classes.

After the attribute has been added to a product or product class, you can configure it, as shown in Figure 16.16.

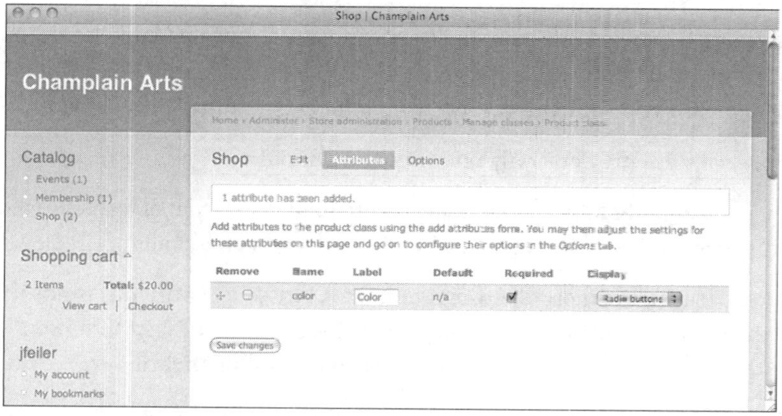

FIGURE 16.16
Configure the
attribute.

From the editing page for a product class or a product, you can click the Options button to configure options for all of the attributes for the product class or product, as shown in Figure 16.17.

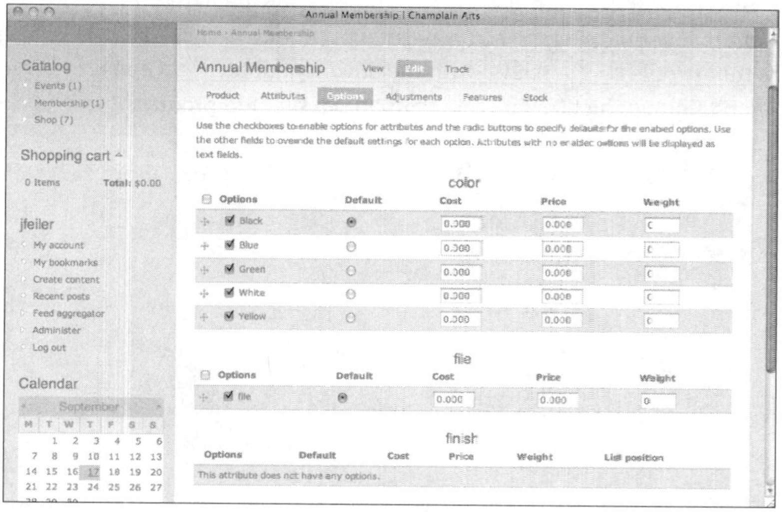

FIGURE 16.17
Configure
options for an
attribute.

Finally, note that for each product to which an attribute is assigned, you can turn on or off each of the options by clicking (or unclicking) the check box for the option in question.

You have now seen the basics of the Ubercart product implementation. These concepts (products, product classes, the catalog taxonomy, attributes, and options) are used over and over as you create your store. The following sections walk you through each type of product.

Working with Downloadable Sales

In some ways, downloadable sales are the simplest type of sale. There is nothing to ship, and you do not have to worry about inventory, because whether one item or 1,000,000 items are downloaded, there is no difference (except for bandwidth).

The first set of steps are done only once for your Drupal site.

Begin by checking Administer, Store Administration. At the bottom of the page (shown previously in Figure 16.3), you will see an indicator showing the status of File Downloads.

If you do not see it, the most likely explanation is that File Downloads is not enabled. Enable the module at Ubercart—Core (optional) File Downloads. At that point, you will see the status of File Downloads, and it is quite possible that an error exists.

Go to Administer, Store Administration, Configuration, Product Settings, Product Features (admin/store/settings/products/edit/features), as shown in Figure 16.18. Note that the directory for your downloadable files should be outside the Drupal directory for security reasons. In Figure 16.18, you can see that it is next to the Drupal folder (not inside it).

Set permissions for the roles you want to be able to download files in uc_file. This is the end of the one-time setup. Now, you can upload files to that directory and create products that people can purchase with the downloadable files. The basic sequence is to create and upload the files first and then attach them to products.

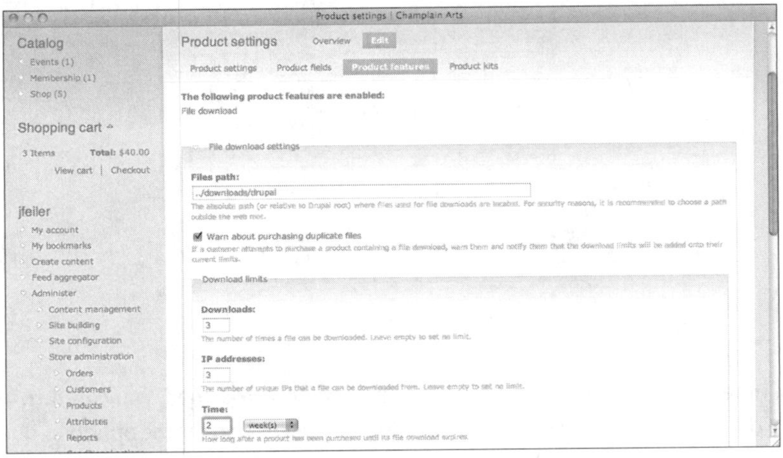

FIGURE 16.18
Set the download folder.

Try It Yourself ▼

Set Up a Download Product

1. Create the file that you will be downloading. Upload it by going to Administer, Store Administration, Products, View File Downloads (`admin/store/products/files`). Click the Upload File button to open the page shown in Figure 16.19. Select the file and upload it.

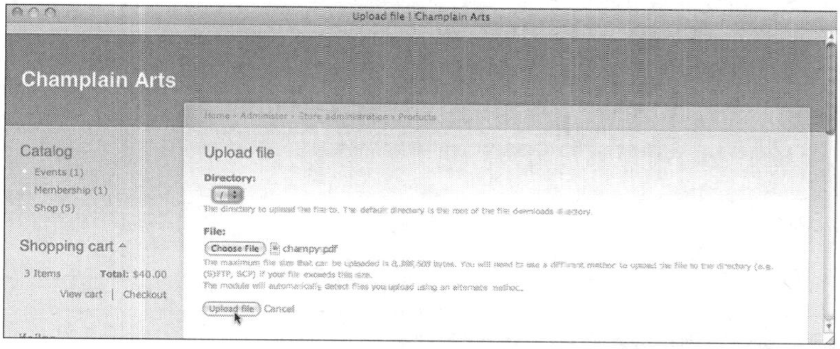

FIGURE 16.19
Upload the file.

2. Now, create the product to which the file will be attached. Do it the same as you would any other product. Unless you are automatically sending printed materials (which defeats the cost savings of a downloadable file), make sure that you mark the product as not being shippable. This check box is just below the prices in Product Information Be sure to save it.

3. Return to the product and click Edit. Now, click Features to add the File Download feature, as shown in Figure 16.20.

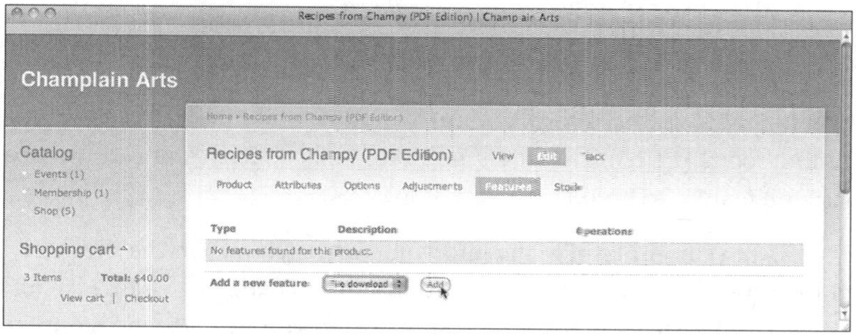

FIGURE 16.20
Add the File Download feature.

4. Select the SKU for the product and enter the filename. Override any download settings if necessary, as shown in Figure 16.21. (By default, the correct SKU is filled in, but you have a choice to add the download to any product.)

▼

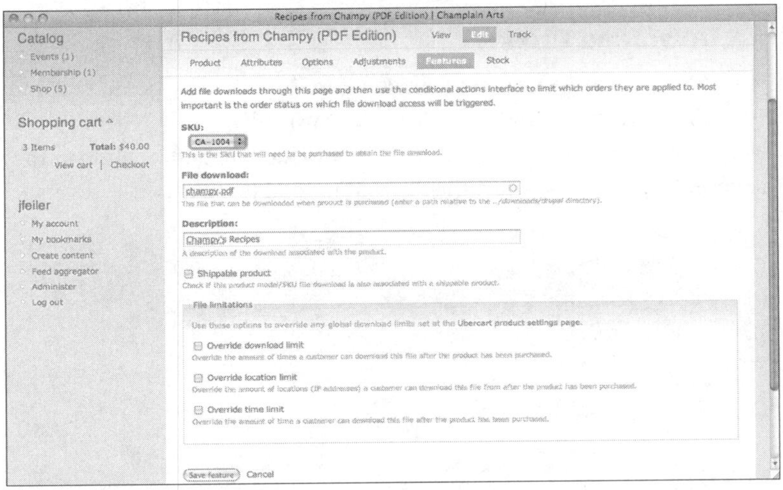

FIGURE 16.21
Attach the file to
the product.

Managing Reservation Inventory

This is for managing unreserved seats. In other words, you can sell 300 tickets or some other given number. Your reservations are for an unreserved seat. If you want to sell seat A101 and A102 (and not sell them twice), you need another strategy. Also note that this works best for relatively small events (a few hundred at most). It is a good demonstration of how Drupal's power can provide the biggest bang for the buck for small businesses and nonprofits. If your club can accommodate 100 people, this is a perfect tool to manage paid-in-advance reservations. If the venue is a 70,000 seat stadium, this will not work.

Working with Reservation Sales

When you are selling reservations, you cannot allow unlimited sales; the theater, stadium, dining room, park, or classroom has a limited capacity. You can use Ubercart's stock tracking feature to handle this situation.

Drupal tracks the current level of inventory and alerts you when the inventory drops beneath the threshold (although it will not prevent an overstock sale). Like all inventory management systems, Ubercart has some issues you need to watch out for. First, there is no way of knowing what your actual inventory level is without counting it. Through clerical errors or what is euphemistically called "shrinkage," some of your inventory may come and go without your knowledge. In addition, if you are selling tickets or reservations to events that are typically sold out, there is no way to avoid monitoring last-minute sales very closely. Everyone from airlines to restaurateurs knows that if you have 1,200 seats to fill, you need to factor in some last-minute arrivals and last-minute cancellations.

Try It Yourself

Set Up a Reservation Product

1. Create and go to the product for which you want to track inventory. Click Edit and then Stock, as shown in Figure 16.22. Enter the inventory level you can sell and the threshold when you want to be notified. Also, make sure to mark the item as Active with the check box.

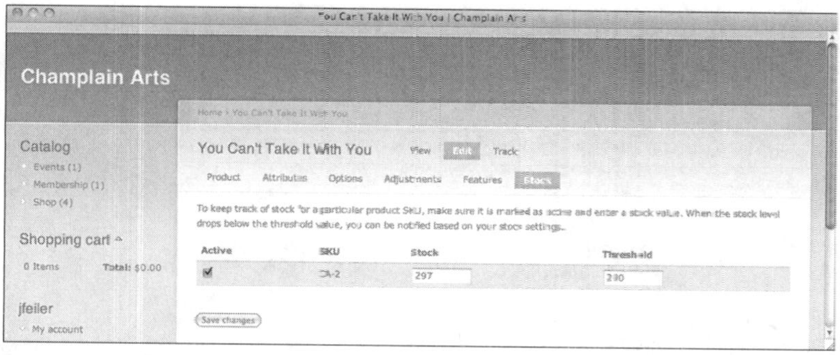

FIGURE 16.22
Manage inventory.

2. You have to manage the process of admitting people. Two automated email messages are generated for each sale. In practice, most people bring their confirmation email. You also receive an email message for each sale. People using this technique often revert to the simplest and most old-fashioned method of management: They print out the confirmation emails and alphabetize them by name. You can add a checkout message to the confirmation email at Administration, Store Administration, Configuration, Checkout Settings (admin/store/settings/checkout) reminding people to bring that email with them to events they have purchased.

3. Periodically, return to that Edit, Stock page shown in Figure 16.22 to check how things are going. Alternatively, go to Administer, Store Administration, Reports, Stock Reports (admin/store/reports/stock/threshold) to view the report shown in Figure 16.23. Note that you can export the values to a CSV file for further analysis.

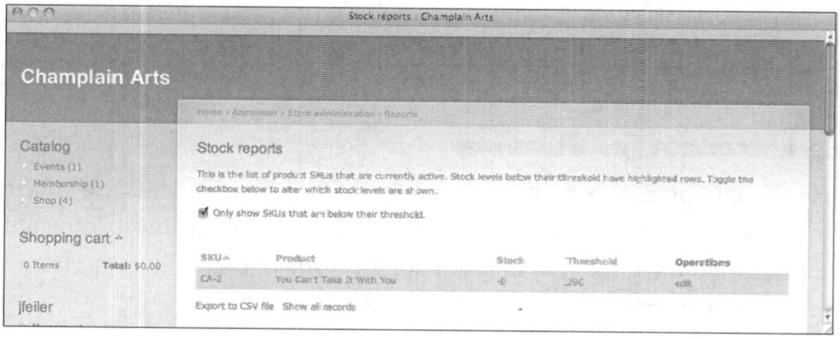

FIGURE 16.23
View stock reports.

Working with Physical Sales

You need to set up a mechanism for shipping if you are handling physical items. There are two parts to this process. Go to Administer, Store Administration, Configuration, Shipping Quote Settings (`admin/store/settings/quotes/edit`), as shown in Figure 16.24. The default settings are usually OK here, but you may want to customize the messages.

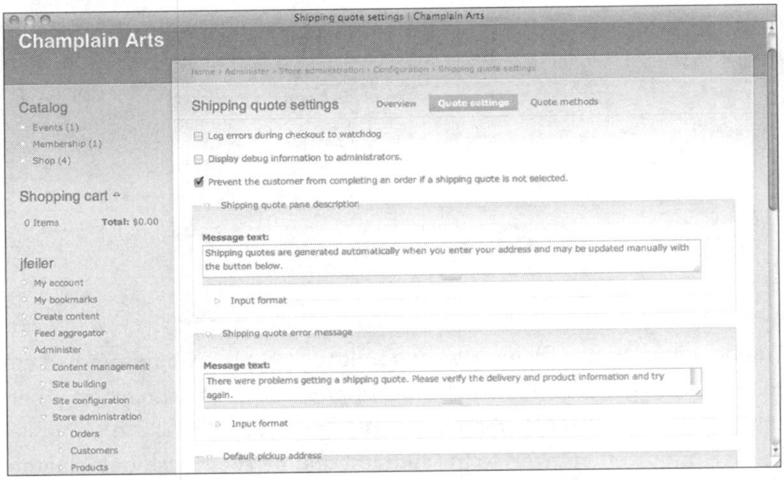

FIGURE 16.24
Configure Shipping Quote Settings.

Now, click Quote Methods at the top right to open the page with the various shipping methods you have chosen. The choices depend on which shipping modules you have installed. (For example, if you have enabled UPS and have a UPS account number, that will be one of the choices.) Note that at the bottom of this page is your default pickup address for the product (scrolled out of view). Enter it here to avoid having to reenter it for each product. You can always override it on specific product editing pages.

This has to be done only once for your store unless you change your shipping methods. You can build on what you have learned from downloadable products and reservations for most of the e-commerce process. The only two tasks that are different are the definition of the product and the fulfillment of the purchase (shipping and delivery).

▼ **Try It Yourself**

Set Up a Product for Shipping

1. Use Create Content to create the product. In this example, it is the Shop product class, but you can use whatever you want. Provide the basic information of name, description, and catalog categories. None of this is different from the nonshippable products you have dealt with before.

▼

Set product information for SKU and dimensions.

2. Scroll down to add an image and the product prices. This, too, is the same as for other products.

3. Scroll down and mark the product as shippable in the Product Information section.

4. Now, you must enter the weight and shipping dimensions. This is all new.

   Scroll down to enter shipping settings, as shown in Figure 16.25. Note that this is where you can override the default product shipping location that you set in Shipping Quote Settings (admin/store/settings/quotes/edit). The product is now ready for people to purchase it. Watch your email for confirmation of sales.

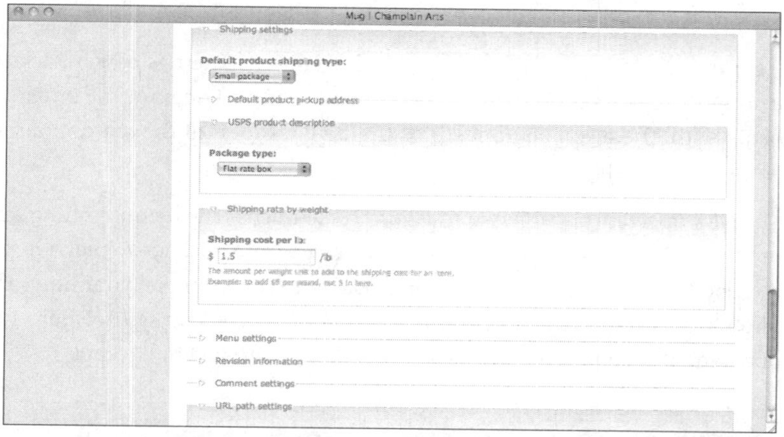

FIGURE 16.25
Complete shipping settings.

The next steps in the sequence of e-commerce sales are up to your customers. You have set up the products and they do the rest. Of course, you should monitor the store and consider using all of your Drupal communication tools, such as blogs, articles, and newsletters, to get the word out. When you are notified of a sale, here is what you do.

Try It Yourself

Fulfill a Shippable Sale

To continue, it is important to understand two basic concepts:

▶ **Package**—This is a box or other container that contains one or more products.

▶ **Shipment**—This is one or more packages that are shipped together. For track-able services, such as FedEx or some USPS products, a tracking number exists for the shipment.

In many cases, these distinctions do not matter. If someone orders one product, it is shipped in one package, which is its own shipment. Nevertheless, to be able to han-dle more complex sales, Ubercart walks you through the process of creating both a package and a shipment. In the example shown here, the customer has ordered two T-shirts and one mug. They will be shipped in two packages. The first one will have one T-shirt and the mug, and the second one will have the other T-shirt.

When it comes time to ship a product, here is what you do:

1. Go to the list of orders at Administer, Store Administration, Orders (admin/store/orders) as shown previously in Figure 16.8.

2. Near the top of the list should be unshipped orders. There is now a Package icon for those orders. Click it to open the page of packages for the order. To begin with, there will be none. Click Create Packages (at the bottom of the empty package list).

   The New Package page shown in Figure 16.26 opens. The default setting for each product is Sep. (separate). That will create a separate package for each item. This is a good setting if products come prepackaged. (For example, your mugs may already be boxed to keep them from breakage.) As you can see in Figure 16.26, one item of each product has been selected to be shipped in Package 1.

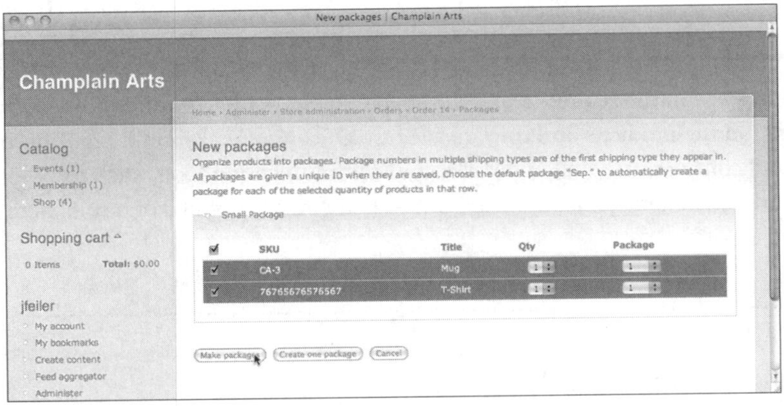

FIGURE 16.26
Set up the first package.

3. After that package is created, you can create the final one. There is only one more product to ship (the second T-shirt), so you create a package for it. You can now view the list of packages by clicking Packages at the top of the page, as shown in Figure 16.27.

4. Now, it is time to create a shipment. Click Shipments at the top of the page to create a new shipment.

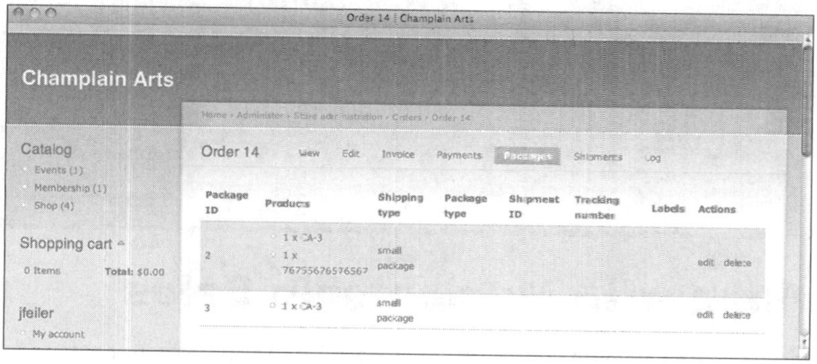

FIGURE 16.27
Review the packages.

5. The page shown in Figure 16.28 lets you choose which packages to ship. In this case, both packages will be shipped. However, if you are temporarily out of stock for some items, you might create only a partial shipment.

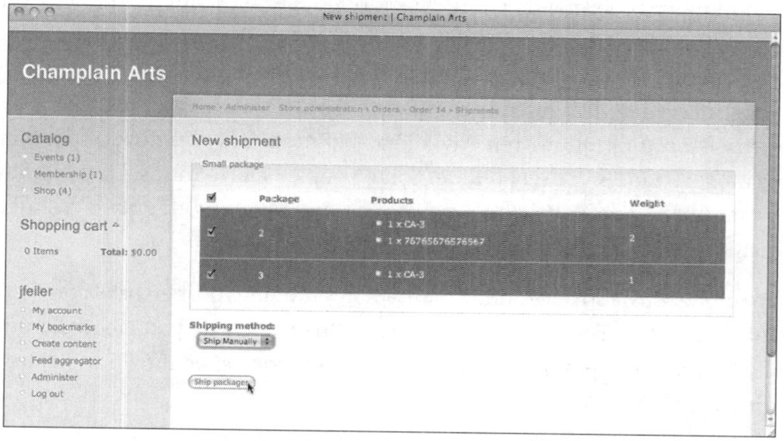

FIGURE 16.28
Ship the packages.

6. You are asked for the shipping data, such as origin and destination. You will need to supply the carrier, tracking idea, and dates for shipping and expected delivery.

7. The shipment will be logged to the order, as shown in Figure 16.29. Mark the order complete, as described previously in Figure 16.9 and Figure 16.10, if this is the last shipment.

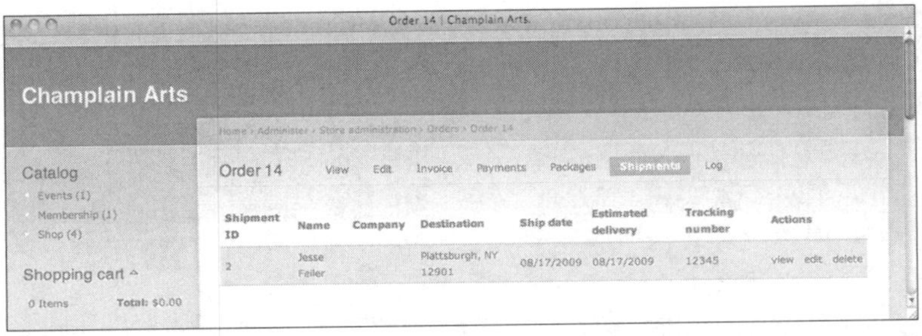

FIGURE 16.29
Drupal keeps
track of the ship-
ment data.

Working with Membership Sales

The last type of product you can sell is a membership. People pay to become a member of an organization or to have access to a site. You manage this by providing a Drupal role that provides the access that they need. You then provide a price and a period of time that the membership will cover.

Because this process is automated, this can be an efficient way for nonprofit organizations to manage their membership. This is often a weak point in finances, particularly for small nonprofits. As the 2008 U.S. presidential election demonstrated, the use of the Internet to collect many, many small donations into very impressive sums is not to be sneezed at. It is already a well-established idea to ask people to support a project, cause, or nonprofit with a PayPal contribution. You can now create a membership category that is entirely online. Some people believe that such a membership category should be priced at a very low level so that people with only a casual interest participate, and then renew at a similarly low renewal rate.

To sell memberships, make certain that the Roles module in Ubercart—core (optional) is enabled. Then, create a product in the same way you created a download for Champy's Recipes. Add a Role Assignment feature, as shown in Figure 16.30 (compare with Figure 16.20).

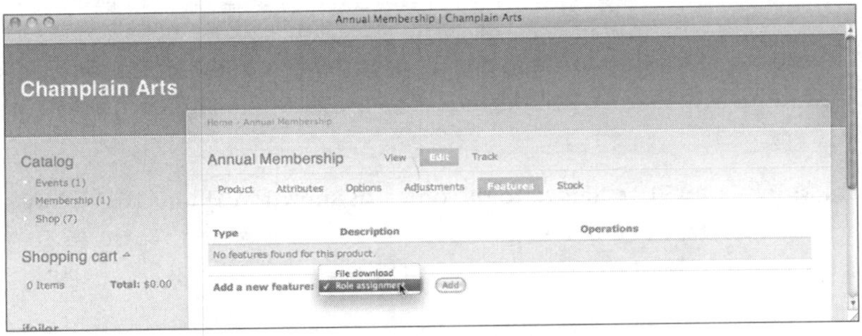

FIGURE 16.30
Add a role
assignment fea-
ture.

After you click Add, the next page lets you set the expiration of the role, as shown in Figure 16.31. For many organizations, an annual membership fee is such an administrative burden that it is not prorated. Here, however, you can specify that the role access is for a given period of time from now. In addition, you can choose to configure it so that if people purchase multiple items, the term is extended.

When the membership expires, you do not have to worry: Ubercart will notify the member.

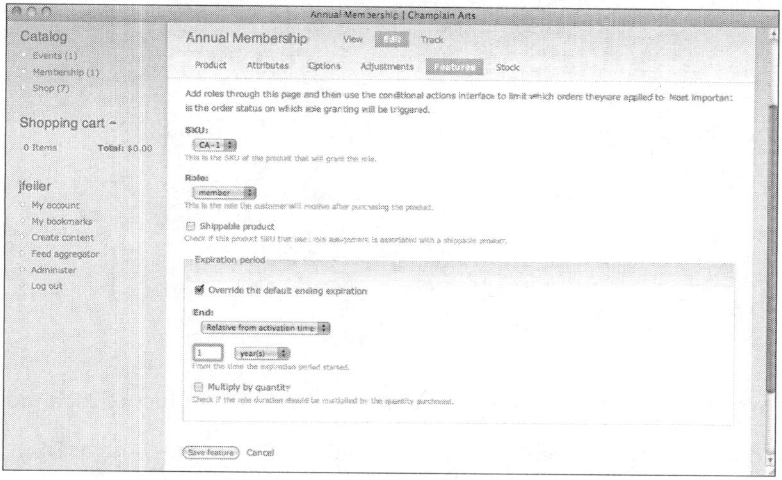

FIGURE 16.31
Specify the expiration.

Using Product Kits

Another Ubercart feature is worth considering. If you have installed and enabled Product Kit in Ubercart—extra, you can make a single item of two or more products. Begin by using Create Content to create a new Product Kit. Give it a name and catalog information, as shown in Figure 16.32.

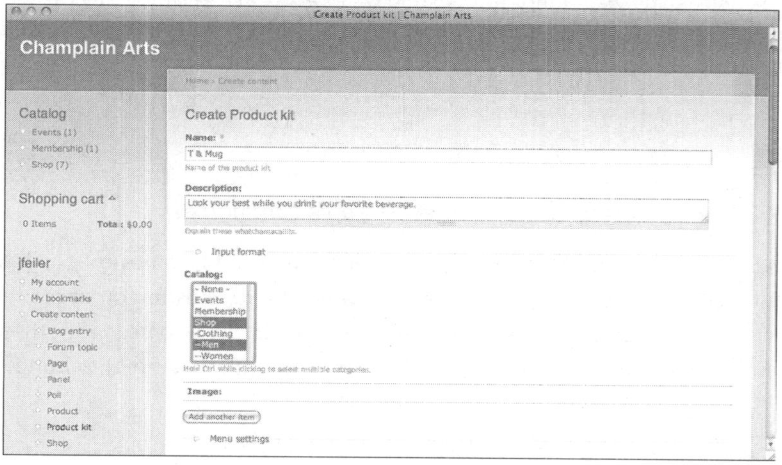

FIGURE 16.32
Create a product kit.

Next, select the products for the kit, as shown in Figure 16.33.

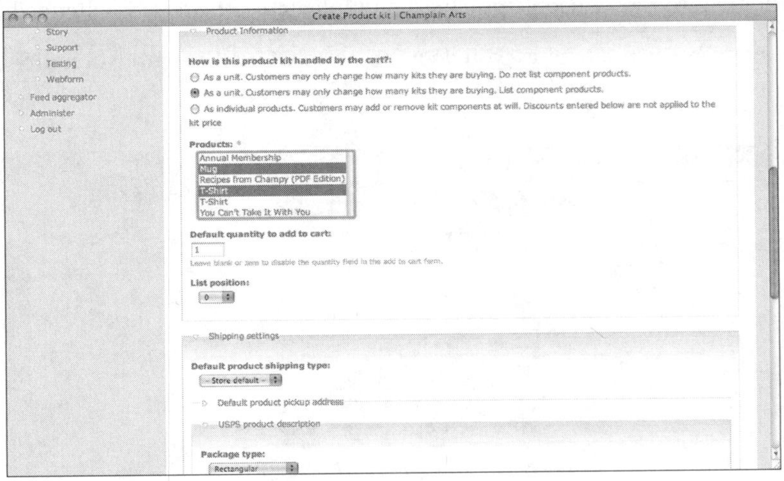

FIGURE 16.33
Select the kit
products.

Click Save and Continue; the next page asks you for the quantities of each product.

The product kit is now added to the catalog, and people can purchase it. From here on, except for the possible discounted pricing, the order appears exactly as it would if the customer had separately added the component products to the cart.

Summary

E-commerce is becoming central to all aspects of the economy from the smallest organizations to the largest ones. Ubercart builds on Drupal's powerful features to implement a set of modules that can handle most of the features that you need to sell successfully on the Internet.

Q&A

Q. What is the biggest obstacle to setting up e-commerce?

A. No matter the size of the organization, no matter if it is a for-profit or a not-for-profit organization, the greatest challenge for an existing organization is usually a reluctance to try something new. For example, a nonprofit that moves its annual membership fee to Drupal and allows Drupal to handle reminders worries that people will be offended in some way. On the other hand, a company that has used a third-party e-commerce site is reluctant to bring that operation in-house because it doesn't have the skills. Use the Test Gateway and a test installation to experiment and see if you can win over the doubters. Remember that this is a common issue.

Q. *What are all those other options in Ubercart?*

A. Explore Ubercart in a test environment so that you can try everything. The process outlined in this hour will help you create the basic types of products. For example, Ubercart has features to handle automatic product substitutions. You can customize email messages and notifications on confirmation pages. But, the best place to start is with the basic structure outlined here.

Q. *We have several types of memberships for different prices. How do we implement that?*

A. There are two basic strategies. You can create separate products with separate prices (such as Basic Membership, Sponsor, and Donor). Alternatively, you can create a single membership product with a Member Type attribute. Use the capability to add to the basic price so that the Sponsor option adds $100, and the Donor option adds $250 (or whatever your levels are). You can combine these so that the membership products are for different time periods (a month, 6 months, year, and so forth), and the Member Type attribute for each one adjusts the price. Ubercart can handle this as long as you decide what you want. And that is one of the benefits of Drupal and Ubercart. As you work through the process, you will confront issues that you may not have thought of.

Workshop

Quiz

1. What is the difference between an attribute and an option?

2. How do you test with fake credit card numbers?

3. How do you add a new category to the catalog?

Quiz Answers

1. An attribute is attached to a product or product class. It is named something like Color or Size. Each attribute can have many options assigned to the product or product class (black, white, red, and yellow, for example). An individual product can add the attributes from the product class and can select only certain of the options.

2. Enable Test Gateway in Payment Settings, turn on Operate in Credit Card Debug Mode, and turn off Validate Credit Card Numbers at Checkout.

3. Edit the Catalog Taxonomy as Administer, Content Management, Taxonomy (D6:`admin/content/taxonomy`, D7:`admin/structure/taxonomy`).

Activities

Select a few e-commerce sites that you think are good. Now, think about how you would implement them in Ubercart. What would the product classes be? Are there product kits? Then, try to build a composite site with the features you like in a test environment.

HOUR 17

Building Your First Live Site

What You'll Learn in This Hour:

- ▶ Reviewing Your Configuration and Implementation
- ▶ Protecting Against Intruders
- ▶ Using Terms of Service and Other Legal Modules
- ▶ Exploring Drupal Advertising Modules

Introduction

Now that you have seen an introduction to Drupal (in Part I) and an in-depth look at Drupal's socializing and communication tools, including e-commerce (in Part II), it is time to focus on building your site. This part deals with the nuts-and-bolts issues of choosing a theme for your site, working with panels and pages, using menus, and other overall site issues.

In this hour, you prepare for creating and deploying your site. You gain some basic housekeeping information—everything from how to manage terms of service (TOS) and protection from bots on your Drupal site.

Reviewing Your Configuration and Implementation

You have experimented with Drupal, and you may have set up more than one site. Now, it is time to do it for real. Think about the problems that you have had, and come up with a plan for the production site (or, if possible, the production and development sites). Many problems arise with shared hosting, but they generally are solvable. (For example, you may be limited to a certain number of installations.)

Go back through the basic settings for roles and permissions and come up with the final version that you will use for production. You also may have experimented with custom content types that might be useful or might need to be consolidated. If at all possible, start by creating your new site from scratch.

One critical point to remember is that the first user you set up has complete access to the site and database. You normally do not run under this account, but you may need it to run update.php and some other maintenance tasks.

Many people use a password that they know well for this account. If you have done so, come up with another one. Although, in general, it is a bad idea to share accounts and passwords, the password for the primary user account must be sharable (so, it cannot be your bank PIN). You will need to share this password when you go on vacation or if you move on to another Drupal gig. It can always be changed, but it is very risky to be in a situation in which you and only you can change the password to something nonsensitive before it can be given to someone else.

Treat this account password as very secure, but secure in a different way than your private passwords.

Protecting Against Intruders

Unless your site is behind a firewall on a private network, you will soon find traces of unauthorized visitors. If you review the log, you will see login attempts by bots; these are often recognizable by the users list. You will see a user who registered a week (month or year) ago, and who has never returned. This is quite possibly legitimate, but it may not be. Malware is now able to recognize forms on websites, register for them, and even send messages. This may be malicious or just frivolous (or both—it can be a dry run for a soon-to-come malicious attack).

You may want to protect your site with software such as CAPTCHA that can distinguish between a person and a bot. Other modules are available, but many people use Completely Automated Public Turing test to tell Computers and Humans Apart (CAPTCHA). Download, install, and enable it, as shown in Table 17.1. (reCaptcha, which is described later in this section, is a web service version of CAPTCHA. You may want both.)

TABLE 17.1   CAPTCHA/reCaptcha Module Reference

Download from	project/captcha, project/recaptcha
Enable in section	Spam Control
Permissions	
Captcha Module	administer CAPTCHA settings, skip CAPTCHA
reCaptcha Module	administer reCAPTCHA
Administration	
Administer, User Management, Captcha (admin/user/captcha)	

There are now several versions of CAPTCHA; they all build on the CAPTCHA base. The idea behind all the CAPTCHAs is that they present a problem that cannot be solved by a computer bot. Only a person can solve the problem. This can be a problem that involves arithmetic and logic—"What is the third word of this sentence?") or one that involves recognizing text that has been distorted to prevent bots from reading it.

Figure 17.1 shows examples of the various types of CAPTCHAs. The final one (reCAPTCHA) is one of the most frequently used. This is partly because it is fast and efficient, but it is also chosen by a number of webmasters because of what is happening behind the scenes (see the sidebar "How reCAPTCHA Works").

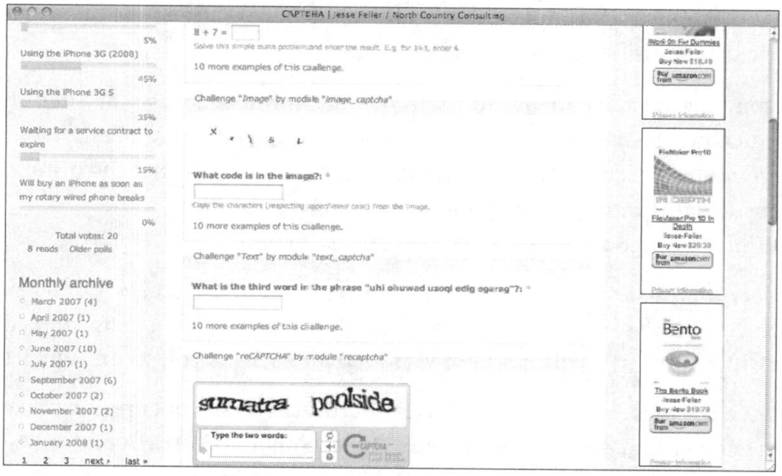

FIGURE 17.1
Different CAPTCHAs are available.

How reCAPTCHA Works

As you can see at the bottom of Figure 17.1, reCAPTCHA presents two words that are slightly distorted. To pass reCAPTCHA and convince the system that you are a person, you must correctly read the two words. Most people do not have a problem with this; if you do, you can always ask for another set of words. (reCAPTCHA also provides an audio interface.)

reCAPTCHA is a web service, so the words are sent to the page from their server on an as-needed basis. There is where the intriguing part of reCAPTCHA lies. If you are trying to gain access to a site, your task is simply to recognize the two test words and type them in. After that, you have passed the test.

From the reCAPTCHA side, only one of the words is a test. The other word comes from a scanned image. Optical Character Recognition software (OCR) is not

perfect, just as scans of old documents are not perfect. As a scanning project proceeds, a list of words that were scanned but not recognized is built. One by one,
each of those undecipherable words is presented next to one that is known.

If the user types the known words properly, the test is passed. In addition,
reCAPTCHA keeps track of the user's interpretation of the unknown word. After a
number of attempts have been collected, reCAPTCHA can provide a word for the
recognizable scanned word. The reCAPTCHA project began at Carnegie Mellon University's School of Computer Science. It was purchased in 2009 by Google for use
in its Google Books and Google News Ardhive Search projects.

You need to download code from the reCAPTCHA site so that the reCAPTCHA
module can call back. The code can be downloaded from
recaptcha.net/plugins/php/index.html in an archive file. Expand the archive and
install the folder inside the reCAPTCHA module folder.

When you have installed the reCAPTCHA module, it will be located at .sites/all/mod-
ules/recaptcha. The downloaded and expanded files are placed inside that folder in
their own folder, which is also called recaptcha. You can check that the installation is
correct by looking for recaptchalib.php. It should be located at
.sites/all/modules/recaptcha/recaptcha/recaptchalib.php.

After everything is downloaded and installed, go to Administer, User Management,
Captacha (admin/user/captcha). You will see all the forms on your site, and you can
choose which form of CAPTCHA (if any) is used for each, as you see in Figure 17.2.

If you have downloaded and installed reCAPTCHA and it does not appear, make sure
that it is enabled and permissions are properly set both for CAPTCHA and reCAPTCHA.
Go to admin/user/captcha and click the reCAPTCHA tab. You will find fields to enter
the public and private keys you have obtained from http://recaptcha.net/api/getkey.

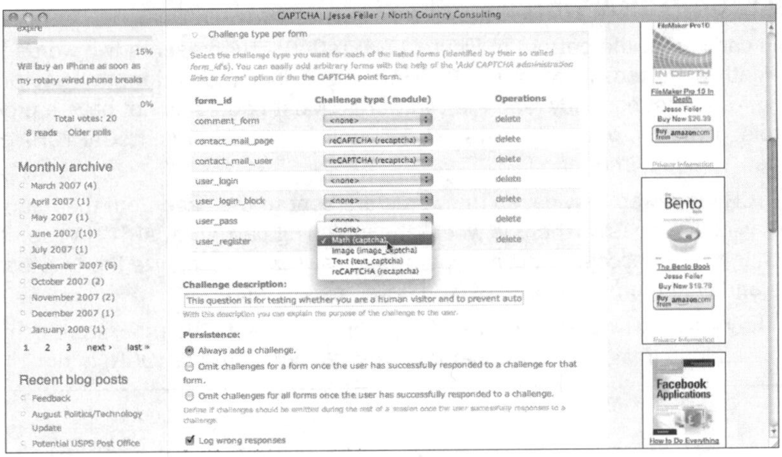

FIGURE 17.2
Set a CAPTCHA
for each form.

Using Terms of Service and Other Legal Modules

You may be launching a site that is larger and more complex than any other site you have been involved with. You should think about two areas of legal issues.

Preparing Legal Notices

Depending on the type of site you are developing, you may need a number of legal notices. These are the most common:

▶ **Copyright notices**—The conventional wisdom used to be that you should protect your site and its contents from unauthorized use and copying, and that the simplest way to do that was to stick a copyright notice on each page. Things are much more complex now. For example, if your site contains open source content, its terms of use may prevent you from copyrighting it again or may require you to continue to post the original copyright or license terms. (Drupal is open source software, but this section applies to your site's content, not its software.) In addition, you may not be able to copyright your site's material. (This applies to government sites in the United States.) The new conventional wisdom is twofold: Know what your copyright status is, and then post the appropriate notice.

▶ **Terms of Use**—You may impose limitations on how your users can use your site. This may be phrased as "by using this site, you agree to..." or it may be a formal document that the user must accept, as described in the following section.

▶ **Terms of Service**—Whereas terms of use refer to how users can use your site, terms of service typically refer to what you will provide to the user. If you are allowing users to update the site, create blogs, and post content, you will be providing a service to them.

▶ **About Us**—This page on the site can be simply informative, but it may need to have credits and notices. This is particularly true for nonprofit sites where grants and even public funding may support the site. The terms of the grant or funding may include notifications you must post.

Adding Legal Interactions

Several modules let you administer legal options.

Terms of Use

The Terms of Use module (`project/terms_of_use`) lets you implement agreement with terms of service on the account registration form. If the user does not check the I Agree box (you can change the wording), the user cannot register. You can specify the text of the terms so this module works for both terms of use and terms of service.

Legal

The Legal module (`project/legal`) implements a similar functionality. One of its features is that if you change the text of the terms, users will be required to accept the revised terms before they can log in again.

Finding More Modules

In the last part of this hour, you will find some references to modules you can use for advertising on your site. That brings up a critical issue for you to consider: How do you find and evaluate new modules for the site?

In Hour 4, "Administering Drupal, Themes, and Modules," you saw how to download modules and find them on drupal/org/project/modules. In the best of all possible worlds, you would have three Drupal installations: your production version, a development version, and a disposable version for module and theme tests. The difference between those last two versions is that a development version should be pretty much a copy of your production site with all the modules installed. The disposable version can be just that—a fresh installation into which you can install a module you want to evaluate. Not having other modules there is beneficial so that you can focus on the new one. If you are pleased, you can install it into the development version and then take down the disposable version.

From the listings on Drupal.org, you can look at comments and at the number of users. As noted previously, very small numbers are not necessarily adverse. When you go looking for specific types of modules (for example, modules to support wish lists), look at the usage numbers. You will probably find several modules with roughly similar numbers. You will get an informal sense for what the number of users of a module in this category should be. (You would not expect it to be less than 10 or more than 30,000, although those numbers are appropriate in other categories.)

Experiment with the module as you would want to use it. Now that you have more experience with Drupal, look for implementations that could use built-in Drupal functionality but that do not do so (rules, taxonomies, CCK, and so forth). These may be indications of a module written some time ago that has been maintained but not structurally updated.

Exploring Drupal Advertising Modules

For many websites, advertising is a critical source of revenue. In fact, as is the case with many print publications, advertising may pay for the support of the site. (In the case of print, there frequently are dual income streams: revenue from advertising is supplemented by revenue from subscribers and purchasers of single copies.)

As the web has grown, advertising revenue has been critical. The economics of the web (very low cost of delivery and presentation along with potentially very large audience numbers) have meant that only highly automated ad delivery services can succeed in many cases. There are Drupal interfaces to Google's AdSense, along with others.

In addition to these networks, a parallel advertising world has grown up on the web. It consists of everything from an ad on a website offering a T-shirt with the company's logo to ads specifically promoting websites (rather than the purchase of goods). The next section looks at both areas.

Advertising with an Ad Service

These programs all function in basically the same way. You create an account with the company and are assigned an ID. Your pages are configured to be able to retrieve dynamic ad content based on either a user's search or the content of the page. That dynamically created ad is placed on your site along with your ID. You are reimbursed based on the responses to those ads.

Do not confuse Google AdSense (in which you earn money) with Google AdWords (in which you pay to place ads such as these on other sites). In its simplest form, an advertiser can pay to have an ad placed on pages with a keyword such as *dog bed* using AdWords. If you have a page related to dog beds, Google AdSense may place the ad paid for by the AdWords user on your page; you are then paid for displaying the ad.

Typically, your account with the ad service provides extensive statistical reporting. If you are already using an ad service, find out if they have a Drupal module implementation.

Google AdSense Module

By the Way

> **AdSense and Generated Ads**
>
> The AdSense terms of service and other documentation envision a process whereby you manually create an ad and paste it onto a page. As more people generate pages dynamically with tools such as Drupal, this idea of copying and pasting an ad is a quaint relic of the past. There is more on the `project/adsense` page.

This module (`project/adsense`) implements Google AdSense on your site. It can be integrated with Drupal roles so that ads are displayed (or are not displayed) only for some roles. This can provide you with an implementation for a subscriber role where the user pays a fee for add-free content. The code for the ad is generated on-the-fly in accordance with Google's formatting.

Amazon Module

This module (`project/amazon`) implements the Amazon e-commerce APIs. This is a somewhat different approach from Google AdSense because the revenue that is generated is not generated by the ad. Rather, if someone clicks through to Amazon with the customized link on your website, purchases earn a commission that is credited to your account. Thus, the revenue is based on sales, not advertising.

Advertising with Custom Ads

Rather than having ads served up by a service that pays your account for the displays you provide, you can create and place your own ads. (This includes publishing ads that are provided to you by your clients.) Modules supporting this functionality typically provide their own statistical reporting.

Advertisement Module

This powerful and popular module can be found at `project/ad`. It can be a good module to experiment with if you want to get started, in part because of its extensive reporting features that help you understand how the ads are working on your site.

Rotor Banner Module

This module (project/rotor) does exactly what its name says. It lets you serve up banner ads in a predefined rotation. Although it is designed for banner ads, you can use it to rotate through any content.

Summary

This hour covers some of the issues you need to consider as you start to launch a live site. You have seen how to protect against spammers and bots using CAPTCHAs and their derivatives. You have also seen how to find new modules and, specifically, how to deal with legal notices and the opportunities for earning money from ads on your site.

Q&A

Q. *What is the best way to find the legal requirements for my site?*

A. Look at comparable sites (in the same government jurisdiction). If your site is part of an existing business or organization, use trade group resources to find out how laws apply to you and your site.

Q. *What legal liability do I have (or receive) if a contributed module does not work properly?*

A. In most cases, you assume all the responsibility. Do not think that this is an artifact of open source software. Reading the license for a commercial product is not for the faint of heart.

Workshop

Quiz

1. Does Drupal work with Google's AdSense?

2. What is the difference between terms of service (TOS) and terms of use (TOU)?

3. Can I sell advertising directly on my Drupal site?

Quiz Answers

1. There is a bridge module available (as for eBay, Amazon, and more).

2. TOS refers to the service you provide; TOU refers to what users can do with that service.

3. Yes. You do not have to use an intermediary such as AdSense, but you may find it easier not to do your own advertising marketing.

Activities

This hour provided a jumping-off point for the last part of the book. Go for it and set up (if you can) three sites: production, development, and disposable. Use the process as part of a learning and training program. If several people are working on the project, it can be a good idea not to work together. If each of three team members puts up the three sites, together you have put up nine sites and you should have created a fairly strong institutional knowledge. This is one case in which working together can be detrimental. By working together, it may turn out that no single member of your team is comfortable setting up a Drupal site from scratch.

HOUR 18

Choosing a Theme

What You'll Learn in This Hour:

▶ How to Evaluate Drupal Themes

▶ Where to Find New Themes

▶ How Much Do Themes Cost?

▶ How to Install and Configure Themes

Introduction

Themes provide the look and feel of a Drupal site. One of the core design principles of a Content Management System (CMS) such as Drupal is that the handling of the content is separated from the handling of its presentation. As with modules, Drupal provides several themes, and third-party developers contribute themes that you can use. Because this is all open source code, you can modify it. In the case of modules, it is usually a poor idea to modify the code, but in the case of a theme, you can modify the code. (Some themes are specifically designed for such modifications in their design.)

In this hour, you will see how to choose, download, and install themes. You will see how to use the extensive customization tools that Drupal provides as well as how (if necessary) you can consider doing your own customization.

Keeping the Train on the Track

For many people and organizations, a discussion about a new or revised website has a tendency to quickly veer off track. Everyone has an idea of what it should look like, and those suggestions can sometimes be less than valuable.

Here is a list of some critical website features drawn from several planning discussions about new websites. The requirements for the new website included the following:

▶ Flash

▶ Can be updated by client rather than consultant

▶ Must be object oriented

▶ Should use green as a predominant color (for an environmental organization)

▶ Should look corporate

▶ Should not look corporate

Whether you are a website designer, a consultant, a client, or anyone else involved in the creation of a website, you can probably add to this list of requirements. It is a long and varied list, and each item absolutely must be in the finished website.

Whatever your role in a new website will be, if you are using Drupal or are seriously considering it, you should quickly realize that none of these items refer to content; they are all presentational. A major part of your job will be keeping the focus on track. For some reason, people find it much easier to talk about colors and Flash animations than about the content, which is the actual reason for the website.

One way to get the most out of Drupal is to understand how you can use themes to change the site's appearance. This hour is a good way to start to understand that structure and functionality. After you feel comfortable with your ability to replace your site's interface, you may want to put that task aside. If you know that you can always come back to make modifications, you can build your Drupal site with one of the generic themes distributed with Drupal. Add data and experiment with it. Do as much testing as your time and budget allow.

Push the data and the interface that you already have. Chances are the interface won't have the boss's favorite color so it will be totally unacceptable, but you can work with it and push it to see where it functionally needs changes. (A color scheme is not a functional change.)

At that point, you can start to build a revised list of requirements that can evolve from your experiments. Such a list might contain the following items:

▶ Can accommodate articles and stories with up to six images in each one. There must be at least two images in each article or story.

▶ Can display a paged list of items with up to 20 one-line summaries on each page.

▶ Uses the boss's favorite color (learn to pick your battles).

As you work on the site, you can change the theme periodically using the themes that come with Drupal or downloadable themes. If you have gone through this exercise in refining your goals, you will be able to evaluate the themes from a functional point of view, and you will gain experience and confidence with switching themes.

As your site comes along, you can then refine your requirements list to make it theme oriented. For example, you may have learned that certain layouts will work for your data and others will not. At that point, whether you use an existing theme, create a new one, or modify a theme, you will know more about what you are doing.

Looking at Themes

Here is a selection of themes and sites. They all use themes included in Drupal itself or downloaded as contributed modules. Compare them with one another to see how you can use themes to transform your site.

About the Screenshots in This Hour

In this hour, some figures have been captured at higher screen resolutions, meaning that the size of the type and images in the figures are smaller than in other hours. Do not worry if you cannot read the text; the point is to show the overall page layout.

By the Way

Three Themes for Plattsburgh Green

Plattsburgh Green is a community group focusing on the environment in Plattsburgh, New York. Figures 18.1 through 18.3 show the site with three different themes.

Figure 18.1 shows the Acquia Marina theme developed by TopNotchThemes in partnership with Acquia for its commercially supported Drupal distribution. It is available for free download at drupal.org/project/acquia_marina.

This is a typical Drupal front page with recent postings in reverse chronological order. Blocks display a welcome message, a calendar, and other features that are scrolled out of sight at the bottom.

Whether you like the look of the page shown in Figure 18.1 or not, there is one important lesson to be learned. You cannot judge a Drupal theme by looking at it in

Go To ▶
HOUR 19, "USING BLOCKS," for more on adding blocks to themes.

isolation. Only by comparing it to other themes do the features of each of the themes stand out. For example, Acquia Marina is a fixed-width theme. If you know what to look for, you can see that in Figure 18.1, but it is easier to notice it in Figures 18.2 and 18.3.

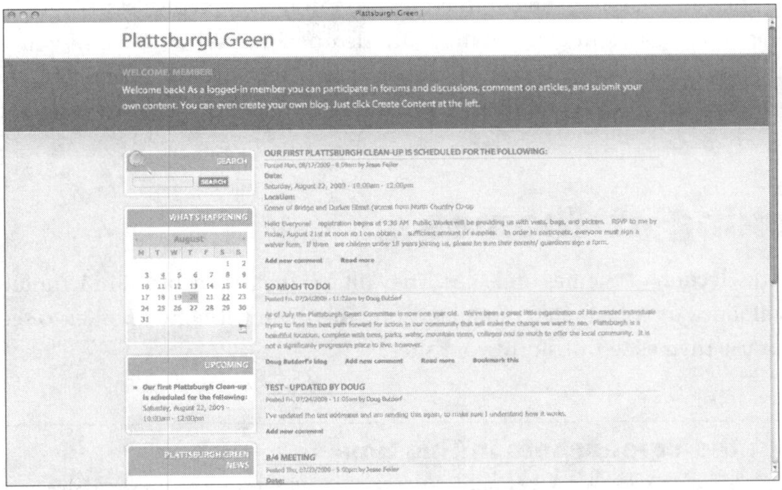

FIGURE 18.1
Acquia Marina in action on the Plattsburgh Green site.

Figure 18.2 uses Garland, a theme that is provided with Drupal. Rather than being a fixed-width theme, it is a liquid theme. A *liquid* theme expands or contracts horizontally to fill the window.

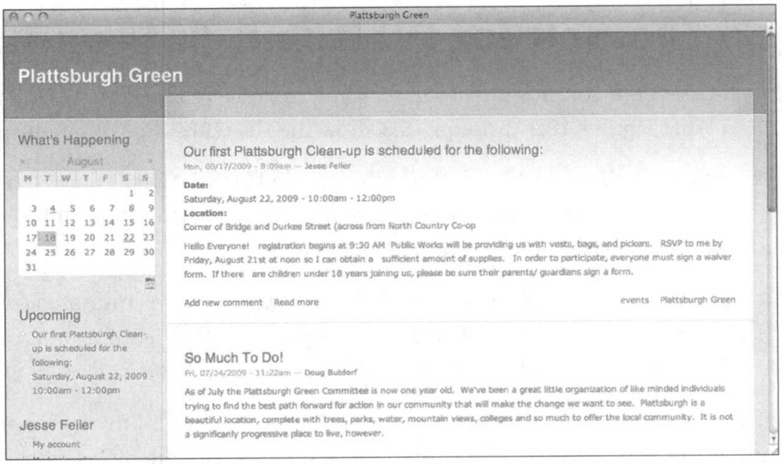

FIGURE 18.2
View Plattsburgh Green in the Garland theme.

Minnelli, another theme provided with Drupal, is a fixed-width theme, as you can see in Figure 18.3. If you expand or contract the window horizontally, the content will remain the same width and will be centered in the window.

FIGURE 18.3
View Plattsburgh Green in the Minnelli theme.

Many people think that liquid themes make more sense because the window's area is used most efficiently. If a user resizes the window, the added space is used. (There is a lower limit: if a window is resized to be less than a certain width, the content is not further reduced, and scrollbars are enabled.) This certainly sounds like the best choice. But hold on.

Looking at Other Sites and Themes

Look at Figure 18.4, which shows the author's website during the late summer of 2009. It uses another free Acquia theme, Acquia Slate from Top Notch Themes (www.topnotchthemes.com/theme/free-drupal-theme-acquia-slate). It is a fixed-width theme, and it demonstrates the main problem with liquid themes. Note that the page features a large image. Smaller images appear on internal pages, but the front page shows a North Country scene that is vaguely related to the season of the year.

For text-based sites, the text can re-wrap as the width of the page changes. But, what do you do with images? You either distort them, which is almost always a mistake, or keep them a certain size and wind up with possibly large margins or blank spots in the enlarged page. For a page design such as the one shown in Figure 18.4, fixed-width is usually the only choice.

If your content contains embedded images, a fluid theme such as Garland is once again feasible. That is because the images embedded in the text can flow as the window is resized. Consider the page shown in Garland in Figure 18.5. The window is relatively narrow.

FIGURE 18.4
Late summer
2009 at the
author's website.

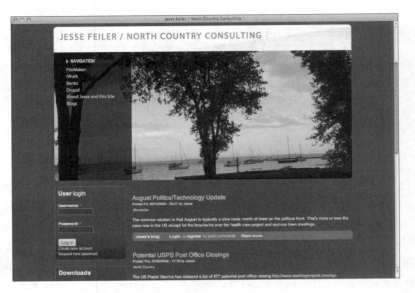

FIGURE 18.5
Garland can dis-
play embedded
images.

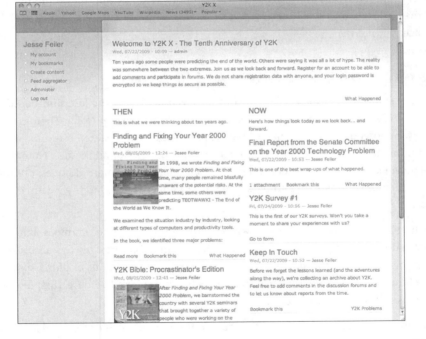

As the page is widened, the text reflows, as you see in Figure 18.6. The images reflow
but are not resized, so there is no problem. (The fact that the images are relatively
small is a key element in all this.)

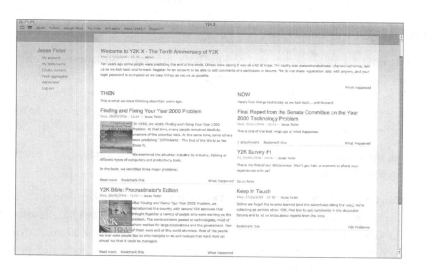

FIGURE 18.6
Embedded images flow with the text.

Evaluating Your Theme Choices

Although the general idea behind themes is that you should be able to switch them back and forth, certain characteristics of your content and of the theme itself (particularly full-page images) may have to enter into your choice of themes. In some cases, you can finesse the issues because some themes come in both fluid and fixed-width versions. Experiment with themes using sample content from the site. Do not use boilerplate text; instead, use real examples of your content (in all of its variations). There is an interaction between theme and content, and you need to be comfortable with it.

Experiment with the configuration options of themes that interest you to see how much flexibility you have. It also can be productive to examine configuration options of sites that do not interest you at all. Sometimes, a simple check box can turn on a function that makes such a site a top contender.

As you explore themes, pay particular attention to whether or not they support the Color module that lets you change a theme's color scheme as described in Hour 4. This means that there is a built-in capability for the theme to let you customize colors. For sites with a background image, look to see if it is possible to easily change that image. You can find this on the theme's Drupal page. If it is not there, either the feature does not exist or the documentation support is poor.

Find themes on Drupal at drupal.org/project/Themes. These are all contributed themes that you can download and use for free. You can also use a search engine to search for Drupal themes; this will uncover some commercially available themes.

Go To ▶
FOR INFORMATION ON CONFIGURING THEMES, SEE HOUR 4, "ADMINISTERING DRUPAL, THEMES, AND MODULES", P. 47.

Buying Themes

If you do not find a theme that you can use with standard configurations, and if you do not want to build your own (or add code to an existing theme), you may be in the market for a theme. As with everything Drupal, this is an expanding and changing market, so you can get the best feel for it by starting from a search engine to find the latest information.

However, the outlines of the market are not likely to change much. There are three main sources for themes:

▶ **Contributed (free) themes on the Drupal site**—You can find these at drupal.org/project/Themes. Like all contributed modules, they are covered by the GPL license. The developer may offer customization and add-on advice and services for a fee. As with all software (not just open source software), price is only a rough indicator of quality.

▶ **Theme developers and consultants**—You can find developers and consultants to help you with your theme. As is always the case, the more you know about what you want, the easier it will be to make the best use of a developer or consultant. (That means the more thinking you do up front, the less thinking you will have to pay for.) Paradoxically, if you are starting out, you may want to plan for two sets of consultations. You may want a consultant to guide you through options and issues; this is a relatively short-term consultancy to get you up to speed if you need more background than this book provides. Then, you can do some more thinking and work with the same (or another) consultant on actual theme development.

▶ **Commercially available themes**—A number of people and companies have developed themes that they sell. One such company, Top Notch Themes (www.topnotchthemes.com), has an interesting pricing model. It has a number of themes that you can download, and its prices are usually around $300. Each theme also has a buy-out price: If you pay that price, no further copies will be sold. Buy-out prices are from around $2,700 to $3,800. Several themes are shown on each page; click a theme and find a full page of details about that theme. At the bottom right of the details page, you can find the number of copies that have been sold. This means that if one of these themes interests you, and if you want to have a more-or-less unique theme, for somewhere in the vicinity of $3,000 or a little more, you can have a theme that is shared by no more than 5–20 other people in the world. (These numbers are based on randomly selected themes on the site.) And you may be able to buy out a theme that has no other users yet.

Installing and Switching Themes

You can set a theme to be used for administration other than the general sitewide default theme. If you are going to be switching themes, and particularly if you will be experimenting with a theme you have not used before, it makes sense to set your administration theme to one of the basic Drupal themes, such as Garland or Minnelli. (Garland is probably the better choice because it is fluid and administration pages flow nicely as you enlarge the window.) If your new theme seems to have a problem, after you have set an administration theme, login with ?q=admin and you will be in the Administration setting using your old administration theme. From there, you can switch the current theme to a safe version that you have used previously.

Not only is an administration theme a safe one when you are changing themes, but it also can be a reminder that you are in the administration area. For that reason, using a default theme, like Garland, with a particularly distinctive (even garish) color scheme can be a good idea. You have the option to treat content editing as administration for the sake of the theme. If you want people to be very aware when they are editing content, use the check box described in the sections following to apply the administration theme to content editing.

Setting an Administration Theme

This process is different in Drupal 6 and Drupal 7.

Drupal 6

In Drupal 6, go to Administer, Site Configuration, Administration Theme (admin/settings/admin), as shown in Figure 18.7. The pop-up menu lets you choose from the installed themes. You can also use the check box to determine whether content editing should use the site default theme or the administration theme.

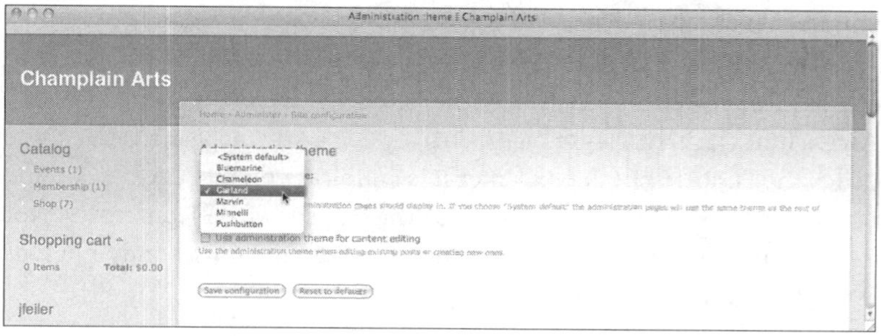

FIGURE 18.7
Set the administration theme (Drupal 6).

Drupal 7

In Drupal 7, the administration theme is set with the pop-up menu at the bottom of the list of themes. The check box for content editing is just below the pop-up menu. Figure 18.8 shows the list of themes in Drupal 7 along with the pop-up menu to select the administration theme. The check box is just below that, but it is scrolled out of sight in Figure 18.8. Go to the list of themes in Drupal 7 with admin/appearance or use the Appearance button at the top of the window.

FIGURE 18.8
Set the administration theme (Drupal 7).

Switching Themes

After you decide on a theme, download it if it is not included with Drupal. Much as you do with modules, do not install it in the main themes folder; instead, drag the downloaded and expanded files to `.sites/all/themes`. Thus, your `.sites/all/folder` will have your downloaded modules and themes.

After you download and move the files for a theme, it will be added to your list of themes. Figure 18.8 shows the list of themes in Drupal 7. With the exception of the administration theme pop-up button at the bottom, it looks the same in both versions. Access it at D6: `admin/settings/admin` or D7: `admin/appearance`. For your new theme, click the Enabled check box. After it is enabled, you can click a Configure link to its right. That takes you to a page such as the one shown in Figure 18.9. Note that each theme's configuration settings are different, so what you see may not look the same as the figures shown here.

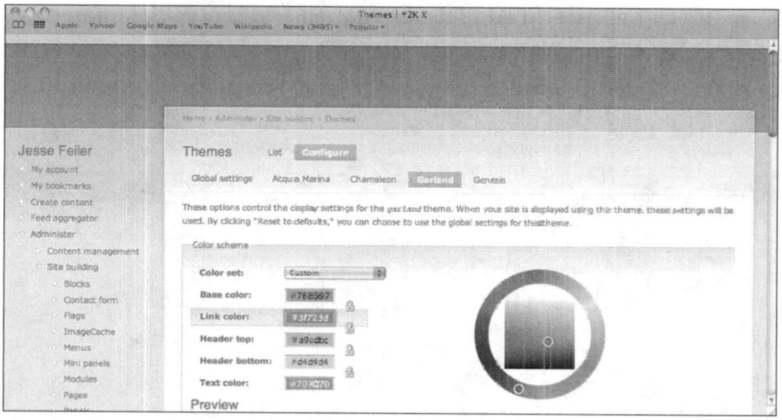

FIGURE 18.9
Start to config-
ure your theme.

At the top of the page, you can see the various themes. If you started from your new theme, you do not need to change the settings. If your theme supports the Color module (as Garland does), the first settings are the color settings (discussed in Hour 4).

Next down the page is a preview of what the theme will look like, as shown in Figure 18.10.

Immediately beneath the preview are settings that you can set for various theme options. Most are check boxes that you can turn on or off.

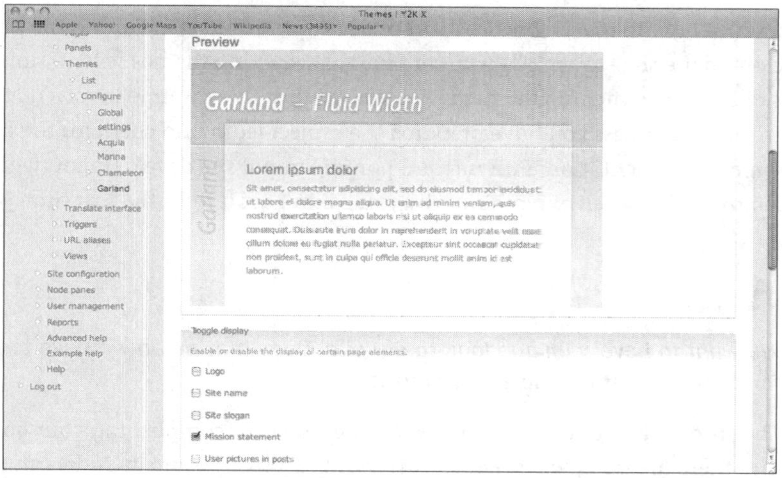

FIGURE 18.10
A preview of the
theme in the
configuration
settings.

The page ends with more check boxes and paths to files that may contain the site icon, as shown in Figure 18.11.

Make sure that you save your settings. Return to the list page and click the Default radio button next to the theme you want to use. When you click Save, it will become your theme. If you have set an administration theme, you may not immediately see anything different. However, if you have changed your site's default theme, navigate to the front page to see it in action. (Any other page except for an administration page will also show it.)

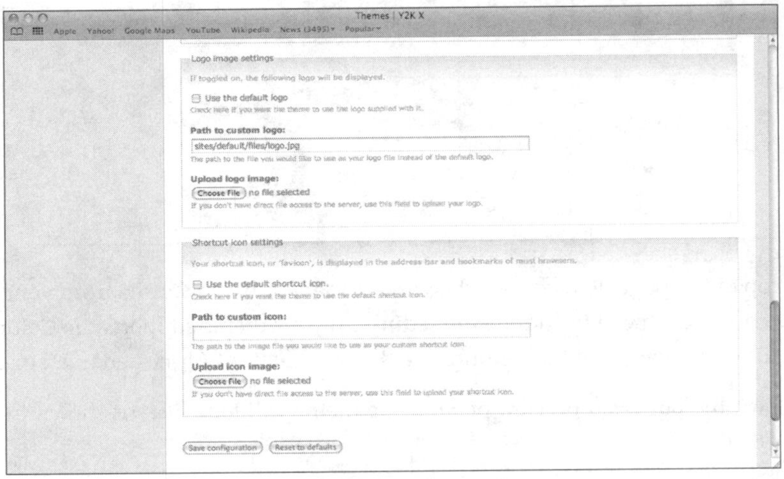

FIGURE 18.11
Complete the configuration.

Summary

Choosing the right theme is a critical part of developing your site. During the process of developing the site, you might want to plan for switching themes several times. The process of actually switching themes is not lengthy, but there is time involved in finding themes. And, unless you have prepared the project team and client for the fact that theme experimentation is an integral part of Drupal site development (which it is), you may find yourself explaining why you "didn't get it right the first time."

Q&A

Q. We want to have a unique look to our site. Does that mean we have to pay for a theme that no one else will use?

A. That is certainly one absolutely legitimate way of accomplishing your goal. But, there are other ways. Remember that the look of your site is determined by your content. If your content lends itself to having images included in articles and stories, those images can define the site. For example, a music or book site might feature new or popular releases on its front page, with each item including the image of an album or book cover. If this is generated automatically (as is usually the case), your front page will always look different. There may be occasions that you will look back on with amusement, such as the day when by sheer coincidence all 10 of the top-selling books and records had brown covers. That automatically generated page would deserve to be printed out! Many people argue that, if your site's differentiation comes about because of its content, that is the best form of differentiation.

Q. Someone has found a WordPress site with a great design. Can we use it?

A. Track down the designs from other sites. Many companies that release themes for other products will repurpose their designs for Drupal. Start from the initial source and check their website. The main work of developing a site design is in the design, so if an individual or company can reuse it for several environments, that can be cost-effective for them.

Q. We are planning to use a number of contributed modules. Do we have to worry about compatibility?

A. Leaving aside themes or modules that are not well written, there should be few problems. You are most likely to encounter problems with themes or modules that are pushing the Drupal envelope. If certain modules are essential for your site, install and enable them before you start evaluating themes. You also can try a search for the module and theme names to see if there are any reports of incompatibilities (or of particular successes).

Workshop

Quiz

1. How many themes can you install?

2. Where are themes installed?

3. How can you avoid image resizing issues when using a fluid theme?

Quiz Answers

1. At any given moment, you can have only one site default theme and (optionally) one administration theme. You can have any number installed and enabled.

2. Themes that are part of Drupal, such as Minnelli and Garland, are packaged in the Themes folder when you download it. Install your own downloaded themes in `.sites/all/themes`.

3. Do not place images in banners, headers, or other places where they would need to be resized. Place them in text that can wrap as the page size changes.

Activities

Even if you have chosen a theme and do not intend to change it, practice downloading, installing, and configuring at least half a dozen themes. Make sure that you are comfortable with the process so that if the time comes when you want to experiment with a new theme, you do not hesitate to do so. If the first time you switch a theme is on a production site with several hundred megabytes worth of data, you are right to feel some trepidation. Add Drupal theme switching to your basic toolkit. It is not a difficult process.

Using Blocks

What You'll Learn in This Hour:

▶ Understand the Basics of Using Blocks

▶ Create Blocks

▶ Place Blocks on Your Pages

Introduction

This hour explores a major component of Drupal—the *blocks* that can appear in various regions of your site's pages. Figure 19.1 shows part of the front page of the author's site (northcountryconsulting.com). Nothing about it indicates that it is a Drupal site. In fact, the layout of the page could be created with any number of site-building tools, including hand-crafted HTML.

What you cannot see are some of the Drupal features that are built in to the block structure. As is so often the case with Drupal, it takes care of many of the issues that you would have to manage with scripts or carefully structured HTML. In this hour, you will see how to create your own blocks and use blocks that are provided as part of Drupal or contributed modules. You learn how to use options so that blocks are or are not displayed under various circumstances, and you learn how to arrange and rearrange the blocks on your pages.

Introducing Blocks

The center of the page shows blog entries, but the left and right margins contain blocks. Each Drupal theme can define its own regions for blocks; the standard ones are *left*, *right*, *header*, *footer*, and *content*. Many themes define additional blocks. If you change a theme, you may have a little rearranging to do, but your blocks should work properly in their new locations.

In Figure 19.1, you can see blog entries in the center content section. The left and right regions contain blocks. Starting in the upper left, these are the blocks:

- **User Login**—Standard Drupal block. If a user is logged in, it does not appear. (You do not even have to click a check box for this behavior.)

- **Downloads**—Below User Login is a Downloads block. You can create a block of your own with a title and text. Figure 19.2 shows how the Downloads block is specified. You give it a name, a title, and its text. If you want to be sophisticated, you can limit its visibility. In this case, the block is shown only to anonymous (non-logged-in) users. A companion block is shown to authenticated (logged-in) users; it contains download instructions.

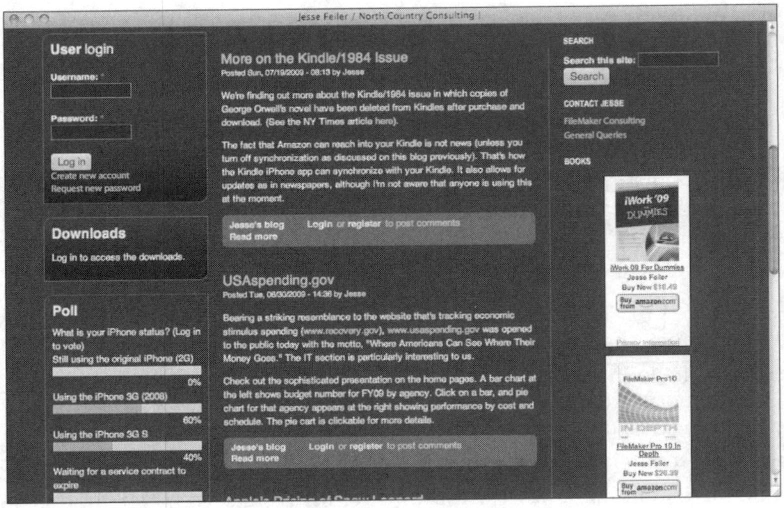

FIGURE 19.1
Use blocks to display information in specific page regions.

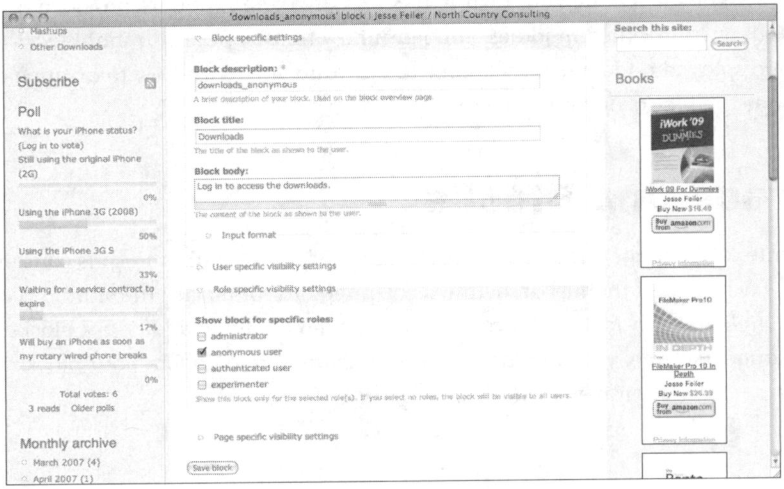

FIGURE 19.2
Create a simple text-only block.

▶ **Poll**—Provided by the Poll module that is part of Drupal.

▶ **Search**—Also a Drupal block.

▶ **Contact Jesse**—Like Downloads, this is a user-created block. Unlike Downloads, it is not just text; it is HTML that provides links to a site-wide contact form as well as to a Webform.

▶ **Books**—A user-created block that contains HTML. The difference here is that the HTML was generated by Amazon.com and contains links to its associate's site.

As you can see, blocks have relatively few limitations, particularly because if all else fails, you can write HTML code. You will find a variety of blocks in Drupal and its contributed modules. Functionally, blocks fall into several categories:

▶ **Basic functionality**—These Drupal-provided blocks implement log in, search, and so forth. Primary and secondary links, as well as menus, are in this category; they are discussed in Hour 21, "Working with Menus."

▶ **Dynamic blocks**—Automatically updated by Drupal. They can provide up-to-date and changing information to your users with no effort on your part other than placing the block. Example are New Forum Topics, Active Forum Topics, Archive List, Recent Blog Posts, Recent Comments, Latest Image, Random Image, Popular Content, and Who's New.

▶ **Your own blocks**—Whether plain text or HTML, you can do whatever you want in your own blocks.

▶ **View blocks**—As you saw in Hour 14, "Working with Views," you can create various types of displays for your views. One of those displays is a block display. This means that you can create your own block from a view and display your own data.

▶ **Contributed module blocks**—This is an area of great interest to the Drupal community, and the offerings are growing rapidly. The Simplenews contributed module which is used to construct newsletters in Hour 12, "Using Blogs and Newsletters" installs a block that people can use to sign up for newslettters, for example.

"Search the modules pages for the keyword "advertising" to see some powerful, useful, and even profitable blocks and modules.

Creating and Using Blocks

You have seen the basic components and features of blocks. The way to master their use is to actually start to use them.

Add a Navigation and User Login Block

The blocks that are available to you depend on your Drupal installation—particularly the contributed modules.

1. Open the block administration at Administer, Site Building, Blocks (D6: admin/build/block D7: admin/structure/block), as shown in Figure 19.3.

2. As you scroll down the page, you will see that most of the blocks are at the bottom in the section of disabled blocks shown in Figure 19.4. In both Figures 19.3 and 19.4, you can see labels identifying the regions of the page. You can drag blocks up and down. If you make any changes, you will see an asterisk next to the affected blocks. After you save the blocks, the asterisks will go away.

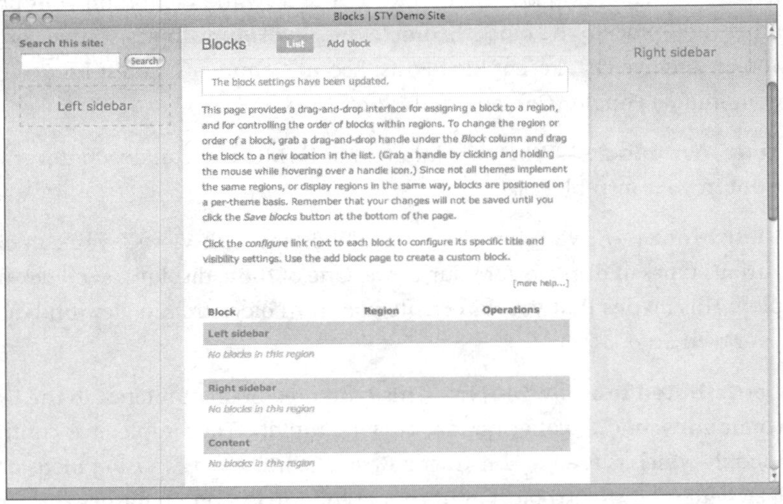

FIGURE 19.3
Open the block administration page.

3. Find the Navigation block and select the left sidebar for its location, as shown in Figure 19.5. Alternatively, you can drag it to the left sidebar section of the block list. (You drag to the section of the block list, not to the actual region of the page.) Click Save Blocks at the bottom of the page.

▼

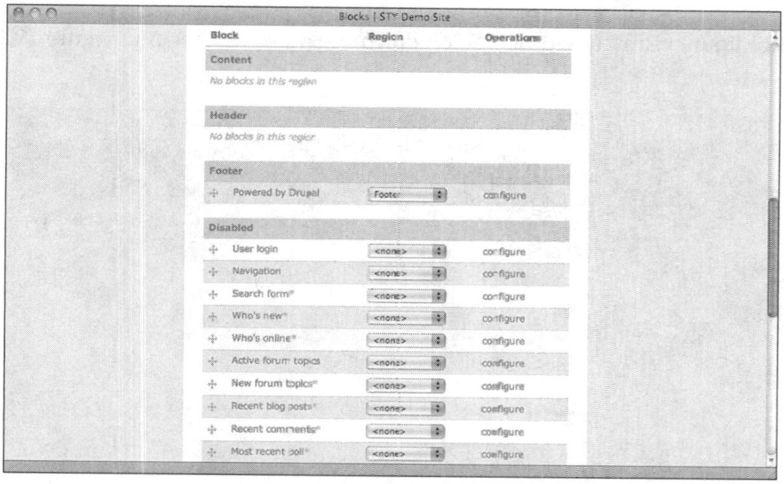

FIGURE 19.4
Disabled blocks are at the bottom.

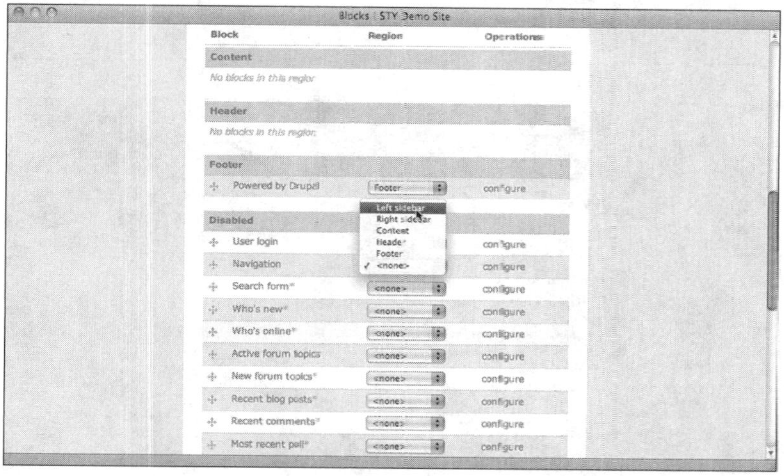

FIGURE 19.5
Select the left sidebar for the Navigation block.

4. Configure the block by clicking the Configure button to open the page shown in Figure 19.6. The most important configuration is the title. Leave it blank for the default title (Navigation, in this case), enter <none> for no title, or enter your own title. You can also allow users to show or hide the block. In most cases, the default option (no user choice) is the best. If you are rearranging

blocks and configuring them, make sure that you save the rearrangement before you click the Configure button.

5. Configure visibility settings. Scroll down the page, as shown in Figure 19.7.

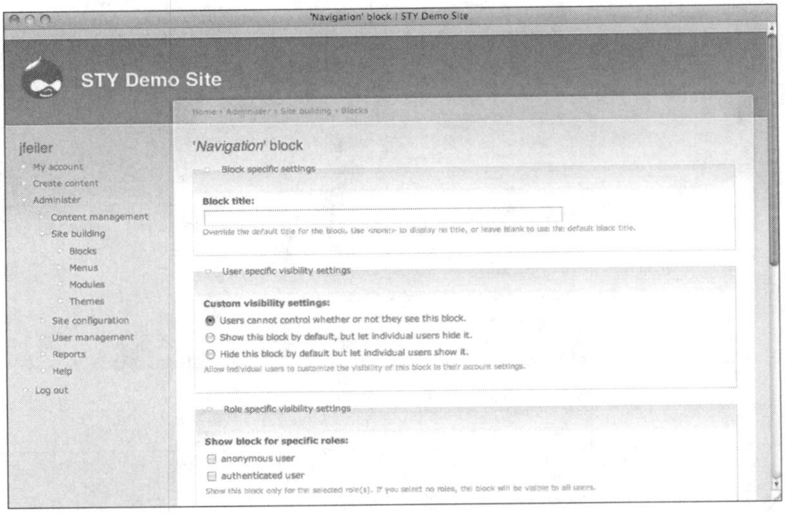

FIGURE 19.6
Configure the
block.

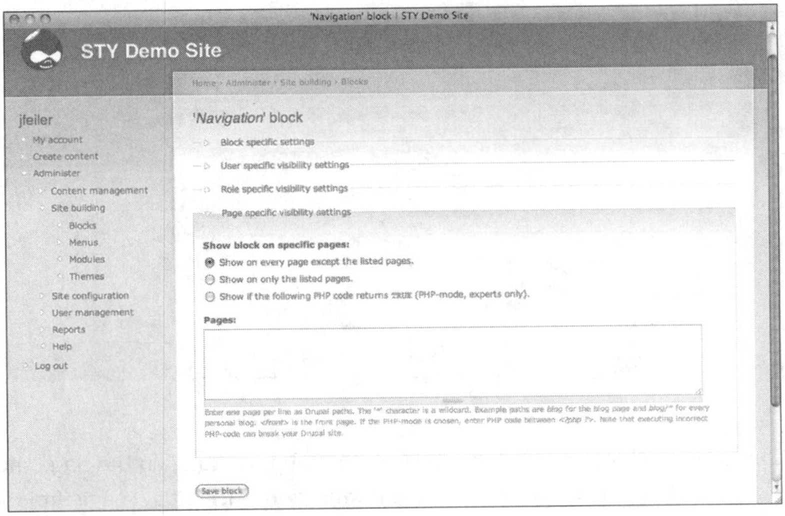

FIGURE 19.7
Configure visibil-
ity settings.

The most common page visibility settings rely on roles. Some blocks should be seen only by logged-in (authenticated) users, and others only by not-logged-in (anonymous) users. If you have a webmaster or supervisor role, you may select some blocks to be shown only to those people. In some cases, Drupal blocks, such as Who's New, are appropriate for supervisors, but not for casual visitors, even authenticated users. As you place the blocks in their regions, just stack them together if you have role-based versions. Only one of them (if any) will appear, but it is a good idea for any variant of a given block to be shown in the same place.

6. List pages on which the block is shown or not shown. The most common such page is the front page (<front> is used in this entry field). This is the simplest answer to people who want a different front page. You also may use this section in conjunction with blocks containing menus. There is more on this in Hour 21. Save the block.

7. Using the same steps, add the Log In block to the left sidebar. If you follow this sequence, it will automatically be placed below the navigation block. Drag it so that it is above the navigation block, as shown in Figure 19.6. Click Save Blocks.

8. Click the Log Out button in the Navigation menu. You will see the User Login block and the abbreviated Navigation menu available to anonymous users, as shown in Figure 19.8.

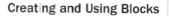

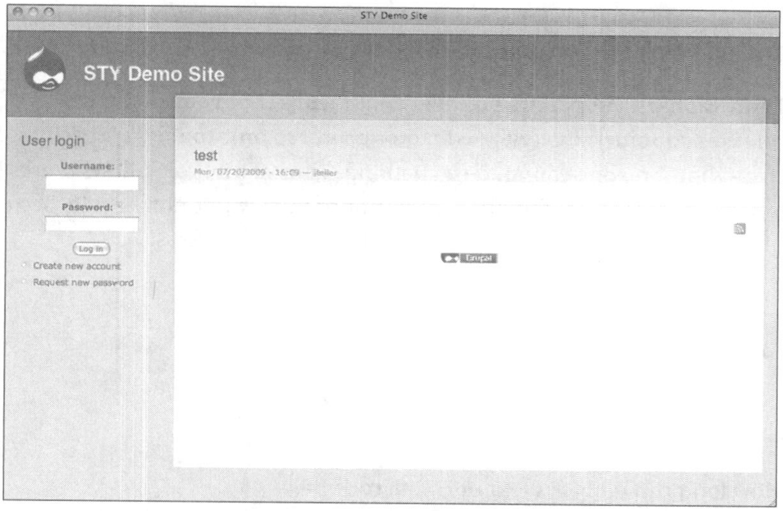

FIGURE 19.8
Log out to see the User Login block.

Summary

Blocks help provide a look-and-feel to your site. Because blocks appear in the same general place on all pages on which they are shown, they provide anchors to the content on the pages.

You cannot work with blocks effectively unless you work with themes at the same time. It is a matter of taste, as well as of your website's purpose, whether you want a lot of blocks in a lot of regions or a few blocks in a few regions. Fashions of web pages come and go; there are ardent proponents of a single sidebar design (in Drupal terms, all blocks at the left or right of the page). In general, regions of a page collapse if nothing is in them, so you can have cluttered pages for webmasters and administrators and sparse and elegant pages for your authenticated users.

Q&A

Q. *My HTML in a block does not work. Is there a simple solution?*

A. Make sure that you are using the Full HTML input format.

Q. *If a user falls into several roles, which role determines visibility of a block?*

A. Permissions in Drupal are positive. That means that you specify that a certain role can do something (view, edit, delete, and so on). You never specify a negative—that someone cannot do something. Thus, if any role allows a user to see a block, that is what is applied. It cannot conflict with another role, because other roles are silent on access, rather than blocking access.

Workshop

Quiz

1. How long can a block's text or HTML code be?

2. What determines the top-to-bottom order of blocks?

3. How do I change the module title?

Quiz Answers

1. There is no real limit, but if it is too lengthy, it may distort the page.

2. Drag them up and down in the block list using the four-way arrows. Remember to save the new order with the Save Blocks button before continuing with configuration.

3. Enter a new title, leave it blank to use the default, or use <none> for no title.

Activities

The number of combinations and permutations of blocks, roles, pages, and visibility quickly becomes enormous and unmanageable. Using pencil and paper (or a white board), draw the basic page design for your pages. Then, assign subregions for each block you intend to use. Annotate the subregion with the modules it will contain and their conditions. Having a consistent layout makes your site easier to use.

Laying Out Panels and Pages

What You'll Learn in This Hour:

- ▶ How Panel Pages Are Built
- ▶ Creating a Front Page from a Panel Page
- ▶ Adding Content to Panel Pages

Introduction

You have seen how Drupal provides default and automated mechanisms for displaying your content without your having to do anything special. For many people, these defaults are sufficient to build a remarkably cost-efficient and effective site.

But, Drupal does not end there. Many people want the control and fine-tuning that they can achieve with hand-crafted HTML. Drupal's panels let you lay out displays in a traditional way.

In this hour, you will see how to get started with panels and the pages that use them. The Panels module has evolved over the past few years into an extremely powerful tool for site design. It has gone through three major versions. Panels 3 makes significant improvements to the user interface. In addition, as you will see in Hour 23, "Using Arguments and Modifying Built-in Pages," this structure makes it possible to totally reconfigure the Drupal user interface for everything from log in and registration to the creation of content.

The demonstration site for this hour is Y2Kx.net—a site dedicated to exploring the 10 years since the Year 2000 Technology problem.

Looking at a Panel Page

There are at least three meanings for the word *page* in Drupal:

▶ Everything that you see on a website is presented as an HTML page.

▶ One of the two default content types for a Drupal site is a page. This is a basic Drupal node into which you can type or paste text, including filtered or full HTML. Thus, you can copy the HTML source code for an existing web page on your current site into a Drupal page content type. (Remember to use the Full HTML filter.)

▶ With the Panels and Chaos Tool Suite installed, you can create and manage pages that can contain laid-out content from one or more nodes. This type of page is the topic of this hour: a *panel page*. A panel page has one or more panel variants within it, but only one variant is displayed at a time. You set the rules by which Drupal determines which variant is displayed.

Did you Know?

Panels 3 and Chaos Tool Suite

The current version of the Panels module is Panels 3. Two modules are involved with Panels 3: Chaos Tool Suite and Panels. If you have used previous versions of Panels, Chaos Tool Suite will be new to you. Some internal reorganizing occurred with the advent of Chaos Tool Suite.

As is the case with views, you can unleash your creativity with pages: your pages are likely to look very different from these. Figure 20.1 shows a page; it uses the Acquia

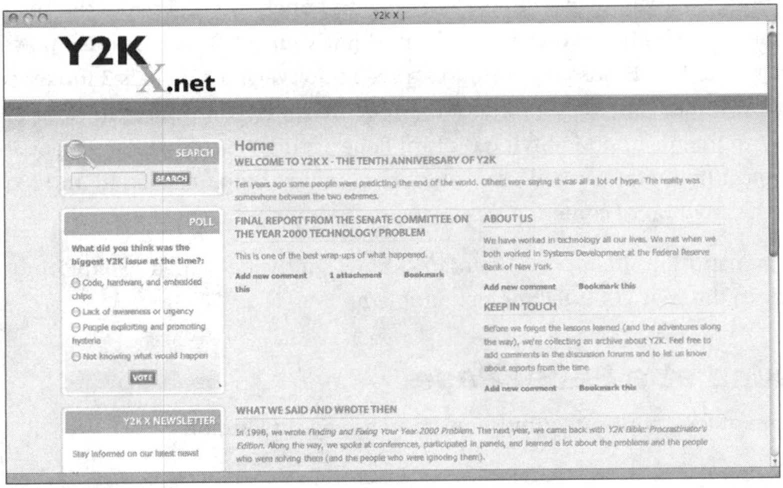

FIGURE 20.1
Explore a panel page.

Marina theme (downloadable without charge from Top Notch Themes at www.top-notchthemes.com).

A panel page such as this is composed of three sets of components:

It contains the normal Drupal regions and blocks that you have seen before.

▶ The center of this page has four *panels* in it. There is one at the top ("Welcome to Y2KX"), one at the bottom ("What We Said and Wrote Then"), and two spread across the middle of the page with one on the left and one on the right (In some documentation, panels are referred to as *regions*. Do not confuse them with Drupal regions at the top, bottom, left, and right of pages.)

▶ Each panel has *panes* within it. A panel contains content in the form of a node, a view, a block, or other content. Panels are bottomless; their left, top, and right locations are part of the panel page layout, but they extend downward to accommodate the nodes and other content within them. The panels at the top and bottom of the page shown in Figure 20.1 each have a single pane in them. The panel at the left center has a single pane ("Final Report..."), and the panel at the right center has two panes within it ("About Us" and "Keep in Touch").

That is the basic structure of a Drupal panel page. The only other point to know is that you can hide the Drupal regions, as shown in Figure 20.2.

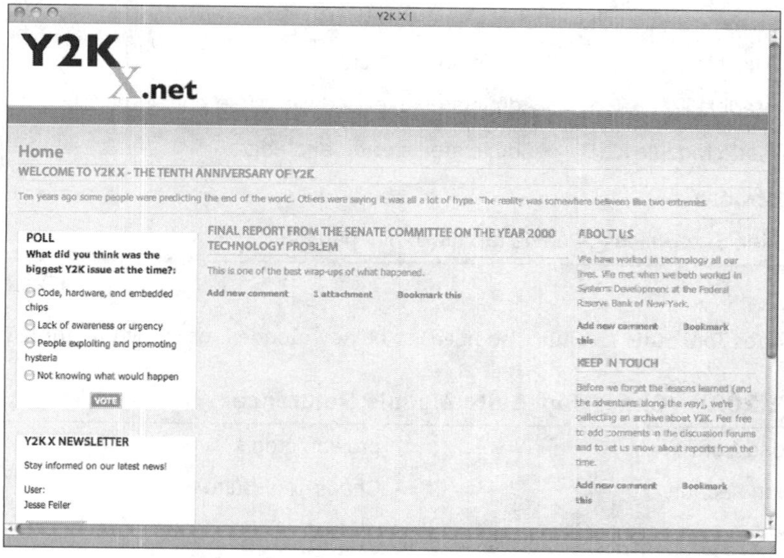

FIGURE 20.2
Hide Drupal regions.

If you look closely at Figure 20.2, you will see that the Drupal regions that contain blocks have been hidden. You have to look closely, because a panel's panes can contain blocks. Thus, in Figure 20.2, there are three panels across the center of the page. The left panel contains blocks in its panes; it could just as easily contain nodes of any kind.

After you have set up your page, you can move content from one panel to another; you can also change the page's layout, adding or removing panels. One of the biggest differences between panels and views is that you specify the content for each pane in a panel. In a view, the query dynamically specifies what content will be displayed at runtime. If you need both, you can place a view with dynamically selected content inside a pane of a panel.

For even more flexibility, this architecture of panes within panels can be applied to objects smaller than a page.

Getting Started with Panel Pages

The starting place, as always, is downloading, installing, and enabling the Panels modules along with the Chaos Tool Suite. There are three modules in Panels; their settings are shown in Table 20.1.

TABLE 20.1　Panels Module Reference

Download from	project/panels
Enable in section	Panels
Permissions	
Panels Mini-Module	Administer and create
Panels Module	Administer, use, and view; use panels dashboard
Panels Node Module	Administer, create, and edit
Administration	
Administer, Site Building, Panels (admin/build/panels)	

The Chaos Tool Suite module also needs to be downloaded, as shown in Table 20.2.

TABLE 20.2　Chaos Tool Suite Module Reference

Download from	project/ctools
Enable in section	Chaos Tool Suite

TABLE 20.2   Chaos Tool Suite Module Reference

Permissions

None

Administration

None

After the Panels and Chaos Tool Suite modules are installed and enabled, you have one additional step to prepare for creating a panel page. Because a panel page (or any other panel structure) contains content that you specify, you need to make sure that you have the content at hand. If you are experimenting with a new Drupal installation, make sure that you have half a dozen or so stories ready to be placed in a panel page. If you leave the default Drupal setting on so that new items are published on the front page, you may wind up with stories that you can use, as shown in Figure 20.3. (These stories are used in this hour's example.)

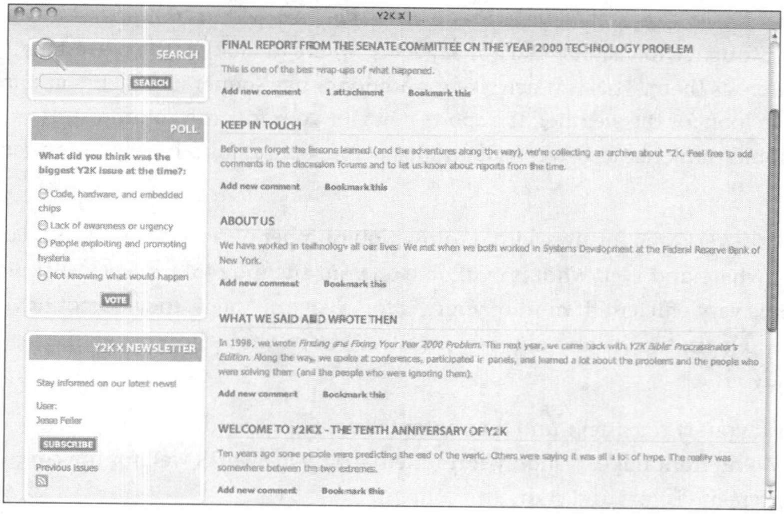

FIGURE 20.3
Create stories for your new panel page.

In fact, more than one page has had its genesis in this process. Someone sets up a new Drupal site and starts to add content. It is great that it shows up on that bloglike first page. Then, a little more visual structure is required. That is okay, because you can make some of the articles sticky so that they are always at the top. You can add a little more structure with blocks in the margins of the page. And before you know it, you—or your users—want to push the envelope a little more, and there you have it: a new Drupal page with panels.

Two tasks are ahead of you: You need to create the panel page, and then you need to arrange its panes and content. This second task has two variations: You can use the Drupal regions that contain blocks, or you can hide them. In any case, all the steps you will be taking can be edited and revised later on.

Creating a Panel Page

Creating a panel page can be very simple and efficient. After it is created and set up, you can customize it just by changing the content displayed within its layout and panes. Many sites have such a page for a formatted front page. It can appear like a newspaper or other periodical in a format that people become accustomed to.

Pros and Cons of Consistent Formats

Whether this is a good idea depends on your site. Sites with a consistent front page can be attractive to visitors who quickly learn where to look for the newest content that interests them. This is much like a traditional newspaper in which you know where to look for the weather, the sports news, or your favorite columnist. However, you should think about two considerations before opting for a highly formatted front page:

This works very well for sites with a fairly high number of repeated visitors. Learning what is where and even what is available on your site may take a few visits; thereafter, it is very efficient. If most of your visitors visit only once, they do not have a chance to learn the ins and outs of your site. They might be happier with a less structured layout.

If your layout is consistent and the content is unchanging, all you have is an unchanging front page. A highly formatted front page works well for the combination of repeat visitors and changing content.

Managing Panel Pages

You manage your panel pages using Site Building, Pages (admin/build/pages). That will open the list of pages shown in Figure 20.4.

These are your site's panel pages. The interface to panel pages is similar to the interface to views. You can create new pages just as you can create new views. In addition, there are a number of built-in pages for Drupal just as there are built-in views. You can override the pages in the same way you override views. The built-in pages are part of the Drupal code installation, and on this list they are identified as being in code, in contrast to the normal storage for pages you create.

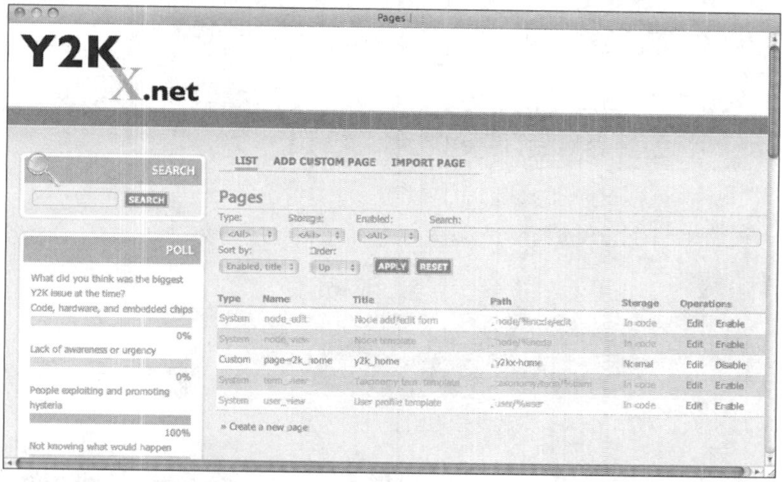

FIGURE 20.4
View a list of panel pages.

From here, you can click Edit to edit a page; you can also toggle the enable/disable status of each page.

Using a Panel Page

You can create a panel page in three steps.

Try It Yourself

Creating a Panel Page

1. Click Add Custom Page at the top or Create a New Page at the bottom of the page, shown previously in Figure 20.4, to start the process. Provide the page name and path information, as shown in Figure 20.5. Everything can be changed later except the internal (machine) name of the page. There is a set of optional settings at the bottom of the page; they are not visible in Figure 20.5. You can leave them unchecked in most cases (and change them later if necessary). Remember to check the box if you want this to be your site's front page.

2. Select the layout for your page from the choices shown in Figure 20.6. Do not worry; you can change the layout later, and you will not lose any data you have entered, even if the changed layout does not have all the panes from your current layout.

3. When you click Continue, you go to the final page, as shown in Figure 20.7. Here is where you specify the content for your page. As with the previous page, you can modify these settings later. For now, click Finish.

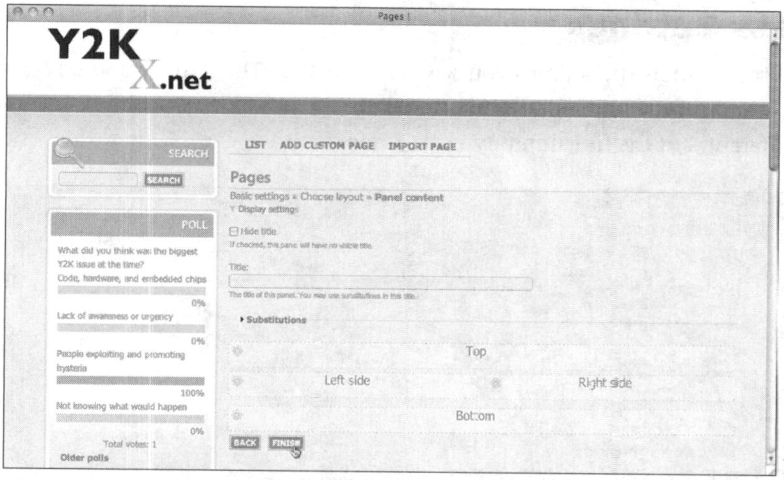

FIGURE 20.7
Finish your page.

Editing a Panel Page's Settings

In the previous section, you saw how to create a new page. After you have done so, you can come back to edit it by clicking Edit at the right of the listing of the page as previously shown in Figure 20.4. (The only thing you cannot edit is the machine name.)

Basic Settings

Clicking Edit takes you to the Summary page, as shown in Figure 20.8.

The settings for the page have been set up when you created the page. The Basic settings are those that were shown previously in Figure 20.5.

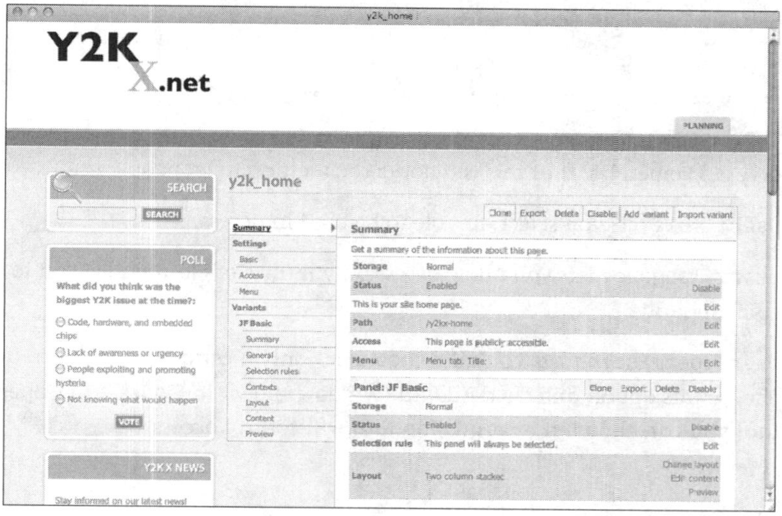

FIGURE 20.8
Manage your page.

Access Settings

Click Access to show the settings you see in Figure 20.9. These are the same types of access settings that you have seen in other Drupal contexts; this interface is somewhat different, but the functionality is the same.

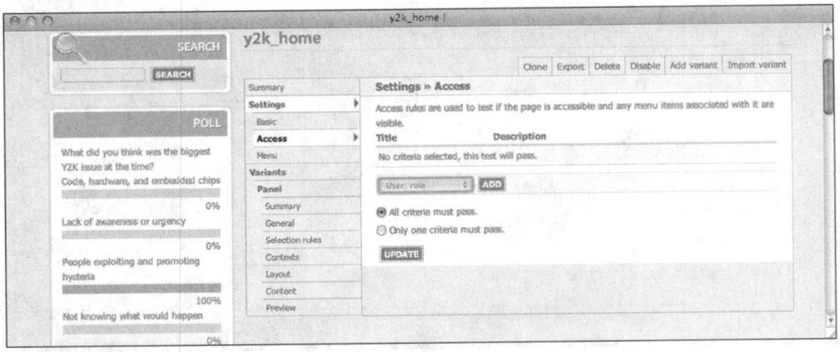

FIGURE 20.9
Configure access settings.

From the pop-up menu, you can choose from four categories of access settings. When you click Add, a window opens that lets you configure the setting. Figure 20.10 shows the window that opens for you to configure user role settings. In this and the other windows that you use to set access, icons at the right of the title bar let you close the window (without saving) or configure (or reconfigure) the settings.

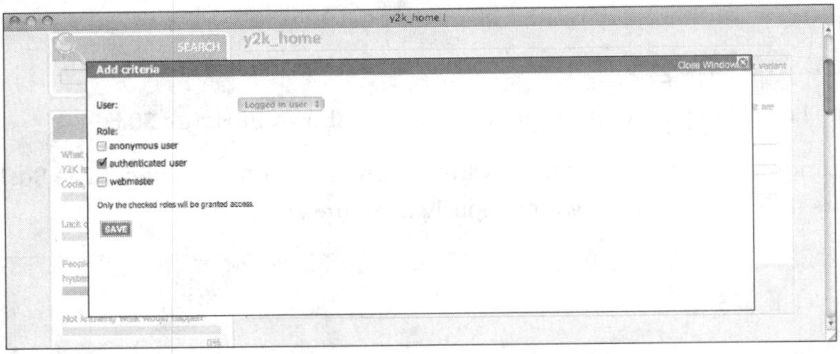

FIGURE 20.10
Configure user role settings.

▶ PHP code lets you enter code that will be evaluated to true or false to control access. (Remember that this is a dangerous setting to let people use.)

▶ User: role lets you select the role to be used in access.

▶ User: language lets you allow access only if the site's language is set to a specific language.

▶ User: permission lets you allow access for only a certain permission. If you choose this option and click Add, the window shown in Figure 20.11 opens so that you can choose the permission that will control access.

After you build your list of access rules, you can use the radio buttons to indicate whether all the rules must pass or only one. These access settings are very useful.

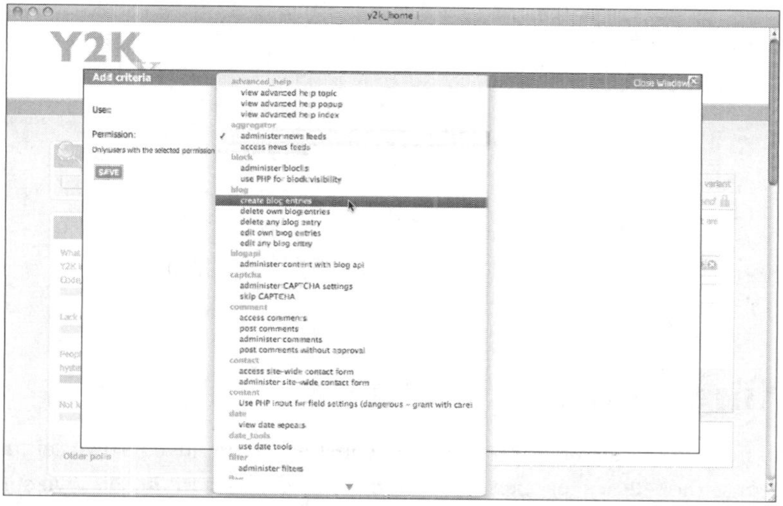

FIGURE 20.11
Select permissions for access.

Drupal already provides sufficient tools for you to use to control access to nodes, but a page that contains a panel may contain many nodes with varying access rules. Left to its own devices, Drupal will display whatever nodes are allowed on that page. After you build your list of access rules, you can use the radio buttons to indicate whether all the rules must pass or only one. These access settings are very useful. Drupal already provides sufficient tools for you to use to control access to nodes, but a page that contains a panel might contain many nodes with ranging access rules. Left to its own devices, Drupal will display whatever nodes are allowed on that page. But setting access for the entire page with these settings means that you can avoid a partially completed page.

For example, four nodes are to be displayed on a page, and a user has access to three of them. By setting the page's access settings, you will either display all four or none. In some cases, that is the correct behavior; in other cases, you want to display the three to which the user has access.

Menu Settings

Menu settings are shown in Figure 20.12. These are the settings for the page you have created, and they are the same as menu settings elsewhere in Drupal.

FIGURE 20.12
Manage menu
settings.

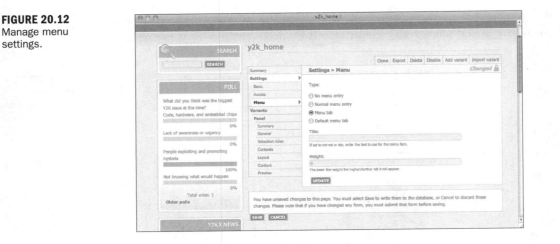

FIGURE 20.13
Manage variants
on a page.

Editing Variant Settings

You can have multiple panels on a page. Because each can have its own settings, and because the settings for each can be complex, each variant has its own summary, as you can see in Figure 20.13.

General Settings

General settings are shown in Figure 20.14.

Here is where you can set your on CSS for the page. It also is where you can disable Drupal blocks and regions, if you want.

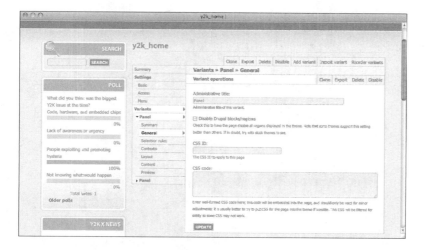

FIGURE 20.14
Configure General settings.

Selection Rules

As noted previously, a page can have multiple variants. The Selection Rules are used to determine which variant is shown. The interface is the same as for Access settings: You can select from PHP code, User:role, User:permission, and User:language. In addition to specifying the values for each criterion, you can also specify whether all or only one needs to pass. Drupal examines each variant in turn; the first one that passes the selection rules is displayed.

Layout

You can change the layout of a panel using an interface similar to that of Figure 20.6. Drupal will manage the rearrangement of content so that nothing is lost. For example, if you have a layout that is the two-column stacked layout used previously in this chapter, you can change it to another layout, as shown in Figure 20.15.

When you click Continue, you will be asked how to manage the content, as shown in Figure 20.16. The settings are the same whether you have more or fewer areas on the new page; provide the mapping from each current area to its new location.

Content

The heart of panel building is adding content to it. When you create a new page and panel, the content is initially empty, as you saw in Figure 12.7. That layout uses the two-column stacked layout. Four regions can contain content in the layout:

▶ Top

▶ Left Side

▶ Right Side

▶ Bottom

FIGURE 20.15
Change a layout.

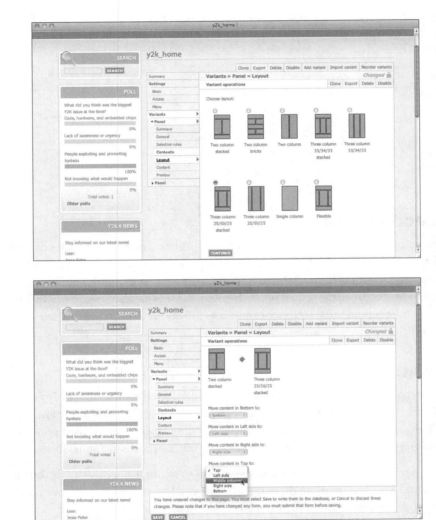

FIGURE 20.16
Map the data in
the new layout.

Each region is bottomless: You can add as much content to it as you want and it will continue to grow vertically. At the upper left of each region is a small control that brings up a contextual menu, as shown in Figure 20.17.

You can set the style for each region. The standard choices are

▶ List

▶ No style

▶ Rounded corners

▶ Default

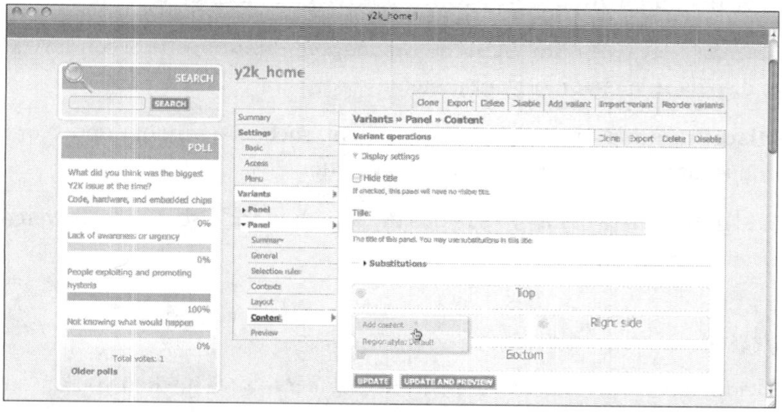

FIGURE 20.17
Configure each
region.

This gives you a variety of choices. For example, you could use a standard style for all the regions on a page, but highlight the right side, top, or bottom with distinctive styling, such as rounded corners. Whatever choices you make, they should be consistent and logical. Just scattering different styles around the page is not helpful to users.

Most of the time, you are interested in the Add Content choice. This will open a new pop-up window that lets you specify the content you want to add, as shown in Figure 20.18.

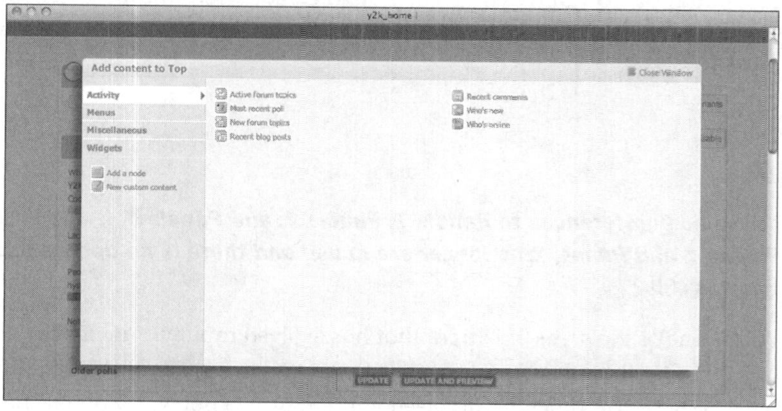

FIGURE 20.18
Add content.

The choices that you see are dependent on what content exists in your Drupal site. The options shown in Figure 20.18 are typical.

▶ **Activity**—These are valuable additions to your page because you do not have to do anything for them to be present and to change. They reflect the activity on your site. Anything that you can automate on a site is particularly valuable, and displaying activity (when it is relevant) is often a valuable addition.

▶ **Menus**—Here, you can select the Navigation, Primary, and Secondary Menus to display in a region of your panel.

▶ **Miscellaneous**—These are image content, such as a random image or latest image, as well as blocks, such as a newsletter.

▶ **Widgets**—These are items such as the Search block, User Login, Powered by Drupal, and so form.

Preview

This provides a basic preview of the page. Remember to save it when you are satisfied.

Summary

Panel pages let you lay out content in a traditional way—very much the way in which newspapers have been laid out for centuries. By using Drupal's teaser structure, you can make each item on a front page (or any panel page for that matter) be the same general length so that the page looks good. (You can change where the teaser break occurs in each node as you enter it. Longer teasers for longer stories make sense.)

By adding panes that contain dynamically updated data (recent comments, for example), your panel page and its layout can automatically be updated as your site's content changes.

Q&A

Q. *I have seen references to Panels 1, Panels 2, and Panels 3. It appears that Panels 1 and Panels 2 no longer are in use and there is no update path. What is this?*

A. This is one of the areas of Drupal that has evolved rapidly. Panels provide functionality that is essential to newspapers and newspaper-like sites. The people who need this functionality need it intensely. Do not worry about the evolution of Panels; rather, consider it a good sign. Remember the Drupal mantra: that whatever happens, the data will not be lost or corrupted. The nodes that you have created for any version of Panels are still there. You may have to modify some layouts, but your data is safe.

Q. *I took your advice and made my site's front page a panel page. Now it looks sparse and empty. Did I do something wrong?*

A. No. Panels (like all of Drupal) organize your content very efficiently. When you move an existing site to Drupal or when you create a panel page, the large amount of content that you have in an old site or in your collection of front page articles can look puny in the more highly structured environment. So, one answer is that this is perfectly normal. If it is a problem, consider lengthening your teasers in the nodes that you include, not using a teaser in a main article or story so that it is significantly longer, and using images either by themselves or as parts of nodes or views.

Workshop

Quiz

1. Where do you turn off Drupal regions for panel pages?

2. What is the easiest way to make a dynamically updated panel page?

3. How do you make a panel page your site's front page?

Quiz Answers

1. Use General settings in the panel variant editor.

2. Configure your panes using any of the automatically updated nodes, views, or blocks, such as new users, recent comments, or active forum topics.

3. Set the path in Administer, Site Configuration to the URL (path) of the panel page. You can also set it when you first create a panel page.

Activities

Experiment with panel pages for your front page. Create them as described in this hour, but do not set them to the front page. Depending on the size of the pages, either print them or make screenshots of them. Then, sit with your users, clients, or colleagues to discuss which you like best (or which features of each you want to combine).

This can be particularly useful if you use the same node content in each of the panel pages. It takes just a few moments to arrange a panel page, and if you use the same content in all of your examples, it is easy to compare the designs.

For a heterogeneous group of users, not all of whom may be experienced in design or technology, seeing the side-by-side examples can be extraordinarily helpful. To make the experiment even more productive, do not use made-up content. Take content from an existing newsletter or website. Many little quirks manifest themselves when you are using real data, and these items can be accidentally omitted from made-up data.

Working with Menus

What You'll Learn in This Hour:

▶ Creating Menus and Adding Content to Them

▶ Creating Content and Adding It to Menus

▶ Creating Custom Menus and Using Them in Blocks

Introduction

When people start to think about the structure of a website, one of the first things they often think about is the menu structure. They worry over that structure to make sure that all the needed information is planned for and laid out in the most useful way.

Remember that in a Content Management System (CMS) such as Drupal, data has no location other than being somewhere in the database. It can be difficult for some people to think about a menu structure in which menu items can appear in multiple places and some of the data appears nowhere. Further muddying the waters is the fact that interface designers for some time now have been having second thoughts about the traditional menus and menu bar. The rise of web-based applications has helped this along. In traditional applications, the menus control the application; in a web-based application, the menus control the browser, and the menus for the web-based application are implemented with HTML (in old-fashioned interfaces) or in a modern tool such as Drupal.

As this hour explores how Drupal handles menus, think about the opportunities that you have. Many modern websites have no internal menus; buttons and other interface elements control navigation. You can do that with Drupal. Other modern websites have hierarchical menus for specific areas of the site and perhaps the entire site. Buttons and other interface elements interact with traditional hierarchical menus so that you can jump in and out.

In this hour, you will see the basics of Drupal's menu implementation, as well as the specifics of the implementations in Drupal 6 and Drupal 7. One of the major changes in Drupal 7 has to do with the menu structure. Basically, what has happened is that Drupal's menu structure has grown a bit too large for convenient management. (This is far from uncommon: <insert name of your favorite office productivity tool here> is a classic example.) The solution in Drupal 7 is to break the menu structure apart so that the remaining component parts are, once again, manageable. The general structure of menus, however, has not changed between Drupal 6 and 7.

Looking at Drupal's Menus

The easiest way to become familiar with Drupal's menus is to explore some examples. Here is a walk-through of some of the basic concepts. Remember that you can customize just about everything.

Figure 21.1 shows two parts of a menu structure in Drupal. At the left, you can see a *primary links* menu (you can change the name to anything you want). This is a traditional looking menu with two menu items, each of which has two subitems. As you will see, you can control their order and hierarchy as well as whether the subitems are shown by default.

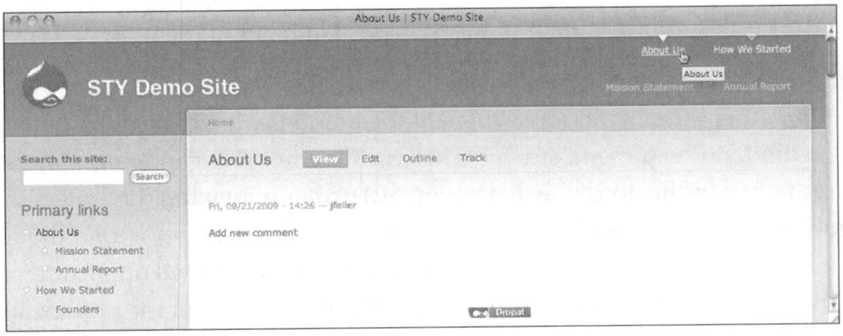

FIGURE 21.1
Drupal can build a links menu.

At the upper right, the primary links menu is shown again. At the top right of the page, the two main items are shown. As you can see by comparing Figure 21.1 and Figure 21.2, clicking one of the primary links brings up the appropriate sublinks. Compare the hierarchical menu at the left in both figures with the menus at the upper right.

The links in the upper right can also be independent. Note in Figure 21.3 that the top line links at the right represent the main links in the primary links menu, but the lower line (Shop Online and Upcoming Events) are totally separate links. Note, too, that at the top left of the page those other links are shown again: this time, they are arranged hierarchically and are preceded by their title. (You can change Secondary Links to anything else, such as Services or Products.)

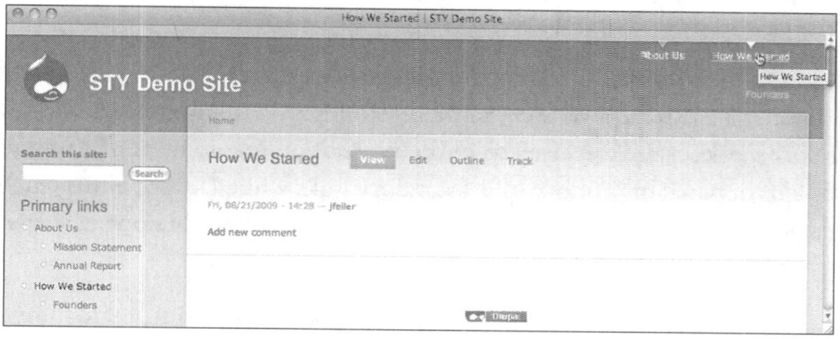

FIGURE 21.2
The links menu can also be shown in a hierarchical structure.

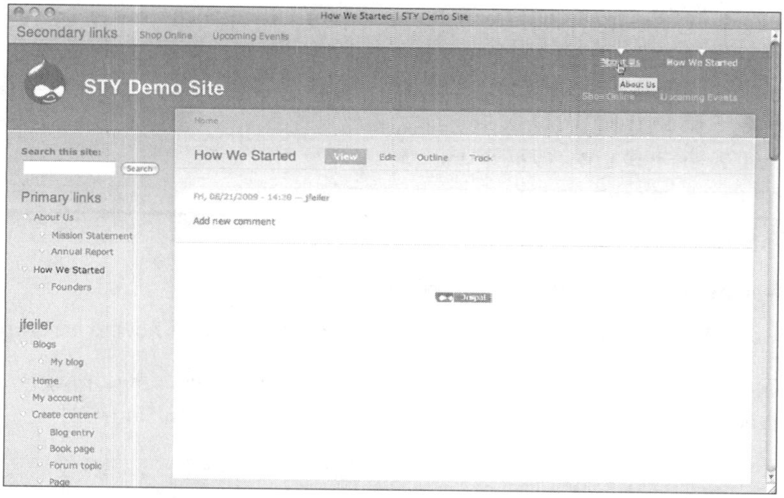

FIGURE 21.3
Links need not be hierarchical.

Here is what you have been looking at in Drupal terms:

▶ **Primary links theme display**—Drupal supports a primary links menu. It is usually an option in a theme so that you can display it or not. Each theme has its own way of displaying primary links. In the Garland theme used here, primary links are shown at the top right of the page with small triangles above them. You turn them on or off in the theme configuration, but you usually cannot change the location.

▶ **Primary links block**—A primary links block is one of the blocks that you can configure. You can place it in any region of the page (a sidebar, the header, the footer, and so forth); you also can choose not to show it at all.

▶ **Secondary links**—This is another set of menus and submenus, as shown in Figure 21.3. They can be shown in a secondary links theme display, in a secondary links block, or neither. They can be hierarchical, as shown in Figures 21.1 and 21.2, or unrelated, as shown in Figure 21.3.

In addition to the primary and secondary links, another set of links make up the *navigation* menu. Although your content and standard Drupal paths can appear in primary or secondary links as well as in the navigation menu, in most cases, your site's content appears in primary and secondary links while Drupal paths (such as Administer, Create Content, My Account, and Log Out) typically appear in the navigation menu.

The names Primary Links and Secondary Links imply a hierarchical structure to many people. As you work with them, you may want to think of them simply as two different sets of links (Red and Green, for example). Hierarchical menus are another matter.

By the Way

Drupal 7 Menus

In Drupal 7, Primary Links is now Main Menu.

▼   **Try It Yourself**

Set Secondary Menus to Be Hierarchical

If you want the behavior shown in Figures 21.1 and 21.2, here is how to accomplish it.

1. Go to Administer, Site Building, Menus, Settings (D6: `admin/build/menu/set-tings`; D7: `admin/structure/menu/settings`), as shown in Figure 21.4.

FIGURE 21.4
Configure the secondary menus to be hierarchical.

Go To ▶
NEW MENUS IN DRUPAL 7 ARE DESCRIBED IN "STARTING FROM THE MENU" LATER IN THIS HOUR.

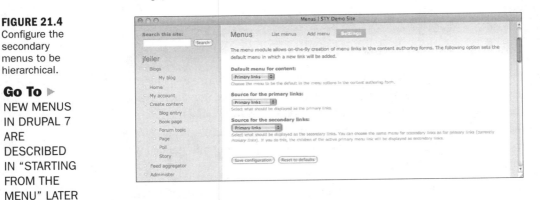

▼

2. Set the source for Secondary Links to Primary Links, as shown in Figure 21.4. Any menu can be hierarchical and contain submenus. This setting takes the second-level hierarchy from the Primary Links (or Main Menu).

Building a Menu and Using Hierarchies

You have seen the basics of using menus in a theme display and in a block on your site. Before going deeper into those issues, it makes sense to look at exactly how menus are built and where they come from. In Drupal, it is difficult, but not impossible, to create a menu with dead items. It is simple to disable a menu item so that it is grayed out, but having a menu item that points to nothing requires a bit of fiddling—and that is a good thing most of the time.

To help you build menus that function, Drupal gives you two ways of building a menu:

▶ **Start from content**—Whenever you create a node of any kind, there is a fieldset for menu choices, and you can set them there. Because you start from content, you will always have a working menu item, provided that you enter the menu data. If you do not enter menu data, you will have a node that is not referenced by any menus, and that is perfectly legitimate. Not everything needs to be accessible from a menu.

▶ **Start from the menu**—You can add a menu item to a new or existing menu. You can also edit an existing menu item and rearrange items and hierarchies. In this way of working, you have the menu item, and you must provide the path to its content.

Most people use both methods at various times.

Starting from Content

Here is how you can use the first method to build a hierarchical menu. The second method is shown later in this hour.

Try It Yourself

Select a Menu for Content

Here is how you can add new or existing content to a menu. This example shows you how to construct hierarchical menus. This will create a hierarchy of

— Primary Links

— — About Us

— — — How We Started

1. Create or edit a node.

2. In the Menu Settings fieldset, provide a name for the item and select the menu in which it should appear. Figure 21.5 shows how you add an About Us item to the Primary Links menu.

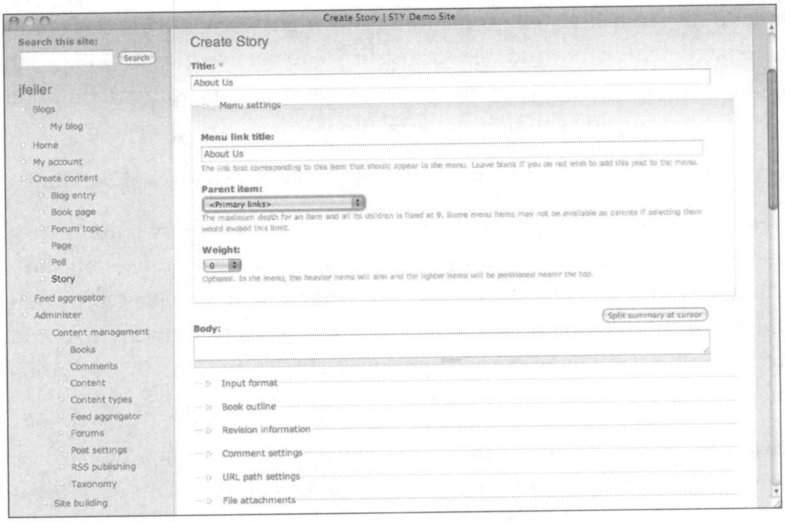

FIGURE 21.5
Add a menu item.

3. To add another node as a submenu, create or edit the new node, provide a name for it, and select the menu item under which it should appear. In Figure 21.6, you see how to add How We Started to About Us.

4. Figure 21.7 shows the pop-up for menu links as these links are being built. Note that you can choose any menu item or subitem as the parent of the new menu item.

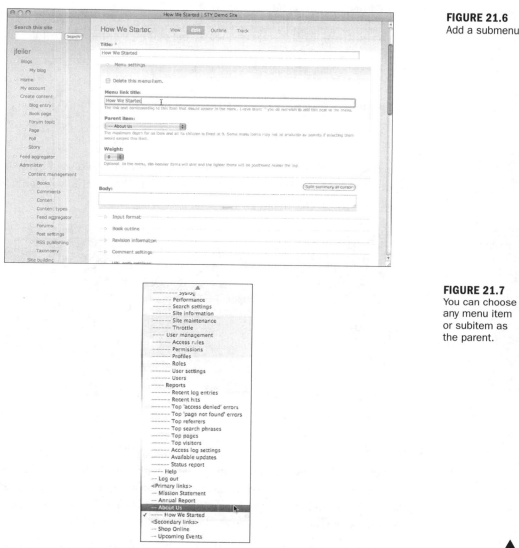

FIGURE 21.6
Add a submenu.

FIGURE 21.7
You can choose
any menu item
or subitem as
the parent.

Starting from the Menu

This section helps you manage the default menus in Drupal as well as add new ones
of your own. One of the most visible changes between Drupal 6 and Drupal 7 is in
the default menus.

Drupal 6

There are three default menus in Drupal 6:

▶ **Navigation**—This menu contains all the default commands including My Account, Create Content, Administer, and Log Out.

▶ **Primary Menu**—Initially empty, you can add items to it as described previously.

▶ **Secondary Menu**—Also initially empty, you can add items to it.

You can add items to the default menus and create your own menus.

In Drupal 6, go to Administer, Site Building, Menus (admin/build/menu), as shown in Figure 21.8. From the list of default menus shown in Figure 21.8, you can add new menus or edit the menus.

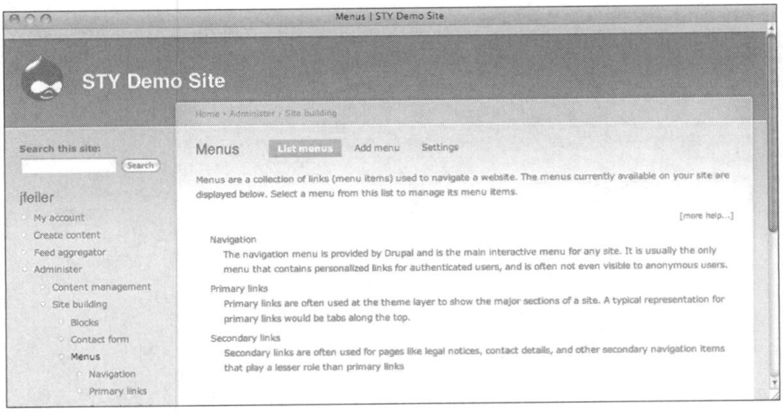

FIGURE 21.8
Configure menus in Drupal 6.

Drupal 7

In Drupal 7, menus have been rearranged along with the administrative interface. In fact, the rearrangements are not drastic, but they improve usability. The following is a guide to the default menus in Drupal 7. As is the case in all versions of Drupal, you can rearrange menus and their items:

▶ **Administration shortcuts**—The Add, Find Content, and Dashboard commands shown at the top of the window when you are administrating Drupal. You can add or remove items from this menu.

▶ **Main menu**—The menu known as Primary Links in Drupal 6 and previous versions.

▶ **Management**—The main submenu items (Content, Structure, and so forth) appear across the top of the window.

▶ **Navigation**—The navigation menu from Drupal 6 and previous versions with management and user items (such as log out) removed.

▶ **Secondary menu**—The secondary links menu from Drupal 6 and previous versions.

▶ **User menu**—Contains user account commands as well as Log Out.

Although the list of default menus differs from Drupal 6 to Drupal 7, the way you manage those menus and their items is the same.

Go to Administer, Structure, Menus (admin/structure/menu), as shown in Figure 21.9. You can also use the Structure button and then the Menus link.

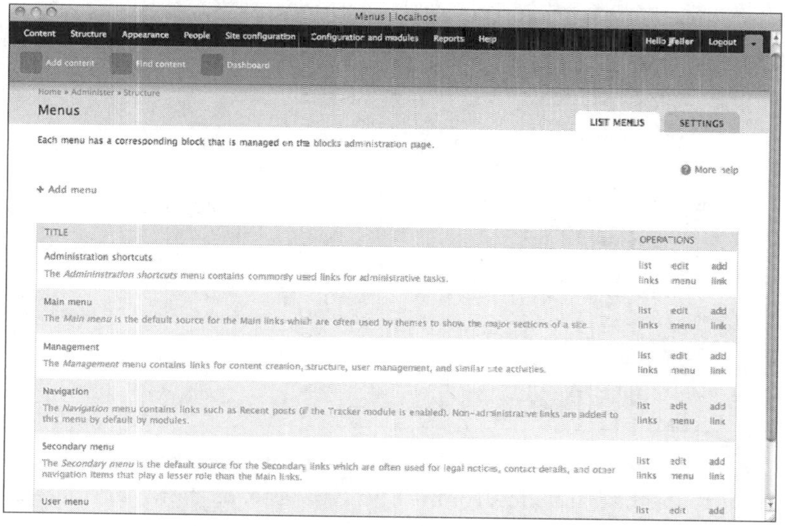

FIGURE 21.9
Administer menus in Drupal 7.

Try It Yourself

Add a Home Menu Item (Drupal 6)

To begin, make sure that the Blog module is enabled in Core. Figure 21.10 shows the basic Navigator menu for a user with permission only to create, edit, and delete blog and story content. This is the default, provided you have enabled the blog module.

In this Try It Yourself, you will see how to modify the Navigation menu so that it contains a Home item that takes you to the site's front page.

1. Go to Administer, Site Building, Menus (D6: admin/build), as shown previously in Figure 21.8.

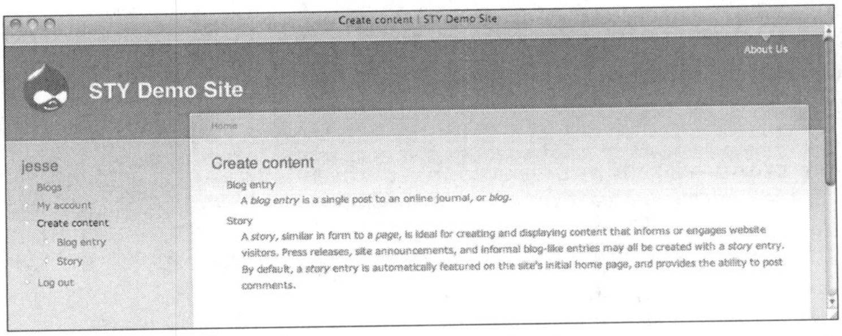

FIGURE 21.10
A user with lim-
ited permissions
has a limited
Navigation
menu.

2. Click the Navigation menu to open the list of links shown in Figure 21.11.

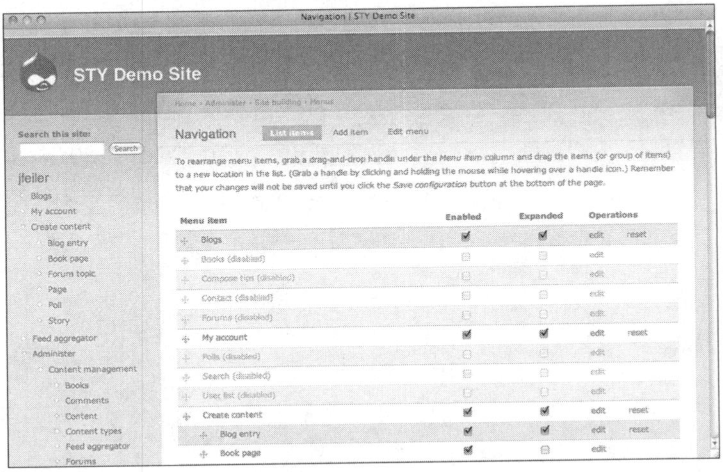

FIGURE 21.11
Begin to edit the
menu.

3. Click Add Item at the top to add a new menu item. For the path, type in
`<front>` for the front page. For the title, type Home, as shown in Figure 21.12.

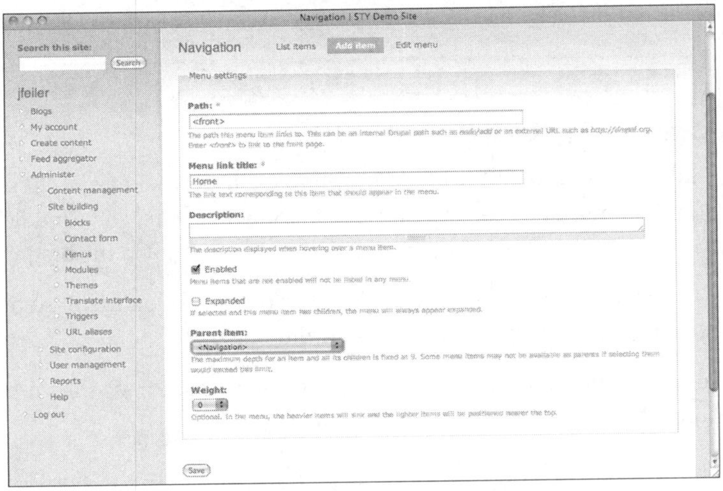

FIGURE 21.12
Add the Home
menu item.

The parent item in Drupal 6 should be Primary Links (the default). Click Save to return to the list shown in Figure 21.11.

4. Use the four-headed arrow to drag the new Home menu item to the top of the list, as shown in Figure 21.13, and then click Save Configuration.

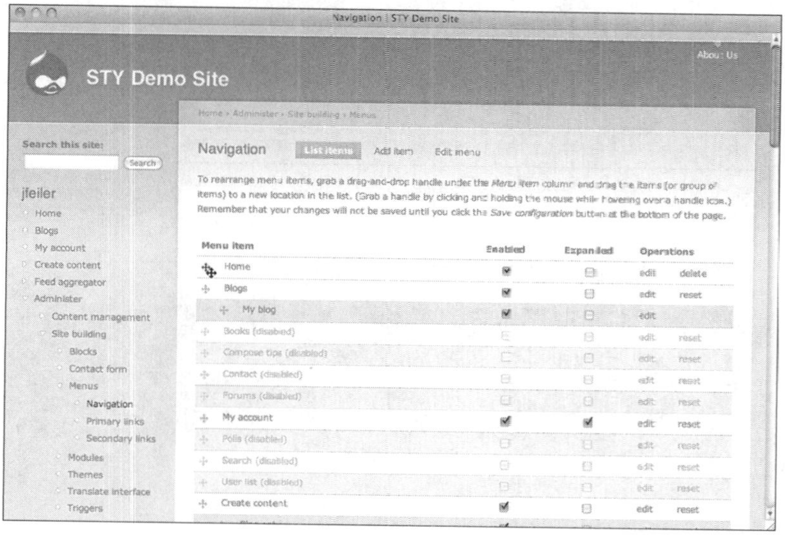

FIGURE 21.13
Rearrange the menu list items.

You can experiment with moving the new menu item up and down as well as in and out of another menu. (It would be a very poor interface design to place it as a submenu under Blogs, but you can do that as an experiment.)

Try It Yourself

Add a Home Menu Item (Drupal 7)

To begin, make sure that the Blog module is enabled in Core. Figure 21.14 shows the basic Navigator menu for a user with permission only to create, edit, and delete blog and story content. This is the default, provided you have enabled the blog module.

In this Try It Yourself, you will see how to modify the Navigation menu so that it contains a Home item that takes you to the site's front page.

1. Go to Structure, Menus (D7: admin/structure/menu), as shown previously in Figure 21.9.

2. In Drupal 7, click List Links next to the Navigation menu. The list of links shown in Figure 21.15 will open.

3. This step is the same as in the Drupal 6 version.

4. This step is the same as in the Drupal 6 version.

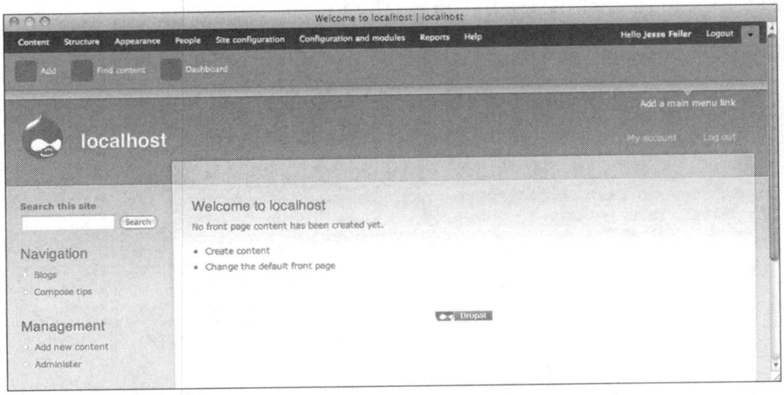

FIGURE 21.14
A user with limited permissions has a limited Navigation menu.

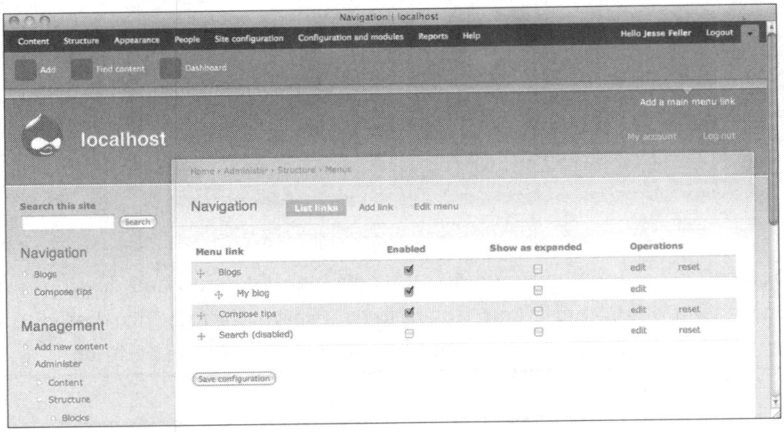

FIGURE 21.15
Begin to add a Home menu item.

Building a Custom Menu for Specific Pages

You can put your new menu-building expertise to good use in building customized menu blocks for specific pages. You can let Drupal maintain secondary links and primary links/main menu links based on the hierarchies you have created in your menus. But how do you handle the frequent need to put a marginal menu structure on specific pages? (This process is the same for Drupal 6 and Drupal 7.)

For a large site, you may have sections of the site devoted to specific areas. For an organization's management structure, those areas could be the following:

▶ Human Resources

▶ Policies

- Forms
- Product Information (Internal)
- Product Information (For Public)

This type of site organization lends itself well to a hierarchical approach. For example, the secondary links under Human Resources could be

- Performance Evaluation
- Payroll Policies
- Employee Benefits

One issue may draw your attention: Why is Payroll Policies under Human Resources and not under Policies? The answer is that Drupal content has no location. The same page can be listed as submenu links for both topics.

But, you may want to have a customized set of links in a block in the margin of Payroll Policies that contains links such as

- State Labor Laws (off-site reference)
- Federal Labor Laws (off-site reference)
- Our Personnel Forms

You already know how to do this. Go to the Menus page shown previously in Figures 21.8 and 21.9. Click Add Menu to create a new menu, as shown in Figure 21.16.

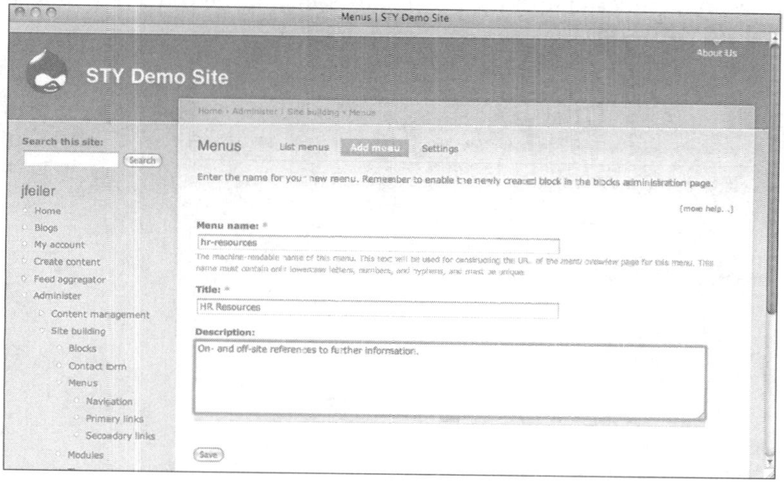

FIGURE 21.16
Add a new menu.

The new menu needs a unique internal name (such as hr-resources) and a user-friendly name (such as HR Resources). It will now appear on your list of menus, and you can add items to it the same as you did with the Home menu link. Now that it has been created, you can use it when you create content to specify the Parent Item of new content.

Drupal automatically creates a new block for each new menu that is created. The name of the menu is used for the name of the block; it will appear in the Disabled section of the blocks list, as shown in Figure 21.17. Place it where you want it either by using the pop-up menu or by dragging it. Remember to save the blocks when you are finished.

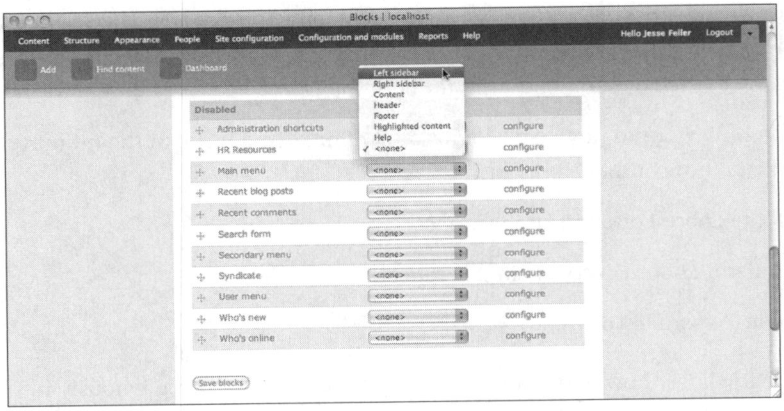

FIGURE 21.17
Drupal automatically creates a block for each new menu.

With a few nodes created under the HR Resources menu, you could have a block such as the one shown in Figure 21.18.

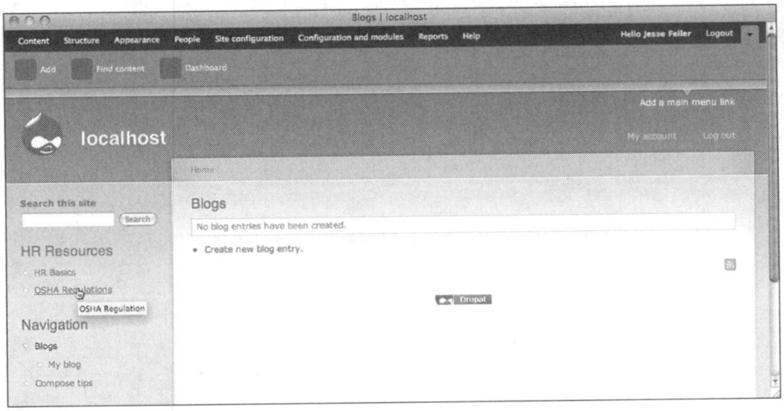

FIGURE 21.18
You can assign content to the menu.

Here is where the block-specific settings you set in the Configure links on the blocks list can come in handy. The HR Resources block that you have created can appear only on specific pages (or on all except specific pages). Remember that paths can appear in multiple menus. You can create several menu-based blocks for sidebars or any other page regions. The process is exactly what has been described here. You might have half a dozen such blocks, each of which appears (or does not appear) on specific pages. Thus, in addition to your basic navigation to major sections of the site, you can have reference menus such as these. If some pages need a number of these menu-based blocks, you can create new, composite menus for their own blocks.

Figure 21.19 shows a menu-based block (HR Resources)

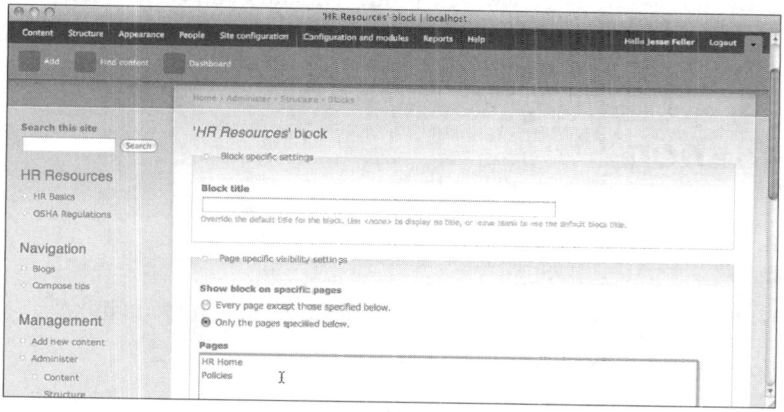

FIGURE 21.19
Use menu-based blocks.

Summary

After you have mastered the basics of menus, you can repeat the process over and over. The use of menu-based blocks, particularly when tied to specific pages, can be an effective way of providing navigation for your end users (and, after you have set it up, it is very easy to implement and reimplement).

Q&A

Q. *We are going to be converting from Drupal 6 to Drupal 7. What is the best way to avoid confusing our end users with the changed menu structure?*

A. This is an issue only if you expose the Navigation menu to your users. If you use your own menus, users will not know that things have changed (although administrators will know). Depending on your time frame, you might want to think about implementing and exposing a site-specific navigation design that is independent of the underlying structure. If you have enough time, consider beginning to implement any part of the navigation that will be visible to users in advance. For example, you can build a Users menu in Drupal 6 so that people are used to it.

Q. *Are there limits to the sizes of menus?*

A. Many people would say that the answer is, "Unfortunately, no." There is research to indicate that long lists of menus (particularly pop-up menu items) are unmanageable. If you have ever navigated through a pop-up menu containing more than 100 countries, you know that unless you live in an early alphabetical place, such as Austria, it can be tedious and frustrating. Particularly with the advent of new web technologies that allow for partial page loads, you can frequently refine the interface choices as people move along.

Workshop

Quiz

1. Where do I set the text to appear when hovering over a menu link?

2. How do you create a menu-based block?

3. How do you create hierarchical menus?

Quiz Answers

1. This is the menu link description field.

2. Drupal does it for you automatically when you create a new menu. (The blocks are for the menu, so if you add or remove individual menu links, blocks are updated accordingly.)

3. There are two meanings to this question:

a. When you create a menu link, set its parent link to the menu link you want to be its parent.

b. For default primary/secondary link behavior, set the secondary links to be primary links so that the hierarchical submenus of primary links will properly appear in the secondary links tabs.

Activities

Laying out your site's menu design is something that benefits from more rather than fewer people. Try out your navigation architecture on paper or in a mock-up to see where people have problems.

If your site is button-centric, experiment with a menu-centric interface and vice versa. Do anything you can think of to force yourself and your colleagues to think of your site's structure from a different perspective.

HOUR 22

Managing the Site

What You'll Learn in This Hour:

▶ **Using Actions and Triggers**

▶ **Understanding Tokens**

▶ **Using Rules**

▶ **Automating Your Site's Maintenance and Support**

Introduction

With Drupal, much of the work of building, maintaining, and managing a website can be taken off your shoulders. You have seen how to use the social and communication aspects of Drupal to let users contribute to the site in various ways. This chapter shows how you can set up the site to perform many maintenance tasks—not just reminding you (or others) when things have to be done, but, in many cases, actually doing them.

There are two sets of automation tools you can use with Drupal:

▶ **Actions and Triggers**—These modules are built in to the core, and they provide many actions that can help automate the site.

▶ **Rules**—This module supports a more complex structure, including more dynamic rule creation. Although it is more complex, it is more powerful in part because so many modules support it. As a result, many people prefer it.

Using Triggers

Triggers and actions work together. When a certain event occurs (the *trigger*), an *action* is executed. Together, they form an automated process that, after it is set up, fires itself off whenever necessary. To begin, install and enable the Trigger module, as shown in Table 22.1.

TABLE 22.1   Trigger Module Reference

Download from	Core
Enable in section	Core—optional
Permissions	
None	
Administration	
Administer, Site Building, Triggers (D6: `admin/build/trigger`; D7: `admin/structure/trigger/node`)	

When you start to administer triggers (D6: `admin/build/trigger`; D7: `admin/structure/trigger/node`), you will be able to manage triggers in a variety of areas, as you can see in Figure 22.1. The installed triggers are listed. To activate a trigger, you assign an action to it.

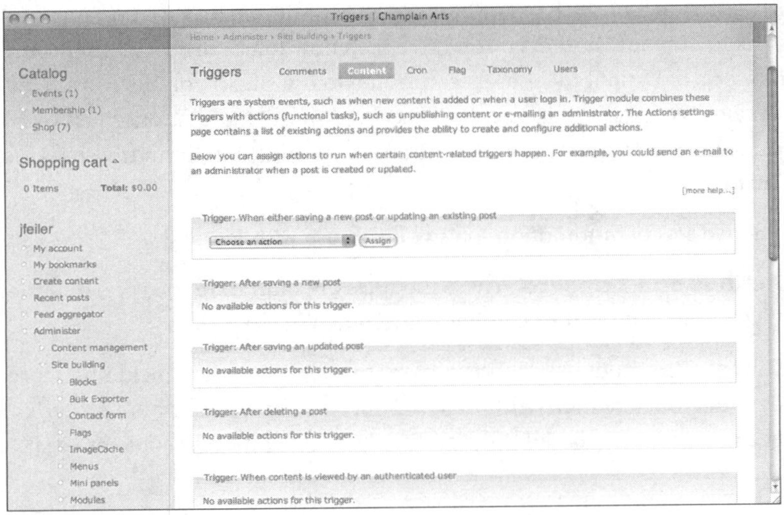

FIGURE 22.1
Start to configure content triggers.

Figure 22.2 shows the actions available for saving or updating a post.

Note that some of these actions (such as making an item sticky) can be accomplished with default settings, but others cannot.

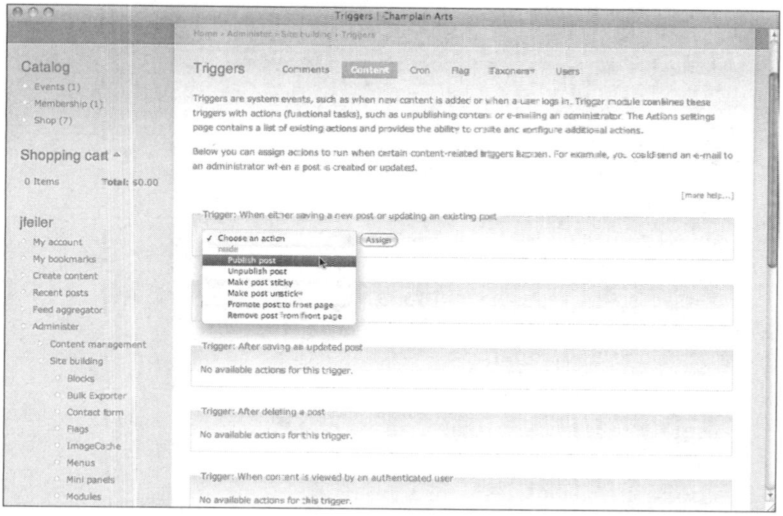

FIGURE 22.2
Set actions for saving or updating a post.

After you assign an action to a trigger, it is shown on the Triggers page. In addition, you can unassign any action, as shown in Figure 22.3.

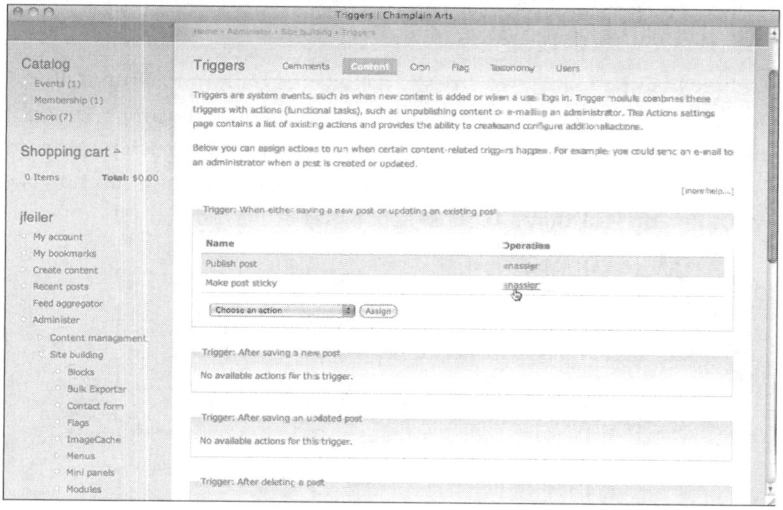

FIGURE 22.3
You can unassign actions from triggers.

The actions for various triggers differ. Figure 22.4 shows the triggers for comments. The trigger/action combination shown in Figure 22.4 enables you to automatically move a post to the front page whenever a comment is saved to it. This has the effect of keeping the front page populated with recent posts (default Drupal behavior) as well as those that have recently elicited comments. In other words, the front page consists of active posts. Anything that you can do to automate the site can be a big help.

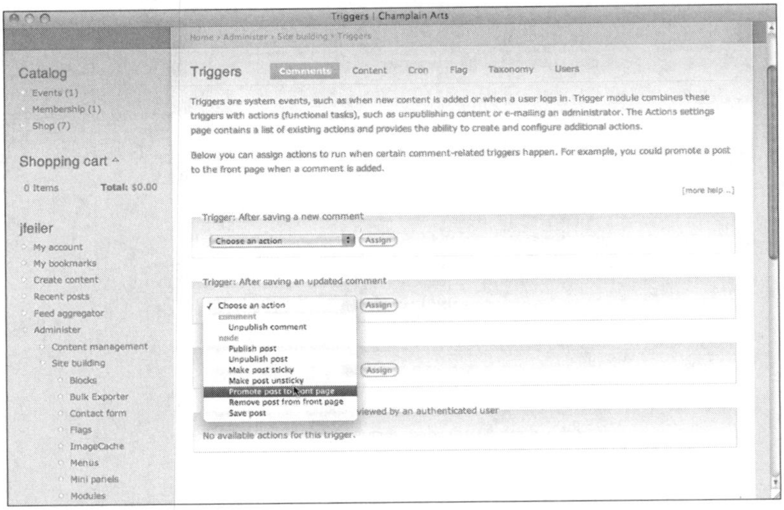

FIGURE 22.4
You can move a
recently com-
mented-on post
to the front page
automatically.

Using Actions

Triggers are enabled only when you assign an action to them. To configure them, you need to set permission at System Module: administer actions.

As you can see in Figure 22.5, two types of actions are built in to Drupal. Basic actions act on the current user, node, or comment without requiring additional information. Advanced actions require additional information such as an email address to which to send a message when a trigger fires. You get to this page from Administer, Site Configuration, Actions (`admin/settings/actions`).

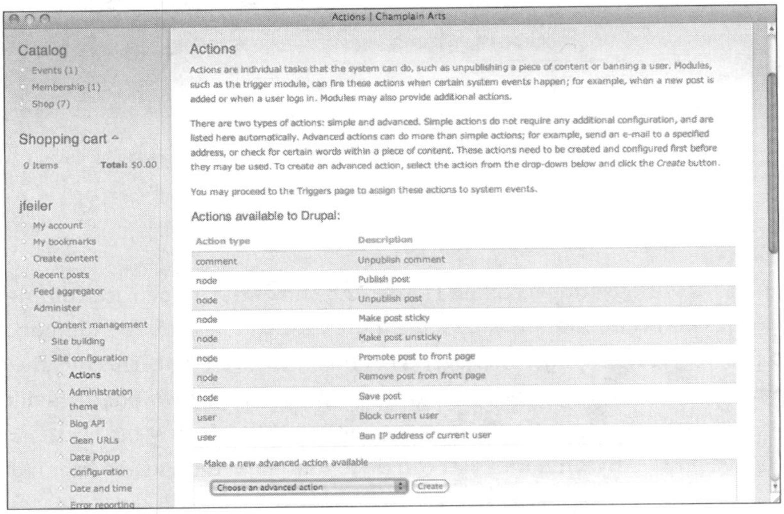

FIGURE 22.5
View basic
actions and con-
figure advanced
actions.

Figure 22.6 shows the ways in which you can configure advanced actions.

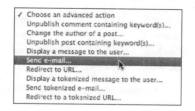

FIGURE 22.6
Select an
advanced action
to configure.

Using Tokens and Customized Actions

The number of customized actions that you can create is unlimited. If you have the Token module installed, you can insert a variety of tokens into the actions. For example, you can trigger an email message to certain recipients when a trigger fires. The action you customize contains the email addresses; you can use tokens to automatically compose the message, as shown in Figure 22.7.

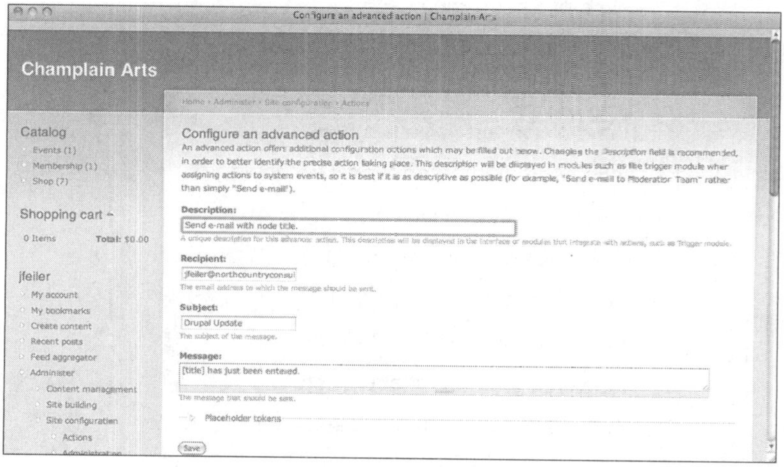

FIGURE 22.7
Create cus-
tomized actions.

Table 22.2 shows the tokens available for nodes. Note that some of them are marked as raw. These are the unchanged versions of user inputs that could have dangerous characters in them. They are later modified by PathAuto, if you have it installed. The best choice is to enable Path and PathAuto and then to use the raw versions if you want to. That lets the Token module use the best representation of the data, and any potentially dangerous characters are stripped by the Path module.

TABLE 22.2   Node Tokens

Token	Replacement Value
[nid]	Node ID.
[type]	Node type.
[type-name]	Node type (user-friendly version).
[language]	Node language.
[title]	Node title.
[title-raw]	Unfiltered node title.
[author-uid]	Node author's user id.
[author-name]	Node author's user name.
[author-name-raw]	Node author's user name.
[author-mail]	Node author's email.
[author-mail-raw]	Node author's email.
[term]	Name of top taxonomy term.
[term-raw]	Unfiltered name of top taxonomy term.
[term-id]	ID of top taxonomy term.
[vocab]	Name of top term's vocabulary.
[vocab-raw]	Unfiltered name of top term's vocabulary.
[vocab-id]	ID of top term's vocabulary.
[yyyy]	Node creation year (four digit).
[yy]	Node creation year (two digit).
[month]	Node creation month (full word).
[mon]	Node creation month (abbreviated).
[mm]	Node creation month (two digit, zero padded).
[m]	Node creation month (one or two digit).
[ww]	Node creation week (two digit).
[date]	Node creation date (day of month).
[day]	Node creation day (full word).
[ddd]	Node creation day (abbreviation).
[dd]	Node creation day (two digit, zero-padded).
[d]	Node creation day (one or two digit).
[mod-????]	All tokens for node creation dates can also be used with the mod- prefix; doing so will use the modification date rather than the creation date.

TABLE 22.2 Continued

Token	Replacement Value
[menu]	The name of the menu the node belongs to.
[menu-raw]	The name of the menu the node belongs to.
[menupath]	The menu path (as reflected in the breadcrumb), not including Home or [menu]. Use Separated by to separate items.
[menupath-raw]	The unfiltered menu path (as reflected in the breadcrumb), not including Home or [menu]. Separated by /.
[menu-link-title]	The text used in the menu as link text for this item.
[menu-link-title-raw]	The unfiltered text used in the menu as link text for this item.
[flag-bookmarks-count]	Total flag count for flag Bookmarks.
[flag-rsvp-event-count]	Total flag count for flag RSVP.
[termpath]	As [term], but including its supercategories, separated by /.
[termpath-raw]	As [term-raw], but including its supercategories, separated by /.
[termalias]	URL alias for the term.

The actual tokens that you have available depend on the modules that are installed. For example, the [flag-bookmarks-count] token is available only if you have installed the Flag module and created a bookmark flag. Ubercart installs a large number of tokens that you can use in email messages to identify products, orders, and more.

Table 22.3 shows the tokens that are available for CCK. They are available only if you have installed CCK. Furthermore, they can be dependent on your use of CCK. For example, the text token [field_location-raw] exists only if CCK is installed and you have created a field called location.

TABLE 22.3 CCK Tokens

Token	Replacement Value
File Tokens	
[field_image_cache-filefield-fid]	File ID
[field_image_cache-filefield-description]	File description
[field_image_cache-filefield-filename]	Filename

TABLE 22.3   Continued

Token	Replacement Value
[field_image_cache-filefield-filepath]	File path
[field_image_cache-filefield-filemime]	File MIME type
[field_image_cache-filefield-filesize]	File size (in bytes)
[field_image_cache-filefield-filesize_formatted]	File size (pretty printed)
[field_image_cache-filefield-view]	Fully formatted HTML file tag
[field_image_cache-filefield-onlyname]	File name without extension
[field_image_cache-filefield-extension]	File extension
Date Tokens	
[field_date-value]	The raw date value
[field_date-view]	The formatted date
[field_date-timestamp]	The raw date timestamp
[field_date-yyyy]	Date year (four digit)
[field_date-yy]	Date year (two digit)
[field_date-month]	Date month (full word)
[field_date-mon]	Date month (abbreviated)
[field_date-mm]	Date month (two digit, zero padded)
[field_date-m]	Date month (one or two digit)
[field_date-ww]	Date week (two digit)
[field_date-date]	Date date (YYYY-MM-DD)
[field_date-datetime]	Date datetime (YYYY-MM-DDTHH:MM:SS)
[field_date-day]	Date day (full word)
[field_date-ddd]	Date day (abbreviation)
[field_date-dd]	Date day (two digit, zero-padded)
[field_date-d]	Date day (one or two digit)
[field_date-time]	Time H:i

TABLE 22.3   Continued

Token	Replacement Value
[field_date-to-????]	If the field has a to-date defined, the same tokens exist in the form: [to-????], where ???? is the normal token.
Text Tokens	
[field_location-raw]	Raw, unfiltered text
[field_location-formatted]	Formatted and filtered text

Table 22.4 and Table 22.5 show tokens for users and site globals. The actual tokens have different prefixes. For values for an author, replace xxx with author. For values related to the acting user, replace xxx with user.

TABLE 22.4   User Tokens

Token	Replacement Value
[xxx:user]	User's name
[xxx:user-raw]	User's unfiltered name
[xxx:uid]	User's ID
[xxx:mail]	User's email address
[xxx:reg-date]	User's registration date
[xxx:reg-since]	Days since the user registered
[xxx:log-date]	User's last login date
[xxx:log-since]	Days since the user's last login
[xxx:date-in-tz]	The current date in the user's time zone
[xxx:account-url]	The URL of the user's profile page
[xxx:account-edit]	The URL the user's account editing page

TABLE 22.5   Global Tokens

Token	Replacement Value
[xxx:site-login]	A link to the site login page
[xxx:site-logo]	The URL for the site logo
[xxx:user-name]	The name of the currently logged in user
[xxx:user-id]	The user ID of the currently logged in user

TABLE 22.5   Continued

Token	Replacement Value
[xxx:user-mail]	The email address of the currently logged in user
[xxx:site-url]	The url of the current Drupal website
[xxx:site-name]	The name of the current Drupal website
[xxx:site-slogan]	The slogan of the current Drupal website
[xxx:site-mission]	The mission of the current Drupal website
[xxx:site-mail]	The contact email address for the current Drupal website
[xxx:site-date]	The current date on the site's server
[xxx:site-date-yyyy]	The current year (four digit)
[xxx:site-date-yy]	The current year (two digit)
[xxx:site-date-month]	The current month (full word)
[xxx:site-date-mon]	The current month (abbreviated)
[xxx:site-date-mm]	The current month (two digit, zero padded)
[xxx:site-date-m]	The current month (one or two digit)
[xxx:site-date-ww]	The current week (two digit)
[xxx:site-date-date]	The current date (day of month)
[xxx:site-date-day]	The current day (full word)
[xxx:site-date-ddd]	The current day of week (abbreviation)
[xxx:site-date-dd]	The current day (two digit, zero-padded)
[xxx:site-date-d]	The current day (one or two digit)
[xxx:page-number]	The current page number for paged lists

Because the list of available tokens is subject to change as you add modules, it is best to install the modules you will be using before you set up actions, triggers, and rules that may use the tokens.

Using Rules

Another set of triggers and actions is available with the Rules module. It interacts with a variety of other modules so that the triggers can be launched from those modules. You can view a list of modules supporting rules at groups.drupal.org/node/10270/rules-modules.

Module support for Rules is very important and powerful. For example, CCK allows you to support a trigger that is dependent on a specific value in a CCK field. It also lets you create an action that sets a value in a CCK field. By combining these two features, you can create a trigger that fires when a node is about to be saved. If a field called location contains the value *here*, the action can replace that value with *on-site*.

This is a simple data substitution issue, and you could probably achieve the same results (clean and consistent data) by changing the location field to be a pop-up menu rather than allowing free-field input. If *here* is not a choice, most end users will figure out that they should select *on-site*.

But the true power of the Rules module—very much like the Token module—is when its functionality allows two modules to be combined in new ways. For example, instead of creating both a trigger and action that are based on a CCK field, consider these mix-and-match module scenarios.

▶ For a cat lover's website, a node with text containing the word *dog* could be automatically deleted. You can construct more serious scenarios involving obscenity. (An action exists that can automatically delete based on keywords, but you can customize it further with your own action.)

▶ Similarly, although the node may not be deleted, a cautionary email can be sent to a site administrator. You might also want to send an email to the end user so that a warning is provided. Rather than censoring the material, it may be just as easy for the end user to revise it.

▶ Among the events that can trigger a rule is a user login. You can pair a user login (perhaps constrained by specific role) with an email message.

It is also worth noting that the combination of trigger and action in the Trigger and Action modules is not directly mappable to the Rules module. Although the concepts are similar, in the Rules module, a trigger is fired by an *event*. When the trigger is fired, a *condition* can be applied. If the condition is true, the *action* occurs. This terminology means that you can have a Rules trigger with no conditions. The trigger may fire when a node is about to be saved and when the condition is a certain data value in a given field. Another trigger may fire when a node is about to be saved, regardless of any data values or conditions.

To get started, download, install, and enable the Rules module, as shown in Table 22.6.

TABLE 22.6   Rules Module Reference

Download from	project/rules
Enable in section	Rules
Drupal 7	
D7CX	
Permissions	
Rules Admin Module	Administer rules
Administration	
Administer, Rules (admin/rules)	

You begin to work with rules by going to Administer, Rules (admin/rules) to open the page shown in Figure 22.8.

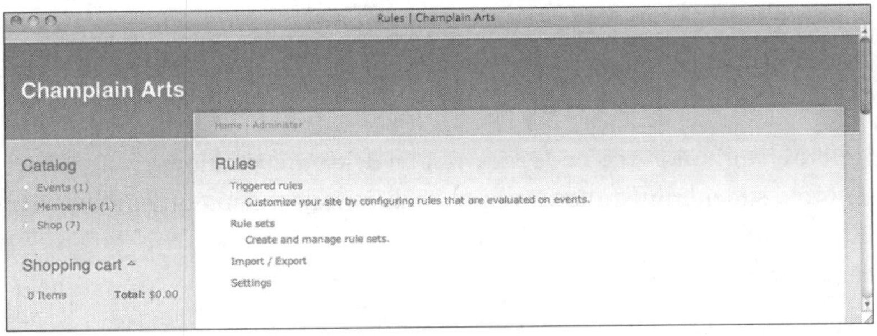

FIGURE 22.8
Administer rules.

When you click Triggered Rules, you will find a list of any active rules, as shown in Figure 22.9. You are started out with an example and you can add your own.

Exploring Rules

This section deals with the first choice, Triggered Rules. The others are well worth exploring after you master triggered rules.

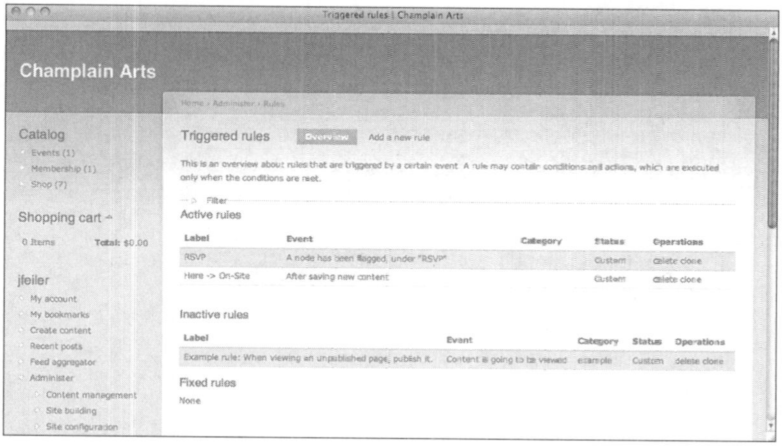

FIGURE 22.9
List the triggered
rules.

All the rules function in similar ways, and they have similar interfaces. The details of the interface change from one triggering event to another and from one action to another, but after you master the basics, you can explore the wealth of options in the Rules module.

Try It Yourself

Send an Email When a User Logs In

This rule has no conditions. It simply sends an email when a user logs in. It also posts a message to Drupal's watchdog, the log of events on your site. Posting the message to the watchdog is useful for debugging, particularly when the action involves sending an email. An email message can fail in many places during testing so it makes sense to know that you have actually tried to send the email or carry out whatever action it is.

1. From the list of rules shown in Figure 22.9, click Add a New Rule to open the page shown in Figure 22.10. Choose User Has Logged In as the triggering event. Click Save Changes.

2. Click Add an Action, as shown in Figure 22.11. You will be presented with a list of available actions; the list varies depending on the modules that are installed and enabled. For this example, choose Send a Mail to a User.

3. Configure the action as an email message, as shown in Figure 22.12. You can greet the user by name using a token. Click Save.

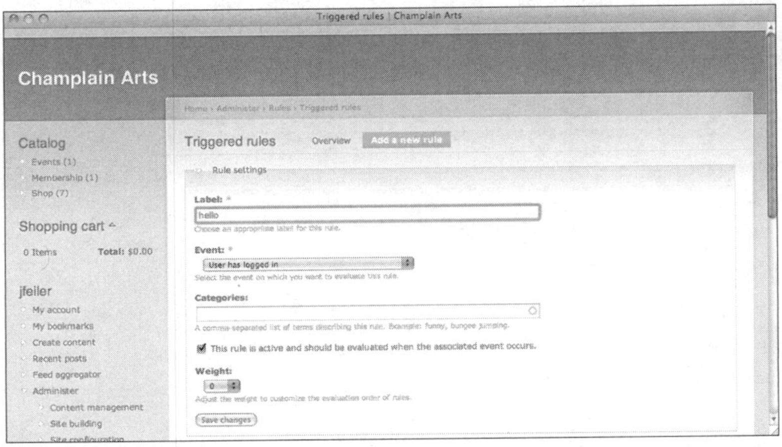

FIGURE 22.10
Specify the triggering event.

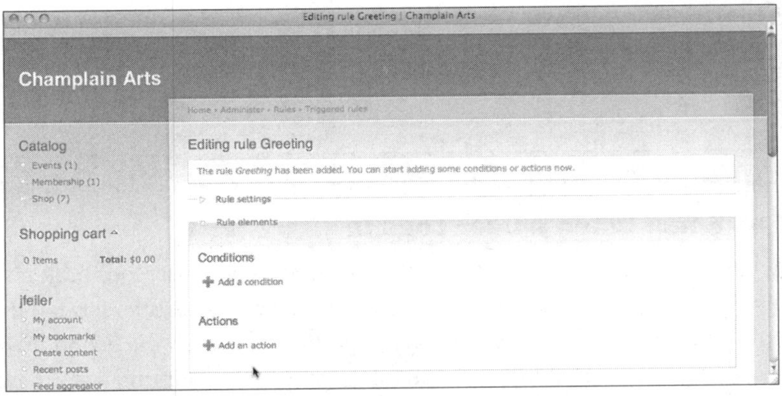

FIGURE 22.11
Add an action.

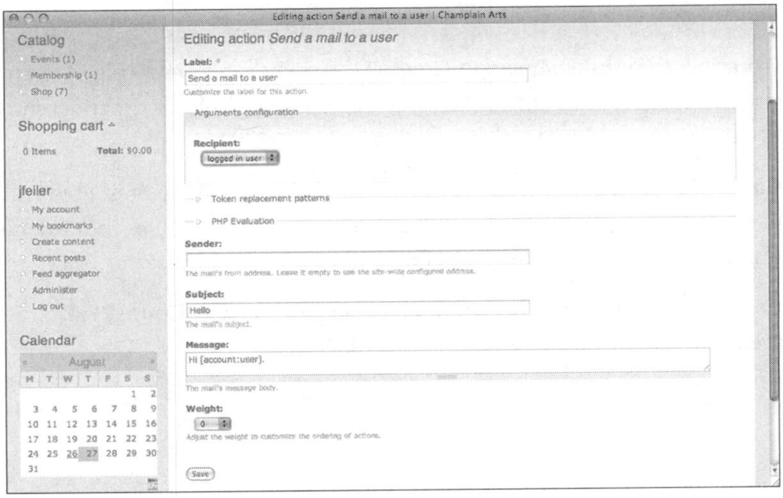

FIGURE 22.12
Configure the action.

4. You can add conditions and other actions, as you can see in Figure 22.13. Conditions can including checking on the user's role or any other information available to Rules. A useful action to add is Log to Watchdog; you can see the results of the rule in Administer, Reports, Recent Log Entries (`admin/reports/dblog`).

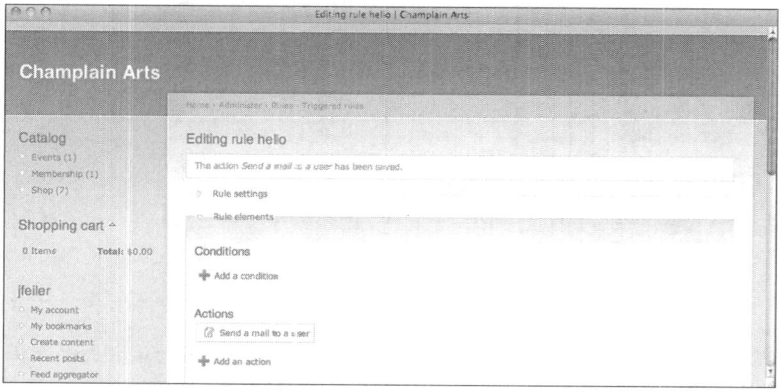

FIGURE 22.13
Add more conditions and actions as you want.

Try It Yourself

Modify Content

Here is a way to modify content. This scenario replaces the value *here* in a location field with the value *on-site*. This is a more complex scenario than the preceding one, but you will soon notice a rhythm to it. As you build the rule, you fall into a pattern that will become familiar:

▶ Add a condition or action.

▶ Specify its details or data.

This can serve as the basis for many rules on your site. For example, the same basic trigger (a data condition) could send a warning email to supervisors or the user.

1. From the list of triggered rules, click Add a New Rule.

2. Enter the data and choose the event. In this case, use After Saving New Content. (For a similar purpose, you can choose After Updating Existing Content; you may need rules for both events, depending on what you are trying to do.) Click Save Changes. The next page lets you review the basic settings and change them, as well as add conditions and actions. Figure 22.14 shows the top of the page with Rule Settings.

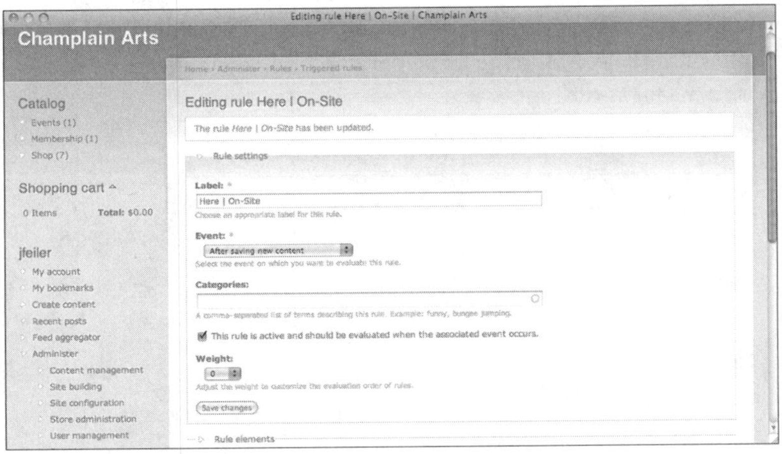

FIGURE 22.14
Review rule set-
tings.

3. After you create the rule and click Save Settings you add conditions and
actions, on the next page, as shown in Figure 22.15.

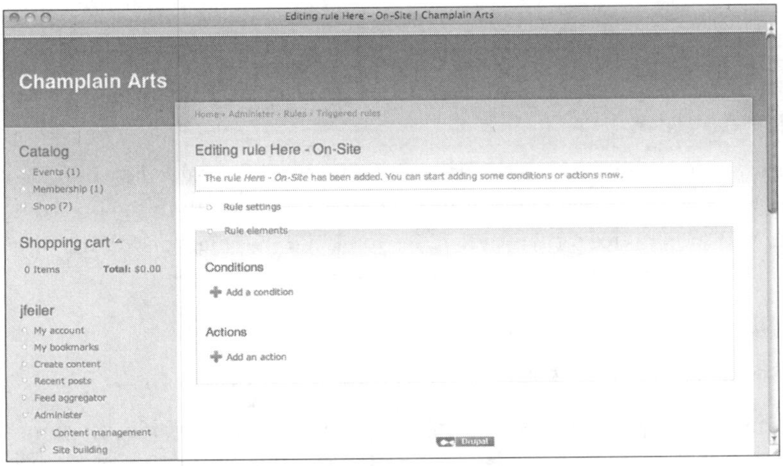

FIGURE 22.15
Add conditions
and actions.

4. Click Add Condition. On the page shown in Figure 22.16, choose Textual Comparison and click Next.

5. Specify the textual comparison. Use the token for the location field's content—
[node:field_location-raw]—and the word *here* in the second field, as shown in
Figure 22.17.

6. Now, add an action to populate the CCK field, as shown in Figure 22.18.

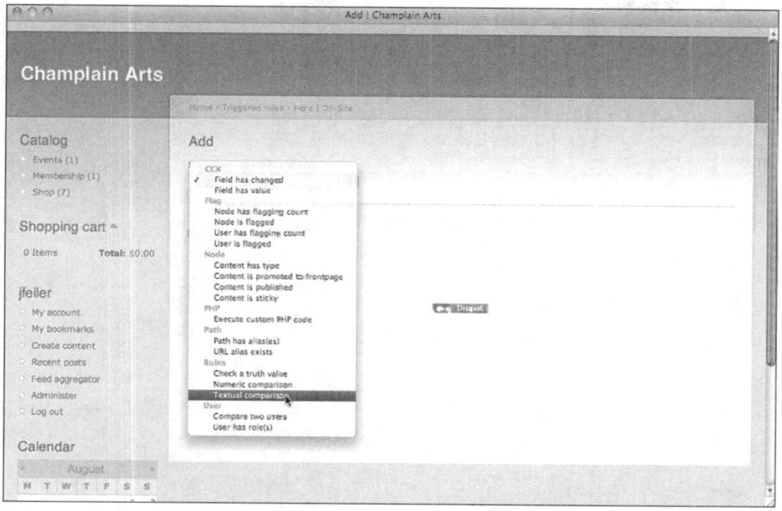

FIGURE 22.16
Add a textual comparison condition.

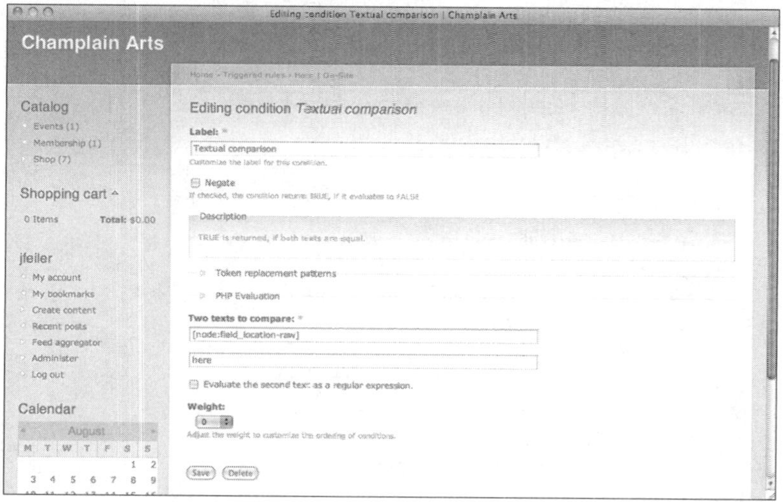

FIGURE 22.17
Specify the condition.

7. Specify the data to populate the field, as shown in Figure 22.19.

8. Create content with a location field in it, as shown in Figure 22.20. Enter *here* for the location. If you followed the sequence in this book, the Date content type that is linked to a calendar is a good content type to use because it has a CCK location field.

9. Now, view that node. This node was associated with the calendar. You can open it from the calendar, as shown in Figure 22.21. Notice that the location field has been changed to *on-site*.

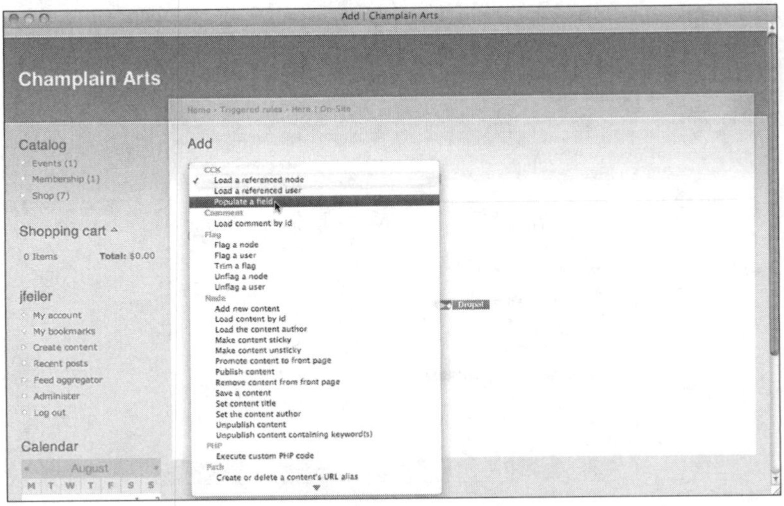

FIGURE 22.18
Add an action.

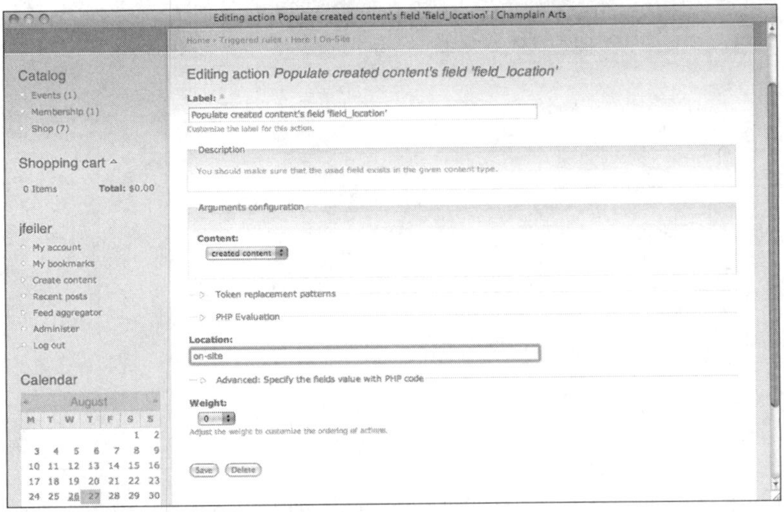

FIGURE 22.19
Specify the action.

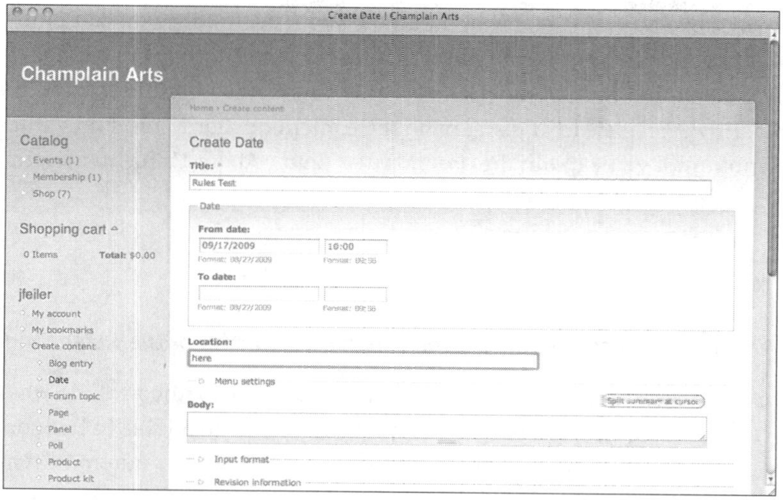

FIGURE 22.20
Create a Date
location field
with value *here*.

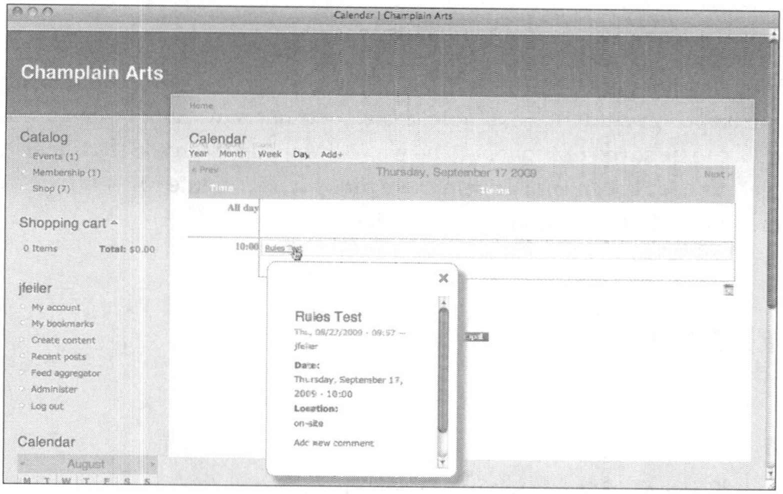

FIGURE 22.21
Confirm that the
location has
been changed.

Summary

Triggers, actions, and rules help you automate your site. In fact, you can plan your site around what can be done automatically. For example, a front page that contains recently entered information as well as recently commented-on information can be valuable. However, instead of just having the content appear to randomly fluctuate, make certain that you explain the ground rules (in an About Us menu or perhaps a block shown only on the front page).

Q&A

Q. *Which is better to use: the trigger/action combination or the Rules module?*

A. In some cases, you may not have a choice; only one method will do what you want. Sending email messages using tokens may be available in both architectures. Look carefully at additional things you might like to automate. One thing is certain: Automating your site using either method is preferable to not automating it at all.

Q. *Do all rules fire at the same relative time?*

A. Many of them fire when something has happened, but some valuable triggers fire before an event. For example, there are triggers available when a node is about to be saved or is about to be viewed. You can intercede to change it or to alert someone. In a similar vein, note that you can create rulesets in the Rules module so that several rules fire together.

Workshop

Quiz

1. Can the same trigger cause more than one action to fire?

2. Do triggers, actions, and rules degrade site performance?

Quiz Answers

1. Yes.

2. Generally not, because they are very efficient in their design and implementation.

Activities

Drupal's automation tools are one of the keys to getting the most out of Drupal. As you select modules, look for those that support Rules so that you can build Triggers and Actions on top of them. Rather than thinking of how you can automate the site (which is a pretty large and complex issue), think about where you can create specific triggers and actions. Then, think about how those small components can help to automate the site.

For example, the fact that you can create targeted email messages with tokens identifying exactly what has happened can be coupled with mail filters you can create on your site. Messages can be filtered based not only on email addresses but also on the subject lines that you can create in actions. You may find that thinking about triggers, actions, and rules leads to new standards for email subjects and categories.

Using View Arguments and Modifying Built-In Pages

What You'll Learn in This Hour:

- ▶ How to Create Dynamic Views
- ▶ How to Create and Set Arguments for Dynamic Views
- ▶ How to Make the Built-In Pages More Useful in Your Environment
- ▶ How to Use User and Node Reference Fields

Introduction

This hour builds on views, panels, and pages to show you how to build dynamic content views and modify pages—including Drupal's built-in pages. You can use and reuse the components and complexity that you have now mastered to help you build large and complex sites that are, nevertheless, simple for end users, as well as easy for you and your colleagues to design, build, and maintain. In addition, you will see how to move beyond websites to incorporate content and database management features that take advantage of Drupal.

Constructing a Dynamic Page

In Hour 14, you saw how to construct a view that retrieves and displays data from the database. You saw not only how to hard-code the selection criteria, but also how to expose the interface, as shown in Figure 23.1.

Go To ▶
REVIEW
HOUR 14,
"WORKING
WITH VIEWS,"
P. 237 AND
HOUR 20,
"LAYING OUT
PANELS AND
PAGES,"
P. 337.

In this hour, you will see how to construct a dynamic view—one in which the data is selected based on an argument that is passed in as part of the URL. Figure 23.2 shows a dynamic page in which the data is specified in the address rather than being hard-coded in the view or set by the user.

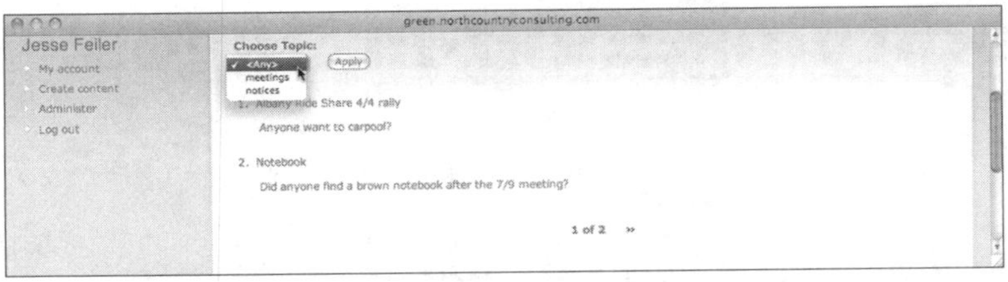

FIGURE 23.1
Allow users to select the data to display in a view.

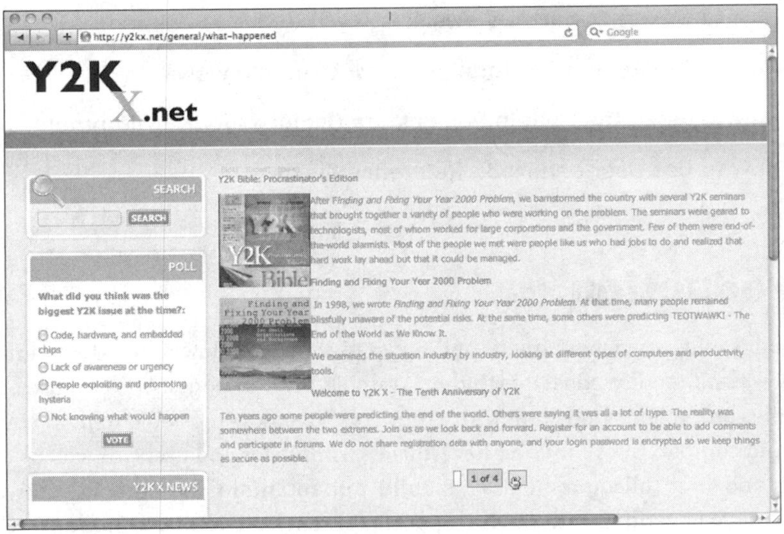

FIGURE 23.2
Create a dynamic page.

Understanding Dynamic Views

Automating the process of data selection can make things much easier for your users. If nothing else, it eliminates an unnecessary step in which they have to go to the page that will display the data, choose the data, and then wait for the page to be refreshed.

In addition to simplifying the user interface, the idea of using arguments in the path gives you, the site designer and implementer, much less work to do. You lay out the view as you want it to be shown, regardless of the content that is displayed. Then, to show one set of data or another, you vary the arguments. For example, assume that the view is named myview, and that it can show information from data identified by a taxonomy term. That term can be used to select data, and thus, after you have built myview, you can use any of the following Drupal paths:

myview/personnel

myview/news

myview/press-releases

myview/documents-public

and so forth. Note that it is common to use hyphens to replace spaces in arguments for these pages.

Arguments can be used for more than just selecting data. For example, you can specify that one argument is used as the title. It does not matter which one: it is up to you to associate each argument with its use. As far as Drupal is concerned, these two arguments could be functionally equivalent:

myview/documents/public/

myview/public/documents

URL Conventions

Drupal users and the documentation are inconsistent on terminology in this area, so here is how this book handles these fragments of URLs. First, in this hour, we assume that you have installed and enabled Pathauto as described previously in Hour 6, "Managing URLs: Cleaning, Redirects, and PathAuto," p. 87. As a reminder, addresses on your website are provided as partial URLs. Thus, the first partial URL shown in the previous section actually resolves to yourwebsite.com/myview/personnel. Drupal will disassemble that into a path (myview) and an argument to that path (personnel). Multiple arguments can exist for a single path so that the fourth example would resolve to two arguments: documents and public.

By the Way

Creating a Dynamic View

Building a dynamic view has just a few variations from building a static view. After the view has been created, you can create a page variant so that your page will be complete.

This example is built on a section of the Y2KX.net site that has been shown previously. For now, all that is important to know is that there is a taxonomy vocabulary called Site Tags. Its identification and content settings are shown in Figure 23.3. (Whether forum topics are included as requiring a tag in this vocabulary depends on your particular data.)

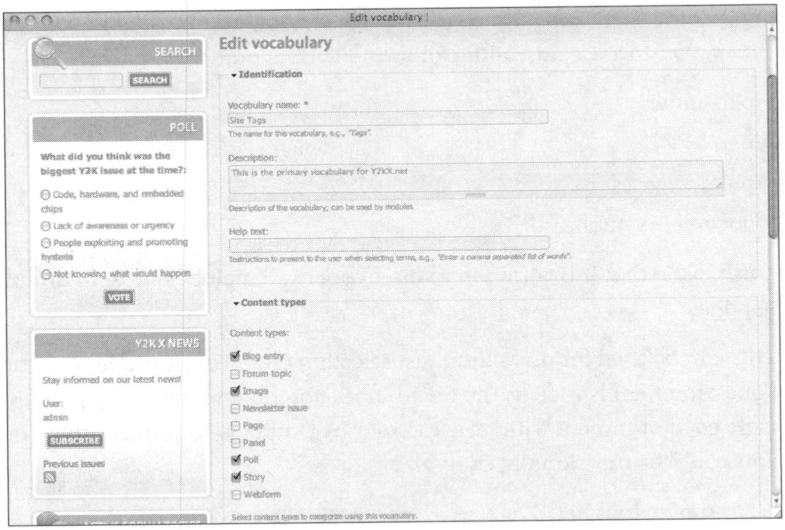

FIGURE 23.3
Use a new or
existing vocabu-
lary to tag your
site's data.

The settings shown in Figure 23.4 mean that you can rely on every node in every major content type having at least one Site Tags tag. This is not required at all for this example to work. However, if you will be relying on taxonomy tags to retrieve data, you are better off if you know that the data has been properly tagged. (In other words, it is not only nice to have those tags, it is essential. Without them, data can be lost forever.)

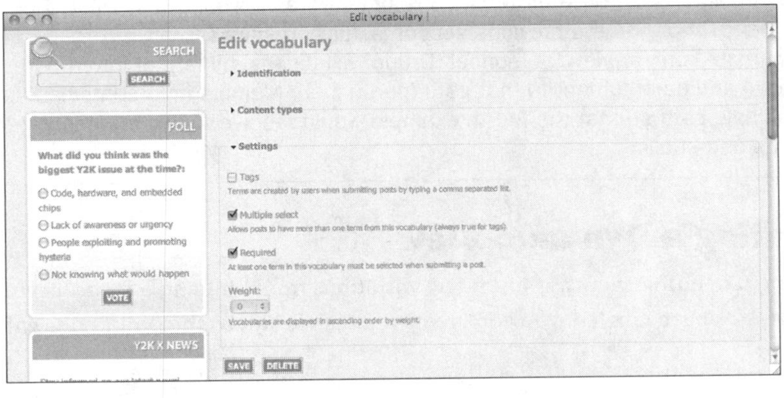

FIGURE 23.4
Your site is more
robust if at least
one tag is
required for each
node.

▼ **Try It Yourself**

Building a Dynamic Page

This is similar to building a static page or a page with a user-selected search criterion. After each step, you normally click Update. Click Save when you are finished. If your Internet connection is not reliable, or if you want to be certain not to lose your

▼

work, you might want to click Save several times to save intermediate versions of your work. If you do this, you may get some error messages that some items have not been provided. Do not worry; you will get to them in a later step.

1. Create a new view. Go to admin/build/views and click Add. This opens the page shown in Figure 23.5. Name the view and provide a description. Because this view is designed to be reused, it is called general_view. The description (seen only by administrators) reminds that it is driven by dynamic arguments. A view like this will show any type of node with the appropriate vocabulary term. Make certain that you choose the Node option for the view's content. When you are finished, click Next at the bottom of the page.

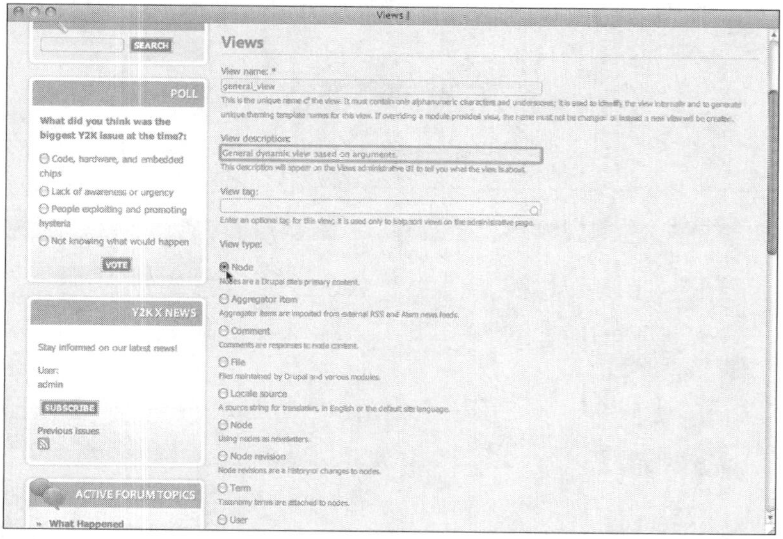

FIGURE 23.5
Add a new view.

2. After you click Next, the familiar view editor appears, as shown in Figure 23.6.

3. Add three fields by clicking the plus sign (+) next to Fields in the center of the view. The fields you want to add are Node: Title; Node: Teaser; and Taxonomy: Term. Adding Taxonomy: Term will make debugging easier as you check to see the proper data is being retrieved. You can easily remove it later. Because these fields are in both the Node and Taxonomy sections, you need to set the pop-up menu to <All> so that all of them are displayed in the list. Check the three check boxes and click Add at the bottom of the page. This was described previously in "Adding Fields to the View" in Hour 14, "Working with Views."

4. You are now walked through the settings for each field. The first one, Teaser, requires no changes to the default settings unless you want to remove the label from the field. Just erase Teaser from the Label field. When you are finished, click Update. Drupal moves on to the next field, Node: Title, as shown in Figure 23.7.

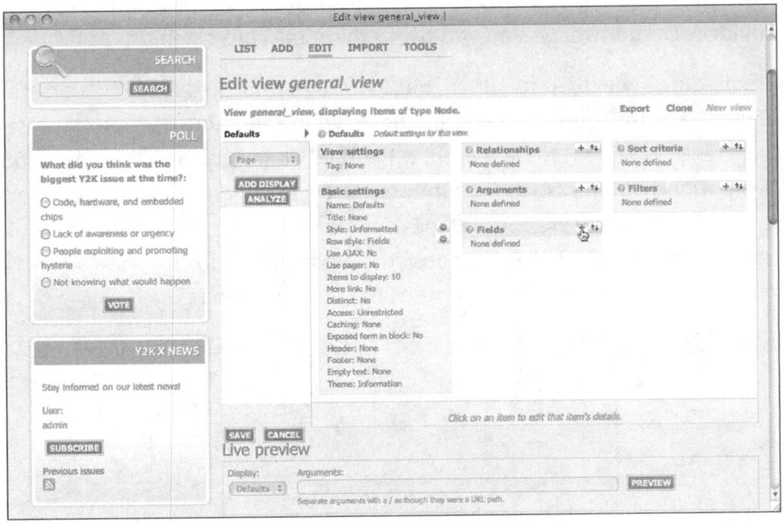

FIGURE 23.6
The view editor opens.

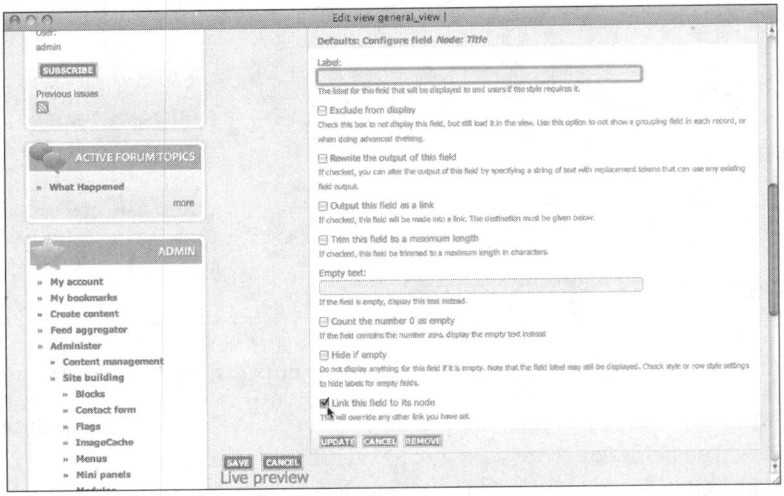

FIGURE 23.7
Adjust the label and link status for Node:Title.

5. Remove the Title label if you want to, and click the last check box to link the title field to the full node. Click Update and move on to the final field where, again, no changes are necessary. When you click Update for the last field, you will see a preview of the data, as shown in Figure 23.8.

6. As you can see, the data is a bit of a jumble. Go back to the view editor and click the double-headed arrows next to Fields in the center of the view editor. This lets you rearrange the order, as shown in Figure 23.9. Move the title to the top; it is up to you whether teaser or term description should come next. As soon as you click Update, the preview display will look much better.

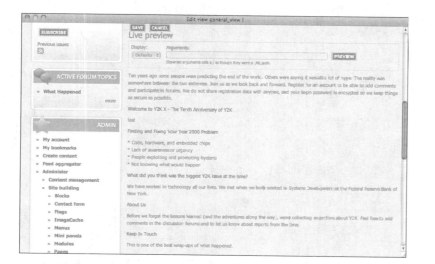

FIGURE 23.8
View the pre-
view.

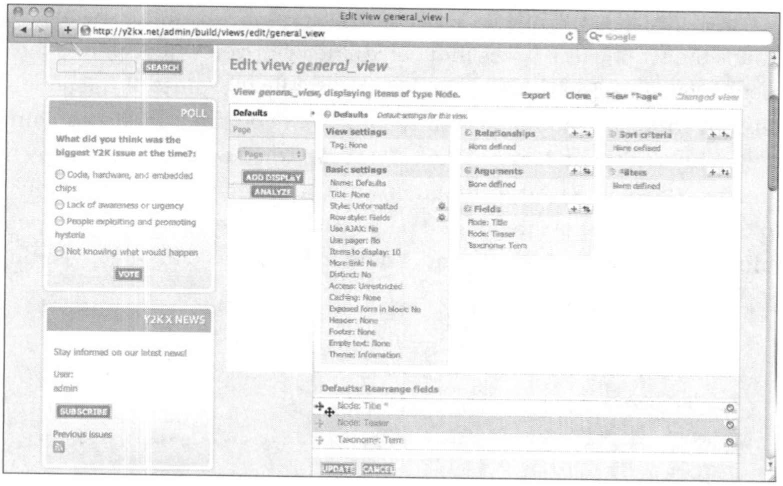

FIGURE 23.9
Rearrange the
field order.

7. When you were building a static view in Hour 14, you next selected a filter for the desired data. Do not create a filter for a dynamic view; instead, create an argument by clicking the + next to Arguments, which is to the left of Filters and above Fields. You will be able to set the argument, as you see in Figure 23.10. The field that you want to set will be Taxonomy: Term. It is actually more efficient to use Taxonomy: Term ID, which is a number, but for now, the term itself can make debugging easier and provide a more robust interface. (Add this to a to-do list so you can come back to it if you want.) Click Add to add the argument.

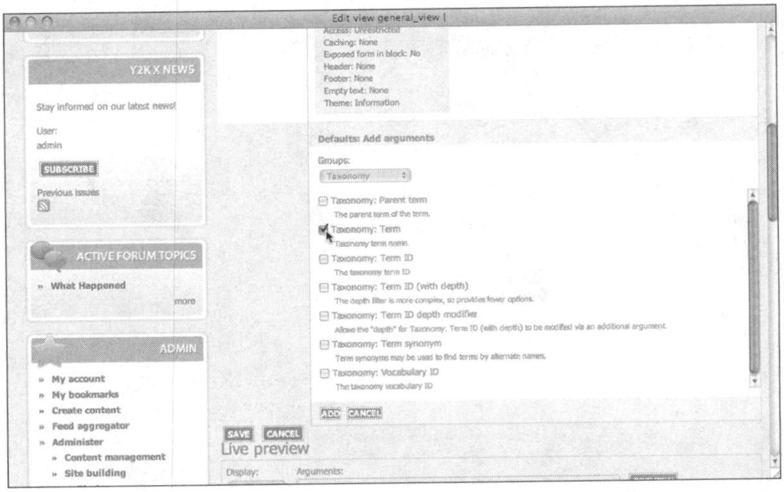

FIGURE 23.10
Attach the first argument to a field.

8. Specify the way in which this argument will be handled. The next page that you see is shown in Figure 23.11. You can accept the defaults. The most important is the set of check boxes that determine what you will display if the argument is missing. The two best choices are usually all values or the page missing error. Depending on your site and how you program it, searching for a taxonomy term that does not have data associated with it may or may not be an error. (If you are worried that a missing argument will cause too much data to be retrieved, rest assured that a pager will be placed on the results pages to minimize the maximum amount of data to be retrieved at any given time.)

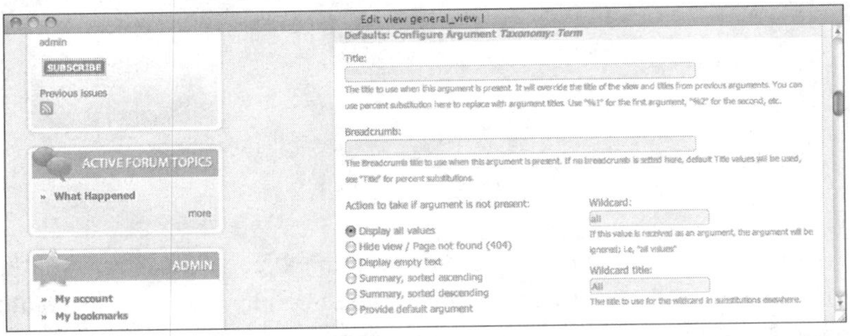

FIGURE 23.11
Set defaults for a missing argument.

9. You have specified how the argument will be used. Further down the page, you can specify how the argument is validated. You know that this argument is a taxonomy term, so you can ask Drupal to validate it. If you were using the argument as the title of a page, no validation would be necessary. You can validate for users, nodes, and taxonomy terms. Figure 23.12 shows the validation options for a taxonomy term. You set the action to take if it does not validate.

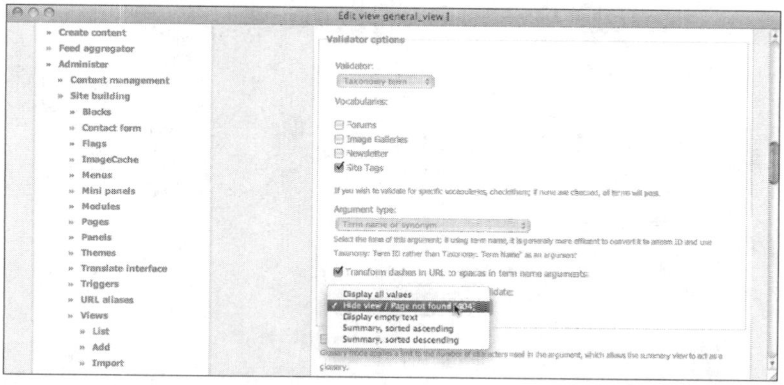

FIGURE 23.12
Set the argument validation options.

10. Complete the process at the bottom of the page, as shown in Figure 23.13. You can specify capitalization rules for the argument (this makes sense if you are using it for a page title). You typically transform spaces to dashes in the URL. And, if you are retrieving data that might have no values, you can choose not to show the items in the summary. In this case, you do not have to worry, because one of the items you are retrieving is the node title and every node has a title. Click Update when you are done. You can add another argument if you want. Remember that you assign the arguments in sequence, so you determine which argument is used to select data, which is used for a title, and so forth. It is solely by sequence.

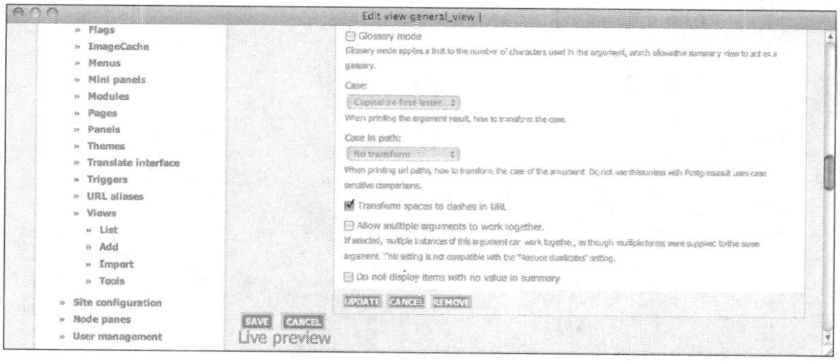

FIGURE 23.13
Complete the argument specification.

11. So far, you have been building the default view. Save it after your last update. Now, add a page display, as shown in Figure 23.14.

You will immediately have an error, as shown in Figure 23.15. A page requires a path.

12. In Page Settings, the path is set to None. Click None to set a path, as shown in Figure 23.16. If this is going to be a utility view, you may want to give it a generic name, such as general.

FIGURE 23.14
Add a page
display.

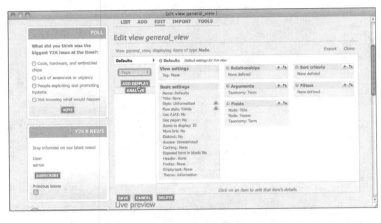

FIGURE 23.15
You need to have
a path for a page
display.

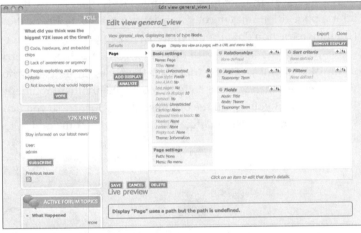

FIGURE 23.16
Set a path for
the view.

13. You are ready to test. Open a new window and type in your path. In this case, the full URL would be yourwebsite.com/general/y2k-problems (if that is one of your taxonomy terms). Remember to replace spaces with dashes.

14. You can tidy up the view using any of the other view settings. One common change is the addition of a pager, as shown in Figure 23.17 (and in the resulting view, shown previously in Figure 23.2). You may want to sort the data, for example. If you have followed the steps here, it may be time to remove the Taxonomy: Term field, which is most useful for debugging.

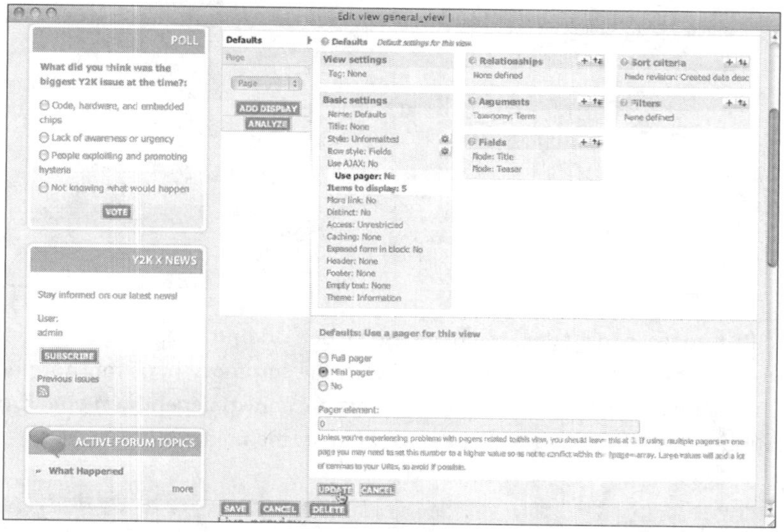

FIGURE 23.17
Add a pager.

Modifying a Built-In Page

You can use pages and panels to modify built-in pages. You will recognize some of the interface from the view editor—in particular, the notion of pages that are in code and that can have variants you create. This enables you to override built-in pages. The example shown here lets you override the basic Create Content page.

Why would you do this? One reason is that you might like it laid out differently for your use or the use of your colleagues. But, particularly with a site that has extensive user contributions (or contributions from advanced users), the data entry pages may need tweaking to make them more specific. You may want your logo on them, for one trivial point. You can relabel fields, but by modifying the entire page structure, you have the ability to make it fit into a corporate look and feel. In any event, it is worth experimenting with; you already know the basics (and a lot more!).

Go to Administer, Site Building, Pages (`admin/build/pages`), as shown in Figure 23.18. You will see any pages you have created there. You will also find some built-in pages that, by default, are disabled.

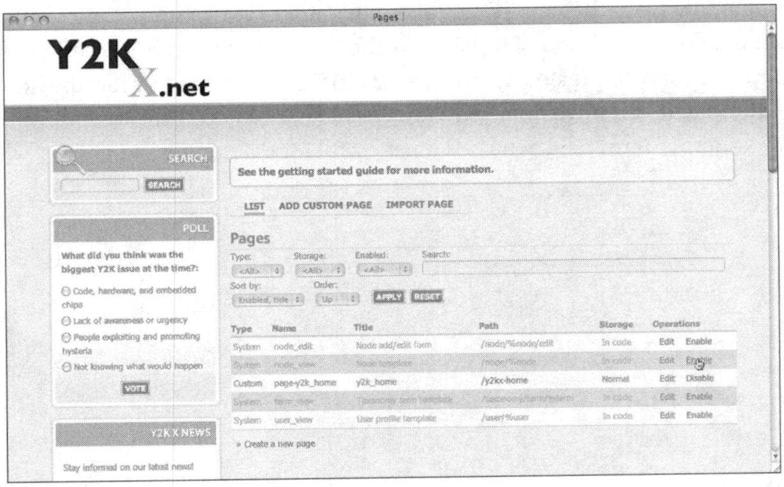

FIGURE 23.18
See existing pages.

Edit the first page—`node_edit`, the page used when adding or editing a node—by clicking Edit. After you click Edit, you will be on the summary page for that page, as shown in Figure 23.19. Whether or not variants are shown depends on your Drupal installation and settings. You will add a new one in the next section.

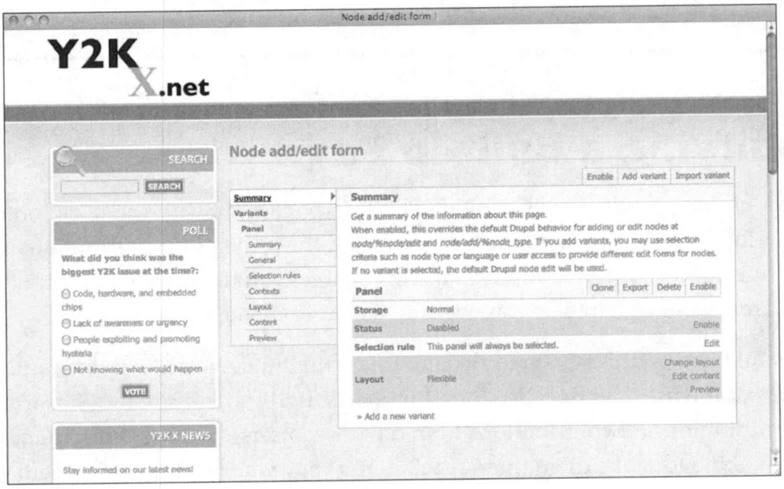

FIGURE 23.19
See the summary.

Click Add a New Variant at the bottom. The page shown in Figure 23.20 opens.

FIGURE 23.20
Add a new variant.

Set the page title if you want. Then, click Create Variant to open the now familiar page shown in Figure 23.21. You choose the layout for your variant.

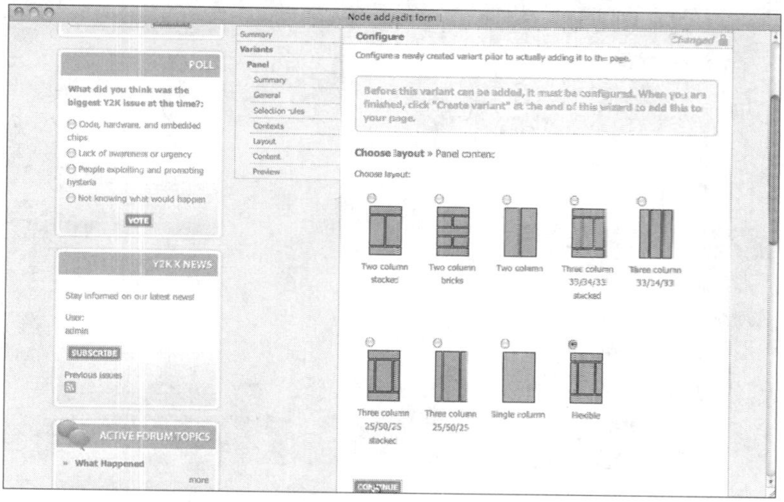

FIGURE 23.21
Choose a layout.

After you choose your layout, click Continue. As you can see in Figure 23.22, you are back in the world of pages and panels. The only difference now is that you have some additional panels you can add. Click Add Content, as shown in Figure 23.22.

You have new categories of content that you can add in addition to the content types you have seen before. Figure 23.23 shows the Form content choices. These are the components of the Add Node form.

FIGURE 23.22
Add content.

FIGURE 23.23
Choose from new components.

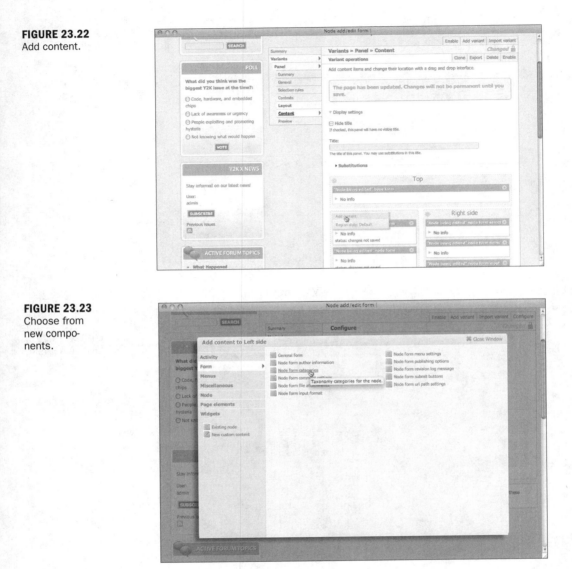

Figure 23.24 and Figure 23.25 show the top and bottom of a Create Content page created in this way. (The basic layout is the Flexible layout.)

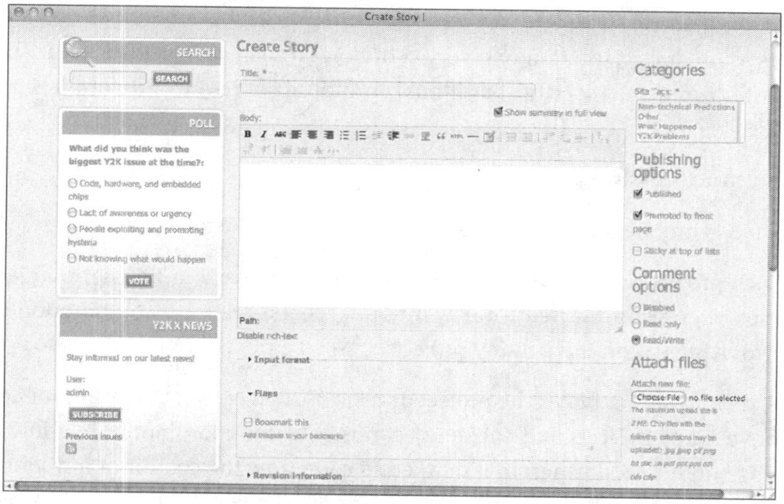

FIGURE 23.24
Create content:
top.

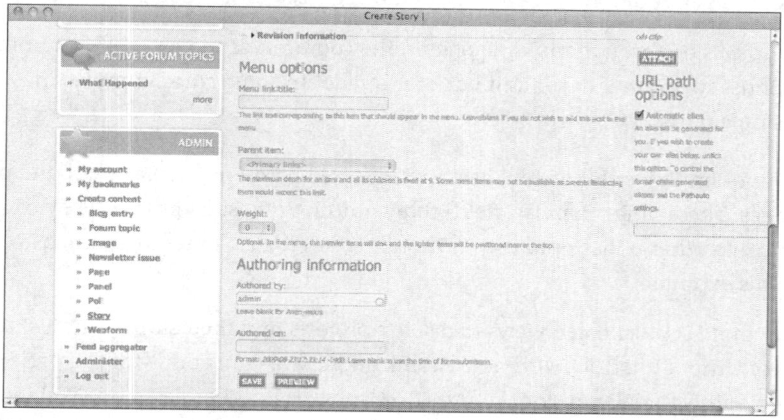

FIGURE 23.25
Create content:
bottom.

Using Node Reference and User Reference Fields

The emphasis in this book has been on developing websites with Drupal because that is how many people think of using it. But, remember that Drupal is a Content Management System (CMS), and in some ways, its web capabilities are extensions of that core. You can use Drupal to build powerful database solutions that, subject to your security settings, might be visible on the web to the public or visible only to a limited group—perhaps certain users or perhaps only people on your intranet.

This section describes how you can combine Drupal core functionality and built-in modules to produce a solution to a very common problem: project tracking. The example shown here is specific, but it has a multitude of real-world parallels in various fields.

The data structure is simple:

▶ *Projects* are the focus of the system. They will be a custom content type.

▶ Each project is associated with one *client*. If you have a multi-client project, most organizations create a new internal "client" that is a combination of the two. A client can have many projects.

▶ A *coordinator* manages the project and keeps it on track. A coordinator can have many projects, but each project has only one coordinator. In a law firm, this might be a partner; in a marketing company, the coordinator might be a traffic manager. Whether the coordinator is the client contact varies depending on how the company is organized and the work that it does.

▶ Projects go through multiple *phases*; the coordinator moves a project from one phase to another or sends it back for a redo. In some cases, a project has only a single phase.

The Drupal implementation will use two CCK field types: node references and user references. These differ from the fields that contain data, such as text. They contain references to other nodes or to users. Drupal makes it easy to set these up, as you will see in this example.

You can build sophisticated views to display projects and their status, but just using the basic Drupal interface with no customization, you can work with the project tracking data you will develop. Figure 23.26 shows what a project node will look like.

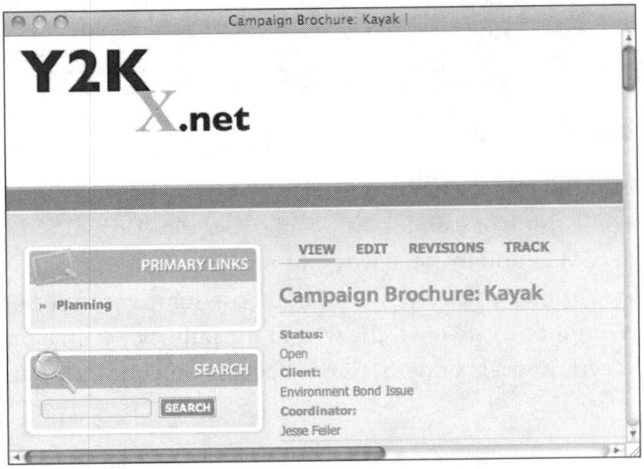

FIGURE 23.26
Build a project tracking system.

The project node is a custom content type that has three fields added: status, client, and coordinator. Status is a text field, client is a node reference field, and coordinator is a user reference field. In the default display shown in Figure 23.25 both client and coordinator are displayed as links to the appropriate data.

Figure 23.27 shows the revision log for a project. This requires absolutely no work on your part other than entering the data in the log for a new revision. Revisions are built into Drupal.

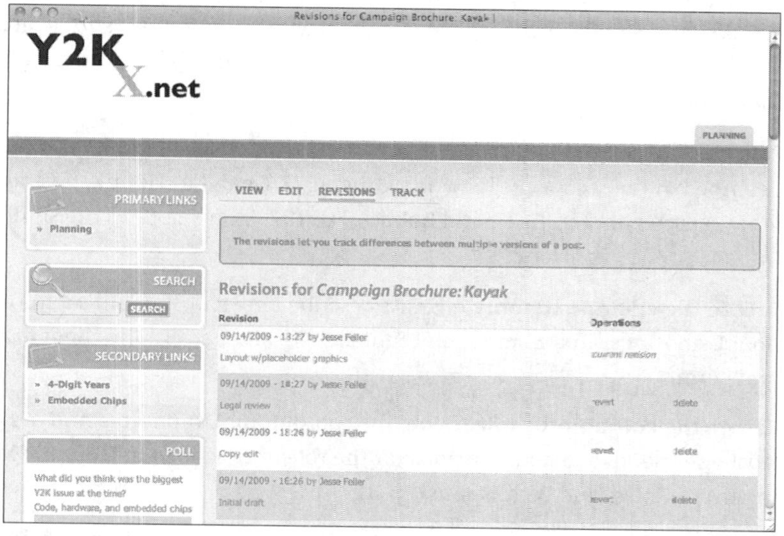

FIGURE 23.27
Drupal revisions manage project phases.

As you see in Figure 23.28, Drupal automatically maintains the link between coordinator and projects. Figure 23.28, all the projects for a given coordinator are shown in the Related Content area of the user's profile, and they are presented as links on which you can click.

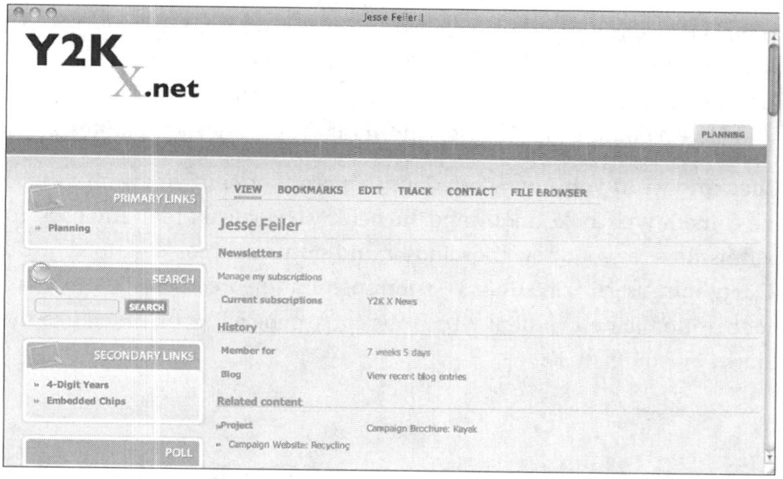

FIGURE 23.28
Drupal tracks projects for a coordinator.

▼   **Try It Yourself**

Build a Project Tracking System

Here is how to build the project tracking system. As you will see, it brings together many of the things you have learned how to do with Drupal.

1. **Set up clients.** You can create a new content type for clients or use the default story or article content type. In either case, you will need to add three custom fields: status, client, and coordinator. Coordinator will be a Drupal role for specified users, and clients will be identified with a taxonomy term. (Clients may or may not be a custom content type.) Adding the fields is described in the following steps.

2. **Add the status field.** This field contains status options. Use the techniques described in the section, "Managing Other CCK Fields" in Hour 7, "Using Content Construction Kit (CCK) and Images," p. 107. Status options are similar to the color options of Hour 7.

3. **Create the client taxonomy term.** As described in Hour 9, "Finding Information: Using Tags, Taxonomies, and Searches," p. 145, create the client taxonomy term.

4. **Create the coordinator role.** Create the coordinator Drupal role and assign at least one user to it. Set permissions for the role as described in Hour 8, "Managing Users, Roles, and Permissions," p. 127.

5. **Add the coordinator field.** As described in Hour 7, add a coordinator field. It will be a user reference field. For the widget, you can choose autocomplete or check boxes/radio buttons. In this example, check boxes/radio buttons is the option chosen. When you click Save, you will need to complete further configuration of the coordinator field. The important settings are shown in Figure 23.29.

   In most cases, you want to implement reverse links from the user's account page to the record containing this field (shown previously in Figure 23.28). Also, as you see at the bottom of the page, select all the roles you want to be used for screening potential users; normally you want Active status users.

6. **Checking what you have done.** This step is optional. If you want to see how the content type looks, rearrange the fields to a logical order and click Save. Set permissions for your new coordinator and status fields as described in Hour 8 (D6: admin/user/permissions D7: admin/config/people/permissions). Create a node using the new content type. Your entry page will look much like the one shown in Figure 23.30.

▼

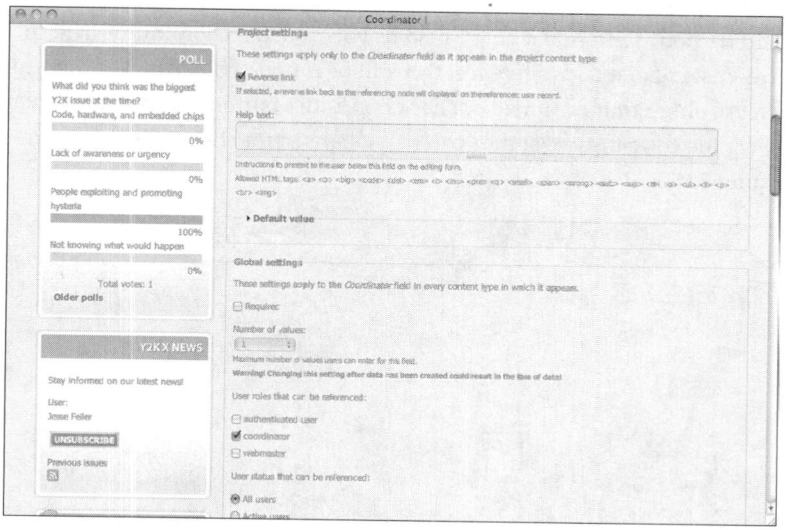

FIGURE 23.29
Configure the coordinator field.

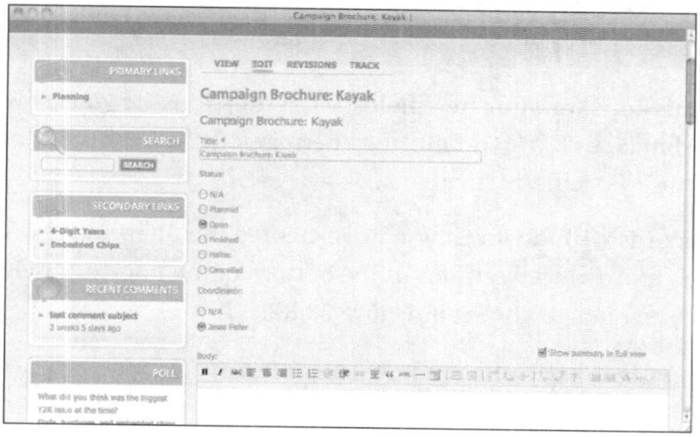

FIGURE 23.30
Check your work.

7. **Create a client view.** Because there are usually relatively few roles, using check boxes/radio buttons is an easy way to select the roles available for a user node. For clients, however, you may have many more. You can use the autocomplete widget option, but you can also filter potential clients using a view. If you have created a custom content type for projects, you can use the same basic interface that you used for users. However, if you are using a more generic content type, such as articles or stories, the number of candidates can be large. Create a view that uses the relevant content type and that filters based on the taxonomy term client created in step three. This was described in Hour 14, "Working

with Views," p. 237. Create a path for the view and test it. (You will have to enter some client data to do so.)

8. **Add a client field.**Add a client field as you added a coordinator field in step five. Instead of a user reference, this will be a node reference. For the widget, choose either autocomplete or check box/radio button. On the next page, select the content type(s) that can be referenced for clients, as shown in Figure 23.31.

9. **Set permissions for your new fields.**Set permissions for your new fields as described in Hour 8 (D6: admin/user/permissions; D7: admin/config/people/permissions).

10. **Filter records with a view.**If you have created the filtering view described in step 7, go to Advanced settings at the bottom of the page and select the view you have created, as shown in Figure 23.32.

11. **Finish up.**Click Save. You can now enter data.

You are ready to use your project tracking system. Here is all you have to do:

▶ Create a node for each new client using your custom client content type or a default article or page content type. Make sure to use the client taxonomy tag. You should only need to do this once.

▶ Create a user account for each coordinator and assign it to the coordinator role. You should only need to do this once.

▶ For each project, create a new project content type. Select the appropriate client and coordinator. Attach relevant documents using the standard file upload mechanism. To start a new phase, click the New Revision check box and enter a log description—perhaps identifying who is responsible and what the phase is. You do not need to create a new project for each phase: the Drupal revision mechanism handles everything automatically. The only want you can break it is if you forget to create new versions or if you forget to complete the log.

Summary

You have seen how to build views that are driven by arguments placed in their URLs. One view can serve up any number of different permutations of data without changing any links or code. You have also seen how to extend the new Drupal interfaces into the data entry area.

Q&A

Q. *A friend says it is easier to write PHP code to retrieve custom data from Drupal. Is she right? Should I start studying?*

A. Most of what you can do in Drupal can be done in code (it has to be able to be done in code because that is how Drupal implements it). For experienced programmers, it often seems as if writing code is the fastest and most efficient way to get the job done. One of Drupal's great strengths is exposing its power through a graphical user interface rather than a PHP interface. And a further problem arises: The code that you write today will undoubtedly need some maintenance and modification over the years. Going the code route locks you into code forever. Working with Drupal's new tools, such as node and user reference fields, views, pages, and panels, locks you into...a graphical user interface.

Q. *I showed my users how easy it is to create views. Now, they want customized views for each department, and they all display the same data. What do I do?*

A. Creating many customized views that display the same data in different formats and combinations may seem like wasted work, but it can be useful. There may be reasons each department wants its own format. In any case, bending the technology to the wishes of the users is a good idea whenever possible.

Workshop

Quiz

1. Does the fact that a Drupal URL may have embedded arguments in it mean that it can't be used for people outside the Drupal world?

2. Can I move the Submit button for new content to the top of the form?

3. How do I use a path to a dynamic view?

Quiz Answers

1. No. There is nothing about a URL with embedded Drupal arguments that makes it look any different from any other URL. Access is dependent on the regular Drupal security mechanism (such as logging in).

2. Yes, but make sure that you don't run into interface issues. If you use panel pages for multicolumn input, you can make the vertical dimension of the page much less, so a Submit button at the bottom of the page is not so far off as it otherwise would be.

3. Type it into a custom block, put it in a story, or use it anywhere you want. It is a URL, plain and simple.

Activities

If you have a lot of user-created content, sit with the users to find out how they would like their data entry page to look. Gathering a focus group together can be useful. Do the same for dynamic views. Try to avoid one-on-one interviews; you will wind up with at least as many choices as people you have talked to.

Customizing Themes and Their CSS

What You'll Learn in This Hour:

- ▶ Look Inside Theme .info Files
- ▶ Override Theme CSS Files
- ▶ Change Background Images

Introduction

One of Drupal's greatest strengths is its robust and flexible architecture. With the exception of a very few critical aspects of core, you can override just about everything in Drupal. Its architecture provides a reliable way of doing so, as you have seen with the sites folder, which can contain folders for your own themes, modules, and libraries. By providing you with a place to put your customizations, many people find that they never need to touch Drupal's code. If you do need to write code, you write what you want and place it in your sites folder where it is separate from Drupal's code. However, Drupal uses code from the sites folder if it finds it, so the link between your customizations and Drupal's code is clearly defined without you actually touching Drupal's code.

As Drupal has evolved, many people have modified the code and added modules and themes to Drupal using this structure. Those modifications have focused on two areas: new functionality (such as the contributed modules described in this book) and improvements to Drupal's usability for its users who are building websites.

Drupal is now at a time of transition as the increases in usability have made Drupal available to people with no skill or interest in writing PHP code (and who may also not be interested in studying thousands of pages of documentation or figuring out how things work by reading the code and experimenting with it). If you think back on the topics covered in this book—polls, shopping carts, user-contributed content, dynamic views, panel pages, RSS feeds, and the rest, it is truly amazing that they are all available to you without writing any code. This is one of Drupal's greatest strengths compared to traditional handcrafted HTML. Think of how you would create an HTML-based website with those features and without writing code.

This hour is the closest you will come to code, and the "code" here is not programming code. Like many websites and systems today, Drupal uses Cascading Style Sheets (CSS) to modify the appearance of its pages. You can customize the CSS for your site so that it looks exactly as you want it. Many people make the mistake of thinking that they need to create custom themes for their Drupal site. Although that is true for some sites, it is not true for all of them. In fact, starting from a basic theme (either one of the themes distributed with Drupal or a contributed theme), you can achieve amazing customizations using two simple techniques:

Go To ▶
YOU CAN
DOWNLOAD
THE THEMES
DISCUSSED
IN THIS HOUR.
ACQUIA SLATE
CAN BE
FOUND AT TOP
NOTCH
THEMES
(WWW.TOPNO
TCHTHEMES.
COM/). ZEN
CAN BE
FOUND AT
DRUPAL.ORG/
PROJECT/ZEN.
GARLAND IS
PART OF THE
DRUPAL
DISTRIBUTION.

▶ **CSS**—Customize the CSS. CSS files are designed to be modified. Sitting down to write a CSS file can be daunting for someone who has not done it before. But, most people do not do that. The most common way of working with a CSS file is to modify it by changing fonts, colors, and dimensions. That is a much less complex task than starting from scratch.

▶ **Background images**—Nothing customizes a theme more than a background image of your own. You can easily do that with CSS.

This hour walks you through the basic and highly effective ways of customizing your site.

Looking at an Info File

Files distributed as part of Drupal are located in the themes folder. Themes you download should be placed in your `sites/all/themes` folder (you may need to create it). Each theme consists of a folder containing all its files. The key file you need to be aware of is the `info` file. It includes the theme name so that, for example, the Garland info file is garland.info.

The `info` file contains a summary of the theme; the section you may need to modify relates to CSS files.

A number of Drupal themes are specifically designed for customization. One of them is Zen, which provides step-by-step comments to help you customize particular aspects of your site.

Looking at Garland

Here is the Drupal 7 version of garland.info. If you compare it to the list of themes displayed in Drupal, you will see that the description is what is shown on that page. Two CSS files are listed: style.css is used as the default, and print.css is used for print media. (The media type is the key in the first set of brackets.) By default, a file named style.css is the file that is used, but you can rename or replace it.

The first few lines of the file with the ID, name, description, and version information not for you to modify, and the final lines, which have been added automatically by the Drupal packaging script, are also not for you. You worry only about the lines between; in Garland, those are the two style sheets lines.

```
; $Id: garland.info,v 1.7 2009/08/11 12:27:37 dries Exp $
name = Garland
description = Tableless, recolorable, multi-column, fluid width theme.
version = VERSION
core = 7.x
engine = phptemplate
stylesheets[all][] = style.css
stylesheets[print][] = print.css

; Information added by drupal.org packaging script on 2009-08-18
version = "7.x-dev"
core = "7.x"
project = "drupal"
datestamp = "1250618833"
```

If you want to customize the Garland CSS file, here is the simplest and safest way to do so.

Try It Yourself ▼

Modifying a Theme's CSS File

Here is the simplest and safest way to modify a theme's CSS file. If there are several files, you need to decide which one to modify. The names are usually self-explanatory. You may see variants of files marked rtl. These CSS variants are used for right-to-left scripts. Note that this Try It Yourself *modifies* the theme's file; in the next section, you will see how to *override* specific parts of the theme's file.

1. To be absolutely safe, copy the entire theme folder to a backup location.

2. Locate the CSS file you want to change. Duplicate the file and provide a new name. If it was style.css, you might rename it mysite.css (substituting your

▼

site name). Make your changes (you may want to make one or two to test) and save the CSS file.

3. Open the theme's `info` file and locate the style sheets line you want to change. Change the style sheet name to `mysite.css`.

4. Save the `info` file.

5. Go to (D6: `admin/settings/performance`; D7: `admin/config/development/performance`). Click Clear Cached Data (D6) or Clear All Caches (D7). Click Save Configuration.

6. Check your site.

Looking at Acquia Slate

Acquia Slate is a free downloadable theme from Top Notch Themes. It is shown in Figure 24.1.

It is much more complex than Garland, but even so, the `acquia_slate.info` file is not long and follows the same basic structure as that of `garland.info`.

Again, it is the style sheets lines that you care about. You can see where the theme's regions are defined, and you can see that the theme exposes its options, such as whether to display the logo or the name. These are of interest, but all you need to do is locate the style sheets lines:

```
; $Id: acquia_slate.info,v 1.1 2009/02/28 23:33:58 jwolf Exp $

name = Acquia Slate
description = <a href="http://www.acquia.com">Acquia's</a> Slate theme is ideal
  for corporate and business sites. Includes advanced theme settings and 12
  flexible content regions for a variety of layouts. By <a href=
  "http://www.topnotchthemes.com'>TopNotchThemes</a>

core = 6.x
engine = phptemplate
stylesheets[all][] = style.css
stylesheets[all][] = dblog.css
;stylesheets[all][] = local.css
scripts[] = script.js
scripts[] = jquery.overlabel.js
regions[sidebar_first] = sidebar first
regions[sidebar_last] = sidebar last
regions[banner] = banner
regions[header_top] = header top
regions[header_first] = header first
regions[header_middle] = header middle
regions[preface_sidebar] = front preface sidebar
regions[content_top] = inner content top
regions[content_bottom] = content bottom
regions[postscript_first] = postscript first
regions[postscript_middle] = postscript middle
regions[postscript_last] = postscript last
regions[footer] = footer
regions[node_bottom] = node bottom
features[] = logo
features[] = name
features[] = slogan
features[] = mission
features[] = search
features[] = favicon
features[] = primary_links
features[] = secondary_links

; Information added by drupal.org packaging script on 2009-05-16
version = "6.x-1.x-dev"
core = "6.x"
project = "acquia_slate"
datestamp = "1242432037"
```

Of the three stylesheets lines, the third one is commented out with the semicolon at the beginning of the line. This theme uses a slightly more structured approach to your customization than does Garland and some other themes. It includes this commented-out line so that you can easily uncomment it.

There also is a `local_sample.css` file as part of the theme's files. It is an empty shell. Copy it, change its name to `local.css`, and you have the file to match the uncommented style sheets line. Because CSS files are applied in order, by having this file as the final one, its settings will override the CSS files that precede it. Thus, your `local.css` file needs to contain only your customizations.

Changing a Theme's Images

Nothing changes the look of a theme more than its images. These images are used for buttons and icons as well as sometimes for background images. If you keep your replacement images the same size, you minimize your work (and maximize the effect).

▼ **Try It Yourself**

Replace Button or Icon Images

Use these steps to customize your site very quickly:

1. Begin by making a copy of the entire theme, in case you need to revert to it.

2. Locate the `images` folder in your theme's files. Open it and you will see the images used for icons and buttons.

3. For the images that you want to replace, open each one and note its size. Then create a substitute image that is the same size.

4. Name the replacement images with the same names as the originals and place them in the images folder (this is why you have a backup, in case anything goes wrong and you need to revert).

5. Go to (D6: `admin/settings/performance`; D7: `admin/config/development/performance`). Click Clear Cached Data (D6) or Clear All Caches (D7). Click Save Configuration.

▲ 6. Check your site.

In the case of a background image, start from a theme that already has an image of the size and shape that you want. Most downloadable themes ship with a stock image (if there are any images at all), so make your choice based only on size and shape of the background image. By picking a theme with the right size and shape for the image, you minimize your work.

Replace a Background Image

After you locate a theme with a background image of the right size and shape, you can download and install it and then replace the image. Explore the theme sufficiently; it may have several versions of the image. For example, there may be a large version on the front page and smaller versions on interior pages.

1. Locate the background image or images that ship with the theme. Many themes use an images folder, and some have a subfolder for background images. In the case of the Acquia Slate theme used as an example in this hour, the background images are located in images/cropped. The front page image is seascape.jpg, and the smaller one for interior pages is seascape-header.jpg.

2. Open each of the images in an application, such as Preview or Photoshop. Note the exact size of each image.

3. Adjust your image (or images) to be exactly the same size as the corresponding stock image. Check that the resolution matches so that you are not accidentally downloading an enormous file.

4. Give the images new names and place them in the folder with the stock images. (You can place them anywhere you want, but this is usually easiest.)

5. Locate the code that places these images. The easiest way to do this is to use the existing CSS files and search for the image name. For example, in Acquia Slate's style.css file, you will find this code to place the large image on the front page:

```
#preface-wrapper {
  background: transparent url('images/cropped/seascape.jpg') no-repeat left
top;
  height: 420px;
  margin: -33px 0 20px;
  overflow: hidden;
  position: relative;
  width: 960px;
  -moz-border-radius: 0 0 10px 10px;
  -webkit-border-bottom-right-radius: 10px;
  -webkit-border-bottom-left-radius: 10px;
}
```

Here is the code to place the smaller image at the top of content pages:

```
#content-top {
  background: transparent url('images/cropped/seascape-header.jpg') no-
repeat left top;
  padding: 0;
  overflow: hidden;
}
```

6. Create a file for your CSS overrides. In the case of Acquia Slate, it will be `local.css`, as described in the previous section.

7. Add to that file the code you located in step 4. Change the names to the names of the new files. Here is what your override file might look like now:

```
/* $Id: local_sample.css,v 1.1 2009/02/28 23:33:58 jwolf Exp $ */

/****************************/
/* LOCAL CSS               */
/****************************/

/* Put your custom css and css overrides in this file and  */
/* rename it local.css.  By restricting your css changes    */
/* to local.css, your changes will not be overwritten when */
/* upgrading to a new version of this theme.               */

/* Steps to activate local.css:                        */
/* 1. Add your custom css to this file                 */
/* 2. Rename this file to local.css                    */
/* 3. Uncomment (remove leading semicolon from ) the   */
/*    following line in your theme's .info file:       */
/*    ;stylesheets[all][] = local.css                  */
/* 4. Clear cached data at admin/settings/performance */

#preface-wrapper {
  background: transparent url('images/cropped/jflarge.jpg') no-repeat left
top;
  height: 420px;
  margin: -33px 0 20px;
  overflow: hidden;
  position: relative;
  width: 960px;
  -moz-border-radius: 0 0 10px 10px;
  -webkit-border-bottom-right-radius: 10px;
  -webkit-border-bottom-left-radius: 10px;
}

#content-top {
  background: transparent url('images/cropped/jfwide.jpg') no-repeat left
top;
  padding: 0;
  overflow: hidden;
}
```

8. Go to (D6: `admin/settings/performance`; D7: `admin/config/development/performance`). Click Clear Cached Data (D6) or Clear All Caches (D7). Click Save Configuration.

9. Check your site.

Summary

Adding your own graphics and images to your website is the fastest way to give it a totally customized look. As you have seen in this hour, it is easy to do this kind of customization.

One of the criteria that you should use in selecting themes for your site is the ease of this type of customization. Check that themes use the standard file structures and naming conventions so that you can make changes just by modifying the info file and customizing or overriding a CSS file.

Q&A

Q. *In addition to modifying CSS and images, what other major design changes to a Drupal site are easy to do?*

A. Explore the Charts module (project/charts) if you have quantitative data. Look through Drupal modules for wrappers to mapping services. Consider adding a CCK image field to your primary node types so that your site is less text heavy, if that is a problem.

Q. *What are the laws about using copyrighted images as background images?*

A. They vary. You can license stock images that you can use without worrying. However, most people find that the simplest way to get customized background images is to take them yourself. If people are present, you may need a model release from them so that you can use their likenesses.

Q. *If I want to use different size images, how difficult is that?*

A. This depends on how different they are. The simplest way is to try one or two to see if there is collateral damage from an image that may not fit into the space on the page allotted for it. In many cases, there are few problems. As long as the center of interest in the image is in the center, slight cropping of the edges is often not an issue.

Q. *I like the transparent effect. How hard is that to achieve?*

A. The effect itself is easy to achieve with CSS. The challenge is creating an image that works with transparency. Look at background images that have type laid over them, and you will often see that one part of the image (usually top or bottom) is lighter or darker than the rest. This lets you place dark or light type on top of this area and have it be readable. You may have to work backward from the overlaid text to find the type of image that works best behind it.

Workshop

Quiz

1. How do I determine what CSS files are used on my site?

2. In addition to checking the size of new images, what else should I check?

3. What are those rtl CSS files?

Quiz Answers

1. They are listed in the theme's info file.

2. Check the resolution so that you are not downloading large files unnecessarily.

3. These files handle right-to-left scripts.

Activities

You have considered all the major aspects of developing a Drupal site. The only activities left are contributing to the Drupal community. This may mean contributing themes and modules, or it may mean volunteering to help with testing.

There are frequent conferences of Drupal developers, and you may want to participate in these. You can go to groups.drupal.org to find groups of people who may be interested in the same type of projects you are working on.

As Drupal moves into its next phase, there are increasing opportunities for Drupal users who are not interested in writing code for themes and modules to share experiences and advice in the development and maintenance of Drupal sites.

APPENDIX A

Updating Drupal

Periodically, Drupal checks for updates to modules and themes. Depending on your settings, you may see messages about downloads. You can also go to Administer, Reports, Status Report (admin/reports/status) to check the updates.

Before proceeding, back up your Drupal installation files and the database. It is also a good idea to take the site offline.

Download and install the updates where the original files were installed. You will be replacing the existing folder for the theme or module: There might be more or fewer files within the new folder. To be absolutely safe, totally remove the old module folder and move the new one into its place.

At that point, you update Drupal's internal configuration by running update.php (from your site's root directory using the URL www.mysite.com/update.php). This will reflect newly downloaded versions of modules and Drupal itself. The messages that you receive will vary, but they come in pairs. Figure A.1 shows the message of updates that are about to be attempted.

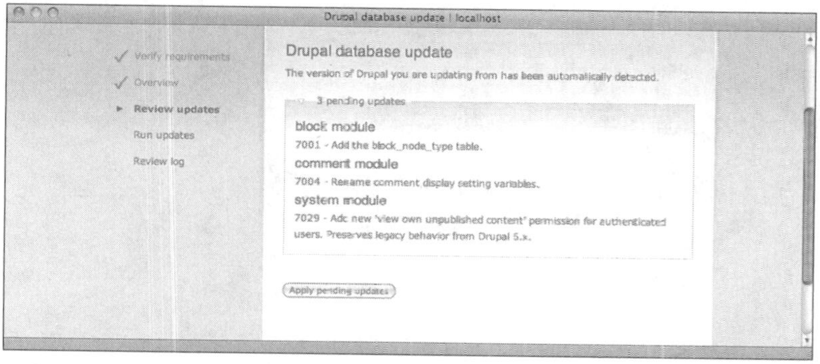

FIGURE A.1
Updates are needed.

Figure A.2 shows the results of updates that have been installed. You can see that the database is periodically updated as modules are changed.

Deal with any errors. Because you have a backup, you can revert the database and your files if you want to. Do a search on the Drupal site to see if other people are having issues, and if a specific module has an issue, look at its page. Read the error message carefully: Depending on your site and your temperament, you may decide to bring the site back online without resolving the issue. If you do decide to postpone dealing with the issue, make certain you do. It will not go away by magic.

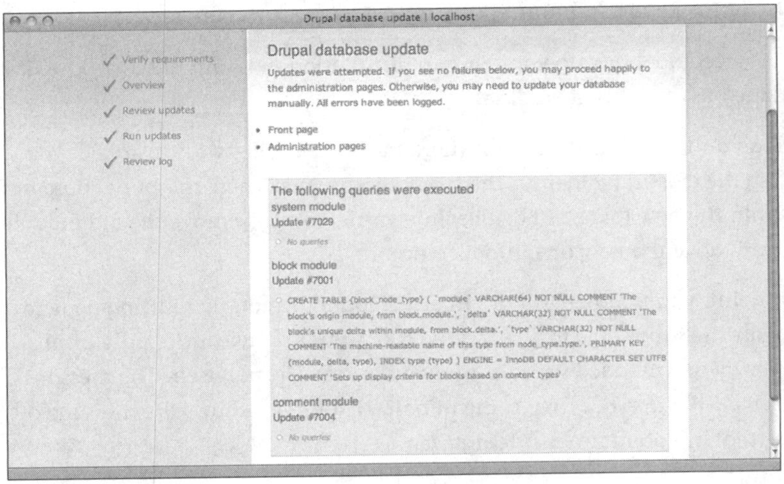

FIGURE A.2
Updates have
been completed.

APPENDIX B

Drupal Background

Drupal's origins can be traced back to 2000, when Dries Buytaert and Hans Snijder, then students at the University of Antwerp, set up a wireless network to share a high-speed Internet connection. It quickly grew into a shared news website, and the software that Dries had worked on was released to others in January 2001 as Drupal.

By the Way

> **Birth of Email**
>
> It is interesting that the precursor of the Internet—ARPANET (1969)—also began as a way to share computer resources and files. One of the first applications added to DARPANET was email (1971).

Drupal has gone through major releases since that time, and it is now used around the world by a variety of government, commercial, and tax-exempt organizations. The current release of Drupal is version 6, and version 7 is just arriving. Because Drupal always supports the current and one prior release, version 5 and earlier are not discussed in this book.

Drupal's Evolution

As Drupal has evolved, its basic standards and underlying structure have remained intact, but new ways of doing things have been adopted. Among the tools and features that have been introduced in recent versions are a new way of handling fields (introduced in the Content Construction Kit [CCK]), views, and panels. If you look at the changes to Drupal, you may see that the entire architecture has been refined over time in much the same way that programming languages have evolved.

The evolution of programming languages provides an interesting parallel to Drupal's development, particularly with regard to how the users of languages and website tools have responded to advances.

► First-generation languages were machine instructions. They were different for each computer, but required no compiler or interpreter to run. The programmers just wrote down the instructions. Computers executed nothing except machine instructions.

▶ Second-generation languages (generally known as assembly languages) were specific to computers, but they had somewhat more humanly understandably syntax. They were turned into machine instructions by programs called *assemblers*. Programmers who were familiar with first-generation languages protested that their code was more efficient. Allowing people to write the slightly abstracted assembler code allowed for confusion, or so they said.

▶ Third-generation languages were turned into machine instructions by *compilers*. They were designed usually to be machine-independent and portable. This allowed for an even easier syntax for humans who used the language. Examples of such languages were COBOL, ALGOL, FORTRAN, C, and, more recently, C++, C#, Objective-C, and Java. Second-generation programmers complained vehemently that this introduced two abstraction levels and even more possibility for confusion. Furthermore, many considered it an outrage that valuable computer resources would have to be used to run these new-fangled compiler programs.

Grace Hopper

Grace Hopper, one of the great pioneers of programming, recounted asking her boss for permission to write a program that would manipulate symbols and turn them into computer instructions—the first compiler. He refused her request. Some time later, he walked past her desk and asked what she was working on. When she replied that she was writing a compiler, he was enraged and reminded her that he had forbidden her to work on it. She replied that he was mistaken. He had not forbidden her to build a compiler; he had said it was impossible.

It has been the same with the web. Initially, websites were handcrafted with HTML. Then, tools such as scripts and templates abstracted and automated the process. Starting in the late 1990s, the integration of databases created database-driven websites in which the actual pages presented to a user not only had never been touched by a developer's hand, but the pages, in many cases, had never been seen before or since by anyone. The pages were built on templates and structures using data from the database.

At every step of the way, people have complained that the old way was faster and better, and that the new way would not work.

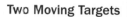

Drupal's Cost Versus Older Techniques

It is absolutely true that developing with Drupal or any other modern website management tool adds complexity. But, that should not be the end of the discussion. The economics of web page development are pretty much linear. It can take only a few minutes to create a basic Hello World web page. After the fairly simple learning curve has been mastered, the next page takes about the same amount of time. As does the 10,000th page.

Yes, it is much harder to create a simple web page in Drupal. Writing a Hello World web page in Drupal and hosting it on a server is not the simple task it is with hand-crafted HTML. Many people who are still objecting to using Content Management Systems (CMS), such as Drupal, end the discussion there, which is a mistake.

The discussion has to be extended out to those 10,000 pages, each of which might cost the same amount to develop in a traditional environment. With Drupal, the first page can take much longer than the first handcrafted HTML page, but the 10,000th page, or even the 100th page, takes a fraction of the time of the corresponding hand-crafted HTML page.

This conversation (or argument) is still common, although the rapid rise of CMS sites demonstrates that a lot of people are finding a lot of value in the technology. An informal survey of Drupal projects drawn, in part, from job postings on drupal.org suggests that a number of such projects exist in large companies that have to manage large websites, and many such projects exist in smaller organizations for which the low cost of open-source software and the speeded-up development time are major attractions.

Drupal has benefited from the ideas that are current in today's software environment and that, in many cases, are hallmarks of open-source software. For example, Drupal contains a database abstraction layer so that it can function with a variety of databases. In the past, web server applications (which is, in some ways, what Drupal is) were often tied to proprietary databases. Companies bought into the proprietary web server application and the proprietary database, and that was the end of the matter. Getting their data out of the proprietary environment was another matter— usually for other people.

Two Moving Targets

Drupal is evolving over time. Many of the recent architectural advances have made its future evolution more predictable, and a number of people expect that some of those advances will minimize upheavals deep in the Drupal core. It is a moving target—it will always be a moving target (as is true of every useful technology)—but its speed is gradually decreasing.

The web is also moving. In the second half of the 1990s, major new standards were added to the web to support new media and e-commerce. The pace of standards changes has slowed down now that we have reached a basic plateau of web functionality.

During the 2000s, one basic tenet of the web did change. Until then, the web protocols were very simple (that simplicity helped the web function and grow). The smallest unit of the web was a page. If you wanted more data, you asked for another page. In 2000, the developers of Microsoft Exchange Server proposed the concept that is now `XMLHttpRequest` and that has been codified in a working draft specification by the World Wide Web Consortium since 2006. This paved the way for partial-page loads, and coincidentally, rendered moot some bandwidth issues.

However, there is no rest for the weary. Just as people got used to ever-more focused and smaller web requests, ever-faster processors, and ever-larger and higher-resolution computer displays, cell phones started ringing. Everything that we know about designing a web page is questioned when that page is shown on a portable device.

And what does that have to do with Drupal?

It is very simple. Developing a web page that displays "Hello World" on a desktop computer is soon going to be a bit like wearing a historical costume in a parade. The web is not on the desktop for many people. It is not in an office. No one knows for sure what the web will be tomorrow, but it is pretty clear that websites will be bigger and more complex. It is also abundantly clear that the cost of building and maintaining tomorrow's websites needs to be brought under control.

What technology will help you develop a website for today that will still be viable tomorrow? A lot of people believe it is Drupal. Its primary consideration across new versions of the code is that data in the database will be preserved even if interface elements change.

And one thing is certain: The changes we have seen in the web so far will not end.

Index

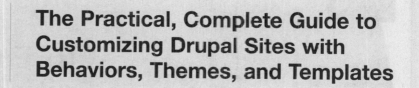

The Practical, Complete Guide to Customizing Drupal Sites with Behaviors, Themes, and Templates

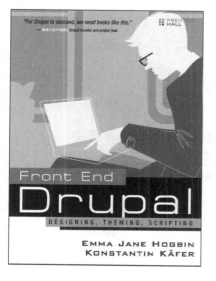

"Drupal faces a common problem on the Web—the relative lack of new, high quality themes. *Front End Drupal* tackles this problem directly and is designed to help both experienced designers and rank novices get an understanding of how Drupal theming works. In fact, I'll be the first to admit I learned a lot from this book."

—Dries Buytaert, Drupal founder and project lead

ISBN-13: 9780137136698

Front End Drupal is 100% focused on issues of site design, behavior, usability, and management. Emma Jane Hogbin and Konstaintin Käfer show how to style Drupal sites, make the most of Drupal's powerful templating system, build sophisticated community sites, streamline site management, and build more portable, flexible themes. You'll also gain hands-on experience through several case studies that walk you through the customization of everything from page templates to Web site forums.

24 Proven One-hour Lessons

Sams **Teach Yourself**

Drupal

in 24 Hours

SAMS

FREE Online Edition

Your purchase of **Sams Teach Yourself Drupal in 24 Hours** includes access to a free online edition for 45 days through the Safari Books Online subscription service. Nearly every Sams book is available online through Safari Books Online, along with more than 5,000 other technical books and videos from publishers such as Cisco Press, Exam Cram, IBM Press, O'Reilly, Prentice Hall, Que, and Addison-Wesley Professional.

SAFARI BOOKS ONLINE allows you to search for a specific answer, cut and paste code, download chapters, and stay current with emerging technologies.

Activate your FREE Online Edition at
www.informit.com/safarifree

> **STEP 1:** Enter the coupon code: ANFCKFH.

> **STEP 2:** New Safari users, complete the brief registration form.
> Safari subscribers, just log in.

If you have difficulty registering on Safari or accessing the online edition,
please e-mail customer-service@safaribooksonline.com

Addison Wesley · Adobe Press · ALPHA · Cisco Press · FT Press FINANCIAL TIMES · IBM Press · lynda.com · Microsoft Press · New Riders

ILLY · Peachpit Press · PRENTICE HALL · Que · Redbooks · SAMS · SAS Publishing · Sun microsystems · WILEY